Public Matters

The Renewal of the Public Realm

edited by Patrick Diamond

POLITICO'S

First published in Great Britain 2007 by
Politico's Publishing, an imprint of
Methuen Publishing Ltd
11–12 Buckingham Gate
London
SW1E 6LB

1

Copyright © Public Service Reform Group 2007

A CIP catalogue record for this book is available from the British Library.

ISBN 978-1-84275-211-2

Typeset in Bembo by SX Composing DTP, Rayleigh, Essex
Printed and bound in Great Britain by Biddles Ltd, King's Lynn, Norfolk

Contents

Part IV: Tailoring reform to public service challenges

Preface: the Public Service Reform Group

Improving public services has been a central goal for the Labour government, just as it is for many public service managers and professionals. In June 2005, I discussed with colleagues in government the need for a more systematic assessment of public service reforms, what we could learn from our experiences and how we could contribute to progressive thinking about reform. We noted that no other organisation had this as its central focus, nor had there been much cross-government debate and research about reform strategies.

We thought it important to harness the experience of people who had been at the forefront of the reform agenda, including David Albury, Michael Barber, Paul Corrigan, Patrick Diamond and Robert Hill, and if possible to continue their participation in thinking about the future of public services. So we formed the Public Service Reform Group in September 2005 to engage with public service reformers, academics, public service professionals and politicians. The group has met regularly since, and this book is the product of our discussions.

The chapters, commissioned by the PSRG, explore the critical challenges for a progressive approach to public service reform. The core theme of *Public Matters* is that Labour needs to go back to first principles and develop a new agenda for public service reform after ten years in power. At the forefront of this is a redefined relationship between citizen and state, requiring a redesigned and smaller central state with much greater involvement of individuals and civil society, as well as new forms of governance. The central state cannot and should not attempt to solve every problem by itself. It must assess the limits to its competence, where it can add most value and how it can get much better outcomes where it does act. It must focus much more on how it can support individuals, communities and local institutions to achieve their goals. This will require significant changes in how central government and the civil service operate.

The introductory chapter to the book, written by Patrick Diamond with the other five PSRG governors – David Albury, Ben Lucas, Gerry Stoker, John Williams and me – sets out our central argument for change. We hope everyone will read and engage with its argument.

The PSRG is enormously grateful to the Policy Network think tank for facilitating our programme of work, especially to Patrick Diamond, who has edited the book – working with the editorial group of the PSRG's governors – and to Constance Motte for her tireless dedication and research support. We would like to thank the authors for working to tight deadlines and producing original and challenging ideas.

We would also like to thank the many people who have offered advice and support: Lord Best, Paul Corrigan, the Edge Foundation, Lord Gavron, Robert Hill, Ben Page and the excellent Policy Network staff. I especially want to thank Keith Coleman and other senior staff at Capgemini for their positive support to me and to the PSRG.

Public Matters is intended to stimulate discussion across the political parties and among public service practitioners, professionals and those who use public services. We invite people to engage in a debate about the issues raised in the chapters by accessing our website at www.policy-network.net.

Lord Filkin
Chair, Public Service Reform Group
April 2007

Part I

Introduction: our argument for change

1

Public services

A radical settlement for the next decade

Patrick Diamond

Introduction

The aim of *Public Matters* is to launch an expansive debate about the future of public services. The debate about the role of the British state and the management of public services is at a crossroads. There is now a de facto consensus among the political parties about the size of the state, but major disagreements persist about the underlying purpose of government action and the relationship between citizens and their public services. The issue is not merely how the state itself is run and organised. The basic foundations of the public realm in contemporary Britain are at stake: how will the values of equity, citizenship and service be sustained in the next generation?

This is also the moment to reflect on the governing achievements of the last decade:

- The 1970s-style public services that the incoming administration inherited in 1997 have been upgraded. There are no longer endless trolley waits or creaking Victorian buildings in the NHS. Teacher shortages have been tackled in secondary schools. There are record police numbers while volume crime is falling.

- Two previous decades of under-investment and neglect have been substantially reversed. The public realm has been rehabilitated in British national life. Indeed, 'public service' is once again a virtue rather than an embarrassment: service to others is celebrated, not reviled as it was in 1980s Britain. The terms of political argument have shifted in a progressive direction, ensuring the culture change necessary for a successful and sustained period in power.

- In an increasingly wealthy and educated society, expectations have risen exponentially over the last decade. But there is increasing evidence that the Blair government's strategy has reached its limits. Recent research from MORI shows the depth of public dissatisfaction.[1] It indicates a loss of faith in the government's capacity to generate public service improvement. In 2001, Labour had a 20-point advantage on whether the public believed that further improvements in the National Health Service and schools would occur. By 2006, this had sunk to a 20-point deficit; 51 per cent of citizens say that public services fall a long way short of their expectations.

The centre-left in Britain should reinvent its model for improving the delivery capabilities of public services, enriching the relationship between services and citizens. It should learn lessons from the Blair years, while recognising that the broader context in which progressives seek to govern has changed dramatically over the last decade: the contours of a new political landscape are steadily taking shape.

Some observers will conclude that public service reform should not be the driving theme of the next decade. The electorate believe that Labour has had long enough to sort out education and health. The government should instead focus on emerging challenges, from environmental sustainability to the appetite for a new localism, pursuing deeper changes to the structures of power and opportunity in society.

This is a tempting conclusion, but it is mistaken. From narrowing the gap in life-chances to enhancing social cohesion and quality of life, public services are pivotal to realising progressive aspirations. Meanwhile, there is the recognition that Britain's problems will be tackled neither by the tried and trusted methods of the post-war social democratic state, nor by the Thatcher-era theory of new public management (NPM). Despite some useful innovations over the last decade, the UK still awaits the radical reforms that will recast the state, enabling it to cope with new challenges.

The future challenges for public services

Any future strategy for public services will need to reflect on the fundamental debates that now face the UK. The most salient emerging trends are:
- the impact of technological change, the decline of traditional manufacturing and the shift in comparative advantage to the rising

economies of eastern Europe and Asia;
- the consumer revolution in post-industrial society fuelling rising expectations of public services;
- greater taxpayer resistance since the 1970s, with growing fiscal and structural pressures including the ageing society and the weakening of the traditional family;
- the new anatomy of inequality, driven by deeper income and wealth polarisation in the post-industrial countries, creating new clusters of social exclusion and fuelling greater inequality of life-chances;
- the emergence of global challenges such as international criminal networks, contagious diseases and terrorist threats that cut across national boundaries, making the task of governing society within the confines of the nation state more problematic;
- the threat of climate change demanding action from national governments and global institutions, while suggesting limits to existing patterns of consumption and growth.

Progressive and conservative approaches to public service reform

In response, today's Conservative Party wants to frame the debate about public services as a choice between the big and the small state. They want to project Labour as the party of the centralising and ineffective state.

The centre-left should not fall into the trap set by the right. The purpose of the state is to enable and empower individual citizens and communities – and that requires a radical shift in the nature and governance of public services. The answer is not to withdraw altogether, as the Conservatives believe. The challenge is to reinvent the state and public services, not to dismantle them.

For progressives, an essential element of public service reform is to redesign the state: to delineate the roles and functions of the state in relation to public services, and to distribute power between different levels of the state – national, regional and local. The state remains a crucial actor in the public domain, as there are many progressive goals that only the state can realise. Greater equity and efficiency in British society requires the state's capacities to be carefully harnessed: Britain needs a state that works not withdraws.

There is a fundamental divide between the right and the progressive left on the role of the state and public services in British society, reflecting contested conceptions of personal liberty and social justice. The right continue to believe that empowerment is about freedom from restraint. Their claim is that people get control over their lives only when the state gets out of the way. Government should vacate civil society wherever possible – leaving the ethic of what David Cameron terms 'social responsibility' to fill the void. This would create patchwork provision, however, neglecting 'hard to reach' families and communities where reform often implies cutting back or limiting the scope of public services.

In contrast, progressives believe in empowerment as an expression of positive liberty – not merely freedom from interference, but the capacity to do and to be as enabled by public goods and public services. That requires an enabling and empowering state. This is what the development economist Amartya Sen envisages in the concept of 'capabilities'.

Sen argues that we need to think about inequality in relation to an individual's 'capability functioning'. What does society enable people to do or not to do, reflecting the skills and resources that they are equipped with? An individual's capability 'refers to the alternative combination of functionings that are feasible for him or her to achieve. Capability is thus a kind of freedom: the substantive freedom to achieve an alternative functioning combination – or less formally put the freedom to achieve various lifestyles.'[2]

The implications of this approach for public services are important:

- The capabilities approach does not mean treating people the same but treating people according to their circumstances.
- Those circumstances need to be defined by the individual who receives the support, hence the importance of choice and personalised provision.
- The capabilities approach emphasises the importance of local and tacit knowledge, hence the value of devolution.
- The capabilities approach does not demand equality of outcomes, but rather that people are enabled to make choices about the outcomes of their own lives. It is not authoritarian but enabling.

This understanding reflects the commitment to redistribution and greater equality that is at the heart of social democratic politics. Public services should remedy rather than reflect or reproduce patterns of social inequality. The individual is conceived as the agent of their own interests – empowered within the collective framework of provision that constitutes the enabling state. The emphasis is on strengthening personal autonomy, interdependence and self-esteem.

Rather than pursuing equalisation through the dispensing of state benefits alone, progressives believe in equalisation through empowerment – enabling individuals and communities to take greater responsibility for their own lives. In accordance with the approach elaborated by Sen, that requires public services to focus on supporting those most in need – within a universal framework encompassing all sections of society.

Sustaining the public service coalition

As William Beveridge understood when the modern welfare state was founded in the late 1940s, public services need to retain the allegiance of the middle classes, who predominantly fund the public realm. The coalition between the disadvantaged, who depend on public services, and the professional classes, who have traditionally upheld the ethos of public service alongside an enduring commitment to democratic public institutions, is vital. For generations the middle class contributed heavily to the cadre of public service professionals in Britain. Such a coalition is central to sustaining long-term support for public provision.

The nature of the public service coalition also has consequences for the relationship between the individual citizen and the provider of public services – schools, hospitals, the police and local government. In a society where individuals regularly experience highly responsive services, their encounters with public institutions might feel bureaucratic, even dehumanising. Users sometimes feel that public services do not treat them personally – prompting the flight of the affluent into private education and healthcare.

Emotional literacy and the recasting of relationships with customers and clients in public services are emerging as key tasks for the future. Substantial progress has been made, but in today's diverse and demanding society, public services should forge a relationship with users characterised by humanity and sensitivity – with the continuing emphasis on high performance. The drive to meet clinical targets in the NHS, for example, should not crowd out the importance of caring for the patient. Accessibility is vital. So too is a recognition of the requirements of diverse groups. Above all, people rightly expect to be treated with respect, dignity and fairness. Progressives need to ensure that public services live up to these aspirations.

The recent history of public service reform in the UK

Many of the issues that are addressed in this volume have been wrestled with by previous governments. The focus of *Public Matters* is the traditional sphere of public service provision in the UK: health, education, criminal justice and local government – though other areas outside the formal public sector are considered, such as economic development. Some historical reflection is necessary, since too often reformers have merely reinvented the wheel in public service reform while perpetuating an unhealthy culture of permanent revolution.

The Thatcher/Major governments 1987–92

After the 1987 general election, the Conservative administration focused heavily on the introduction of quasi-markets into schools, hospitals and welfare services. This involved a major bureaucratic offensive against the traditional structures of the public sector in Britain. The aim was to improve both efficiency and service outcomes by exposing such services to greater internal competition. 'Next steps' agencies were created to make the civil service leaner and more efficient. The introduction of grant-maintained schools also meant greater devolution of resources at the school level, bypassing local education authorities (LEAs). Meanwhile in the NHS, this shift led to the introduction of a purchaser/provider split between health authorities and NHS trusts, with GPs acting as independent purchasers. This emphasis on greater devolution was combined with greater centralisation in other areas, including rate-capping in local government, removing responsibility for further education from LEAs, and the intensification of audit and inspection in the NHS.

The Citizen's Charter 1992–7

The incoming Major administration sought to address widespread and vocal dissatisfaction with levels of accountability in public services. This led to the introduction of the Citizen's Charter in 1991, building on reforms initiated during the Thatcher years. In fact, many of the ideas behind the Citizen's Charter grew out of Labour local government, especially innovative local authorities in York, Southampton and Lewisham. The NPM theory was also influential. The aim of the Citizen's Charter was to increase the efficiency of public services, ensuring they were answerable to the consumer by providing information about their cost and management, while setting targets for delivery. This meant that public administration would be increasingly sensitive to the aspirations and interests of 'customers', while adopting techniques and incentives that prevailed in the private sector.

The Blair years, phase 1 1997–2001
Before 1997, leading Labour politicians emphasised that change would be incremental, intending to build confidence in Labour as a party of government. The incoming administration took the sharper edge off quasi-markets, but did not completely dismantle the architecture that was inherited from Margaret Thatcher and John Major. Some features of the NHS internal market were removed during Labour's first term. An intensive target-setting and inspectorate regime was introduced with top-down managerial pressure from central government, as exemplified by the literacy and numeracy hour in primary schools and the NHS plan launched in 2000.

The Blair years, phase 2 post-2001
The reform process has been a journey as ministers, government departments and public service agencies have sought to learn from their mistakes. Since 2001, the Blair administration has amended its reform model, acknowledging the limits of centralised command and control in the delivery of public services. This meant greater use of quasi-markets, plurality of provision and stronger internal competition between providers in health, education, social care and local government. It was argued that choice and competition would ensure greater equity in public service outcomes, as well as stronger efficiency and responsiveness to customer demands. As Robert Hill argues in Chapter 15, the Prime Minister emerged from the 2005 election determined to make public service reform even more self-generating – to create self-improving public service systems.

Empowering citizens and communities through public services

Public Matters acknowledges the limits of these approaches to change. It accepts that errors have occurred over the last decade:
- There has been a simplistic faith in individual choice as a lever for diffusing power in public services;
- The notion that the private sector is the solution to every problem

facing public services is ill conceived, as is the contrary belief that it should have no role;

- There has been too little acknowledgement of tensions and trade-offs in public service reform;
- The role of local government has largely been ignored: too many programmes have been managed in a top-down, centralised fashion, while the distribution of powers at the central, regional and sub-regional level has been inadequately defined;
- The opportunity to engineer major institutional reform in central government, including the civil service, has been missed;
- The importance of outcomes and value for money in public services has too often gone unrecognised.

It is important to contrast the argument of *Public Matters* with those of leading critics of public service reform,[3] understanding the debates of the last decade while forging a strategy for the next ten years. There are three main areas of disagreement about the desirability of allowing mechanisms such as competition and contestability a major role in shaping public services:

- The first disagreement concerns the general hostility to markets, the suspicion that competition is wasteful, and the assertion that contestable markets lead to unacceptable patterns of inequality – with the general preference for monopoly suppliers as the pinnacle of productive efficiency in public services. This is unsustainable in a society where citizens' demands are ever more differentiated, and where most observers recognise the benefits of managed competition in raising standards within a regulatory structure that also gives priority to equity.[4]
- Second, critics of public service reform often deride the desires of consumers. For them, consumers are often ill informed about their 'true' needs and misled, for example, by advertising. Such critics do not generally regard consumption as a reputable activity. The spread of consumption in industrialised societies since the 1950s, however, could be regarded as an agent of aesthetic and moral advance. It is mistaken for public services to ignore consumer sensibilities: in a recent survey, 81 per cent of respondents said that Britain's public services 'need to start treating users and the public as customers'.[5]
- Finally, critics of competition and contestability in public services tend to assume that the motive of service is all the incentive needed by producers. This is a utopian assumption: it is clear that monetary

incentives are often necessary to play some role in any functioning public service. Regulated markets have positive virtues, bringing constraints, disciplines and incentives to bear on individual behaviour. Social democrats should never put the interests of service providers before those of service users. They should focus first and foremost on the public interest, refusing to settle for what Wright and Gamble term 'the equity of universalised mediocrity'.[6]

The contributors to this volume set out a progressive agenda for public service reform that acknowledges the limits of states and markets, rather than setting up the two in opposition to each other. They reject the tendency to define the state and the market as in opposition. The provision of public goods benefits from both solidarity and competition, though there will be specific instances in which it is hard to reconcile them. To debate the balance between states and markets misconstrues the issue nonetheless; the question is: what kind of state and what kind of market do social democrats want to frame? In the model developed in this book, there are two central components of empowerment that should inform all public services: empowerment of individual citizens and communities, and empowerment through the decentralised strategic state.

Empowerment of individual citizens and communities
The following measures are proposed to pass power back to citizens and localities:

- Both individual and collective choice should be extended through greater use of the commissioner/provider split in education, the NHS, criminal justice, social care and local government. For example, children with special educational needs should be given personalised budgets. In the prison service, there should be greater competition and discretion for commissioners to invite bids from private and voluntary sector providers.
- It is right to encourage co-production in public services – but that requires the codification of rights and responsibilities for both users and public service professionals. One example is the use of home–school contracts. Where citizens abuse or misuse a public service, sanctions should prevail such as fines for missed NHS appointments.
- There should be greater scope for individual citizens and communities to exercise voice alongside choice, since the two are complementary.

That requires giving local people more control over local public provision and opening up public services to mutual forms of ownership and involvement by local communities.

- The Commission for Equality and Human Rights will provide a statutory framework to monitor fair access and treatment, but the human rights model will need to be more strongly defined in relation to public services.
- Public services need to have clear rights of redress for citizens, while framing their roles and responsibilities to Parliament. The NHS, for example, should introduce a written constitution. This constitution would define in statute the rights and responsibilities of central and local organisations in the NHS; public, private and voluntary sector providers; professional groups; and those who use the NHS. It would defend and uphold the public interest.
- Citizens should have greater freedom to own, manage and direct public assets. There should be greater scope for shared equity in social housing, enabling more people to get on the ladder of property ownership – while the state should continue to invest in the social sector. Co-operative ownership of public goods such as leisure centres, galleries and parks should be encouraged, capturing the spirit of the early Labour movement.

Empowerment through the decentralised strategic state
We propose the following measures to build a strategic centre:

- The structure of Whitehall and all central government departments should be reviewed, alongside deep and lasting reform of the civil service, as Michael Bichard elaborates in Chapter 8. The regulatory structure imposed on public services by central government is often stifling and over-bureaucratic.
- There should be a new settlement for local government, as Dermot Finch advocates in Chapter 13, with an appropriate distribution of responsibilities at the regional, local and neighbourhood level. These must be 'place sensitive', reflecting the particular needs of localities, as David Albury reiterates in Chapter 10.
- There should be a new deal between central government and public service professionals, as Charles Clarke argues in Chapter 9, entailing a substantive shift in managerial power from central administrators to front-line managers, including headteachers and hospital chief executives.
- The delivery of public services is conditioned by the relationship that

prevails between citizen and state, as Gerry Stoker suggests in Chapter 3. The new model of public service reform requires a coherent approach to constitutional change. That means a democratically elected House of Lords, proportional representation in local government, and a Bill of Rights to enrich the citizen–state relationship – alongside deliberative mechanisms that will help to ensure deeper public engagement.

Shaping effective public services

But reinventing public services does not only require the empowerment of individual citizens and communities. It means making public services more effective in achieving their outcomes – ensuring greater efficiency, productivity and value for money while addressing the effectiveness of service design, as Geoffrey Filkin argues in Chapter 14.

Consequently the role of the central state must change, focusing only on essential tasks and devolving greater responsibility to localities. In 1926, John Maynard Keynes distinguished between the agenda and non-agenda of government. He wrote: 'The important thing for government is not to do things which individuals are doing already, and to do them a little better or a little worse; but to do things which at present are not done at all.'[7] Since the 1920s, there has been a dramatic expansion in the scope and scale of the state. But the state has to be effective at securing outcomes that are important to the public if confidence in the power of collective action is to be sustained. If it fails, the terms of political trade will sooner or later turn against progressive politics.

Future elections are set to be a contest between parties over who is best placed to get most value from existing levels of public expenditure. The projections set out in the 2006 pre-Budget report would reduce public spending by 0.5 per cent of national income over the next three years. Any further rise in general taxation appears unlikely in the foreseeable future. But while the rate of increase in spending is slowing, the government has challenging aspirations both to improve public services and to reduce child poverty. Consumption patterns mean that demand for public services is rising inexorably. The tension for centre-left parties across the world is that as societies get richer, the willingness to pay for public services often declines sharply. This gap between willingness to pay and demand creates perceptions of under-funding, fuelling the tendency towards opting out.

This represents a fundamental challenge to strategic thinking on the centre-left. *Public Matters* sets out a radical response to what is an enduring progressive dilemma:

- Governments should accept that the central state has a limited role, and that some issues will have to be resolved by localities and individual citizens acting together, including levels of funding and payment mechanisms for local public services.

- That requires a radical review of what the central state does, prioritising functions it alone can do. For example, the negotiation of terms and conditions for staff might be devolved in certain circumstances.

- All central government policies and programmes should be submitted to a public value test. Inevitably, some will be decentralised, other services may be reformed, but some will be cut altogether.

- Cutting wasteful programmes will enable resources to be focused on dealing with the challenge of acute social disadvantage, while switching to more effective evidence-based solutions.

- There should be a new contract between citizen and state. That will require greater conditionality, for example in the benefits system. User contributions already exist in public services, for example through university tuition fees and NHS dentistry – and are here to stay.

- At both the central and the local level, the state's role should change from provider to commissioner, securing outcomes from a mixed economy of public, private and third-sector provision. This should encourage local innovation and entrepreneurship, but it will require active management of the supply side in public services, for example supporting the growth of voluntary and third-sector providers by moving away from the absurdity of one-year funding contracts.

- Where service delivery is inadequate, the central and local state must act quickly to impose sanctions on under-performance, being prepared to see incompetent providers fail.

- The public should be empowered with high-quality performance data, alongside trigger mechanisms to ensure rapid intervention in failing public services.

The approach to public service reform set out in this book draws largely on European rather than North American experience, reflecting the commitment to social cohesion and equity that lies at the heart of modern conceptions of citizenship. It advocates diverse and pluralistic models of public service organisation and delivery – rooted in the principle of solidarity with access determined by need, not ability to pay.

Tailoring reform to public service challenges

In Chapter 15, Robert Hill argues that governments have to recognise the need for a range of levers and change drivers tailored to the particular problems facing a public service. The challenge is to select the right levers to effect change and achieve service improvements. For example:

- In health (Chapter 16), Simon Stevens proposes financial and non-financial incentives to supplement the traditional reliance on collegial and hierarchical approaches in NHS management, including a greater emphasis on co-production. The introductions of patient choice, the tariff system and new surgical providers should all produce major reductions in NHS waiting times, in part through greater competition.

- In education (Chapter 17), Hill sets out options for reform in five key areas: providing individual students with more choice over what and how they learn; major changes to how the curriculum is structured and assessed; releasing the energy of school leaders and investing in their skills; involving and engaging parents in schooling; and reforming school funding. These should be combined within a sustainable programme of educational change.

- In tackling early disadvantage (Chapter 18), Patrick Diamond sets out the case for a major shift of control over programme design and implementation from central government to local parents and communities. In addressing social exclusion, governments should reclaim the localist and participatory principles of Sure Start as it was introduced in the late 1990s. Participation by citizens and communities helps to create pressure for organisations to perform well.

- In criminal justice (Chapter 19), Ben Rogers focuses on increasing the accountability of the police, giving local authorities a greater say in determining how resources are used. Local councils should have increased responsibility for local crime prevention, including the early identification and treatment of high-risk offenders.

- In skills (Chapter 20), David Coats, Laura Williams and Alexandra Jones argue that educational institutions must respond effectively to local demand. There are limits to the role of markets in delivering work-orientated training and the development of human capital. What is required is a regulatory regime that addresses both under-performance and gaps in provision that arise in particular localities.

Trade-offs and tensions in public service reform

This model of public service reform outlined in *Public Matters* also acknowledges the importance of facing up to dilemmas and trade-offs. Some advocates of reform have been too optimistic or Panglossian, assuming that different techniques and institutions can be combined in an unproblematic fashion.

The future role of the state will depend on how intractable dilemmas are finally resolved.[8] In public services, there is a constant struggle to raise standards and to maintain the morale and support of those working in them. While it is legitimate to decentralise power and give greater control to individual citizens, welfare states still require a sense of solidarity and national community. This requires a stronger spirit of citizenship, but in the face of growing nationalistic and xenophobic pressures. Finally, the public agenda is shifting from the satisfaction of material needs to quality of work and quality of life – but these are values beyond the state and the market, suggesting limits to both.

In response to critics on the left, reformers appeared to suggest that seemingly incompatible values, interests and institutions could be reconciled in the public interest. This has turned out to be a mistake that has played into the hands of their opponents. Not all private sector bodies are capable of acting in the public interest. Too much choice will ultimately drive out voice. Reformers need to be alert to tensions and difficulties in exploring how public services are organised.

As Albert Hirschmann warns, progressives are inclined to over-state their arguments by suggesting that 'all good things can be combined'.[9] The argument is that reformers should not leave it to their opponents but should themselves explore the possibility of some conflict or friction between a proposed and past reform – or between two currently proposed programmes. If progressives do not acknowledge that any reform is likely to impose some costs, they will concede ground immediately to their opponents. Progressives should make a convincing case for the policies that they advocate on the grounds that they are right and just, rather than alleging that they are required to stave off an impending disaster.

Conclusion: Public Matters

The aim of this book is to develop an agenda that will revitalise the public realm through stronger, fairer public services. It seeks to build intrinsic support for public services so that these institutions cannot be swept away by future governments – embedding an enduring progressive settlement in British society.

In an age where citizens are better educated, less deferential and ever more demanding, public institutions will increasingly need to share and spread power. Thirty years ago, the electorate may have been content to elect a government and leave them to get on with it. Not so today: citizens are experts as well as voters, producers as well as consumers.

Public services need public involvement to achieve their mission. Our radical agenda focuses on how an enabling and empowering state helps individuals to gain greater control over their lives. Progressives must demonstrate that their approach empowers citizens to seize new opportunities, while helping them to cope with all the complexity, uncertainty and insecurity of the modern age. This is the future challenge.

2

The context for reform and why progressives need a new narrative on public services

Ben Lucas

This chapter looks at the context for public service reform, argues that progressives need a new narrative on public services and proposes what the key tenets of such a narrative should be. The starting point for this should be a renewed clarity about why public services matter for the centre-left. The mechanisms for improvement are clearly important, but the fundamental question is: what are public service reformers trying to achieve? This chapter argues that progressives need to spell out how public service reform will improve the lives of individuals and local communities and what the relationship is between this and the historic social democratic values of social solidarity, social equity and individual empowerment.

The political challenge New Labour now faces is by far the most serious it has had to confront since 1992. Not only has Labour lost much of its local government base to a resurgent Tory party, which under David Cameron has happily plagiarised from New Labour, but even more seriously we look in danger of losing the argument as well. Since the mid-1990s Labour has set the political agenda, the only question for the Tories being whether to push themselves further into the wilderness by opposing it or whether to come to terms with the new settlement. But that policy and political hegemony is now under serious threat. At the heart of this is the public services debate. The danger is that Labour's approach to public service reform has begun to look increasingly incoherent in terms of policy, competence and communications. Competence has been a big strength for the government since 1997, but this reputation is now being undermined by confusion about the public service reform strategy.

Despite very substantial increases in public spending on key services such as education and health and, despite actual improvements in those services, the public is not convinced that these services are improving. Where once the government enjoyed very strong public support for its approach to public services, now it faces deep public scepticism. Recent Ipsos MORI research shows that the public does not now believe that the government's policies will improve public services. Only 31 per cent of the public believe that the government's policies will improve public services, compared with 59 per cent who don't, a net score of minus 28 per cent. Reports from focus groups reveal deep scepticism about the government's public service claims and confusion about what its messages are.[1] For the first time for nearly two decades Labour has lost its lead over the Conservatives as the party most trusted with the NHS.[2] The only glimmer of hope here is that on the whole people's own experience of public services such as hospitals and schools is more positive than their assessment of the performance of these services nationally. According to Ipsos MORI research this 'local good, national bad' perspective can also be read across to who people trust on public services – broadly they believe front-line professionals and don't believe administrators, national media and ministers. The danger for Labour is getting the worst of both worlds – neither getting the credit for improvements so far, nor being trusted to improve things in the future.

At the heart of the problem is a confusion about what it is that Labour is trying to do with public services. That is why Labour now needs to go back to first principles to develop a new narrative for public service reform. This must demonstrate that the money that has been spent so far has achieved real results and that there is a clear purpose and direction to the next stage of the reform programme. This narrative must perform a number of functions: it must show why public service reform is at the heart of Labour's social justice mission; it must link the record of Labour's first, second and third terms to create a coherent reform story; and it must provide a clear direction of travel for future public service policy. As New Labour prepares for a new era, with a new Prime Minister, in an economic environment in which public spending will not be able to maintain its current rate of increase, a new social democratic consensus about public service reform will be required. This should not be a fudge between different reform strands but rather a radical approach to transforming public services. The twin planks of Labour's approach so far have been investment and reform. As the pace of investment slows in the next spending round, so it will become even more important to spell out what progressives mean by reform.

The back story

But the starting point for this has to be an analysis of where we are now. Labour inherited public services which were on their knees because of the Tory philosophy that there is 'no such thing as society'. Social solidarity and community had been hugely eroded by the Conservatives. It wasn't just that the major services had been run down but, equally importantly, the public spaces which underpin community had been allowed to fall into decay – parks, squares, libraries and museums. The Tory view was transactional rather than transformational: if you could, you used your own means to buy the best service by opting out of public services. As a consequence, public services by 1997 were becoming increasingly residual, with many schools and hospitals in a shocking physical state, literally crumbling. Transport, and particularly rail, was in chaos because of botched privatisation. The private sector was cast as the preferable alternative to public provision, not as a partner which could help improve public services.

The story of Labour's first two terms in office was about stopping the rot and beginning to rebuild public services. Primarily this involved investment and the use of targets and prioritisation to drive up standards. Labour's huge investment programme in schools and hospitals has massively improved the physical infrastructure of our key services. This combination of investment and targets has been able to achieve lasting results not just in new hospitals and schools but in reduced waiting times, improved literacy, smaller class sizes, better exam results and a falling crime rate. There has been a big increase in the number of front-line public service workers and professionals: more teachers, doctors, nurses and police, and these public service workers are better paid and more respected. In order to drive efficiency and innovation, the private sector has been used to share risk, inject capital, add specialist expertise and improve performance through contestability. Welfare has been reformed for the able bodied through a rights-and-responsibilities compact which has seen a huge reduction in unemployment. The New Deal targeted youngsters, while Sure Start and the working families tax credit have helped parents, in particular single parents, to get back into work. Specific initiatives have been taken to deal with particular educational challenges such as the literacy initiative. Other initiatives have been addressed at behavioural issues affecting urban Britain, such as anti-social behaviour. And some reforms have been introduced which aim to empower people more directly in the way in which they access services, such as GP choice.

The success of Labour's approach has changed the political landscape. The election of David Cameron as Tory leader is proof of how much New Labour has embedded a new consensus about public services. One of Cameron's first acts was to symbolically accept the new public services settlement and distance himself from the Thatcherite approach of the 1980s by saying that 'there is such a thing as society'. The core of this new settlement is on the traditional Labour territory of funding for the key public services – the Tories dare not now argue openly for public spending cuts to fund tax cuts. Their repositioning has gone so far as to lead them to claim that they are now on the side of public service professionals, against cuts and reorganisation in the health service; though how this squares with a desire to reduce taxation by up to £22 billion is still to be resolved. The Conservatives have so far not been subjected to a rigorous and critical analysis of how their public services policy platform stacks up, partly because their policy commissions have yet to publish their final reports. But it is already clear that there are considerable tensions within the Conservative approach – for example how to reconcile a smaller state with maintaining spending levels on health and education, or how, on the one hand, Cameron can be on the side of public service professionals against public service reorganisation and then, on the other hand, want to position himself as being in favour of greater citizen and patient empowerment.

So the apparent new settlement on the importance of maintaining decent levels of funding for public services masks some major policy and political challenges. The reality for Labour is that despite its successes there have also been significant limitations to its public service reform approach. A centrally driven target-based drive for improvement can only get you so far. It has improved standards but at the risk of stifling innovation, creativity and participation at a local level. Public services are now plateauing in terms of improved standards and their impact on people's lives. As Jim Murphy MP has argued, those who are most in need of public services which can transform their life-chances cannot afford to wait for the gradually rising tide of universalism to do the job.[3] While the general standard of public services is much better, this does not mean that there are not schools which are still failing kids from the most deprived backgrounds or social housing which is still concentrating inequality. And the extent of improvement has been patchy across public services, with some areas, such as large parts of the welfare/ benefits system, being left, until recently, mostly unreformed.

The limitations are not just to be found in what has been achieved but also in the policy framework and the reform narrative. From the second term onwards, there has been a greater emphasis on reform and moving away from a simple reliance on national targets to trying to put in place self-sustaining reform processes. But reform has meant different things at different times, embodied by different and sometimes competing concepts. Choice, contestability, national standards, earned autonomy at local level, specialisation and even some mutualisation have been reflected in a variety of specific policy initiatives, which have been patchily implemented across different public services. While it is right that policy makers should have a variety of tools and levers at their disposal it is necessary to have conceptual clarity as to the overall objectives and destination of travel. It sometimes appears as if the government has fetishised private sector service provision of public services, but this should never be an end of public policy and the reality is that it is only ever likely to be some aspects of some services, rather than all public services, which could be run by private firms. Similarly choice has sometimes been presented as an instrumental good for driving improvements in quality and sometimes as a good in itself.

Labour in power has also been at times too keen to claim for itself an exceptional position within international social democratic thinking, implying that everyone else must always have to learn from New Labour. The problem with this is that instead of being able to demonstrate that the British road to reform has some important common characteristics with other Continental social-democratic reform approaches, Labour has too often found itself under attack as if it were the only progressive government experimenting with different models for public services. The reality is that within Continental social-democratic models for public service, diversity and localisation of delivery have long played an important role.

Public service reform in Scandinavia

The Scandinavian countries have long been associated with a social settlement which is based on high-quality, generously funded public services. But that does not mean that there has not been significant experimentation and reform within these systems. In Sweden, in response to the economic recession of the early to middle 1990s, there was a significant shift in spending priorities away from compensatory towards productive public spending. In particular this saw a reduction in the social security bill and a substantial increase in spending on the provision of childcare services. As a result of this, Sweden now has a higher proportion of women in the workforce than any other developed country. At the same time choice is an important feature of the Scandinavian reform model. For example, parents can choose between municipal and non-municipal childcare providers, but within a system which is collectively funded through taxation.[4] Choice has also been introduced in the form of voucher models in Denmark and Sweden within the health and social services. This started with care for the disabled and the elderly, where direct payment voucher-based approaches were introduced in the late 1990s to enable service users to be the employer, using their state voucher with whichever provider they choose, whether in the state or private sector.[5]

Societal change and the new challenge for public services

It is no accident that across the developed world progressives are grappling with new models for public services, because the same social and economic forces are driving the need to make these changes. The most important contextual change for public services has been in the nature of society itself. There are five interrelated developments affecting society which public services have to respond to: technological change, the consumer revolution, globalisation, global warming and the new anatomy of inequality.

Technological change has changed the terrain fundamentally for public services. The impact of the knowledge economy on every aspect of people's lives means that public services are now judged against benchmarks which didn't even exist a generation ago. Today's 24-hour society has changed beyond all recognition people's expectations of services in terms of constant real-time access, responsive to the individual's needs. If public services can't keep up with these expectations then they risk losing the confidence and usage of large sections of the public. At the same time these technological advances have generated possibilities for public service change which simply weren't there before.

Technological change has also helped to quicken the pace of what is sometimes called the consumer revolution. This is actually broader than just consumerism since it relates to much more than the power balance between people, producers and the market. It is a cultural and political change which started to gather pace in the 1960s and has to do with a fundamental shift in how people see themselves in relation to their own lives. Deference has given way to a strong scepticism towards and often mistrust of people in authority, whether this be politicians, business leaders or school teachers. People are much more demanding in terms of their expectations of services, whoever they get them from. The experience of more choice and competition in relation to a wide range of services delivered by private sector companies has given many more people a taste of being able to pick and choose, moving their custom whenever they can get a better deal on price, service and quality. From a social-democratic perspective there are both negative and positive elements to this societal change. The negative is the development of a 'me first' attitude, but on the positive side the tendency towards people wanting greater control over their own lives offers the prospect of a more participatory democracy.

A similar tension exists in relation to globalisation. What is undeniable is the impact which globalisation is having on people's lives. It is reshaping the economy, the type of work people do and the nature of the labour market. A number of challenges arise out of this. Balancing national and community identity with globally driven change is one of these, which has had a particular impact on some communities in relation to the consequences of immigration and the diversity it brings. Public services are often at the centre of these frictional changes, for example in relation to housing policy. But the challenge is also much broader than this: given the competitive threat which the UK faces from the emerging BRIC economies (Brazil, Russia, India, China), the need to significantly improve the skills base of the British workforce will be the biggest single driver affecting education and training policy. That is why public services need to become much more ambitious. The aim of ensuring that state education matches private education outcomes is critical because it is about ensuring that excellence becomes not just an aspiration but a reality for all. Progressive universalism will require public services which are not just good but world class in order to give Britain the competitive edge in the global economy.

The consequences of global warming for public service strategy are also very serious. Following the Stern report, a new settlement, as significant as that in relation to health and education funding ten years ago, is in the process of being developed. This will affect everything from fiscal strategy through personal and corporate responsibility to transport policy. As befits a new policy priority, which is unconstrained by the institutions which have developed in response to earlier policy priorities such as welfare, health and education, the pace is being driven from the bottom up. The innovators are schoolchildren, third-sector organisations, community groups and local authorities, with their urban emission reduction targets. Government is racing to catch up and the issues go to the heart of the relationship between behaviour, responsibility, regulation and intervention. That is why the Environment Secretary, David Miliband, has rightly framed his climate change policy as an environmental contract between citizens and government. Moreover, from a social democratic perspective this is a classic issue of social justice, with the poorest countries potentially suffering the most from global warming.

But for the Labour Party, inequality within the UK should be just as pressing an issue. The anatomy of inequality has changed over the past few decades – we now live in an 80/20 society. While the economy is growing and the government has succeeded in taking large numbers of children out of poverty, stark inequality continues to divide our society. Social mobility has stalled among a large proportion of the 20 per cent of the population who are relatively poor and the bottom 2.5 per cent remain caught in a lifetime of disadvantage and social exclusion. Today's poor teenagers are more likely to be poor in middle age than their counterparts a generation ago. Whereas in the past, class politics was based on a broad identity of interest across a working class which stretched from skilled craft workers and technicians to unskilled manual workers and was represented by trade unions, vibrant community and mutual bodies and the Labour Party, now the bottom 20 per cent find themselves increasingly excluded socially and culturally from the mainstream of society. For people and communities trapped in this vicious circle of low expectation and low achievement the danger is of being further and more deeply excluded by societal change and economic globalisation. Whereas popular culture in the era of social mobility championed working-class heroes and lampooned barriers to mobility, now it is 'chav culture' which is the butt of the joke. Labour's first two terms reversed the decline in public services and established decent minimum standards but that is not sufficient to transform life-chances and elevate the excluded from poverty and capability deprivation. For the progressive left this is a particular challenge now that the Cameron Conservatives appear to have accepted the analysis of social-democratic commentators such as Polly Toynbee that relative poverty is the measure which ought to count when it comes to understanding inequality.

What do social democrats want public services to do?

Better public services have been at the heart of New Labour's domestic agenda for an important ideological reason which has rarely been clearly stated:

namely, that social democrats want to see a cohesive society built on social solidarity and equal opportunity, and public services are the shorthand for the range of governmental and public interventions which are the prerequisites for this. Public services should be an expression of community and public value. They are critical to maintaining social cohesion and solidarity through the common experience which they embody. Labour's moral and political base lies in this notion of community; R. H. Tawney, for instance, saw 'fellowship' as being at the core of the good society.[6] Here it is very clear that Labour's vision of the role of public services in underpinning cohesive communities is very much part of the European tradition rather than the more individualistic US one. What happened in New Orleans in the aftermath of Hurricane Katrina provided an object lesson in the danger of allowing social solidarity to wither away.

But public services are not just about maintaining community; they also have a critical role to play in enabling people to overcome disadvantage and inequality. For a previous generation of social democrats, such as Anthony Crosland, education was the key public service instrument though which to promote equal opportunity. But today, given the anatomy of inequality and social mobility, it is clear that public services across the piece need to be transformed so that the socially excluded can overcome capability deprivation.[7] A key challenge for progressives is to build a new consensus for tackling inequality. That means moving away from redistribution by stealth towards recognising that hard choices will need to be made about spending priorities and the highly targeted measures which will be necessary to make a decisive contribution to achieving a more equal society.

There is also a major challenge to be faced in terms of changing the relationship which public services embody between the state, the community and the individual. This goes beyond the 'enabling state', which Neil Kinnock talked about, to the 'empowering state', which gives people the ability to control and determine their own local services, effectively recreating a new public realm. Fragments of this approach can already be seen in some of Labour's more radical policies – Sure Start, the New Deal for Communities, local area agreements and city strategy pilots for worklessness. The linking thread is about providing funding and a policy framework within which to empower local people and local organisations to develop their own solutions to local versions of national issues. At the neighbourhood level there is the opportunity to develop a new synthesis between consumerism and collective action, and this could create a new type of public service which is responsive to individual need and preference and is shaped by local community involvement.

The narrative of change

If public services are to become the vehicle for the re-creation of a more vibrant public realm, based on citizen and consumer empowerment, then this requires a very different narrative than the one which has been developed by Labour up until now. What is required is a much sharper, more political sense of what a reform agenda for public services is all about. The old models have had their day. The post-war Beveridge and Webbian model of universal mass public services cannot rise to the challenges of overcoming inequality and transforming life-chances in the 80/20 society, while at the same time responding to the rapidly rising and individualised expectations of the hard-working majority. But neither can a model based on 1990s new public management theory, as the introduction to this collection suggests. The change which is required is about much more than 'steering rather than rowing', reframed and rationalised targets, earned autonomy, the purchaser/ provider split, and the extension of rational choice initiatives. Progressive public service reform should be about re-engineering public services so that they empower individuals and local communities, both giving people greater control over their own lives and enabling them to have the freedom to develop their own potential.

Progressives must be clear that this is about re-energising the public realm, not privatising it. A mixed economy of providers will be necessary to deliver this, but means should not be confused with ends. Consequently, Labour needs to talk more about the values which underpin improving public services. Embedding public service reform in the values of social cohesion and social justice will not only make it easier to explain why change needs to happen; it will also draw a much clearer battle line with the Conservatives. The means are important but they should not be allowed to either distort or infect the values which underpin Labour's approach to public services. There is much more which can be done with important ideas such as 'public value' to demonstrate that Labour's approach can breathe fresh life into the public realm. Public services and public space can be improved by private endeavour but Labour should be clear that the key value here is that the public realm matters.

Second, there needs to be a clearer story about why reform is necessary. The problem which Labour has suffered from so far is that too much public discussion has been given over to the tools which are necessary for change, rather than to what it is that Labour is trying to achieve. So a greater focus should be put on what the outcomes are which improved public services should deliver and what the public's experience would be of these. There are two levels to this. On the one hand, Labour should be making the case for better societal outcomes from public services, such as closing the education and opportunity gap in post-sixteen education, or closing the health inequality gap. On the other hand, the next stage of reform needs to develop a proper dialogue, mostly at local level, about what people themselves want to see from their public services. The priority here is to ensure that public service strategy is driven both by social justice considerations and by the need to improve people's individual experience of services, through voice- and choice-based empowerment.

Third, we need a clearer view of the role of the state in relation to public services. This will be another important battle line with the Conservatives, whose position can be crudely summarised as 'there is such a thing as society' but it doesn't need to rely on state activity. The political right have always been most comfortable with a small state, what Robert Nozick called the minimal state, whose primary function is to guarantee the security of its citizens and to protect livelihood and property rights.[8] Traditionally the left have argued for an expanded role for the state to promote positive rights, not just to protect negative ones. The left, in addition to seeing the state as the means for achieving social justice, have also seen it as the embodiment of social cohesion or secular society. But this view of the state has come under increasing pressure for both good and bad reasons. There is a tension between the state as a provider on the one hand and an enabler or empowerer on the other. At the same time there is policy confusion about how the state should cope with an increasingly diverse society. The debate about faith schools may only be the start of this; separate treatment within the health service could be the next test and we are already seeing the consequence of effective community segregation in housing policy. At the heart of this is the need to create a new consensus about the role of the state, for example, in ensuring social cohesion and social equity, but not being the sole provider.

Fourth, progressives need to develop a political strategy to deliver change rather than just to signal it. That means thinking seriously about change management, about how to build a movement for change which involves public service professionals and workers alongside the public. Lasting change cannot be done to people, it has to be achieved with them. The temptation to signal a direction of travel on a particular policy area by picking a fight with those employed in the system is ultimately self-defeating. We need large numbers of public service workers and professionals to be part of the reform movement, both because this is the only way in which change can really be effective and also because their witness to what has already been achieved will be far more credible with the public than anything ministers can say. MORI research has shown, perhaps not surprisingly, that whereas doctors and teachers are trusted by nine out of ten people to tell them the truth about public services, ministers, journalists and business leaders are trusted by only two out of ten. The same research study also showed that most key groups of public service professionals do not feel a strong sense of allegiance to their government department.[9] So it's clear that so far as public services are concerned the only trusted messengers are the professionals and they don't trust the message. This has to change – public service workers and professionals have got to be involved in the reform process if it is to be sustainable.

Fifth, public service reform needs to be driven by a more considered strategy, which builds a case and enlists advocates before launching into binary choices on policy solutions. We should pick our priorities carefully and concentrate at any one time on fewer areas for policy change. Trying to achieve change simultaneously on too many fronts risks policy confusion and, worse still, making Labour look incompetent. It also leaves the public bewildered and understandably unclear about Labour's public service message.

Public services for the twenty-first century

As a social-democratic party, New Labour must be clear that its ultimate priority is creating a more cohesive and equal society, in which people are empowered to shape their own destinies. Public service policy must be driven by this objective. That means that Labour's overall approach should be to ensure that public services are re-engineered so that they can much more effectively help reduce inequality while at the same time meeting the fast-rising aspirations of the comfortable majority. Labour's approach will need to maintain a number of explicit values and elements in balance with each other:

- Progressive universalism: at the core of a social-democratic perspective on public services must be universalism, the belief that public services should be for everyone in society, rather than being residual services for the poor. It is this universalist experience which is critical to maintaining social solidarity and social cohesion. Moreover, there is a political imperative to ensuring that the middle class continue to use public services, in order to maintain the current generous political settlement on public spending. Risk pooling is at the heart of key public services, such as health, and this universalist idea is not only more equitable but also more efficient than private systems. The challenge for progressives is to ensure that public services can keep up with rising aspirations in order to continue to justify their universalist character.

- Redistribution: while public services need to be based on progressive universalism, they also have a major role to play in promoting social justice and tackling inequality. Public services or interventions focused on transforming the circumstances of those in the bottom 20 per cent will be redistributive and New Labour needs to be explicit about this; that is the price of creating greater social cohesion. For example, there is now a growing understanding that early-years intervention is critical to reducing inequality. But a progressive agenda on this will need to go beyond just provision of childcare to creating quality pre-school education, with properly qualified and regulated early-years teaching at its heart. Such a reform will require substantial funding from what will already be a tightly constrained public spending total.

- Collective empowerment at neighbourhood and community level: where possible public services should be co-produced with local people at neighbourhood level, which means using technology and networks to enable people to improve their own communities and to exercise control over how they want services to operate. This bottom-up approach will involve a big extension of the role of voluntary sector organisations within public services – not so that they become quasi-public bureaucracies but rather so that they can be at the interface between services and local people, helping empower local communities, as Stephen Bubb elaborates in Chapter 6. Environmental policy will be a key test bed for this. There are few institutions to encumber the development of more socially innovative practice and because the environment straddles the divide between personal behaviour and state action, it is an obvious area in which to promote co-production – for example on recycling, soft and hard transport demand management, and energy conservation.

- Individual empowerment through choice and personalisation: for services which cannot be so easily co-produced then the principle of giving people a greater say should be reflected in structuring services around their needs; in education this will lead to personalised pathways for learning, and in other services this may be reflected in letting people choose how they can access services and offering them greater choice between GPs, schools etc. For this to have real impact, it will have to involve, where practical, devolving budgets to individuals to enable them to make their own choices about what sort of service they need and who they want it delivered by, something which is already beginning to happen in some areas of social care.

- Involving public service workers and professionals: in order to build sustainable long-term change, the next stage of the reform agenda will need to build deeper networks of change managers and public service champions within the main public services; this will require a more strategic and collaborative approach to developing and embedding reform.

- Making public services part of the governance of place: Wherever possible, priorities and delivery for public services should be determined locally, either at the level of the neighbourhood or community or at the more strategic level of the governance of place. This means that substantial decentralisation and devolution should be critical elements within a future public service reform strategy, based on a real transfer of power away from the central state and towards local councils and local communities. Distinctiveness in terms of social, cultural and economic priorities and identity should be the key drivers of public services such as policing, environmental protection, economic development and transport.

- Value for money/efficiency: to earn the support and trust of voters and make best use of national resources, public services will have to continue to demonstrate that they are efficiently run and represent good value for money. That means that there will rightly be a continuous focus on how things can be done better and more efficiently through competition and more joined-up working in terms of processes and cost centres between public services (shared services).

- Diversity of supply: in order to respond to the challenge of improving and reshaping public services, it is clear that monolithic models for service delivery will not be appropriate, something which has long been understood by social democrats in other European countries. That means that there will have to be greater diversity of supply, with an expanded role in public services for the voluntary sector, social innovators and private firms. But progressives need to be more open about where the tensions between this and strengthening the public realm may lie. Stronger local accountability and scrutiny processes need to be built into public service delivery.

Progressives need a new public service credo which explains their overall approach to public services and provides clarity about the future direction of travel. Underpinning this should be the values of social justice, social solidarity, and community and individual empowerment. The new universalism should mean everyone gets what they want and need from public service, but not necessarily in the same way. That means that public services must respond to the needs of all users, helping everyone attain their potential, but given the diverse needs of both individuals and communities, services will need to be delivered in a variety of different ways by different providers and, wherever possible, with and by the people themselves. The guiding principle of this new universalism should be that no community or individual should be poorly served by public services and that the power balance should be reversed so that, as far as possible, ordinary people and local communities determine their own local services. The tools for achieving this will vary; what should underpin all are the principles of empowerment, capability building, and equitable common funding.

Part II

Empowering citizens and communities

3

The state, the citizen and public services
A new collectivist agenda

Gerry Stoker

In today's world the state–citizen relationship is characterised by ambiguity. We want the state to protect us from crime but not to subject us to unnecessary surveillance. We want the state to block terrorist threats but not to usurp our freedom. We want the state to do more to save the environment but not to tax our essential driving trips. Any new agenda for public services needs to take account of this reality. This chapter argues for a new collectivist agenda that encourages citizens to do more for themselves, supports a myriad of community and not-for-profit institutions, and enables citizens to exercise greater control over the operation and functions of the state.

Some progressives think of the state and more particularly public services as expressing a distinctive and positive set of communal values by providing a counterpoint to the selfishness stirred by consumer capitalism. The state promotes other-regarding and communal activity against the self-interested and individualistic decision-making of the market. Colin Crouch,[1] for example, argues that we should avoid contaminating public services with private sector features and practices precisely because they will undermine the quality of universal citizenship and rights expressed in state provision of public services. The state is for all and public services express the values of solidarity and mutual support of a community.

This chapter starts by demonstrating that citizens do not share such 'dewy-eyed' visions of the state and public services. Many citizens – for good reasons – are wary of the state, sceptical about its capacities and uncertain about its motivations and objectives. There are particular pressures in today's world –

such as globalisation and the loss of trust in politics – that add still further to the tension in state–citizen relationships.

To meet the reality of state–citizen relations we need to break with those progressives who insist on the abstract philosophical promotion of the values of the public realm versus the nasty world of commercial decision making. Instead progressives need to recognise the inherent contradictions and the new challenges embedded in the state–citizen relationship and not to reify it as a model of some high ideal of human expression. We approach the state as consumer, citizen, taxpayer, carer, user and supplicant in a jumble of ideas and emotions. We need to think through the complexity of these real relationships and not explore them through the lens of idealised conceptions of citizenship. Above all, progressives need not so much to rehash the case for the state as to recognise that collective judgement can be expressed in other ways than through the state. A new collectivist vision for public services is set out in the middle of the chapter.

The final section of the chapter outlines a strategy designed to deliver that new collectivist vision. It argues for a public service strategy driven by radical decentralisation expressed through both delegation and devolution, an enhanced network management practice for public services, a culture of respect for human rights among public service providers of all sectors, and a determined effort to allow families and communities to take more responsibility for themselves.

Why the state and citizen live in tension

Why should citizens be wary of the state? The traditional answer is that the state expresses the monopoly of legitimate coercion in modern society. It can send people to war, move them from their homes, take a proportion of their income and wealth and imprison them. For this reason that great invention of constitutional democracy is widely seen as the best learnt defence of the citizen against the state. Nothing about the twenty-first century weakens this case and as progressives we should be keen to ensure continuing support for the principles of constitutional democracy. But at the same time we should be looking to improve its practice since it is plain that many citizens in mature democracies find conventional politics a massive turn-off.[2]

Yet in today's world constitutional protection for the citizen through the processes of formal democracy, even if they worked perfectly, would not be good enough. The state now stands considerably beyond a minimum 'watchman' in our lives. It is an institution and an idea that enters every nook and cranny of our lives. Today's state is a 'cradle to grave' affair and the reality is that we need it; yet we have grounds for fearing it at the same time, for a whole variety of new reasons beyond those of traditional constitutional theory. This argument soon becomes clear if you examine each of four dominant expectations we put on the modern state.

The first set of measures provided by the state is designed to promote our basic freedoms, to provide us with protection and justice. Through ensuring the rule of law and creating a range of institutions and practices to achieve that, the effective modern state provides a great service to citizens. By protecting us from terrorism, foreign invasion and domestic crime, the state makes a vital contribution to well-being. Finally, under its broad umbrella the effective state provides access to justice, so that wrongs against us may be righted.

Yet although we welcome these measures we doubt the effectiveness of the state and fear the consequences of its pursuit of them in the modern world. Access to the law for redress remains stubbornly unequal to some degree; fear of crime remains high and the terrorist threat feels at best to be only partially successfully managed. We imprison larger numbers of people than ever before but even the staunchest supporter of a tough justice policy must have doubts about whether the system works as well as they would wish. But beyond these doubts about effectiveness are fears about what the state is doing in this area. The legal and court systems seem to many citizens to be an unwieldy business, lacking a cutting edge to deal with certain types of criminality, and yet at the same time they offer an unwelcoming environment in which to seek justice. The fight against terrorism appears to lead to measures that curtail traditional freedoms, whether they be stop-and-search practices by the police, the introduction of identity cards or extended detention without charge. These measures may or may not be seen as justified but it is difficult to deny that they have an oppressive quality that could make any citizen at least wary of what the state is doing in our name.

The state has also become the actor that we look to to provide services that meet basic and more advanced needs in our lives. It is not just our protector; it is our saviour in providing health, social care, education and in some instances housing and income support. Sometimes this is experienced as organised beneficence as recipients obtain the benefits of the investment made by themselves and others through a redistributive tax system. At their most positive, institutions such as the NHS express communal values of solidarity.

But the state in this arena of meeting needs also rations and redistributes in a way that citizens find difficult to fathom. And gather any group of citizens in a social setting and ask them for examples about waste in the provision of public services and the examples pour out.

For many services there appears to be an unending spiral of public expectations about the quality of what they receive, no matter what level of resources are provided. An Ipsos MORI survey conducted in August 2006 asked people what they thought a reasonable wait was for a GP's appointment, if they had a bad chest infection; it found that 65 per cent of people expected to be seen in one day or less. The government's target is forty-eight hours. Asked how long it should take to be seen in A&E if they thought they had a broken wrist, 66 per cent of people said they would expect to be seen in two hours or less. The government's target is four hours. And for an outpatient appointment for a non-serious back problem some 45 per cent of people would expect to be seen in two weeks or less. The current average wait is just over six weeks and the government target is that no one will wait more than thirteen weeks.[3]

Beyond spiralling expectations citizens are hearing that the state is no longer simply there to provide. Rather it has expectations of your help. It wants you to eat more healthily, be a better parent, take regular exercise and save for your retirement. The state has the character of both a generous aunt and a nagging nanny. Again citizens are left in a position where they are far from sure which of the two faces of the state they are going to experience at any given exchange. Ambiguity and contradiction are inherent in our experience of the state.

We also expect the state to ensure our current and future amenity: the physical environment, transport and communication pathways which are central to how we live. Again the state has much to offer in ensuring our mobility, facilitating the continuing communications revolution and pro-moting care for our environment. Yet here again there are obvious questions to be raised about its effectiveness. But more than that, it appears that the state will need to ask us to change our behaviour in order to save us from ourselves. If we are going to avoid the adverse effects of global warming we may need to cut energy consumption, fly less and source foods more locally. We may need to accept higher taxes to reflect the environmental impact of our activity and road tolls in order to ease congestion and make mobility possible. In short the state has got a message of 'tough love' to sell in this policy area.

Finally we have expectations in the modern world of large-scale migration and changing work and family patterns that the state should promote community cohesion and togetherness. It is difficult to over-estimate the complexities involved in this role for the modern state. We have moved from 'hard-wiring' challenges to a concern with 'soft-wiring' society. It was enough of a challenge to the state to build schools, roads and hospitals and ensure the supply of clean water, gas, electricity and all the requirements of modern life. But now it is required to deal with issues that require a degree of tacit knowledge and depth of understanding that may be beyond it. Moreover the importance of emotional intelligence may be one of the great insights of social psychology at the beginning of the twenty-first century but it would be an extreme optimist who felt that such intelligence was the default position of most arms and agents of the state.

It is vital that the multiple faces of the state as experienced by the citizen are understood. We ask the state to do a lot and it often fails to keep up with our rising expectations. The state gives, supports and nurtures but it also controls, challenges and divides. The state and citizen, unsurprisingly in this light, are not easy companions.

Things have got harder for the state

There are contradictions inherent and embedded in the state–citizen relationship but there are also good grounds for thinking that the relationship has got even more problematic in recent decades. There are tensions and large-scale questions about the state's capture by its employees, its capacity for effective action in a globalised world and its authority in the light of a steep loss of public trust in authority. If you add to this that all is not well in our families and communities it becomes clearer still that the state–citizen relationship is challenging and problematic.

The captured state?
The idea that the state could be captured by inside interests has a long history in progressive thought – witness the arguments in different circumstances of G. D. H. Cole and George Orwell – so it is not some trumped-up charge of the New Right. Public-choice critiques that inspired Margaret Thatcher and Keith Joseph are overblown with their emphasis on how public servants are narrowly bent on the pursuit of power and money, under the guise of public service. As most empirical studies have shown, public servants are neither

entirely knavish nor wholly knightly in their behaviour and cannot be said to have captured the state. Indeed I would go further and argue that many are mission oriented and see the values of a public service ethos as central to their motivation. The issue of the captured state is I think more mundane and in many respects more intractable.

The starting point for our thinking is to recognise just how many people are employed by the state and the scale of the challenge involved in getting them to act in an efficient and effective manner. The largest UK retailer, Tesco, boasted record profits and success in eleven countries in October 2006 and employs 340,000 people.[4] In 2005 UK local government alone employed 2.6 million and one authority – admittedly the one with the largest population in the UK, Birmingham City Council – employed 52,000 people overall, or 37,000 full-time equivalents.[5] The NHS in 2005 had 1.3 million staff.[6] The point is that Tesco management are increasingly concerned that the number of their staff means that it is becoming near impossible to establish a clear ethos and way of working. But how do you get the large numbers of those employed in public service focused on the task in hand and geared up with the right training and support to enable them to do their jobs? How can you as a manager understand what it is like to be at the front line given the scale of many state institutions? It is the humdrum, everyday dependence of the state on such a vast army to get things done that leads, if not to its capture, then at least to a constant tendency for it not to perform quite as its political masters and citizens would like. State employees inevitably have bad days, are diverted by personal problems and may not always have their mind on the job and the scale of the state makes for enormous difficulties in controlling this vast empire.

The weakened state?

Some point the finger at globalisation and the rise of the global economy, dominated by multi-national corporations, as great forces that sweep away state power because the economic power they express is so overwhelming that political organisations cannot resist. There can be no doubt that globalisation brings in its wake substantial changes in the way that economies and societies work, driven by a more rapid communication and a stronger set of connections between different peoples and organisations across the world.

The anti-globalisation lobby fears that globalisation is an unstoppable force driving the world economy into an integrated, borderless whole, in which multi-national companies can move freely to locate where it best suits them and in which innovation and changes in production and consumption are fuelled by avaricious companies and fashion-obsessed consumers and enabled by spectacular technological advance. The degree and intensity with which the world is being tied into a single market makes national resistance pointless. But as Andrew Gamble points out: 'Acceptance that there is something called globalisation, or at least that there are certain trends towards a global market, is not the end of the argument but the beginning of it, since there are so many ways in which states and groups can adjust to these changes.'[7]

Globalisation does mean that the state needs to learn to operate in a different way. It needs the capacity to act in localities and regions where economic activity can be co-ordinated around clusters and it needs a capacity to think and act globally. This weakening of the nation state provides a tough challenge. It requires an appropriate level of local autonomy combined with international governance capacity. The state in the twenty-first century needs in the light of globalisation to become a very different animal. It is necessary to think of the forms and institutions of the state in new ways.

The state in a post-deference society

The environment of British civil society was more benign in the period of the great expansion of the welfare state after the Second World War than it is now. Large-scale projects and programmes were put together with a minimum of public consultation and pushed through. It was only in the 1960s and 1970s that people's protests about, for example, massive slum clearance programmes began to be heard. The state's projects and programmes had been carried along on a sea of deference. No more.

The British seem to have thought for at least two decades that most politicians are untrustworthy. Trusting politicians to tell the truth has been, at best, the view of only one in five of British citizens in various surveys between 1983 and 2004. It does appear that greater levels of trust in government could be observed in earlier periods, in the 1950s and 1960s. Now, you might think that an increased amount of distrust of politicians is a healthy thing, since otherwise why would accountability through elections be seen as important? But it perhaps becomes worrying when a lack of trust in politicians spills over into a lack of trust in information provided by government bodies. According to a MORI survey in 2005, 68 per cent think official figures are changed to support politicians' arguments; 59 per cent think the government uses them dishonestly; 58 per cent think official figures are politically interfered with.[8]

There is a wider loss of the legitimacy of authority in society. The police, judges, teachers and many others in positions of authority report a loss of respect and a greater willingness for their decisions to be challenged. Again there are reasons for thinking that the rise of critical citizens might be a good thing and healthy for our democratic creed. The difficulty is that the evidence points to the emergence of a culture of hopeless fatalism and deeply ingrained cynicism towards public institutions.

Failing families and communities
Sometimes the failings of society are unfairly put down to the state. Take for example the case of children looked after by local authorities. Harriet Sergeant, in a pamphlet published in September 2006, graphically highlights a system that we could all agree is under-performing:

> This year approximately 6,000 young people will emerge from the care of the state. What is their future? Of these 6,000, 4,500 of them will leave with no educational qualifications whatsoever. Within two years of leaving care 3,000 will be unemployed, 2,100 will be mothers or pregnant and 1,200 will be homeless. Out of the 6,000 just 60 will make it to university.[9]

Of course it is not necessary to conclude in the light of these findings, as Sergeant does, that the state is a 'rotten parent'. Rather I would argue that these figures show how difficult it is for the state – notwithstanding all its capacities and resources – to substitute effectively for the care, love and attention normally provided by families and communities in the upbringing of a child. Looked-after children have been failed by their families and communities and the state struggles to pick up the pieces. So what is important is to recognise just how hard it would appear to be to do anything about such problems once they are established. Failing communities and families are the key issue as much as any failings on the part of the state.

And there is evidence that all is not well in our communities. Robert Putnam has achieved considerable influence for his thesis that it is the lack of social capital – civic networks, mutual trust and shared obligations – in our societies that can explain the difficulties we face.[10] Everybody watches too much TV and as a result we have lost our capacity for community engagement, the bedrock of democratic politics. The trouble is that citizens today are self-absorbed non-joiners, generally not taking their civic duties seriously enough. I do not think that the evidence supports the idea implied by Putnam's work that citizens are simply now much less interested in the world around them and therefore less engaged. New communication technologies and TV may have reduced the relative importance of face-to-face exchanges but they have opened opportunities for other forms of exchange. But what is clear is that work demands, changing employment patterns and the rise of a rampant consumerism have taken a toll on traditional collective institutions such as trade unions, political parties and social clubs and as such civil society has to learn to operate in a new way.

The case for a new collectivism

The scale of complexities of state action today and lack of public trust in its decision making mean that the case for the state needs to be presented with even greater care today than in the past. Above all we need to articulate a vision for a new collectivism not premised on using state power and action to remedy society's ills but drawing instead on a more subtle understanding of where the efficacy and capacity of collective action comes from in today's world. It's the collective action of citizens, families and communities that matters. The state's job is to support and facilitate that action. It needs to empower citizens and help them cohere.

Public services are there to help ensure that the capabilities of citizens are realised: that citizens have the health, education and social networks to allow them to make something of their lives. But that job is always done in co-production with others – with families, communities and citizens themselves. The impact of the state on educational achievement is matched and surpassed by the role of parents. Good health depends more on the lifestyles and circumstances of people than the quality of care in hospitals. Citizens are co-producers and the best deciders when it comes to how to make the most of the opportunities they are given. Their empowerment is one key to a successful citizen–state relationship.

The welfare state has the capacity to bring people together, to express solidarity, mutual respect and cohesion. The state–citizen relationship should express in a practical way the idea that 'no man is an island'; to rub along on a crowded planet we need to co-operate with each other and our common humanity tells us we owe each other. The state's role can be to enforce society's rules against individual citizens. More generally and much more commonly it is there to provide the framework in which co-operative and co-ordinating activity can occur, whether that be through recycling, the activities of millions of volunteers or mutual insurance against sickness. The active engagement of citizens is central to any effective expression of solidarity. Public services, then, provide a way of equal citizens achieving freedom and expressing solidarity. The welfare state is not there to make people equal. It is there to allow their equality to find expression by giving them the tools and capacities to make their own choices. Public services are not there to do things for people but to enable people to do things better for themselves. So while expert judgement and the representative political process remain at the heart of defining public services, increasingly citizens themselves are looking to exercise greater control both as individuals and as part of a collective.

Our commitment should be to a new collectivism: a welfare collectivism that is not about a system of public ownership and control but rather takes as its ambition joint citizen ownership of social issues and control over solutions expressed through an enabling state and a vibrant role for community, voluntary and private sector groups.

A strategy to deliver a new collectivism

Empowerment and practical solidarity should be the progressive's goals for public services. We can talk about 'our' values till the cows come home but it is delivery that matters. And delivering on empowerment and solidarity is massively difficult because the tensions in the state–citizen relationship often stall progress and confuse our practice. In this final section of the chapter I spell out a strategy designed to meet these tensions head on and deliver a public services strategy that can make a reality of a new collectivism. I focus attention on four factors: decentralisation; respect for human rights; interventions that promote family, community and civic responsibility; and the virtues of providing services through a mixed market of providers.

Decentralisation has to be a key component in plans to restructure the state–citizen relationship because the scale of the state, the complexity of what it is trying to do and the need to actively engage civil society in finding and implementing solutions mean that more policy and decisions need to be made away from the commanding heights of Whitehall and Westminster. This insight has now become part of the accepted wisdom of our age but a large question mark hangs over what is required to deliver decentralisation. It is important to distinguish between two elements of the strategy: those that promote delegation and those that provide for devolution. The former leaves the setting of ends in central hands but delegates the means to others; the latter hands over both the setting of ends and of means to others. Both are legitimate elements in a strategy of decentralisation but it is important not to confuse the two as their logics are completely different.

The logic of delegation

The logic of delegation can be invoked in a variety of ways. Policy wonks and ministers talk about giving power back to the front line of public service providers or giving others independent power to make judgement calls on their behalf. They are recognising the limits to their capacities and their reliance on others to deliver public services. But more formal theories of delegation start with the idea that the principal (the author of the delegation) prefers the agent to work towards objectives in tune with the boss's wishes. The relationship is defined by the power to set a framework resting in the hands of the principal but an information advantage in the hands of the agent as he or she is the person with direct involvement in the activity. The issue becomes: 'Is the gain produced by delegating the decision to a more informed party worth the loss produced by having someone with different preferences make the choice?'[11] Delegation is about letting go but in the hope of getting outcomes that you value.

Delegation theory would argue against a developed target culture. Intensive monitoring efforts by the principal are undermined in the context of information asymmetry and will be damaging in the long run to the reputation of both principal and agent. So when you delegate you have to let go. Yet you can and should set the rules of the game: influence how the agency can make a decision, who it needs to consult, the speed at which it can be allowed to make decisions. Moreover as principal you can try to delegate to your allies, those that share similar preferences to you. Thus an agency can be given quite broad remit but an environment can be created in which it is more likely to make decisions in tune with the perspective of the principal.

Most delegation assumes that accountability for outcomes remains with the principal hence the justification for steering while delegating. There is one interesting variation identified in delegation theory: the principal creates an insulated form of delegation that keeps him or her away from the decision but still does a job for the principal in that it delivers a credible commitment that decisions are going to be made in the long-term public interest. The best-known example is that of delegating control over the money supply and interest rates to an independent decision-making body to insulate it from short-term political interests. The key point to be made about this form of delegation is that it is a tool to be used only in special circumstances, otherwise there is a danger of creating an entire system of delegation that lacks accountability. Creating an independent agency to manage and oversee the production of official statistics is an example of insulated delegation that would appear to be easy to justify because the accountability issues are not intense, but creating a similar agency to oversee the NHS would raise more serious issues.

Delegation is a great tool to break over-reliance on the target culture. It abandons the logic of monitoring in favour of the idea that those at the front line have an information advantage and therefore more effective capacity to make decisions than those at the centre. But it is a tool that has its own logic. You can delegate with strings and keep accountability lines in place. And in special circumstances you can delegate using a deliberately insulated form but at a cost in terms of loss of accountability that will have to be considered very carefully.

The logic of devolution

The logic of devolution is very different to that of delegation. Under devolution, authority for setting both ends and means is decentralised to another. In short there is a handover of not only delivery responsibility but also accountability for outcomes. You are accepting that someone not only knows more than you but they are better placed to judge what should be done and whether it has been done. Devolution, because it hands over all aspects of a decision, is a form of decentralisation that cannot easily be reversed. The legitimacy and growing confidence of the Scottish Parliament, the Welsh Assembly and the Greater London Authority show that devolution tends to grow institutions that expand their decision-making capacity and once the door to devolution is opened it cannot be easily closed.

The most obvious gaping hole in any devolution strategy for public services is its application to England. The urgency of the need for a new constitutional settlement for England cannot be over-stressed. Whether devolution be to stand-alone local agencies, local government, city regions or regional assemblies, the most important thing is simply to get on with it. And yes, there remains a strong case for a double devolution, not only to formal local institutions but also to more informal networks in communities and neighbourhoods.

A new management through networks

Alongside reforms of delegation and devolution, managers of public services need to become focused less on running their organisations and more on managing a system of delivery. A new collectivism demands a capacity for state, community, voluntary and private agencies to work together more effectively in partnership. As Lester Salamon puts it: 'The "new governance" shifts the emphasis from management skills and the control of large bureaucratic organisations to enablement skills, the skills required to engage partners arrayed horizontally in networks, to bring multiple stakeholders together for a common end in a situation of interdependence.'[12]

Salamon identifies three core sets of skills. The first is activation skills, getting the relevant players involved in helping to resolve problems. Whether that is getting enough 'buy-in' from various participants in a scheme to promote environmental improvement or, on a more hard-nosed basis, ensuring that there is enough of a market in producers of care services for the elderly, a key requirement for the manager in the context of network management is coaxing participants and more broadly constructing an environment suited to their search for public value. A second skill set identified by Salamon is the capacity to orchestrate in order to help the various elements of any network collaborate more effectively. There are skills of diplomacy, communication and bargaining often involved in achieving co-ordination. Finally there is the modulation skill set, in which the central challenge for public managers is to determine what combination of incentives and penalties should be brought to bear so as to achieve the outcomes desired.

The adoption of a human rights culture, not a legal system

In the context of a new collectivism we need an overarching set of values to steer all those engaged in public service delivery. Citizens also need to feel able to challenge the state and demand more respect and dignity. Here the 1998 Human Rights Act has a role to play, not as a formal legal mechanism but as an expression of the values that should drive public service provision.[13] What is required is not a narrow legalistic approach to human rights but rather the encouragement of a respect for human rights principles among all public service providers. The principles that underpin the European Convention on Human Rights provide an ideal backcloth to public service provision. Fairness, respect, equity and dignity (or FRED) are guiding principles that both providers and clients of public services can relate to and regard as appropriate to defining how public services should be delivered. Such an approach would avoid the dangers we now face of creating an overly legalistic culture in public services similar to the litigious environment that pervades US healthcare. FRED principles are about respect and do not inherently promote a 'no risk' practice among professionals or tie us up in knots about what constitutes equal treatment for all clients.

The issue to be addressed is not how to legally enforce these principles through the courts but rather how to ensure that a human rights culture is enshrined in public service practice. If you want services driven by the user, to design services tailored to individual need and to expand and support individual choice then the human rights framework provides the perfect home. If you want public services to protect the vulnerable and weak then again a positive commitment and proactive policy towards human rights in public bodies could provide an important part of the answer.

People should be able to use human rights arguments outside the courts in order to hold public service providers – from the public, private or voluntary sectors – to account for the services they provide and the way they provide them. In any case public authorities should take a proactive stance to establish a culture not just of complying with but also promoting human rights in their organisations. The appeal of a human rights approach is that it could be transformative for public services, both empowering people to stand up for their rights and preventing threats to those rights in that it will encourage public bodies to take a proactive approach to rethink their policies and practices.

Interventions that promote family, community and civic responsibility

It is a truism to say that we have rights and responsibilities. In the previous section of this chapter I talked about how users of public services could make real their rights. But equally we need strategies to ensure that citizens, families and communities realise their responsibilities. There are limits to what we can expect the state to deliver. But the search for responsibility is also a search for empowerment. We need to give people the opportunities and capacities to take responsibility.

For individual citizens there is undoubtedly a fund of goodwill towards supporting others that can be built on. According to the 2005 citizenship survey half of the people in England had in the previous year undertaken volunteering at least once a month, giving a total of 20.4 million active volunteers.[14] Some 78 per cent of people had, according to the same survey, given money to a charity in the previous four weeks. The most common block to volunteering was identified as work commitments. There are measures that could be taken to promote both the giving of volunteer time and charitable donations that have been undertaken but could be developed still further. Employers could, for example, be encouraged to support volunteer schemes among their staff, and further tax changes could be made to support charitable giving.

It is difficult not to agree with John Hutton, the Secretary of State for Work and Pensions, when he argues that progressive thinkers have always been a bit leery of talking about families. Yet as he points out:

> The family is the bedrock of the welfare state. It is the family which cares for the new born, raises children, instils a sense of values, coaxes and encourages children to learn and thrive. It is the extended family – grandparents, aunts, uncles, godparents and family friends – who play a crucial caring role.[15]

The value of this informal care has been estimated at £20 billion a year. But it is difficult to put a value on the emotional support and benefit that comes from these exchanges. This is an area where we cannot afford to have no strategy. As Hutton points out, there are schemes to support and programmes of help but what is required above all is more radical thinking about how 'our welfare society helps support families combine the opportunity to work with the opportunity to care'.[16]

As for communities, it is to be hoped that a number of new opportunities for people to take responsibility will be enhanced. The options are numerous: through engagement in decision making, volunteering and involvement in service delivery or new forms of community ownership and the management of assets. There are many examples of good practice; what is required is a framework in which they can grow and spread.

Concluding note

The relationship between state and citizen is not an easy partnership and never will be. But progressives need to be prepared to think radically and bravely about what to change and what to leave alone. Because if they do not others will. The beginning of the twenty-first century sees demands for another shift in the pattern of the relationship. The state needs to become more decentralised and a better network partner. We need to match a commitment to citizen rights with a culture that expects and demands more from citizens. It's the collective action of citizens, families and communities that matters. The state's job is to support and facilitate that action. A more decentralised state and a more responsible citizenry are the keys to the state–citizen relationship in the future. Empower and support communities and citizens and they will deliver. We need to recognise the richness and potential of a new collectivism.

We need to play to the strengths of all partners in collectivism to a greater degree. Citizens and their organisations are naturally responsive, able to pick up new demands and oriented to bringing into play local knowledge and capacities. The state through its permanence and formality has the capacity for strategic thinking and planning for the long term. Bold thinking and reform could enable us to have the best of all worlds.

The new collectivism is not anti-state but rather demands that the state play a different role, which it is equipped to do by way of its character and essential features. The state is not well suited to be the provider of all services or the sole carrier of our moral commitment to solidarity and fraternity. But it is well equipped to structure our environment to help us individually and collectively to be free. Freedom requires the creation of the positive conditions for people to make their own choices and support one another in doing so. The state, through its legal force, authority and capacity for focusing financial and human resources, has a vital role to play in creating an environment where other forms of collectivism can thrive. Allow the state to step back from taking responsibility for everything and it will become more adept at taking responsibility for that long-term strategic thinking and organising that it is ideally suited to deliver. The enabling state is not a lesser institution but rather an institution that has found its true cause and mission as far as progressives are concerned. The enabling state is there to support and encourage a collectivism that incorporates governmental and non-governmental institutions, community groups, social networks and citizens in a shared practice of collectivism that in turn puts people in a position to make the lifestyle choices that deliver the most benefit to them.

4

Financing public services

Anthony Giddens

What are the public services?

The term 'public services' is often used as though its meaning were simple and straightforward. But it is not. 'Public' itself is an ambiguous and difficult notion. It can mean a body of people, that is, the citizenry – 'the public'. Public services would then refer to services directed to serving the needs of the citizens. This cannot be the whole meaning of 'public services' though, because there are many 'private' organisations that serve the needs of the population at large, such as supermarket chains.

'Public' can also mean 'public-spirited', in the sense of services driven by altruistic motives of some sort. There is quite often a tinge of this idea when people speak of the public services, especially those who speak positively about them. On the political left there is a residue of traditional socialism in this meaning. 'Public' contains the idea of a collectivity, and is hence deemed to be superior to the more mean-spirited world of commercial enterprise, driven as it is by the pursuit of profit. Yet this notion can be doubted. After all, it is a prime tenet of economic theory that profit-driven enterprise often serves the public good better than economic decisions taken by higher authority, even where that authority is acting from impeccable motives.

'Public' can also mean 'open' and 'accountable', and there is an element of this too in the way in which those in favour of public services speak about them. It implies a close connection between public services and democracy. Those who run the public services are accountable to the public, because their masters are elected by the citizenry and because the public can put pressure on their conduct of affairs. However, members of the public are able to exert pressure upon commercial organisations too, since they are able to pick and choose what they buy in the marketplace.

Finally, 'public' can be a synonym for 'state-provided', or 'largely state provided', and this is its most generic sense when people talk about public services. This usage can be dangerous, however, since it can lead to eliding the 'public' and the state. Those who work for the state can imply that ipso facto they serve the public interest, whereas this isn't necessarily true at all. For instance, unions working in the public sector may claim that by definition they are representing the public, whereas in fact they might be acting against the public interest – for instance, defending archaic work practices.

Why all this nit-picking about terms? Is it in any way relevant to a chapter that is supposed to be about the funding of public services? Well, yes, it is. We can't talk about funding public services unless we are clear what public services are, because that decision can make a major difference to what the funding is actually for.

I would suggest defining 'public services' in the following way:

1. The public services comprise organisations that receive substantial funding from the state – that is to say, from the taxpayer. The 'state' can be national or local. I don't think it is possible to be more specific about how substantial the funding proportion has to be, and at the edge there are no clear boundaries. Very few services, however, are funded wholly by the state. We have to speak of 'funding' rather than 'ownership', because 'public services' goes well beyond those that are actually nationalised.

2. Democratic pressure can be put on providers to influence how the service in question is organised, or how decisions are reached. Such pressure is exerted through national elections and the agendas that parties develop to fight those elections. But it can also be mobilised through the variety of democratic options available to citizens to influence political processes, such as seeing one's local MP.

3. The guiding normative criterion is that of the public interest. What constitutes the public interest in any particular context may not be easy to define, and is likely often to be contested. Nevertheless it is a crucial point and one to which New Labour should pay especial attention. The government has failed to develop an adequate political vocabulary to convey it to citizens. Public services cannot be identified with the state in a simplistic way, since what the state does may or may not be in the public interest in a given situation. The state may be inefficient, overly bureaucratic or dominated by producer interests; it may treat its clients poorly; and so forth. 'Privatisation' – turning some services over to commercial deliverers – is not ipso facto a betrayal of the public interest,

but on the contrary may sometimes serve that interest better.

4. There is a public service ethos which has real purchase, even if people in public sector organisations have many other motives and concerns too. Research comparing public service workers with those in business organisations shows overall differences in attitudes between the two. In one study, for instance, managers working in the public sector, the non-profit sector and commercial firms were asked about their views of their work. Among sixteen possible goals, public sector managers placed 'providing a service for the community' first. This aim did not appear anywhere at all in the top ten goals for managers in the commercial sector. Much the same contrast was found between those working in non-profit groups and workers in commercial settings.

5. Clients in the public services are what I call 'citizen-consumers'. In the commercial marketplace, standards are guaranteed primarily through competition. Individuals in this context are more like 'consumer-citizens'. A consumer good that is inferior to its competitors and offered at the same price will be forced out of the market. The power of the consumer in this respect is real power. The state is needed, but mainly in order to oversee the general framework of the market, prevent monopolies and provide the means of guaranteeing contracts. There can, and should, be choice in the domain of public services too. However, standards normally cannot be guaranteed primarily through choice, as in the marketplace. They have to be supervised in a more direct way by professionals and public authorities. Citizenship takes priority over consumerism, which is why I speak of the 'citizen-consumer'. Choice is not the sole means of voice, because of the integration of public services with the mechanisms of democracy. However, since there are no clear-cut divisions between the public services and other sectors, many overlaps and interconnections are possible.

6. The 'services' provided in the public services do not only involve services in the narrow definition of that term. In other words, they include more than only the provision of person-to-person goods – the sense of 'service' in 'service industries'. They comprise also, for example, the procurement or construction of material goods, such as transport infrastructure or housing. This point takes on a new significance when we consider the rising importance of environmental issues.

According to such a definition, what institutional areas are to be included under the general rubric of public services? Education and healthcare certainly, even though there is a considerable amount of private provision in both, interconnected with the 'public' elements in complex ways; defence; policing; the law courts; prisons and their administration; major aspects of transport and communications, although the complexities are well illustrated by the railways, with their mixed system of control; the BBC, which has its commercial divisions; the welfare and benefits system; a diversity of agencies receiving partial state funding, including quangos; local services of diverse kinds.

Funding dilemmas

It follows from what I have said that there is a relationship between the proportion of GDP taken up by taxation and the likely state of the public services; however, it also follows that such a relationship is a loose one. There are different ways in which the public services may be organised to serve the public interest and only looking at the evidence will tell us what is best. Moreover, different countries might choose varying mixtures of provision. For instance, the proportion of students in higher education is everywhere on the increase. In a society (such as Sweden) where the proportion of taxation in relation to GDP is elevated, higher education continues to be funded mainly be the taxpayer. In the UK, following the last set of government reforms, those who benefit from going to college or university pay part of the cost, albeit retrospectively. These are different ways of reaching much the same goal.

When we look at the condition of the public services in the UK, we should be very clear about why they are as they are – that is to say, in some key areas still markedly inferior to those in the best-performing countries. The historically low level of tax revenue in Britain is certainly one reason. For a long while it stood at about 37 per cent of GDP, a considerably lower level than the EU average. It was important to generate more revenue to refurbish and upgrade the public services, as the Labour government has done since 1997. Today the proportion of taxation in relation to GDP stands at about 41 per cent and a great deal of new investment in the public services has been made.

However, there are two other reasons. One is simply the poor economic performance of the UK in the early post-war period, when it was the 'sick man' of Europe, a situation that lasted for well over two decades. Britain simply was not as rich as most of the other industrial countries over that period and therefore had less to spend upon public goods. A second is the impact of Thatcherism. Some of the innovations made by Margaret Thatcher helped improve the country's economic performance relative to that of other countries. Yet the price paid was a heavy one, since Thatcher's governments allowed the public services to decay during the period of their stewardship.

There is an important lesson to learn from the period of Britain's poor economic performance. It is that economic and public policy must be considered together, with the aim of achieving mutual benefits wherever possible. In other words, in considering how public institutions are structured – and how best to fund them – we must always give attention to how they influence economic growth and job creation. There are many observers, of course, especially on the political right, who argue that the sheer volume of taxation affects these factors. Low levels of taxation, they say, are needed if a country is to be dynamic economically.

The evidence does not bear out this view. There probably is an upper limit to taxation levels in respect of adverse effects on economic performance. A case in point might be Sweden, which has the highest tax take among the industrial countries, but where GDP per head relative to other countries has dropped over the past twenty years. By and large, though, there is no direct relationship between tax as a proportion of GDP and economic performance. Thus the other Scandinavian countries, Denmark, Finland and Norway, have high taxation but also excellent rates of economic growth compared with other mature industrial economies.

For the first two years after 1997, the government stuck to the spending plans of the Conservatives rather than immediately investing more in public services and other areas. Although the point is arguable I think it was the right thing to do because of the need to reassure financial markets that the new government was determined to live within its means. From 1999/2000 onwards, however, large amounts of money were channelled into the public services, especially into education and healthcare. Quite correctly, the government argued that investment must be coupled to reform and also looked to other modes of funding, including especially private–public funding projects. They have been roundly criticised for their pains, especially from leftist circles. The reasons are at least in some part ideological – anything that uses the term 'private' must be a betrayal of the public services. As I have said, such an assertion is unacceptable.

This point is essential in assessing the government's support of public–private partnerships. What matters is how far these serve the public purpose in an effective way as compared to state sector provision. They have to be considered in terms of real comparisons, not with a mythical world where state-based organisations are 100 per cent efficient and where they always deliver on time.

A crisis in funding?

The significant increases in funding for the public services made since 1997 have been concentrated especially in the fields of education and healthcare. In spite of widespread doubts about whether the money has been spent effectively, objective indicators show major improvements – with more to come as longer-term investments feed through. However, on current plans the rate of spending growth is due to fall substantially – by 2006/7 in the case of education and 2007/8 in the case of healthcare. The level of public debt is climbing. In September 2006 it stood at £486.7 billion, compared to £446.7 billion a year before.

All good things come to an end or, in this case, taper off. Following the very large sums of money that have gone into the public services, funding is due to flatten out in the next spending review period. Possible reactions are to say that there must be some belt tightening – or the knee-jerk reaction of the traditional left: put up taxes.

We should be more radical than either of these solutions imply. In the short term, various spending adjustments could be made. I believe the government's approach to crime has run its course. You can only get so far by relying on the criminal justice system. One of the only areas where Britain is a European champion is in the proportion of people in our jails. So one saving is: don't go ahead with building new prisons, but explore alternatives that are both much cheaper and more effective. Other suggestions are: look for a different strategy on defence spending – collaborate more with our partners in Europe, defer a final decision on Trident – the idea that a binding decision has to be taken now does not stand up to scrutiny; contain public sector salaries, which have now risen substantially; introduce a ruthless audit of base line expenditure in government departments, as Geoffrey Filkin proposes in Chapter 14; consider new strategies of tackling VAT fraud and evasion, again preferably in conjunction with other EU member states – it has risen steeply in recent years, and is estimated to be costing the country £12 billion in lost income per year. In a recent report, the Institute of Fiscal Studies suggested that Gordon Brown should consider putting off the expenditure needed to reach the government's 2010 target on child poverty. This would be a major mistake. In my view, countering child poverty should be the driving force of the government's commitment to reducing poverty as a whole.

We should press on in short order with the reform of the state. At the core of the state, there is an essentially unaccountable body, the civil service, as Michael Bichard highlights in Chapter 8. More decisive action is needed if the Gershon report of 2004 is to have an effect.[1] When the report came out, with its proposal to slim down public service jobs by over 100,000, it was said to have 'sent shock waves through every government department and agency in the land'.[2] It was supposed to save £15 billion a year, but remains to be implemented. The capacity reviews of the civil service launched in 2005 have reported on departmental capacity in ten main areas. They are a useful beginning, but at the moment their recommendations lack bite, and it is not clear how far they will advance the Gershon programme – which should be one key aim.

Plainly the longer term is where most effort should be concentrated. Reform processes desirable in and of themselves are also directly relevant to funding. Promoting greater innovation in the public services; making breakthroughs in productivity, especially in the NHS; involving citizens more directly as producers rather than just users of services; and expanding the scope of user charging – these are the ways in which the public services should evolve. All can help stabilise and control the deployment of resources.

Could increased user charges help? After all, the level of such charges in the public services in the UK is at a lower level than in most other developed countries.[3] User charges offer potential advantages in addition to financial savings for the state. They can contain demand by limiting the frivolous use of services that are 'free'; and they fit neatly with the principle that citizens should accept responsibilities as well as rights.

Healthcare charges have been in use in Britain for some while – in respect, for example, of prescriptions – although so many are exempt that their scope is in practice very limited. It has been a sacred principle of British political life, however, that so far as direct medical services are concerned, the NHS should be free at the point of delivery. Yet the UK is almost alone in holding to such a principle. User charges for such services are in place in many Continental countries, such as Sweden, France and Germany. In Sweden, patient fees are set at modest levels in order not to deter those who need medical help from seeking it. They contribute only a little over 1 per cent of total funding. France generates a higher proportion of revenue – about 8 per cent – from patient charges, on the basis of payments not fully reimbursed in the public health insurance system.[4] In Germany, the proportion is nearly 10 per cent.

Should there be more co-funding in the NHS? My answer would be yes – certainly at least to the modest level that exists in Sweden. Charges should be levied for visits to GPs and at the same time coupled to the right to see any NHS GP one chooses. The principle that the NHS should be free at the point of use is based on the notion that even a small fee would deter some people from visiting the doctor when they need to, especially poorer people. But the whole point of introducing fees would be to deter people from seeing the doctor – those who come for minor or non-existent ailments. In a society where there is no absolute poverty it is hard to see that a small charge would deter those who really might need treatment. I'm not sure that any Labour politician would ever take the risk, even though responsibility ranks high on the government's agenda.

Care for those at the beginning and near the end of their lives is an area where substantial co-payment already exists, but where the pressure for greater state investment is strong. Investment in children is now recognised to be crucial both to the creation of human capital and to reducing inequality. As in the case of care for the elderly it interacts closely with factors affecting the position of women. The most advanced countries in terms of state provision for children are Sweden and Denmark. The costs, however, are extremely high – over 2 per cent of total GDP. In Britain, the system is more mixed, with a heavy dependence on targeted policies, and much less extensive. Sixty-five per cent of long-term care for the elderly in England is funded by the state, the remainder by individuals and their families. This figure does not involve any costing of the large amounts of care that are provided by unpaid carers. Scotland is alone among the nations of the UK in abolishing user costs for care of the elderly.

In his admirable survey of the subject, Peter Robinson makes it clear that user costs can make an important contribution to the overall cost of public services.[5] However, as he also points out, user charges are at least as difficult to introduce in political terms as are orthodox taxes. After all, the increase in national insurance to help fund healthcare proved less controversial than the decision to bring in student fees.

There is one area where user charging is bound to leap up the agenda: the environment. In just a few months the whole debate about climate change has become transformed. A quite radical shift towards environmental taxation and away from income or employment taxes is on the agenda for the next few years. User charging in this context has a potentially wider application than elsewhere, since many environmental goods have never either been paid for directly by the consumer or properly priced at all. The issues are much too large and difficult to discuss in detail here but are certain to affect both the nature and the economic viability of the public services as a whole.

A concrete example is congestion charging on the roads. A detailed proposal has been put forward by the Institute of Public Policy Research to set up a national system of congestion charging by 2010.[6] It would deploy global positioning technology, which is already in use for environmental charges on large lorries on motorways in Germany. The technology makes it possible to charge road users differing rates according to the roads they are using and the times at which they are travelling. Charges set at the right levels would produce a 7 per cent reduction in road traffic and lower carbon dioxide emissions by over 8 per cent. They could potentially also raise revenue of £16 billion annually at today's prices.

That climate change will directly affect core areas of traditional welfare funding is very obvious, even if the overall implications are difficult to predict. Extreme weather will become more common, including summer heat-waves. Just such a heat-wave, which affected areas of the Continent in 2003, cost an estimated 12,000 lives in France alone. Environmental issues will have to be brought much more within the framework of the obligations of citizenship as we seek to tackle these problems.

Should overall taxation be increased?
Given the need to continue investing in the public services, should Labour be considering further increasing tax rates? Many on the left would answer 'yes'. Citizens, it is said, will pay more tax if the way in which their money is spent becomes more transparent. They will also support hypothecated taxes if such taxes are strictly kept for the purposes for which they are designed.[7]

In some areas I am in favour of hypothecated taxes – including for various areas of environmental taxation. A greater emphasis upon green taxation is bound to be a feature of the next few years, given the central importance of controlling climate change. The proceeds of road charging, for example, might be linked directly to spending on improving public transport, as has happened in London.

In talking of taxation, however, we should concentrate upon the tax take, and how effectively it is spent, not formal tax rates. And the tax take is influenced in a fundamental way by what the consequences of fiscal practices are, and by their interaction with other aspects of economic institutions. Taxes influence behaviour (and quite often, as in the case of environmental taxes, we want them to influence behaviour). Taxation has risen to a higher proportion of GDP not mainly because of the increase in national insurance, but because of success in generating good growth rates and in furthering job creation. We have to look at the intersection of expenditure with policy areas that affect who uses the public services and why.

The challenge will be to maximise policies that help reconcile economic growth and social justice – as tax credits do at the moment, in spite of the administrative problems to which they have given rise. Consider, for example, one of the big difficulties facing the country – the fact that the bottom 25 per cent in the education system fares badly in terms of literacy and functional skills. Improving this situation would increase the fund of human capital, reduce social divisions, improve life-chances and help job creation – all of which would impact positively on public service expenditure at the same time as having much more profound social effects.

There is an important point to be made here: improving the public services or some main parts of them, especially education and healthcare, can itself have major economic multiplier effects. Just as the interaction of fiscal measures with economic performance crucially affects available funding for the public services, the same is true in reverse. How far the public services are efficiently run, and how far they reach their goals, vitally affects the state of the economy, as well of course as overall well-being. This theorem has even greater force as investment in healthcare rises, assuming other things stay the same. Such investment is due to reach 10 per cent of GDP by 2010, even with a shallower growth pattern. It is a very large chunk of national wealth to be in the hands of an organisation with low productivity. We must redouble our reform efforts.

The government has set itself the task of increasing the proportion of the labour force in work to 80 per cent from its current 75 per cent – an already high ratio when compared to most other industrial countries. Having a high proportion of people in work (above a decent minimum wage) is a crucial factor in welfare. An 80 per cent participation ratio, other things being equal, would be the equivalent of a cost injection into the public services of £20 billion a year, taking into account increases in tax revenue and the lower level of welfare payments that would result.

Helping more disabled people get into work, for example, given that the expenditure on them is cost efficient, clearly reduces strains on welfare benefits as well as having a positive outcome for those involved, as John Hutton highlights in Chapter 11. The same applies to policies aimed at persuading older people either to stay in work or to come back to it. In Finland, for instance, as a result of policy innovations of this sort, the proportion of men and women of pensionable age in work has risen to 64 per cent. In the UK it is only 33 per cent.

Policies affecting women will be central to the effectiveness as well as the economic viability of the public services. A high proportion of women are in part-time work, many because they want to be, but also because of lack of opportunity. Schemes that make it possible to move from dead-end jobs into managerial positions could play an important role – at the moment, most have been developed by businesses themselves rather than by the state. Women who do not have consistent paid employment tend to have inadequate pension provision later on and hence become heavily reliant upon public revenue – not a good situation for anyone.

Well, after all this, should we be thinking of putting up taxes? I don't think so, if this means raising tax rates (especially income tax) in order to generate more revenue. The growing prominence of environmental taxes will create difficult problems, which will need very careful overall tax planning to cope with. At the moment investment in sustainable energy resources stands at a low level and will have to increase substantially. Tax incentives and sanctions designed to change behaviour may generate new net revenue, but by definition that revenue will decline as behaviour change actually occurs. Should a major technological breakthrough of some sort occur, say with pollution-free electric vehicles in terms of battery life, or nuclear fusion, it could not only fundamentally alter the environmental field but also have major effects on revenue generation.

Striking a balance between these different components of social and economic policy will determine the future shape of public spending. Increases in environmental taxation should in principle be accompanied by tax reductions elsewhere, especially those that would help poorer groups, and particularly where they involve incentives to work. I don't think it is possible to be too prescriptive about what the proportion of tax in relation to GDP should be. It could rise further without adverse effects – indeed with positive ones – if the policy mix is right. Developing flexibility in the fiscal system will be most important in a world of rapid change, where the outcomes of such change are not predictable.

Conclusion

1. We cannot take decisions about how best to fund the public services without deciding what the 'public services' are – a more complex issue than appears at first sight and one with many implications.

2. The public interest in any given situation or policy area has to be clearly separated from the sphere of the state. The fact that a service is supplied 'privately' in some or large part does not mean that it cannot fulfil public purposes. Conversely, the fact that an organisation or institution is 'public', in the sense of being closely associated with the state, doesn't ipso facto mean that it serves the public interest better than an alternative method of delivery.

3. It follows that there are no intrinsic barriers to combining different means of public service provision, especially when mutual learning processes take place. Public–private partnerships and other non-orthodox ways of organising services for the public have to be assessed in a non-prejudicial way.

4. We can't say 'here are the public services, how shall we fund them?' as if such a question were distinct from issues of economic dynamism, growth and job generation. On the contrary, exploring the interconnections between them is essential for sound fiscal policy.

5. User charging has a key part to play in the public services but more for the discipline and sense of responsibility it promotes than for sheer revenue generation. Nevertheless, it is a principle likely to be ever more widely applied.

6. The coming shift towards environmental taxes will have a radical effect on public service provision. It should be an aim of policy to make such innovations revenue neutral as far as possible. How difficult or otherwise it will prove to introduce new environmental taxes (and tax benefits) will depend a great deal upon how far such a goal can be achieved.

5

From choice to control:
empowering public services

Ann Rossiter and Liam Byrne

Choice and the politics of empowerment

Progressives now have a first-class barometer for the popular success for new thinking: to see an idea picked up and echoed by David Cameron's Conservatives. The concept of the empowering state is the perfect example. Over the past five years, the progressive agenda has being moving beyond the concept of the state as having an enabling role, helping citizens to fulfil their capabilities, to something much more radical: seeing the primary role of the state as empowering people. At its core, this involves a genuine redistribution of power away from government and towards citizens.

Is 'empowering' different to 'enabling'? Absolutely. When the leader of the opposition told the Power Inquiry that his vision was of an 'empowering state', his view of it appears to be very narrowly conceived, based on government 'backing off' and leaving people to get on with it.[1] This is to miss the point. A real agenda for empowerment, as David Miliband has pointed out, must go beyond allowing people the freedom to take control to giving them the ability to do so.[2]

This kind of freedom has deep roots in progressive thinking. The idea was developed by T. H. Green in the 1880s and was the driving force behind the New Liberalism of Leonard Hobhouse and others at the turn of the century.[3] In the 1950s, Anthony Crosland reminded socialists that they should not forget their libertarian roots,[4] and three decades later, Roy Hattersley explicitly placed his arguments in these terms in his book *Choose Freedom*. Hattersley echoed his predecessors, arguing that 'the purpose of the equality we seek is the extension of liberty'.[5] It is not the freedom defined as the absence of constraints; rather it has more in common with what Hobhouse and John Maynard Keynes called 'effective freedoms', or more recently, what Amartya Sen labelled '"capability", to choose a life that one has reason to value'.[6]

This argument, which underpins so much of the United Nations Development Programme's *Human Development Reports*, takes us beyond the idea that impoverishment is simply the absence of income, and beyond the idea that equality of opportunity is on its own enough. It tells us that both income and opportunity might get you to the starting line in life, but without capabilities, you will only get so far down the track – stopping perhaps a long way short of your ambitions – or indeed your potential. This emphasis on capability is vital. It helps us see more clearly the relative value of the different reforms which we need to make. It helps us see that freedom of choice – in public services and lots more besides – is not simply a path to a certain outcome, but something with intrinsic value itself.

By making freedom 'effective', or improving 'capabilities', people are empowered. This richer understanding of the concept of empowerment provides a motivating principle for a whole spectrum of policy, from double devolution in local democracy to new approaches to welfare and the ability for citizens to exercise choices over the public services they receive.[7]

Labour has been poor at communicating how our public service reforms are driven by this conception of government. Too often we have taken it as self-evident that reform should be supported because it represents a redistribution of power. In particular, the choice agenda in public services has been badly explained. Rather than talk about what it is that individual citizens want and need from their services, and how they can best be provided, we have fought running battles with public service workers. But for many voters, public services are synonymous with the people who work in them. Unsurprisingly, therefore, reform has often rebounded with the public.

Worse, the government has allowed itself to get hijacked by the debate about private sector involvement in the public services and this debate has all too frequently overtaken the important argument about the need for diversity of provision if we are to meet the full range of individual needs. It has raised fears of a hidden agenda to privatise public services.

While we have struggled to explain the important distinction between private sector involvement in the provision of services which remain free at the point of use, and privatisation, the bigger argument has risked getting lost. The suspicion about ministers' motives in involving the private sector has been heightened by the apparent fetish which has been made of the private sector, particularly when Labour first came to power. All too often it appeared that government saw the private sector as the repository of productivity, efficiency and customer focus, while the public sector represented the opposite, when even the IMF now recognises that this is not an assumption that can be supported: 'Much of the case for PPPs [public–private partnerships] rests on the relative efficiency of the private sector [compared to the public sector]. While there is an extensive literature on this subject, the theory is ambiguous and the empirical evidence is mixed.'[8]

This problem is not of course without a root cause, which is the way choice has been thought about in the first place. When the Prime Minister says, 'Choice isn't an end in itself. It is one important mechanism to ensure that citizens can indeed secure good schools and health services in their communities,'[9] he is valuing choice for a particular reason: the instrumental good that comes from a quasi-market where through the exercise of that choice, signals about what service users value are communicated to public servants. When funding follows those choices, those signals have the added power of 'rewarding' or 'punishing' organisations chosen, or not chosen, by service users. Choice, in this case, is a means to the more effective delivery of public services.[10]

But there is a more valuable rationale for why we might value choice: because it passes a degree of control back to service users; this is the intrinsic good of empowerment. In this case choice is an end in itself.

The progressive left's discussion of choice needs to recognise not one but both of these ideas. If we take seriously the idea of the empowering state, it suggests that a discussion about choice in public services should proceed from a more developed understanding of what the concept of choice means to citizens. Obviously this is likely to vary between individuals, and between different kinds of public service. It may or may not involve making a choice between providers.

One of the best illustrations of how we can go beyond choice to offer personal control can be found in the individual budgets which the government is piloting in social care. The individual budget pilots still have big questions to answer: How do we translate entitlements to lots of different services into a single 'account'? Can individual budgets be delivered within existing resource envelopes? What has to happen to develop the right supply markets? How do we encourage the take-up of demand?

Crucially, individual budgets help us see just why we have to move the debate about 'choice' to a debate about 'personal control'. First, they put the focus on the individual – and the actual outcomes in life they are seeking. Second, they underscore how achieving those outcomes means that we have to think of the public service 'product' as defined as the package of services needed, rather than the provider.

The concept behind individual or personalised budgets is, like most of the best ideas, a very simple one. The proposal is to bring together the different sources of funding available to social care users in the form of individual budgets; existing resources would be allocated differently, delivering services in ways that meet individuals' needs and giving them choice in how those needs are met. For example, people would be able to live where they choose, perhaps through the provision of housing adaptations, and disabled people would be helped to overcome physical impairments and enter or maintain employment.

There are in fact lots of different ways of conceiving personal choice and control. A number of taxonomies have been proposed[11] but for the sake of simplicity, we can see the options as being

a. a single user exercising choice of a range of providers;
b. an individual user selecting from a menu of services from a single or multiple providers;
c. communities or groups exercising collective choice over which of a range of providers to use;
d. communities or groups having a degree of choice over how services are designed.

This does not include the range of options in which choice is exercised on behalf of consumers, which is beyond the scope of this piece. All of these points (a–d) taken together would give a fairly full description of ways in which public services might be personalised, and we need to find a new language to convey both this richness and three sets of benefits:

- **Empowerment** – involving users in the design of services and the way those services are delivered tends to improve outcomes.[12] The NHS Expert Patient Programme, led by those with chronic medical conditions, is a good example of the potential benefits of this approach. The results show not just a decrease in pain and other symptoms, but an increase in patients' control over their own lives and in their satisfaction with life.[13]
- **Equity** – a stronger sense of personal ownership of public services should lead to greater support for their collective provision. Choice

conceived as empowerment runs contrary to the perception that providing greater choice requires promoting selfish individualism and necessarily results in a degradation of support for state action.

- **Efficiency** – giving service users more say over the design of services is likely to lead to a rise in overall allocative efficiency. In other words, spending on public services is directed more closely to those features that service users want and need, rather than what those running the services believe they might need, or think they ought to need. As a result, overall public value is likely to increase for a given level of public spending.

But delivering these benefits requires some changes to the way we have set about introducing choice and control to date.

Empowerment

One way of considering the impact of choice as empowerment is to ask whether patients feel a greater sense of personal ownership or control of public services. In the absence of this, the closest we can come is asking whether patients are satisfied with the experience of choice. Has the exercise of choice increased overall levels of satisfaction with public services, all other things being equal?

There is evidence to show that those who are offered choice are satisfied with the experience. The Picker Institute, as part of its evaluation of the London Patient Choice (LPC) scheme, explored patients' reactions to the offer of an alternative hospital for treatment.[14] LPC offered patients facing a wait of more than eight months for elective surgery the option of going to an alternative provider in the capital that could offer faster treatment. Most of those surveyed while on the waiting list (82 per cent) responded positively when asked if they would consider going to an alternative hospital. Only 18 per cent said they would not consider it under any circumstances. Uptake was relatively high with two thirds (67 per cent) of those who were offered the opportunity to go to an alternative hospital choosing to do so. An overwhelming majority (97 per cent) of patients who had opted to go to an alternative hospital said they would recommend the scheme to others.

Case study: individual budgets in action

'Joseph' has very limited communication capacity. He was placed in a residential college some distance from his home. It was increasingly clear that he was unhappy with this placement. Because he lacked speech with which to communicate his unhappiness, his frustration tended to boil over into so-called 'challenging behaviour'. It was becoming increasingly clear that his placement (which cost many thousands of pounds a year) would soon break down. Local social workers would then be faced with the difficult task of finding him somewhere else to stay.

The precursor to individual budgets was available. Joseph and his family were introduced to the idea behind it and, after discussing the level of funding they could expect to have at their disposal, were able to develop a scenario in which he moved back to the family home and was supported by somebody he knew well and trusted. In this case, it happened to be an aunt. The flexibility of In Control (individual budget holding) allowed the aunt to be properly paid for carrying out this support work and thus enabled her to give up her previous job.

After only a few months, the young man was back in the family home with his pets and other familiar elements of home life. His parents, who were never happy about him living away from home, but simply did not feel they could cope with him without support, are also much happier. They are delighted with how settled he seems and are beginning to pick up their own life together after so many years of having to put their own needs on hold in order to support their son.

Equity

A progressive analysis of choice systems should also be concerned about their impact on equity. This goes beyond the obvious requirement of retaining a commitment to providing services to all, free at the point of use. The concern here is to ensure that the process of introducing choice does not further extend the advantage that articulate and informed service users have in gaining access to public services. Specifically, the concern is that the process of choice will either squeeze out disadvantaged users or, at the least, improve the access and outcomes that the advantaged users enjoy to a greater degree than those experienced by disadvantaged users.

This is important for a consideration of choice from either an empowerment or an efficiency perspective. However, there is evidence to show that people in lower socio-economic groups value the introduction of choice more than those in other groups.[15] This is unsurprising since these are the people who are likely to have most contact with the public services and to rely on them most heavily. Disempowered in other areas of our market society because they have less buying power, it is to be expected that giving them greater control over public services is valued highly.

To prevent the introduction of choice systems from exacerbating current inequities within public services, they need to be designed in such a way as to

- prevent providers from actively selecting users, overtly or covertly;
- provide an effective government response to failing providers, which could include active support, management change or closure;
- make the freedom to choose meaningful for all users through the provision of information, advice and support, including objective performance data, and assistance with access costs, for example, to cover the costs of additional cover.[16]

Measured against this standard, school choice falls down on a number of fronts. Schools actively select through their admissions policies and parents often do not have a meaningful choice of school since they have to bear the costs of travel, uniforms and so on. As a result, sorting (or segregation) is greater where there is more choice.[17] In health, by contrast, the research to date into take-up of the option of choice shows that there is no bias by socio-economic group. Again, this is unsurprising, as patients have been supported in making decisions and in accessing more distant facilities. Equality of access is made real.

Efficiency
In the absence of cost–benefit analyses, we should ask whether the choice systems which have been established in UK public services accord with international best practice. Have they been established so as to maximise efficiency gains? We know a reasonable amount about the features which are necessary for choice systems to generate improved outcomes from an examination of the international evidence; these include

- substantive freedom for service users to choose a provider;
- adequate demand sensitivity, including the potential for supply to expand with demand at provider level and at system level;
- sufficient managerial and financial discretion so that services can respond to meet user choice;

- funding following the user, and to the appropriate administrative level, e.g. direct to the service provider.[18]

One of the biggest barriers to the effective working of choice systems is the limited scope that exists for expanding provider and system capacity. The secondary school system is a case in point. Although the problem varies considerably from area to area, there are a number of schools, deemed desirable by parents, which are heavily over-subscribed. There is very little scope for those schools to expand to meet demand, leading to a number of parents being refused entry for their child. The decision about which children to admit is made on a variety of criteria, notably catchment area. The result in this case is likely to be house price inflation within the catchment area, pushing out children from less wealthy families.[19] In other cases, schools may exercise a form of covert selection, favouring children with a better academic record, for example.[20]

Defenders of the system will point to a reasonably high level of matching between parents' first preferences and allocated places, with approximately 92 per cent of parents receiving their first preference.[21] However, we should be cautious about taking this statistic at face value. Parents face a difficult decision in stating a preference for a school. In an area in which there is a shortage of good quality places, failure to win their first preference may result in them going to the back of the queue for other schools. So parents have to make a difficult calculation and identify a preference for a school which they are likely to get.

The primary problem highlighted here is that capacity in the school system is 'lumpy'. Schools cannot expand easily to meet demand since they are faced with multiple limitations in the form of management, teaching staff and buildings. This suggests that the English system of school choice fails to meet at least one of the major criteria which are necessary if we are to expect efficiency gains.[22]

By contrast, choice in elective care is quite different. Here the Department of Health has expanded capacity in the system through the establishment of independent treatment centres. Since funding follows the patient, and hospitals have the managerial and financial freedom to respond to patient needs, it would be reasonable to expect efficiency gains to result.

The other major factor to consider is geography. Genuine choice of provider in any sector means that an individual has a choice of a number of hospitals or schools, for example, within easy reach of home and accessible by public transport. Research shows that outside major urban areas, geography places significant limits on choice for many people.[23]

So while choice systems can deliver efficiency benefits, there are real limits to their capacity to do so, including the limits placed on them by geography. If a system is to deliver such benefits, as in health, it needs to be designed with great care and considerable investment must be made in information, guidance and support for those doing the choosing, particularly if we are to avoid exacerbating unequal outcomes.

Where next for choice and personal control?

When choice is conceived as empowerment – in terms of a revolution in personal control of services – it provides a strong motivation for policy makers to expand beyond those areas in which it is possible to offer users a choice from among a range of providers and to consider how other forms of choice can be developed. It helps us see more clearly the spectrum of powers that might seek to put in the hands of citizens – some to be exercised personally; some collectively with other users, and some in concert with the wider community.

Choice and control of services
The government has taken some steps to allow individuals to choose from a range of service options, for example in the secondary school sector. The introduction of specialist schools and academies with particular areas of expertise does provide parents with some meaningful choices between different kinds of school. This burgeoning diversity is to be welcomed, but should also be questioned.

On what basis have decisions been made about the nature of that diversity? It is not at all obvious that what parents seek when they make a decision about which secondary school their eleven-year-old child will attend is a technical specialism in music or maths. The majority of parents are unlikely to be confident enough about their child's abilities in a particular area, or to be clear enough about their future direction, to make a decision on that basis. Instead parents may want to make a decision based on attitudes to learning, to discipline, to breadth of curriculum or to ethos. While schools do exhibit some diversity on these fronts, it is a result of accident, rather than design. The truth is that we simply do not know which criteria parents would prefer to use for decision making.

Simply asking parents on a one-off basis about preferences will not reveal this information either. Rather, engagement with parents in any particular locality will need to be deliberative and consultative, closer to a citizens' jury than an opinion poll. It will not always be possible for service users to be involved in the kind of co-production role with service delivery that Charles Leadbeater recommends.[24] Many people will not want to make the commitment in time and effort that this involves. An effective rule of thumb is that the greater the time and/or energy expended by service users in contact with a particular service, the greater the potential for a co-productive relationship to develop. But a regular, deliberative engagement by local services with their local communities is essential. The information about preferences revealed by this kind of exercise would be valuable for local and national authorities in their commissioning role.

Crucially, in the past, we have thought about 'choice' in a rather technocratic way, as different alternatives between providers. But individuals often do not really think about life in this way. Rather they are seeking an outcome – and will look to a range of providers, or a range of services to be packaged or brokered together, to provide that service. All too often Labour has thought about diversity of providers, rather than how individuals – like individual budget users – might be able to construct a package of services that delivers them the outcome they are actually interested in. This means that if choice is to be introduced in such a way as to be made meaningful for people, government might need to think about more diverse provision, and even about loosening some very prescriptive services.

Collective choice and effective freedom

There are a range of public services where choice of provider has never been an option because the presence of multiple service providers is unfeasible, for example in many areas of public transport or the police service. If a user is not satisfied with the personal protection the police are providing, she cannot (short of employing her own bodyguards) opt for a different provider of the service. There are no alternative providers to the national police force,[25] for example, and thus no choice of provider.

As user choice does not create contestability in this type of service, little attention has been given to how choice might be made meaningful for, or extended to, service users. Currently, users can only influence the delivery of the services they receive – either at local authority or national level – by voice mechanisms such as petitioning local councillors, for example, or by a democratic vote, to bring in a party to change the way in which the police force, refuse collection, or parks, are delivered.

In denying choice to users of single-provider services we are assuming that *who* delivers the service is the only choice worth making. In fact, the *how, when* and *what* of service delivery are equally, if not more, important. These choices can be readily made in single-provider and collective services: for example, which day rubbish is collected or how late in the evening public transport runs.

There is a key difference between what we would define as 'voice' and what we define as 'collective choice'. The difference hinges on where the decision-making power lies. All voice mechanisms – including a vote in a representative democracy – are expressions of opinion. The authority to make final decisions lies with another person – an elected representative, the organisation carrying out the consultation, or the one being petitioned. Collective choice, on the other hand, implies that the authority to make such decisions lies with the collective of service users. In such a system we would expect to see service users being presented with a range of choices about how their service is delivered or who delivers it. They would then decide, collectively, which choice to make. In other words, this form of choice would mean a direct transfer of power away from the service provider to the users of that service.

Opportunities to exercise this type of choice could be delivered in a number of ways. Citizens could be asked to rank local problems according to their importance, to rank broader operational priorities or to be asked for feedback which becomes binding. They may be given the right to choose between competing tenders for local services or to specify levels of service.

Conclusion

Giving service users a choice of which provider to use remains an excellent vehicle for delivering improved outcomes, provided certain conditions are present. However, these conditions are pretty stringent and there are only a limited number of services, notably social care and health, in which they are met in a developed way. Where they don't exist we need to look at alternative models for the introduction of choice in public services, including choice of service or package of services, or collective choice.

Whichever model of choice is adopted, we have to expand our understanding of what choice means for service users. It is not just a mechanism for delivering efficiency gains, but a way of empowering citizens – of redistributing power from the state to the citizen. It is a way of revolutionising individual and community control over public services.

Seeing choice in this light has important implications both for the design of public service reforms and also for the way in which we communicate them. If progressives are going to win the argument for reform, we need to make a much more convincing case which places choice and control centre stage – not because of any long-term benefits that flow from contestability, but because ownership, and ultimately control, of public services lies with the public themselves – a public with rapidly rising expectations and increasingly diverse ambitions. Our ultimate aim should be for a dialogue with users and indeed with public servants to help shape and design services as part of a mutual relationship, which involves long-term detailed engagement.

Perhaps more important for a progressive party is the fact that we can win this argument on the grounds of equity. Choice and control in public services is a recipe for greater, not less, equity in Britain today. Under the monopoly provision of the past, public services have been far from equitable in terms of outcomes. Our test therefore is whether new arrangements take us forward or backwards from this imperfect starting point.

For choice and personal control to work, all sorts of ingredients have to fall into place. It is not simple to get right. To make decisions, parents and patients will need accurate and accessible information about the range of services on offer and may require support in coming to a decision. We have to protect the inarticulate from the risk that the articulate, educated and/or time-rich dominate.

Nor should we shy away from arguing that sometimes choice and control are best exercised by communities not individuals. As Adam Lent and Natalie Arend explain, 'If users make decisions as a group it means the power differentials arising from different shares of individual resources could be levelled out as the advantages of information, interpersonal skills and acquaintance possessed by some are pooled within the wider group.'[26]

However choice and personal control are conceived and introduced, there are a range of tools open to policy makers which can help reduce inequitable outcomes:

- Information about the choices on offer needs to be made widely available and delivered in accessible forms. As Paul Corrigan has pointed out in relation to choice in primary care, this information may be anecdotal or descriptive in form, as well as statistical.[27]
- Sources of explanation and advice will need to be made available to service users as they are in the NHS in the form of patient advisers.
- Policy makers should consider the introduction of mechanisms to redistribute virtual or actual buying power within public services in which there is individual budget holding or in which funding follows the user.[28]
- Staff quality and shortages should be addressed through the introduction of differential pay rates for staff for working in difficult or disadvantaged areas.

Which tools are employed in any particular area of service will depend on the nature of that service and what form choice takes.

Finally, we suggest five core principles which should be adopted when considering the extension of choice in public services:

1. Choice should be seen as providing value in and of itself, irrespective of whether it also has the potential to generate efficiency gains.
2. Other models of choice, other than choice of provider, should be introduced across public services.
3. We should consider diversity in service provision a virtue in so far as it does not impact on equity.
4. We must be guided by the wishes and needs of service users when considering the range of choices on offer.
5. We need to adopt a new approach to communicating the importance of choice which emphasises public ownership of, and responsibility for, our public services.

6

Transforming public services through the third sector

Stephen Bubb

> The making of a good society depends not on the state but on the citizens, acting
> individually or in free association with one another. The happiness or
> unhappiness of the society in which we live depends upon ourselves as citizens,
> not on the instrument of political power which we call the state.
>
> William Beveridge, 1948

'Until August 1914, a sensible law-abiding Englishman could pass through life
and hardly notice the existence of the state, beyond the post office and the
policeman.'[1] So wrote A. J. P. Taylor in his famous history of the twentieth
century. Now, at the beginning of the twenty-first century, we are in need of
a major reassessment of the role of the state in public service provision. And
such a reassessment must be based on a radical change to the role of the central
state, the empowerment of citizens and a concern for outcomes not inputs in
service delivery – key themes of this book.

As we know, Taylor's description of the role of the state masked mass
unemployment, ill health, deprivation and mass inequalities. It was a time
where services to the public were largely provided through hundreds of
charities or municipal authorities. By the outbreak of the Second World War,
it had become clear that the country's welfare system could not cope with the
multiple pressures of growing industrialisation, population growth and
inequity of provision. Clement Attlee in his autobiography used his first job as
warden of Toynbee Hall to illustrate this, when he recalled the work of the
Charity Organisation Society, which believed in Poor Law principles of
deterrence. It advocated giving children only burnt porridge served at
inconvenient times and places.[2]

Beveridge

The post-war welfare state settlement set the national framework which still largely shapes many of our key public services today. Yet was William Beveridge proposing a monolithic top-down state structure? In his report he outlined the principles to be followed in establishing a welfare state.[3] The third of these was:

> Social security must be achieved by cooperation between the state and the individual ... The state in organising security should not stifle incentive, opportunity, or responsibility; in establishing a national minimum, it should leave room and encouragement for voluntary action by each individual to provide more than that minimum for himself and his family.

It is essential therefore that core themes of the reforms set out in this book are seen as a renewal of the welfare state, returning to an approach centred on the citizen, not the state. How do we put the citizen at the heart of public service reform? This is the crucial question to be answered by policy makers. John Stuart Mill wrote, 'The worth of the state is the worth of the individuals comprising it.' How then does government facilitate that worth?

A growing third sector

The last twenty years have seen a significant and growing role for provision of services to the public through the third sector. The most obvious example has been in social housing, where the vast majority of provision is now through a vibrant housing association movement, which manages some two million homes on an asset base of £60 billion. Less well known has been the trans-formation of many day and residential care services for children and the elderly and people with disabilities. Indeed, the majority of social workers are now employed in the independent sector rather than by local authorities; a change that has occurred in less than fifteen years.

Other radical reforms have transformed services for people with learning difficulties and long-term health problems. Institutional care has been transformed into a network of community provision, much of it driven by third-sector organisations. This has brought huge benefits to the users of those services, their families and carers. Children's services are increasingly being provided through third-sector bodies. Services for addiction, rehabilitation, palliative and community care, in academies and educational trusts and in employment services continue to grow. Social enterprises are pushing the boundaries of provision and often leading regeneration of derelict localities and neglected communities.

Yet the third sector's service delivery is still very small judged as a proportion of the total spend. The current government has set out its objective of increasing third-sector provision in five key areas:

- education (through academies and trusts);
- health (particularly in social care and potentially through transferring services to social enterprises);
- offender management (where the ambition is that 10 per cent of services will be provided through the third sector);
- jobs and training (a major new role in providing person-centred employment services);
- growing social enterprises.

Yet for all the talk of an expanded third-sector role, under 2 per cent of overall government expenditure on public services is through the third sector.

The vision and the reality

There has been growing political interest in the potential of third-sector service delivery. Gordon Brown has said:

> A clearer distinction is now being drawn between advancing the public interest and equating the public interest with state ownership, bureaucracy and centralised administration. We can demand that a service be promoted in the public interest without wishing that the government manages that service . . . In the next five years the role of government will shift even more from the old 'directive and controlling' to enabling and empowering voluntary action. Increasingly the voluntary sector will be empowered to play a critical role.[4]

And Tony Blair has reiterated on many occasions, 'What matters is what works, not the delivery mechanism.'

There is an increasing understanding of the significant potential of third-sector organisations both in articulating and promoting user views, and in adding value to service delivery. The Conservatives have strongly supported this proposition. In 2006 David Cameron said:

I have great ambitions for the social sector in this country, and I make no apology for that. I simply do not believe that we will make serious progress in tackling relative poverty and deprivation, in creating communities fit for the twenty-first century, unless we inspire a revolution in social provision. From state welfare to social welfare, the big idea that is at the heart of our plans for social justice.[5]

Consumers and users of public services increasingly demand user-friendliness. Indeed, David Miliband, when Minister of State for Communities and Local Government, argued that 'better health and education and lower crime and environmental sustainability cannot be achieved without citizen participation'.[6]

Many third-sector organisations are composed of service users or their supporters, carers and volunteers, and they are generally trusted by the users of their services. Indeed, it is difficult to see how greater citizen participation can be secured without using the third sector both as deliverer of services and as 'voice' for consumers and citizens. The estimated 55,000 social enterprises are offering a new route for the delivery of services, regeneration and community empowerment, though it is important to take note that these are but one form of third-sector organisation. Many traditional charities are increasingly developing their 'trading' arms and acting in a social entrepreneurial way.

It is sometimes argued that there is little evidence to back claims for added value in the sector, but it is interesting to note that in the recent report of the Social Care Inspectorate, third-sector providers outscored both the public and the private sectors. The 2006 statement of the Commission for Social Care Inspection pointed out, for the second time, that third-sector providers more consistently meet minimum standards in care provision than either the public or the private sectors. In explaining these findings, the commission's experts cited the way in which the best third-sector organisations empower service users to insist on these standards, giving them greater control as well as better services.

If 'empowerment' of citizens is to be effectively realised then this requires

- a diversity of service provision between private, public and third-sector providers;
- a devolution of power to citizens and communities;
- flexible non-bureaucratic services which encourage co-production, innovative delivery mechanisms and choice;
- services based around the citizen, not producer interest.

The third sector can and should be central to the reform process. Why?

The third sector's public value

The particular value of the sector is demonstrated through

- passion and commitment;
- joining up services based on client interest, not producer interest;
- entrepreneurship and innovation;
- the ability to deliver to the hardest to reach;
- flexibility and lack of bureaucracy;
- the ability to grow social capital;
- control exercised by the user, client or carer and the community;
- autonomy from excessive professional control;
- ability to drive social change.

As the anthropologist Margaret Mead once said, 'Never doubt that a small group of thoughtful committed citizens can change the world. Indeed it is the only thing that ever has.'

Transfer or transform?

The role of the third sector in public service reform does not consist only in delivering services. The sector has always played a major role as a voice and advocate, whether for the rights of those who use services or are excluded from them, as a voice for the 'voiceless' or as an advocate for service reform. Indeed, many charities would argue that their role is to act as a voice, as well as to provide services. The RNID, for example, acts as the representative of the deaf and hard of hearing and campaigns on their behalf as well as providing direct services. RETHINK, the mental health charity, delivers services, with a turnover of £42m. But it also campaigns against the stigma that people with schizophrenia suffer in society. The RSPCA campaigns against cruelty to animals as well as providing an extensive inspectorate service. Barnardo's has long been seen as an advocate for the rights of children but runs extensive services for looked-after children.

The strongest case for service delivery through the third sector is not a managerial case. This is not about delivering more services through organisations for their own sake. It is about harnessing their strengths as value-driven and connected organisations capable of challenging established views and articulating the voice of the citizen and the community. This agenda cannot simply be an individual consumer agenda. 'Public services provide not just a private benefit to consumers, but also a public good.'[7]

There are two key reasons why we believe in an expanded third-sector role. Through this role we can achieve

- modernised public services which provide more diversity in providers, choice and flexibility, and
- services which engage more citizens and communities directly in the process of delivery, and therefore support civil renewal and citizen and community engagement.

Our ambition through the public sector reform agenda is to develop a transformed relationship between the individual and the state. The networks and organisations that can enable this to happen are found throughout civil society. In other words, this is not simply an argument about transferring employment services from, say, Jobcentre Plus but also about how we can empower communities to establish mechanisms and organisations that promote employment and training as well as healthy living, and that tackle addiction, anti-social behaviour and mental health problems – problems that get in the way of employability.

However, it is clear from the growth of many third-sector organisations that a burgeoning service delivery role has strengthened their capacity to understand and to influence government policy development and to work for policy change. The homeless charities are a prime example of this: today they campaign for policy change but their understanding of the needs of homeless people through the delivery of services makes them indispensable to government in the development of policy.

So in arguing for a bigger third-sector role in public services, we believe this is both about the transfer of specific services from state provision and about the transformational power of the wider third sector.

> Extending the range of choices available is just one of the ways in which the third sector can contribute to building public value, not just as a high volume provider of public services, but as an agent of civil renewal. While the technical issues that obstruct the operation of the market and cause difficulty for purchasers and providers alike are real and require resolution, the prize is a more dynamic, more responsive, effectively user-controlled set of services. Achievement of this prize requires a cultural transformation of public services which goes beyond the introduction and development of a market of providers.[8]

Securing the consumer voice?

The Future Services Network, an exciting alliance of the CBI, the National Consumer Council and the Association of Chief Executives of Voluntary Organisations (Acevo), has been arguing for the transformation of public services by putting the consumer voice at the heart of the debate, and acting as a countervailing force to the producer voice. Much of the debate on public service reform is dominated by the producer interest; paramount in this have been the trade unions and dominant professional bodies, who are increasingly now attacking third-sector organisations. An example of what to avoid comes from the NHS. There has been a significant growth in spending in the NHS, but a large element of it has been invested in the renegotiation of contracts for doctors and consultants. An opportunity to transform the service through working practices that would benefit patients was lost and it remains remarkable that doctors' surgeries are not available to the public at times the public want.

But this is not simply about individual consumers. The third sector has traditionally worked with communities in securing regeneration for example, or with excluded communities of interest and those who are denied service provision, for instance people with autism or migrants and refugees.

Many third-sector organisations exist to support the rights of citizens who have been marginalised through a disability, by age or social exclusion. A 'consumer' approach cannot properly tackle how the state ensures effective services for people with mental health problems or severe disabilities for example. Thus the role of carers and volunteers, families or organisations who act as advocates is crucial in effecting a service that meets the needs and ensures rights of citizens. It is not sufficient to argue for better services for the mentally ill; what's needed is to organise a service that gives effect to their human rights, while tackling the stigma that attaches to such illness.

Similarly, any reform must ensure the transfer of power to communities. Citizens living in deprived or neglected communities often encounter multiple problems in securing effective service delivery from the state. It is often only by citizens acting in and through community organisations that change can be secured. Take for example the Coin Street social enterprise in Waterloo, south London, which defeated plans to turn over that area of the South Bank to offices, and now has ambitious plans to develop services including a primary academy, a continuing-care centre and leisure facilities.

The scope for change?

Expanded service delivery by the sector has tended to be limited to the margins of existing services. So for example a bigger role is envisaged for the sector in social care but not in acute hospitals. In prisons and probation the sector is seen as making additional contributions but with a significantly smaller role than the private sector. In employment services the sector is seen as playing a role in pilot areas looking after the disabled or in deprived communities, but not yet in mainstream Jobcentre provision.

Martin Narey, chief executive of Barnardo's and previously chief executive of the National Offender Management Service in the Home Office, says, 'We in the voluntary sector can do things economically and effectively. We can do things differently. Our services frequently grow from a local base and are unusually responsive to local circumstances. We are trusted.'[9] So we may need to undergo a step change through outsourcing and asset transfer where that will provide a better service. Indeed, one could argue that what is needed is root-and-branch reform that considers what a 'deconstructed' service might look like if it were reconfigured around the citizen or community.

The National Health Service: promoting health, not sickness
Thinking in the Department of Health (DH) can often be dominated by the interests of acute hospitals and key professional bodies, where encouraging care in the community, healthy eating, exercise and action on smoking is seen as 'alternative' and less exciting than the work in acute hospitals. Community-based services are not regarded as mainstream, and palliative care and care in hospices are seriously under-funded.

However, the establishment of health centres, dental practices, care facilities and the like which are run by either existing third-sector organisations or newly established ones (such as community interest companies) ought to be seriously considered as a way of engineering long-term change in patterns of ill health. It is also clear that more sophisticated measures of 'productivity' are needed. More activity and shorter waiting times do not necessarily mean better health.

The financing of the health service currently incentivises bad health and prevents alternative strategies on provision. Indeed the DH cannot even accurately cost its own provision, which leads to absurdities like penalising hospitals that cut the length of a patient's stay, even though this may be better for the patient and cheaper for the NHS.

Yet broader thinking could unleash huge potential. Community hospitals or health centres that are run by a community organisation with health authority and local authority input could provide a crucial answer to the health needs of rural or isolated communities. Empowering and funding housing associations to work with charity and community groups to provide a range of care from simple health testing, through dental support and straightforward operations, to elder care, coupled with effective community health promotion and action to tackle addictions, is a long-term but potentially hugely beneficial way to encourage healthy communities. Already some third-sector organisations have been encouraged to move into dentistry provision in deprived areas where access to NHS dentists is now becoming unattainable. Les Huckfield, a former Bennite minister under James Callaghan, now says, 'In many areas third-sector organisations have already become the only way in which public services can be delivered, since traditional or mainstream delivery has proved unreliable or too expensive.' He argues that the NHS needs to become a community health service.

Patrick Diamond and Charles Leadbeater and Hilary Cottam argue in their respective chapters for participative public services. Leadbeater and Cottam suggest a major redesign of the health service. Instead of measuring achievement by filling hospital beds, a 21st-century health service would concentrate on, and be funded to provide, disease prevention. The process would begin not with a hospital asking how it can reach the public but the other way round with individuals asking how they wanted to live their lives. 'You organise the system around being well and prevention and have a safety net for cure when you need it.'[10]

Education: expanding real choice
More progress has been made in education, where many third-sector organisations have traditionally been extremely active. The encouragement of academies, new partnerships and trust schools has advanced choice and allowed more freedom. For example, Montessori and Steiner, very active in continental Europe, have in the past been prevented from actively promoting their brand of teaching but are now using academies to do this. The government could move towards enabling child trusts (which ought to be sector-led organisations) to establish schools where there is local demand. Housing and community associations should be empowered, encouraged and financed to work across health, education and job boundaries.

Employment: tackling worklessness

Jobcentre Plus needs radical restructuring and transformation, with a clear split between purchasing and provision. Freeing the state, whose role lies in determining welfare payments and acting as a portal to support and advice, from the task of delivering employment and training services will both improve efficiency and cut costs as well as increasing choice and better delivery of services. It is clear that in tackling the needs of those on welfare benefit for more than a year, a tailored service is needed. The obvious lesson to draw is that third-sector organisations will be better at placing such people into employment and training. For example, an interesting innovation pioneered by Tomorrow's People placed job advisers in doctor's practices. This type of radical approach could help transform this service.

Reforms in Australia eight years ago transformed the Employment and Training Service (ETS). Today, Centrelink (the equivalent of our Jobcentre Plus) is the portal for the job seeker and determines benefit but the work of the ETS is now provided through a range of private and third-sector organisations. A job seeker in Australia is now presented with the choice of two providers. The reforms have driven down the cost of the service, and yet have improved the outcomes for job seekers.

It is well known that for nearly 2.7 million people on welfare benefit, the issue is not so much unemployment as worklessness. Thirty per cent of those on welfare benefit are estimated to have mental health problems. A significant proportion, the largest in Europe, are lone parents. Thus tackling welfare reform requires a more comprehensive and user-focused approach to those seeking jobs than can be provided through Jobcentre Plus. While the government has acknowledged the strength of these arguments, opposition from within the civil service and the trade unions has so far prevented a radical reform that could revolutionise the service we provide to job seekers and those on welfare benefit. It remains to be seen whether the radical approach advocated by David Freud in his report to the government will be implemented.[11]

Crime: genuine alternatives to prison

It is well known that the majority of crime is committed by people who have already been inside prison. Some 60 per cent of prisoners are reconvicted within two years of release. Reoffending costs £11 billion a year. And yet of the £370 million allocated to the Youth Justice Board in 2004, 70 per cent was spent on the youth custodial estate rather than community intervention. Released prisoners are responsible for at least a million crimes a year.

There are high levels of both mental health and addiction problems in prisons. Martin Narey, when chief executive of the National Offender Management Service, said that in 2000, 90 per cent of those entering prison were recognised as displaying one or more forms of mental disorder. Yet little time or resource is spent on rehabilitation, and at present the over-crowding in prisons is seriously hindering any attempt to provide support and, therefore, to help ensure lower rates of reoffending. Interestingly, in the United States since 2000, a massive reduction in prison spending has coincided with massive falls in the crime rate as alternatives to prison have had to be pursued.

A readjustment of financial priorities towards supporting organisations that work with ex-offenders and those likely to offend is more likely to achieve crime reduction than building more prisons. While it may be unlikely that we will see a third-sector prison, joint ventures could offer entirely viable models for containment and rehabilitation. Already one third-sector organisation is involved in the running of a youth offender institution, and more such innovative approaches are needed. Recently the crime reduction charity Nacro suggested taking the 8,000 people in prison for less than a year (where they receive no rehabilitation or support from probation when they leave) and placing them in an emergency third-sector-led programme funded through the money otherwise spent on prison. This would almost certainly prove more effective in preventing reoffending.

Social and community enterprise
Social or community enterprises are an exciting way to expand citizen- and consumer-driven services. The Development Trusts Association has argued that community enterprise involvement in public service delivery and an expansion of that role can deliver high-quality services in local communities that have been badly served by a state-run public sector.[12]. A large expansion of investment in these bodies, together with initiatives to open up access to commercial capital markets, could pay a large social dividend. In Italy Silvio Palmero, a reformed terrorist, leads a social enterprise of young ex-prisoners who design and make T-shirts under the Made in Jail brand. Not so far fetched to think of social enterprise community rehabilitation facilities? However, there is a little of the 'flavour of the month' about politicians' espousal of social enterprise. Tim Smit, chief executive of the Eden Project, is critical of the way the left has patronised social enterprise as 'cottage public service industries', who tackle the marginal and the lost of society.

There is every reason to believe social or community enterprises can be large scale and ambitious: take the example of ECT, which started as a small community transport scheme. Now it runs the refuse and recycling service for the entire London Borough of Ealing (population approximately 300,000) and is expanding elsewhere. This is the model governments should support. However, this approach distresses those who believe 'community' equates with 'small' and to become large and professional is to lose one's soul. Yet large third-sector organisations can still remain closely in touch with clients and communities.

A review of opportunities for the transfer of assets from public bodies to third-sector organisations could offer an exciting way of developing community involvement and ownership in their localities.

Joint ventures

The scope for private/third-sector finance initiatives and joint ventures is undeveloped. However, a long-term finance initiative between commercial and third-sector bodies could open up a new way of providing services and enable expansion, especially where capital investment is needed – in health centres, youth clubs or residential care homes for example. Prisons could be run on a three-way public–private–third-sector venture basis where commercial-sector managerial skills are allied to third-sector people management and rehabilitation expertise.

This chapter can only touch on the possibilities and potential but a mind shift from third-sector providers as a 'sticking plaster' to the mainstream has to be the way to reinvigorate public services for citizens and communities.

The constraints

A more significant role for the third sector will require both it and the government to address a number of significant constraints.

Despite widespread calls for greater involvement, and while many policy initiatives from government departments suggest a central role for the third sector, in most areas this has not translated into practice on the ground. Data on the size and scale of the sector is incomplete, but it is evident that its role in public service delivery remains relatively small. In 2001, the third sector's income from government, including social housing, stood at only £3.7 billion. Although this sum excludes the significant assets gained by the sector through housing association stock transfer, it stands at only 0.7 per cent of total public spending.[13] In comparison, it is estimated that the government spends nearly £100 billion each year on goods and services from the private sector.[14]

Government figures indicate that spending on the third sector is actually decreasing as a proportion of total expenditure, suggesting huge potential for expansion. To ensure that an expansion of third-sector activity is possible and desirable, both government and the third sector will need to pay close attention to a number of significant barriers.

Procurement and finance

The foundation of many of the barriers to change lies in the simple fact that contracts for service delivery between the state and the third sector are not yet fit for purpose. The vast majority of arrangements are short term, highly insecure, under-valued and excessively bureaucratic.

Acevo's recent publication *Surer Funding*[15] illustrated how all parties currently lose out through poor contractual arrangements:

- Third-sector organisations find it difficult to recruit and retain staff, to access and manage finance, and to improve services;
- Citizens receive services that are not as reliable, or as high quality, as they could and should be;
- Government bodies achieve poor value for taxpayers' money in commissioning services.

At present, both the government and the third sector expend a huge amount of time and resources in managing short-term renegotiations of relatively small quantities of money. By placing funding on a more stable, performance-related footing, the government would free resources for greater investment in the front line, producing better services for users and better value for taxpayers. Long-term contracts provide the basis for capital investment and access to the capital markets.

What is key to securing more service delivery through the sector is funding reform based on

- sharing the responsibility for risk;
- full cost recovery;
- cutting waste caused by bureaucracy;
- longer-term contracts.

So far strong commitments from central government to reform have had less impact on the ground, and its vision of a third sector competing 'on equal terms' has not yet been realised. The recent sector action plan, introduced in December 2006,[16] will pave the way for change if the government is seriously prepared to implement the proposals.

Capacity and staffing
Part of the difficulty in building effective procurement relationships lies in the third sector's lack of capacity. In many ways the sector's huge diversity is one of its strengths, enabling highly specialised service offerings and facilitating healthy debate over policy positions. Yet it also raises the problem of scalability.

Of the 200,000 registered charities, just 2,400 of them receive two thirds of the sector's income. The vast majority of third-sector organisations are small, in terms of both turnover and professional staffing. This places limitations on the sector's ability to work effectively with government, both in developing a coherent, large-scale offering and in successfully negotiating an effective contractual relationship.

Many third-sector organisations lack the capacity to invest in strategic development, effective research and monitoring, and good quality staff development and support, particularly in the fields of leadership and management. This reflects a historic failure to recoup the overhead costs necessary for such investment. Until all contracts between government and the third sector reflect the full costs of delivery, in accordance with central government policy, the deficit in capacity can only grow. The sector's deficit in professional development and skills is particularly acute. It currently spends as little as 1.3 per cent of its turnover on training and development, compared with the public sector (2.7 per cent) and the private sector (3 per cent). Even this low figure may be flattering, since the third sector enjoys high levels of provision of goods in kind.

There is real concern that 'scalability' will hinder the scope of sector organisations to meet the challenges of bigger contracts. This requires a greater capacity (which the government can support) and growth in third-sector mergers and alliances. The sector itself needs to address these difficulties and shortcomings.

Governance and accountability
Concern that the third sector is not immune from the general loss of confidence in corporate governance has led to a concerted drive to improve its accountability and transparency. Commentators have argued that the

sector's present standards of governance owe more to history than to effectiveness. Professor Bob Garratt writes:

> The corporate governance of NGOs is a hot topic at present. I have worked with some of them on this very issue and have come away disappointed by their innate conservatism and short-sighted need to keep a firm grip on the levers of existing organisational power. The corporate governance values of accountability, probity and transparency are not yet well developed in many NGOs – but need to be if they are to maintain their own long-term reputations.[17]

There is a specific tension between the voluntary tradition of charitable governance, historically one of the hallmarks of the sector, and the increasing risks and scrutiny to which trustees are subject. The idea of trusteeship as a 'gift of time' does not always sit well with the onerous responsibilities and standards charities are expected to achieve in their accountability to stakeholders, particularly in relation to the rising standards demanded of public service providers. The government has noted a 'general consensus that "one size does not fit all" and that the diversity of the sector means that prescriptive solutions are not always the way forward'.[18] Again this is an issue the sector itself must address.

Costs and risks

Perhaps the third sector's area of greatest expertise lies in its ability to work with the hardest to help. This chimes closely with the government's commitment to use 'the experiences of the bottom 10 per cent as a litmus-test of reform across government'. The third sector has always prioritised the need to 'focus on the disadvantaged and champion them as services are transformed across government'.[19]

There is strong evidence that the long-term financial and social benefits of third-sector work outweigh the costs. The New Economics Foundation has undertaken significant work on social return on investment (SRI), looking at the financial value of the social and economic returns achieved. A pilot study of four social enterprises showed an SRI of between 1.3:1 and 1.8:1.[20]

For some statutory bodies, embracing new risks with the aim of developing more flexible and innovative services will prove counter-cultural. Processes of accountability for public spending incentivise public bodies to minimise the risks they incur, ensuring that expenditure is as stable and predictable as possible.

The state is also a poor decision maker. T. S. Eliot's 'The Love Song of J. Alfred Prufrock' sums up the approach:

> In a minute there is time
> For decisions and revisions which a minute will reverse.

The state as an enabler

Gerry Stoker argues cogently in Chapter 3 for a new collectivist agenda where devolution and decentralisation of public services will allow citizens and communities to play their proper role in service delivery. This revitalised role between the state and the citizen is a key one for the third sector to facilitate.

In local government there is now significant force behind the concept of local authorities as 'place shapers',[21] becoming service providers only where it serves the strategic purpose. The role of an elected local leadership in driving economic regeneration and social welfare is seen as a role that joins together government agencies and combines with the private and the third sectors. The idea of a local authority drawing together or 'joining up' the strategic direction of the many service providers in a locality has great force. The disjointed nature of state services has always been a significant problem in trying to provide user-focused services. The organisational and cultural barriers that exist between local government, the NHS, Jobcentre Plus and other government agencies often inhibit an effective outcome for a service user. For example, a person leaving prison faces a multitude of challenges in finding a job and accommodation and often tackling problems of addiction and mental health. Currently, the state has a limited ability to provide a joined-up service for an individual, yet third-sector organisations can and do provide such a person-centred service. That is why it is argued that services need to be both decentralised and devolved.

However, the state must remain as a crucial actor in the public domain, setting the progressive goals for services and monitoring outcomes, rather than withdrawing altogether. As Ed Miliband, third-sector minister, has said, 'It does not mean government should withdraw. In praising "social enterprise" the motivation must not be to palm off responsibility for welfare and abdicate the responsibility of government. Instead it is to understand how government and social enterprise can both contribute to a fairer society.'[22]

Partnerships or patronage?

Partnership working is much in vogue and is often invoked as a solution to the difficulties of public service provision. It is seen as a cure for many ills, yet is beset by two fundamental problems. Firstly, what is seen as partnership working by the state is often perceived as patronage by the third sector. Secondly, the actuality of partnership working is swamped by bureaucracy and an ever-expanding network of committees and structures to support such working.

Those advocating more 'partnership' do so more in hope than expectation of change. Partnership, without a more equal distribution of power between partners, is unlikely to secure the transformation of public service delivery. At its worst it is a flabby excuse by government to avoid more radical approaches to delivery or community empowerment.

More radical measures are needed, and so the need for a decentralisation and devolution of power from the central state must be accompanied by a real shift in power relationships between those running local services and third-sector organisations.

Towards solutions

Some very specific steps can be taken to move this agenda forward.

* The gradual transfer of certain services to third-sector providers and the opening up of delivery to a diversity of providers must continue, while the framework for such delivery and the establishment of agreed outcomes remains a state duty.

* There should be a radical programme of national and community asset transfer, where under-used or misused assets of public sector organisations in local government, the health service and other agencies would be considered for transfer to third-sector organisations. The government should commit to ensuring that in the sale of national or local assets no longer required, those suitable for community use are transferred to community organisations rather than put up for sale.

* A programme of capital investment is needed. A major injection of capital funds into the existing lead bodies (for example the Adventure Capital Fund and Futurebuilders) and a more co-ordinated approach between the state and commercial and charity leaders must aim to lift funding from the current maximum of only £500 million to more than

£1 billion. Traditionally, one of the constraints to the sector's role has been its limitation to funding through either grants and contracts or philanthropy. It has traditionally had little access to capital markets. A number of new instruments are now being developed and the proposed Social Investment Bank is a good example. But in overall public spending terms, the amounts available are minuscule. Greater capital access must also be built on longer-term funding for third-sector bodies.

- Government commissioning of services should encourage joint ventures between the private and the third sectors. There are a growing number of examples of such initiatives emerging from the sector but these need to be encouraged, facilitated and promoted through the funding and procurement system. The state may also be a partner in three-way public service ventures.

- Partnership Commissioners: moving away from the plethora of partnership committees and working groups, each local authority should appoint a commissioner whose task is to promote public service reform through involvement of the third sector. A commissioner should also be appointed at government level, reporting to the minister for the third sector to implement reforms outlined in the third-sector action plan and to encourage asset transfer and growing opportunities for service delivery.

- The government has begun to address the difficulties of lack of capacity infrastructure in the sector through, for example, the establishment of capacity builders. So far the funding has been limited and a new infrastructure is needed to support capacity building, sector mergers and alliances, and support for growing scalability.

- Commissioning structures must be reformed to incentivise co-production models, joint ventures and innovative ways of delivering community-based service. A much greater use of social clauses in contracts and the education of public servants to use commissioning as investment rather than shopping is crucial.

- The sector itself needs to review its governance arrangements and consider the scope for developing its capacity through greater use of mergers and strategic delivery alliances (which might be through local organisations working with more locally based third-sector bodies).

Conclusion

A greater role for third-sector organisations in public services is both inevitable and desirable: both to provide citizens and communities with choice and to increase their voice. But as Will Hutton has said, 'this will be determined both by political necessity in government and by growing self-confidence and assertiveness in the third sector itself'.[23]

There is a narrowness in the current political debate on public service reform which often revolves around a purely managerial approach. This restricts the range of organisational possibilities through which politicians and practitioners can identify solutions. This book proposes radically different models of service delivery and a changed role for state and citizens, as well as a transformed public sector. Third-sector organisations will be key to this transformation.

So by greater sector involvement we can act, as David Miliband has suggested, as 'the supplier of power to individuals and communities'.[24] At their best, third-sector organisations have compelling advantages in public service provision. They focus on service users not institutions, they put user involvement ahead of staff interest and they have the flexibility to innovate, promote change and work across government silos. And most compelling for governments seeking to empower communities, they build social capital and inclusion, giving direct accountability to communities.

7

The user-generated state
Public Services 2.0

Charles Leadbeater and Hilary Cottam[1]

Caroline Tomlinson's disabled teenage son, Joe, had a problem. He wanted to go to school with all the other teenagers in Wigan, on the bus. But when Caroline approached the Social Services Department to see whether that would be possible, she was told that the department already had a block contract with a local taxi firm to take Joe to school, and sending him on the bus would be an additional cost it was unprepared to pay, especially as in the department's assessment Joe would need to be accompanied by two care workers to make sure he came to no harm.

A few months later, however, Caroline and Joe enrolled on an initiative called In Control, run by a social enterprise for the Department of Health, which helps young people with learning disabilities take control of their own care. Everyone going on In Control gets their own annual budget – the cash equivalent of what they would have got in services – and help to decide how to spend it on the kind of support they need. Caroline and Joe quickly drew up a plan to get to school on the bus, with the help of two fellow sixth-formers who were studying for care qualifications. Joe was happy. He and Caroline were managing the risk rather than the department, so the social workers were content. And, as Caroline put it, 'you give me ten pounds and I will make sure it goes much further for Joe than any local authority'.

Joe and Caroline Tomlinson, and the other families enlisted by Wigan Council onto the project, found their relationship with public services transformed. Where once they were dissatisfied, complaining consumers, in an adversarial relationship with service providers and professionals, they found themselves turned into participants and co-investors in finding better outcomes for themselves. They sought and paid for professional advice and support, but within the context of their own plans. In the past, all too frequently, it had felt the other way around: Joe and Caroline fitted into plans and strategies drawn up by the professionals, trying to bend their lives to fit within the provision the council made available.

It is often assumed that the public have to rely on professionals to deliver public services because, in the economic jargon, there is an 'information asymmetry': the doctor or teacher knows more than the patient or pupil. Yet the families of these children have fine-grained knowledge about what they really need: when they need two carers to support them and when one will do, what risks to take on a trip to the zoo and so on. The In Control initiative draws out this latent, tacit knowledge of users, which is largely kept dormant and suppressed by the traditional delivery approach to services in which professionals are in control and assumed to have all the knowledge. Consumers are thus rendered generally passive because they are assumed to lack the capability of taking charge of their own care, health, learning or tax.

Caroline Tomlinson summed up the benefits of In Control like this:

> You get longer-term funding. It's not week by week so you can genuinely plan for how you will use the money. It gives you something to build around – for example planning a trip out that you might save up for – rather than just managing the service, getting by. It gives you much greater flexibility to commission the mix of services you need, when you need them. For example, my son wants a social life, he wants to be able to go out, without his family, like other seventeen-year-olds. So on those occasions he wants to be accompanied by a seventeen-year-old. That's not something that would be possible under social service rules.

Making In Control work is not simple. Turning service users into commissioners and designers of service solutions is tricky, as Caroline explained:

> You need help to start planning and designing what you need. I was not used to seeing opportunities and possibilities. I just thought in terms of getting by. You get used to accepting your lot, what you get given. You need planning tools to help you visualise and shape the services you want, and that needs to be a continual process, which you adjust. You have to go step by step, building up your confidence to take risks and do things a little differently. It is not easy being on In Control, it's like running a small business, constantly juggling people and money and time. But it's a darn sight better than having to fit into a larger system.

The benefits of In Control go beyond just giving Caroline and her son an individualised budget to spend as they see fit, for the budget brings additional benefits: it mobilises their ideas and know-how to make the money go as far as possible. When they were service users they had no incentive to innovate. Now they have lots of incentives to add their innovations because they stand to benefit, and through the community of families on the In Control programme those innovations are likely to spread.

As In Control shows, services that enlist users as participants are more likely to unlock user-led innovation. Lead users tend to have more extreme and intensely felt needs which put them in the vanguard of change in a field. Lead users often have greater knowledge, they use products more intensively and they have skills that allow them to adapt products. What they want now other consumers will want in due course. Many technology and computer games companies are well versed in working with their most demanding and innovative lead users to work out ideas for future products and applications. Caroline Tomlinson is a lead user of public services. Her family's complex and intense needs highlight how more mainstream services, for example care of elderly people, long-term conditions and learning programmes, could be reformed.

In modern media, software, games and cultural industries, user-generated content is all the rage, spawning social networking sites such as MySpace and Bebo, mass computer games such as World of Warcraft, volunteer-created encyclopedias such as Wikipedia and Citizendium, news services such as South Korea's OhmyNews, which has 55,000 citizen journalists, trading systems such as Craigslist and eBay, and the fast-growing virtual world of Second Life. Most of these examples are built on a dynamic relationship between a company or core organisation that provides the kernel or platform and a large community of users who generate, share, amend and distribute content. What would the public sector be like if it too mobilised mass user-generated content for care, health, safety and education? For the past decade most of the debate about public service reform has focused on delivery, making the public sector value chain work more efficiently, to resemble reliable private service delivery. But you cannot deliver complex public goods the way that Federal Express delivers a parcel. They need to be co-created. That is why these emerging models of mass user-generated content are so intriguing. They point the way to a user-generated state. Put another way, most of these emerging business models enlist users as participants and producers at least some of the time: they move from consuming content, watching and listening, to sharing, rating, ranking, amending, adding. A public sector which treats people just as consumers – even well-treated ones – will miss this dimension of participation which is at the heart of the most successful organisational models emerging from the interactive, two-way internet, known as Web 2.0. What would Public Services 2.0 look like?

In Control provides a glimpse: by turning people into participants in the design of services, they become innovators and investors, adding to the system's productive resources rather than draining them as passive consumers waiting at the end of the line. But In Control only works when professionals play a quite different role. The family chooses which support workers to employ and what hours they should work, and uses money flexibly to spend on treats, outings, different modes of transport, technology at home. The basis for this spending is usually a personal plan drawn up through intensive consultation between the client, their family and social workers. The person-centred plan provides the focal point for organising all care – formal and informal, provided by professionals and friends and family. This is not a formal process of assessment like a means test. It does not involve lots of forms. Person-centred planning has to be collaborative, down to earth and colloquial and plans have to adjust and adapt, as people change, growing in confidence, or their needs change. Critically, people know from the outset roughly what kind of budget they are working with.

By turning people into participants in the process, rather than dependent service users, the clients and their families are more likely to commit their own time, effort and resources. They have an incentive to do so because it makes the money from Social Services go further. With more people becoming participants public services should be able to get higher productivity, better outcomes and more satisfied clients without spending vast extra sums on professional services. The current model of professional service provision means that to get more education you have to employ more teachers and build more schools. That is why public sector output only goes up in proportion to inputs and spending. But what if you could break through that constraint which so limits public sector productivity and do what computer games companies have done? A computer game with a million players needs only 1 per cent of them to be player-developers, adding back content to the game, and it has an unpaid workforce of 10,000. Imagine that logic applied to public services: it would release vast new sources of innovation, ideas and effort. Traditional professional public services will be more effective the more they are designed to help and motivate users to generate their own content and solutions.

That at least is the promise. But the user-generated state will be possible, as In Control shows, only if participative public services are well designed to make sure professional opposition is allayed or defused; risks are properly assessed by participants and professionals; spending is accounted for; people are given support, advice and tools to make informed choices; and those with least confidence and fewest resources are given additional support to make the best use of the choices available. Above all, these approaches need to motivate people to want to help themselves and one another. Public services must not just serve people but motivate them to want to do more for themselves.

Traditional methods to squeeze more productivity and higher quality out of public service value chains – targets, inspection, outsourcing, downsizing, workforce flexibility – are painfully slow at delivering real improvements in efficiency and outcomes. They are running out of steam. That is why promoting participation should be at the heart of a new agenda for public services participation – not in formal meetings or governance but in service design and delivery. Participation offers a way for people to devise more effective, personalised solutions, at lower unit cost than top down professional services. What would it take to apply the principles of In Control to the rest of the public sector? How far could it extend? What kind of benefits would it bring? What are the potential risks and downsides of Public Services 2.0?

Five principles for Public Services 2.0

People are not consumers or users but participants
People will participate in creating service solutions only if they play a much larger role in assessing their own needs, often through consultation with professionals, and devising their own plans for their care, education, re-entry into the workforce, long-term condition management, local amenities etc.

In social care, for example, a large share of the system's resources is taken up with professionals assessing user need and then allocating services to the user. Service users are largely passive in the process. The assessments use professional and bureaucratic language beyond the grasp of most users. Filling in these forms is frustrating and time consuming for many carers: a MORI survey in Scotland found that form filling was one of the most significant activities unpaid carers engaged in.

People will need simple-to-use tools to allow them to better self-assess and plan for their needs. In Bolton, for example, our design team developed a pack of cards for diabetics to use to assess the way they manage their condition and how it could be improved. In the Brazilian city of Curitiba, which has pioneered innovative approaches to participatory budgeting and service design, families in deprived neighbourhoods have been given comic books to guide them to self-assess their needs. Person-centred planning techniques of the kind used in In Control allow people to visualise the kind of life they would like to lead and how their care would have to be organised to make that possible. People make videos and draw pictures to explain what they need. All long-term public service users, whether in health, social care, education or welfare, should be encouraged to self-assess and plan, using simple tools to help them visualise the support they currently get, the life they would like to lead and the kind of support, formal and informal, such a life would require.

This process of self-assessment is often possible only with the advice and support of peers and professionals. At the moment professionals tend to assess people's eligibility in a formal, arm's-length process designed to ration eligibility to state services. A more personalised approach would require professionals to engage in a more informal but also more intimate conversation with clients, over a period of time, to draw up and revise plans together, looking at solutions which lie beyond public services.

Financial frameworks

Giving users greater say will count for very little unless money and resources respond to these choices. The financial frameworks for public services will need to change to support greater participation. In social care, education and health that will mean taking a wider view of the total resources available. If service users can be encouraged to become co-producers, with their carers, then they become part of the productive resources of the social care system, not just consumers of those resources. The development of preventative and community-based care services, to relieve demand on professional and public services, will be possible only with long-term growth in volunteering and scaling up the capacity of voluntary organisations. The unpaid and volunteer services, provided within families and the community, will be vital to the long-run sustainability of the system as a whole. Helping to further develop that volunteer, collective, community infrastructure should be a priority for social care investment.

Public sector budgets need to change as well with more joint commissioning of services and buildings. Councils commission many services –

transport, care packages, meals – as block contracts to reap economies of scale that come from standardisation. External providers, including the voluntary sector, like such block contracts because they provide them with stability. But their inflexibility can also mitigate against personalisation by locking resources in. Councils would need much more flexible models of contracting that would allow people more choice over services.

We also need something much more radical: give the money to the people and trust them to use it wisely. The experience of In Control is that users feel greater control when they can assess how budgets are being spent on their behalf. That also encourages them to take more responsibility for their care and to devote more of their time and effort to it. The key, however, is to find financial solutions that meet people's needs rather than following a rigid formula for disaggregating budgets. Direct payments and fully individualised budgets work for people when they have the self-confidence to make choices, the information they need to compare options, and advice and support from peers and professionals. However, handling direct payments, including employing your own staff, also brings anxieties and responsibilities that many people do not want. Indeed some clients given an individualised budget may choose to spend it on the service they are already receiving. People should have a range of options for how budgets are distributed, with direct payments and individual budgets at one end of the spectrum and traditional services and top-down budget allocations at the other.

Most public services are a public–private finance initiative at the micro level of the family, mixing private, family, voluntary and state resources. The same is true of care for people with long-term health conditions and investments in education. An effective public service would mobilise all these resources, not just the state's portion.

Professionals and workforce reform

Participative public services will work only with the support of staff as well as clients. One of the major obstacles will be professional opposition to ceding control to clients or pupils who 'cannot be trusted'. Now, in many settings people will still want a professional solution. Someone going into hospital with a hernia does not want to be an active participant in the operation. They want to be well served by well-trained professionals. But often we need professional support to find our own solutions rather than a professional service upon which we come to depend. Indeed more participative approaches which relieve some of the management burdens from the shoulders of professionals may allow them to get back to their original professional vocation rather than acting as risk assessors and gatekeepers.

Professionals would still play a critical role within a participative system but they would have to give up some of their power in exchange for a better quality of work. They would have to share assessment, planning and risk assessment with clients. They might have to accept working alongside para-professionals. Professionals would play several roles:

- advisers, helping clients to self-assess their needs and forge plans for their future care;
- navigators, helping clients find their way to the services they want;
- brokers, helping clients to assemble the right ingredients of their service package from different sources;
- service providers, deploying their professional skills directly with clients;
- risk assessors and auditors, especially in complex cases involving vulnerable people who might be a risk to themselves or other people.

Take social work as an example. It could be made more attractive and satisfying as a profession if social workers had less management responsibility, paperwork and bureaucracy. Yet that would mean social workers ceding management control to others. The development of para-professionals such as social work assistants and expanding the role of care workers would relieve some of the burden on social workers, who sometimes seem to do jobs they are over-qualified for. The redesign of the role of social workers would trigger a redesign of the skills, responsibilities and roles of the wider social work workforce, including managers, para-professionals and unpaid carers.

Creating a wider market for services

There is no point giving users greater say over the services they want or even the budgets to commission services if supply is unable to respond to shifting demand. Participation in planning public service provision will mean nothing if services are trapped in rigid blocks, as in the case of Wigan's taxi service to take Joe Tomlinson to school.

The following principles should guide how services are organised to support participation:

- Flexibility, so that provision can be reconfigured easily to meet shifting needs. If resources are tied up in inflexible contracts or in building-based services, they will not have the flexibility needed to meet changing demands.
- Integration, so that different services – housing, social care, health and

education – can be combined, to create a joined-up experience for service users. That will require more joint commissioning of services, more joint planning of provision and more work in partnership between different services. People with complex needs rarely find the services they want within a single department or even within a single local authority. They need support from several different sources. Those supports need to be integrated to be effective.

- Variety, to provide people with real choice over the style of provision. Choice between two standardised services is no choice at all. People should be offered a variety of modes of provision, which might, for example, demand more or less of them as participants.
- Innovation, so that the social care system develops new service options for people. A prime example is exploring the role digital technology might play in more personalised, home-based care support, by allowing more remote monitoring of the health of frail and elderly people to enable more timely interventions, thereby preventing crises or responding to them more effectively.

New measures of success

Too often public service users and staff report that the measures of success reflect macro performance targets and budgets that pay too little attention to user experience. Feedback loops in public services are very extended. Service improvement is driven not by direct user choices or complaints but by external regulation and reviews of services, acting at one remove, often after the event.

More participative approaches to planning services will only work if the participants also define more of the standards and outcomes. We need more person-centred measures of success in education, health and social care, to complement the top-down and macro measures of targets and standards. User panels should be more directly involved in the formal regulation and inspection of services. Users also need more effective direct triggers to force a change in services when they fail to meet agreed standards. Some public service users feel they have no option but to accept the service that is available, no matter how bad it is. Users need to be given a right to options such as direct payments or individualised budgets, so that they can commission alternative provision if the public services they are getting do not come up to scratch. Imagine the eBay rating system applied to public service provision, or a service like TripAdvisor, the travel site where people rate and comment on hotels they have stayed in. Public service users need similar sites and services.

These five themes should be at the heart of more participative approaches to public services:

- Tools to give users more choice and voice, to encourage them to become participants in shaping the services they get and so to take more responsibility for them, investing their own resources and ideas in better outcomes.

- A new financial framework to encourage investment in community-based prevention, allow integration of different public service budgets around shared social goals and devolve more spending directly to users so that services are commissioned around their plans.

- A new division of labour within public service workforces, with the growth of para-professional assistants, support workers and managers, which will in turn allow a revival in professional vocational roles. social work based around the roles of adviser, navigator, advocate, broker, counsellor, risk assessor and designer.

- Continued development of a mixed-economy provision so that user choices can be translated into service provision. That will require services that are more flexible, integrated, diverse, innovative and cost effective.

- New measures of performance which give users greater say over service quality and new rights for users to switch services when quality falls below an agreed threshold.

Radical innovation rarely starts in the mainstream. It often starts in marginal markets with committed, educated and knowledgeable users creating new products or services. In the private sector, especially in media, music and culture, the margins are becoming the mainstream faster than ever: eBay went from 122 participants in 1995 to 122 million in 2005. In the public sector innovations in the margins such as In Control often get trapped on location, never developing and propagating. How would we take the principles of participative public services developed by In Control into the mainstream?

A Health Service 2.0

There is no better example of why participative public services are needed and how they could come about than health. The National Health Service is one of the largest remaining planned economies in the world and the debate is all about how to bring an element of perestroika to a system that, like the Soviet Union of old, depends on people queuing for a long time, rations treatment and provides highly variable quality. All over the developed world the assumption is the same: health is what hospitals and doctors deliver. The more that hospitals can produce high-quality, personalised, mass customised treatment, along a more or less linear patient pathway which looks something like a production line, the better healthcare we will get. The patient goes in at one end ill, is worked on by doctors and nurses, and emerges out the other, like a finished product, well again.

The scale and significance of the hospital reform programmes, focused on acute care, should not be minimised. Quality of care in hospitals is still too variable. But most hospital-focused health reforms seem to be addressing the symptoms of professional stress and organisational breakdown, rather than the underlying causes. The hospital-based healthcare system was a response to the spread of contagious and acute disease born of urbanisation and industrial-isation in the late nineteenth century. Now this system of professional diagnosis, prescription and monitoring has to deal with an epidemic of chronic disease, much of it associated with a society in which people live longer. Even cancer is becoming more like a long-term condition to be lived with and fought against. It is no longer an automatic death sentence.

In the UK, 45 per cent of the adult population have one or more long-standing medical conditions. Among those aged over seventy-five, the fastest-growing group of the population, the figure is 75 per cent. By 2030 the proportion of 65-year-olds with a long-term condition will double. In 1990, heart conditions and cancer were responsible for 19 per cent of deaths: most people died too young to be troubled by chronic conditions. In 2004 circulatory diseases and cancer were responsible for 63 per cent of deaths. They are one of the main reasons people go to see doctors. About 80 per cent of consultations with a GP are about an aspect of a long-term condition. Another 10 per cent are for minor ailments and conditions that are best dealt with through self-treatment and over-the-counter drugs. General practice is increasingly a reassurance service for people who have minor ailments that doctors can do little or nothing about or long-term conditions that are also incurable. Chief among these chronic conditions is diabetes. In the UK more than two million people are diagnosed diabetics and a further million – the 'missing million' – are diabetic without realising it. Internationally the rate of diagnosed diabetes has doubled in twenty years and will double again in the next twenty. If Type 2 diabetes, which is linked to lifestyle, is caught early its development can be kept in check. Yet between 40 and 50 per cent of diabetes is not diagnosed until it is too late. Then people become dependent upon regular insulin injections, which in the UK involve repeat visits to the doctor. Diabetes, in principle a preventable and manageable condition, costs the NHS £5m a day, 5 per cent of total NHS expenditure and 10 per cent of hospital in-patient costs. The hospital-based health system, with heavy fixed costs of buildings and professional staff, is ill designed to prevent and manage these diseases, chronic conditions that arise from lifestyle and need to be managed in the community.

The closed, professionalised system is too centralised and cumbersome to cope with the epidemic of chronic conditions which mainly stem from people's lifestyles. The front line of healthcare is not in hospitals nor even GPs' waiting rooms, but in people's living rooms and kitchens, pubs and clubs, supermarkets and restaurants, gyms and parks. By the time someone realises they have a chronic condition that warrants a visit to the doctor it is too late. We need a health system which catches conditions early or, even better, prevents them altogether and allows people to take action without having to wait to see a doctor. Such a health system would have as its prime aim enabling people to stay healthy and well. That in turn would mean patients and users becoming participants in and producers of their own health: user-generated healthcare. The best way to imagine what such a system would look like is to think of a health system organised primarily around people, their families, homes and communities, supported by hospitals and doctors, rather than a system which is dominated by high-fixed-cost hospitals.

A user-generated healthcare system would have to be highly distributed. Knowledge and resources could not be centralised in specialist hospitals or even surgeries. People want healthcare close to home. Public investment should not be going into more big hospitals, but into creating a home-based healthcare capacity, which is more flexible, personalised and cheaper. The challenge of chronic disease is to enable people to change their lifestyles. That cannot be done through a consultation with a doctor. It has to happen in situ, as people shop, eat, walk and work. People need help, advice, support and tools close to hand, without having to visit a doctor for reassurance and advice. We need to shift towards much greater self-assessment and diagnosis. New generations of intelligent sensors and monitors will allow many of the tests that GPs do to be done at home. The average diabetic sees a doctor or nurses perhaps six hours a year for a check-up, but spends 8,000 hours self-managing their condition. The big gains will come from improving what happens in the

8,000 hours of self-management. The distributed resources of the new health system will include an expanded role for pharmacies, which conduct 600 million consultations, twice as many as GPs.

Solutions would have to be co-created between people and professionals. Giving people a sense of control should be one of the central goals of a user-generated health system, equipping them with tools, knowledge and motivation to better look after themselves and one another. If someone spent nine months with the support of a life coach to prevent the onset of diabetes, the cost would be less than fifteen years' dependence on insulin injections and regular consultations with doctors, which is invariably the result of late diagnosis.

Co-created solutions emerge from interaction and conversation, not from a professional delivering a solution to a passive and dependent patient. People would need to help one another peer to peer, as the families on Wigan's In Control programme found. As consumers their main relationship was with their service providers. As participants they started to look sideways to one another for help and support. Medical professionals do not have all the solutions, even to purely medical issues. They are not the best people to turn to for advice about the social, personal and emotional aspects of health. The best source of support for those issues will not be doctors but other people who have lived with the condition themselves. A participative system will see patients and their carers as part of the distributed knowledge base. We need to create new platforms and spaces – both social and digital – to allow people to share and collaborate. Imagine an open-source approach to building up knowledge about diabetes management, in which people can find different modules relevant to their particular position, life-stage and needs, an eBay-style system for trading help and equipment, or a way of learning about health through a computer game such as *The Sims*.

All this would require new organisational models and professional roles. Chronic conditions arise from our subtly different lifestyles. A centralised organisation that relies on a cadre of specialised, knowledgeable professionals is too cumbersome to deal with such complexity. It cannot hope to gather all the information it needs to work out what needs to be done in highly dispersed and different settings. Far more needs to be done by self-help groups and online forums. The DIPEx website, for example, is a place where people with different conditions can post their own narrative accounts for others to learn from. More and more people are turning to the internet, chat rooms and discussion groups for help, support and information on health.

We will reduce the toll of chronic disease only if we encourage many more distributed participative solutions that also encourage people to help one another. Participation will only flourish if it also breeds collaboration. We will create better public health only by influencing many, many private healths. Fifty years ago daily life – getting to and from work and the shops – involved the equivalent of walking a marathon a week. In 1952 the British cycled 23 billion miles a year, compared to 4 billion now. Only 20 per cent of men and 10 per cent of women work in physically demanding occupations. Activity has been designed out of our routines. A quarter of the English population is officially judged to be obese. Lack of adequate physical activity is closely connected to chronic conditions. A national network of peer-to-peer personal trainers and health clubs – Active Mobs – might be one of the best long-term health investments we could make.

From rhetoric to reality

The government has at least started to acknowledge the need to shift in this direction in some areas, most obviously in social care, with the 2006 White Paper *Our Health, Our Care, Our Say*, which envisaged a move towards much greater use of individualised budgets. In education personalised learning should open the space for more participative approaches. Already the tax system relies on regulated self-assessment and other areas could follow suit. The most impressive welfare-to-work programmes, for example those run by Work Directions in Birmingham, rely on mobilising the motivation of participants to follow through their plans. The 2006 local government White Paper envisaged greater decentralisation of power and budgets – double devolution – which should encourage greater community participation in decision making. Responses to climate change will require large changes in individual behaviour as well as investments in new infrastructures for energy and transport.

Yet despite the rhetorical backing for more participative approaches the progress on the ground has been limited, for three main reasons. First, established, mainstream services still gobble up most of the resources, most clearly in the health system. It is difficult to create a new community-based and participative healthcare system when most of the resources are still locked up in servicing large hospitals. Second, most attempts at promoting participation are locked into the current system: they are sustaining innovations designed to

make the current system work better rather than radical and disruptive innovations designed to create something new. The prime example is the expert
patient programme, which enlists people to become better patients within the
NHS system rather than promoting wider change. Third, creating more
participative approaches is not easy and, as In Control shows, it takes not just
thoughtful design but also a good deal of political struggle to fight off
opposition from vested and professional interests.

Attempts to create the user-generated public sector will have to confront
twelve main issues:

- *Economics: is it too costly?* The assumptions are that participative
  approaches require lots more support from professionals to tailor
  solutions to individual needs and people will tend to want to claim and
  spend more. The evidence from In Control is that participative
  approaches do not have to be more expensive so long as authorities
  employ realistic cost controls and encourage people to mobilise
  complementary resources.

- *Equity: is it just for the middle classes?* The assumption is that opportunities
  for choice and participation will be taken by the most articulate and
  confident. The professionally controlled state system at least protects the
  vulnerable with some guarantee of equity. Yet In Control has managed
  to give voice to some of the most vulnerable people in society. Mass
  state services do not guarantee consistency and equity: they can be
  highly arbitrary and capricious in the way they allocate funding and
  make decisions. Well-designed participative approaches benefit those
  least able to benefit from the current system. The implications for equity
  depend on how they are designed and who they are designed for.
  Choice and participation can benefit the least well off if the systems are
  designed for them.

- *Fraud and risk: will greater freedom be abused?* Previous experiences with
  co-individualised budgets such as individual learning accounts suggests
  there may be considerable scope for fraud and abuse. Yet In Control
  suggests otherwise: most people do not try to over-claim and they are
  very careful spenders of their money. Once it becomes their money they
  tend to look after it very well; as Caroline Tomlinson says, getting
  maximum value from it.

- *Changing roles of professionals.* Professional power is at the heart of the
  public service system of assessing need, regulating risk and measuring
  quality of outcomes. More person-centred approaches to planning will

challenge professional power and so provoke resistance. Successful In
Control authorities have developed approaches that bring clear
compensating benefits to professionals, for example by restoring
professional vocational roles. Strategies for workforce reform and
expansion – bringing in a wider range of skills and support – will be
critical.

• *Supply side response.* Most public service provision is organised around
  inflexible blocks of services: schools, hospitals and prisons or block
  contracts for care. This rigidity, justified by economies of scale, limits
  services' ability to respond to specific needs. Users tend to be fitted into
  the service boxes available to them. Public authorities will have to
  develop ways to procure services that allow for more personalisation and
  flexibility. However, it is also essential there should be 'backwards
  compatibility': the new system must also provide room for elements of
  traditional services that some people will want.

• *Audit and accountability.* How should individuals account for the money
  they spend? Fear that individuals might misspend money is one justification for continued professional control over budgets and onerous
  requirements to account for spending. In Control recognises people
  need to account for how they spend the money but this is made as
  simple as possible and linked to their care plan. The most effective way
  to kill off participative approaches is to distribute funding through
  individualised budgets but then reregulate and audit in great detail what
  people can spend their money on: giving with one hand but taking back
  with the other. Finding realistic, robust but simple forms of accountability will be essential. This needs to be linked to new person-centred
  measures of outcomes.

• *Regulation and risk.* In social care, authorities will be concerned that
  greater individual discretion to shape care might lead people to take risks
  which would put the authority in jeopardy of a breach of duty of care.
  Person-centred plans must involve a redistribution of risk assessment
  and responsibility away from professionals. But this needs to be made
  clear: giving people individualised budgets means them also taking on
  more responsibility for handling risk.

• *Regulation and innovation.* Participative approaches will be at odds with
  regulation that might punish rather than reward or encourage innovation. Innovating authorities need to know how regulators and
  inspection regimes will respond. Most public service regulation and

inspection is designed to guarantee consistency and delivery of standards. In participative public services, inspection would need to encourage and endorse far greater diversity of outcomes.

• *Building participant confidence.* Different participants will come with different levels of confidence, support networks, friends and family. A participative approach will have to be very responsive to their different needs, starting points and resources. Not everyone is ready or wants to be a participant. Most people, some of the time, will want to be consumers. Some people will want to be in that position all of the time.

• *The role of the voluntary sector.* The voluntary sector will be vital to provide additional support and services for people to help themselves. Building the voluntary sector's capacity to support person-centred services will be vital. But some voluntary groups see their main role as advocating better services with the traditional professional service model.

• *Political leadership.* The scale of the transformation and the risks involved will require committed political leadership at central and local level to meet professional opposition to ceding control, media scare stories about risk and fraud, and public concerns that participative solutions are really a back-door route to service cuts.

• *Scaling up.* The biggest challenge in all social and public innovation is how to scale up promising ideas. What is being scaled up? (An idea, a set of principles, a set of tools, an organisation?) How is it being scaled? (Through franchising, policy prescription, campaigning, organisational growth?) In Control is an alliance between enlightened professionals, participants, carers and councils to create a new set of solutions tailored to individual aspirations. The In Control community has an open-source feel to it: ideas and improvements are readily shared. Simon Duffy, In Control's director, talks of it as an operating system for social care, which can be adapted and amended in different contexts applied to different needs. Scaling will also be helped by making the system quite modular, so that people can pick, choose and improve just what they want to focus upon. Most open-source software projects that attract a large developer community have this modular structure, which allows many people to participate in its development. The technology writer Tim O'Reilly calls this an 'architecture of participation', which encourages many people to make contributions and ensures they all add up. The Web has an architecture of participation: it invites people –

most people – to take part. Public services do not always come with such a welcome.

Participative solutions cannot be mandated top down. The centre can help create the conditions for them to emerge – for example by promoting individualised budgets for social care and long-term conditions – but it cannot mandate what outcomes should be achieved. Participative public services are far more likely to spread by word of mouth, peer to peer, just as social networking has.

Public Services 2.0

We need a new way to create public goods that takes its lead from the culture of self-organisation and participation emerging from the Web. The tax system increasingly depends on mass involvement in self-assessment and reporting. Welfare-to-work and active labour market programmes depend on the user as a participant, who takes responsibility for building up their skills and contacts. Neighbourhood renewal has to come from within localities, it cannot be delivered top down from the state. Public goods are rarely created by the state alone but by cumulative changes in private behaviour.

The chief challenge facing government in a liberal and open society is how to help create public goods in a society with a democratic ethos, which prizes individual freedom and wants to be self-organising and 'bottom-up'. Increasingly the state cannot deliver collective solutions from on high, or decide on its definition of the public good and impose it from above, at least not continually: it is too cumbersome and distant. However, it can help to create public goods – such as better education and health – by encouraging them to emerge from within society. Government cannot. Government's role is to shape freedom: getting people to exercise choice in a collectively responsible way and so participate in creating public goods.

Productivity should rise because highly participative services can mobilise users as co-developers and co-producers, multiplying the resources available. Participation allows solutions to be tailored more readily to individual needs and aspirations; people have to share responsibility for outcomes and devote some of their own inputs. Participation is the best antidote to dependency if it equips people with tools so that they can self-provide and self-manage rather than relying on professional solutions and services. Participative approaches are not only vital to create more personalised versions of existing services, such as health and education, but also to address emerging needs and issues, such as waste and recycling, community safety and long-term conditions, where public outcomes depend on motivating widespread changes to individual behaviour. Participative public services connect the individual and the collective in new and far more powerful ways than seeing people as taxpayers, occasional consumers and even more infrequent voters.

The triumph of the modern industrial public sector is the creation of institutions on a vast scale which provide services, such as education, health and policing, that were once limited to just a few. These universal systems aspire to deliver services that are fair and reliable. Yet that in turn requires codes, protocols and procedures, which often make them dehumanising. As people become more dependent on the expert knowledge of professionals, so they lose faith in their own capacity to act. The rise of professional power is mirrored by a loss of individual responsibility. We become cases to be processed by the system. Education and health come to be commodities to be acquired rather than capabilities we develop in ourselves to live better lives. We now identify services delivered by professionals with the ultimate goods we want as a society: health, learning, safety, order, justice.

Public and professional institutions should educate us towards self-help and self-reliance as much as possible. As Ivan Illich put it in *Deschooling Society*: 'Good institutions encourage self-assembly, reuse and repair. They do not just serve people but create capabilities in people, support initiative rather than supplant it.'[2] The golden rule must be that instruction by professionals must never outweigh opportunities for independent learning; any service must be designed to motivate and enable self-help.

We need much greater emphasis on intelligent self-assessment and self-evaluation. That is already the linchpin of the tax system and should play a greater role in education and health. The education system schools us to think of assessments as exams, something we do at the end of the pipeline, checked by a professional. We need an education system that builds up capacity for intelligent self-evaluation, so that we are better equipped to assess and solve problems under our own steam, with the help of our peers and professionals if needed. An education system for the twenty-first century would have constant self-evaluation, much of it through peer-to-peer criticism and support, at its core.

In *Limits to Medicine* Illich described health as a personal task, which people must take responsibility for:

Success in this personal task is in large part the result of the self-awareness, self-discipline, and inner resources by which each person regulates his own daily rhythm and actions, his diet and sexual activity ... The level of public health corresponds to the degree to which the means and responsibility for coping with illness are distributed among the total population.[3]

These ideas are not appropriate to every aspect of public services. People in need of urgent and acute surgery do not generally want to be participants in the process; they want a good service, delivered by professionals. Too often the ethic of self-help can be used to get us, the users, to do more of the work ourselves. Self-service is not the same as participation.

Yet the range of ways we can create public goods is expanding. In energy, for example, nuclear power might provide part of the solution to global warming but so too could highly distributed domestic micro-generation. Schools and hospitals will continue to exist but in an environment where more learning and healthcare can be delivered informally and at home. People will want to be consumers some of the time, participants at other times, when it makes sense for them.

And just for a moment think ahead. Imagine what it will be like in ten years' time, as public services seek to serve people who have grown up with Bebo and social networking, MSN instant messaging, buying and selling on eBay, looking up stuff on Wikipedia, getting their music via MySpace, playing multi-user games and broadcasting themselves across YouTube and its successors. Across much of culture and commerce a huge shift is underway: as technology lowers barriers to entry, people are slowly finding their voice. The people we used to call the audience are taking to the stage, or at least the stages they want to set up. And they are getting used to copying, mimicking, commenting, rating and ranking whatever they see. A public sector that does not utilise the power of user-generated content will not just look old, outdated and tired. It will also be far less productive and effective in creating public goods. The big challenge for public service reform is not just to make services more like FedEx, more efficient and reliable. There is now another big challenge: to make public services as participative, communal and collective as the best of what is emerging from the new collaborative culture. That is why in future every public service must carry with it an invitation to participate.

Part III

Decentralising the strategic state

8

Effective governance and the civil service
The role of ministers and managers

Michael Bichard

Labour returned to power in 1997 committed to improving a swathe of public services from education to health and from local government to welfare benefits. Consequently public expectations were inevitably high and they increased further with the unprecedented additional investment made available from 1998. Ten years on, there have been significant improvements. In addition the nature of the political debate about public services has been redefined so that it is now much more about investment rather than cuts. But few would argue that the improvements achieved have matched the resources invested or that public services have been 'transformed'.

The reasons for this are naturally complex but I would argue that the failure to modernise the civil service itself is central. Some say that the importance of this is over-stated. They argue that the strength of the political vision should be sufficient to deliver the desired outcomes. Some feel that the civil service is less of an issue now that the development of public policy and the delivery of services for the public good are increasingly pluralist. They often argue that the civil service with its proven reputation for honesty, integrity and neutrality should above all be protected not reformed.

It is true that the strength of political will and vision represented in a powerful secretary of state can drive change in particular policy areas for a time – but it is never sufficient to deliver and sustain permanent change. That requires the positive engagement of a civil service which is effective, focused and creative, simply because any civil service which is permanent, like the British one, wields huge power. That power is exercised in its influence over legislation and regulation; in the way it does or does not intervene in public service delivery; in the targets it sets for services and in the culture it creates for business as well as the public sector. That power has to be harnessed if any government is to be successful. But more than that, a government, to be effective, needs to have in place a civil service which has the capacity to respond effectively to the current challenges facing the country – and a service with which it has a positive relationship based upon mutual respect and understanding. The fact that civil service reform has been a preoccupation of successive governments for the past fifty years suggests that none has been content with the constitutional relationship between the political and administrative arms of government or with the service's capacity to deliver. That has remained the case for the past ten years and unless the service is finally reformed further governments will continue to founder on its inadequacies.

In fact, of course, 1997 provided the perfect opportunity to tackle this. There was a new government with high levels of public trust and a large majority which was staking its future on better services. Strangely, however, the government appeared unsure how to take advantage of these circum-stances. So far as the civil service was concerned, it seemed unsure what to do or how to do it. Initially ministers and the Prime Minister seemed excessively grateful that the service had 'smoothed' the transition and behaved impartially. Few seemed to understand how the service worked and how best it might deliver what was an unusually coherent political vision worked on in opposition. In some key policy areas there was a clarity about the delivery as well as the vision – the independence of the Bank of England, the literacy and numeracy strategies and the New Deal all come to mind. But there was no such clarity about how to deliver civil service reform and instead a nervous fear of the power of a beast best left undisturbed – whatever the rhetoric suggested. Indeed there developed a convenient drama where the government advocated reform and the service professed reform. In reality little of substance seemed to change.

Perhaps there was a feeling that reform would cause disruption and conflict at the heart of the governmental process at a time when co-operation was required. Perhaps the fear was that accusations would be made of political interference. Perhaps it was felt that the public were not interested. These are all legitimate concerns but they could have been and in future could be managed by a government with a clear vision well communicated.

A new Cabinet Secretary has now shown some understanding of the need for modernisation but the question today is whether he will receive the political support he needs to succeed – and whether the public trust necessary to reform presently exists. The stark reality remains that to be effective a government of whatever political colour requires a reformed civil service. Better public services, on which so many depend for a civilised existence, require a reformed civil service. Effective governance requires a new constitutional relationship between the (political) executive and the administration. And if there is to be a fourth-term Labour government these are matters that must be grasped.

Some will always argue that we should instead of reform pay more attention to defending the traditional values of the service, and it is true that these continue to be worth defending. But they are not of themselves sufficient to enable any government at home to provide quality public services with limited resources, nor are they sufficient to enable the UK to compete globally. That requires a different kind of service, building new skills and new values onto its long-standing strengths. It is not a question of either just protecting the old or merely introducing something new. It must be a question of reform built upon existing strengths.

But where should we start this process of reform? Well, the most important first step must be to achieve greater accountability of the service.

In fact, government with strong encouragement from the civil service has used external accountability as a way of securing improvements in many other parts of the public services. So we have had comprehensive performance assessments, carried out by the Audit Commission, of individual local authorities, while in education and health, targets, assessments, inspections and league tables have been widely used. There has been much greater reluctance to use external accountability as a way of driving up performance centrally and the reasons for that are not hard to find. They have much to do with the way in which ministers are presently implicated in any criticism of their departments or their civil servants by virtue of the principle of ministerial responsibility. As has been pointed out most recently in the Institute of Public Policy Research (IPPR)'s *Whitehall's Black Box*, 'ancillary to ministerial accountability is the non-accountability of civil servants'.[1] Put another way, the current governance arrangements make it very difficult to distinguish between the performance of the permanent staff of the department and the competence of the secretary of state; they leave ministers exposed by the fact that they accept apparent responsibility for detailed operational decisions of which they can have little or no knowledge; they provide ministers with no real power to hold civil servants to account without breaching the conventions which surround the impartiality of the service; and they protect the service from any real form of external accountability. The only way to introduce real accountability and hence real reform is first to redefine the constitutional relationship between civil servants and ministers.

In the past commentators have been very nervous of such a redefinition for fear of 'letting ministers off the hook'. In reality the current arrangements let everyone off the hook. As a senior civil servant said to the IPPR, 'the accountability fudge . . . protects ministers and officials. Ministers can say, "Not me, guv" while officials hide behind them. This is not in the interests of effective government.'

The central question, then, is how an incoming administration could redefine this relationship without being perceived either to reduce ministerial accountability or tamper with the civil service for political purposes.

There will be those who argue for fundamental change by, for example, replacing the British model of a permanent civil service with something akin to the American system, where administrative officials are so closely aligned politically to the governing party that they leave office with them. But there are many disadvantages in such a system, not least the discontinuity it inevitably produces and the fact that it prevents the development of a skilled and experienced administrative class. More tellingly, however, such a radical departure is simply unnecessary. What we need, instead, is a clear acceptance that ministers must take responsibility for those things over which they have or should have control – but should not be held responsible for actions, events or omissions which they clearly cannot control. That means they should be expected to accept responsibility for policy choices and decisions, for the strategic decisions about how policy is to be delivered, and for delivering the level of resources which are adequate to deliver their policy agenda at that particular time (via a process of negotiation with the Treasury). They should also be responsible for ensuring that once significant specific failings have been identified they are effectively addressed. What they cannot be responsible for is every specific operational failing that occurs unless taken together they become systemic or derive from the strategic and policy decisions the minister has taken.

Of course, no redefinition of ministerial responsibility can ever produce something which is free of potential controversy and the need for interpretation. But that is so endemic in the current arrangements that ministers and in particular civil servants escape accountability by taking refuge in the confusion the system creates. And the distinction between policy and implementation inherent in this redefinition has worked effectively here (e.g. the Monetary Committee of the Bank of England) and abroad.

The current arrangements have, arguably, also forced ministers to spend less time on developing and articulating a clear vision for their policy brief. They have instead become in some cases the chief executive rather than the chair they should be. Most, of course, have had little experience of operational management and are therefore spending their time performing a role for which they are not well equipped – at the expense of the role which probably attracted them to politics and government. A redefinition of ministers' role and their relationship with the Civil Service is long overdue.

If such a redefinition clears the way for achieving greater accountability of the civil service, how can this best be delivered? Gus O'Donnell, the relatively new Cabinet Secretary, deserves huge credit for introducing capability reviews, which provide for the first time a credible and reasonably transparent process for assessing (and benchmarking) departments. But the reviews have two major flaws. First, they do not yet focus sufficiently on performance and delivery – although, to be fair, the first reviews have given this more attention than I for one had expected. Second, although the review teams include external members they are not independent in the way that local authorities' comprehensive performance assessments have been. For the reasons rehearsed above this is not possible currently without implicating ministers (on occasions unfairly). It is unlikely therefore that the Cabinet Secretary will have been encouraged to take such a route even had he wanted to do so. But with the changes suggested above that should be less of an issue and the current reviews could be developed to focus more on performance with much greater independent input. Alternatively, the reviews could be carried out by a totally independent body such as the National Audit Office (NAO) and/or the Audit Commission.

Many do not feel that the NAO in particular is well equipped for this task and I accept that it would need to develop a new set of skills to perform the task effectively. However, that is surely achievable and the independence of the NAO would provide much greater confidence that there was in place for the first time true external accountability of the civil service. The head of the NAO is ultimately replaceable only by the Crown and has the authority and the protection therefore to exercise this difficult scrutiny role robustly. Equally the NAO would be free of any suspicion of political influence. On balance this wholly independent scrutiny remains for me the preferred option.

There should, however, be a third side to this accountability triangle. At the moment NAO reports are presented only to the Commons Public Accounts Committee (PAC), which decides the reports it wishes to examine in public.

Almost invariably the permanent secretary, who is the department's only accounting officer, has the doubtful pleasure of attending for this. Other select committees are not able to use NAO reports for this purpose although they do often hold hearings to consider departmental strategies and business plans. At the moment therefore, no parliamentary committee holds public hearings to address the general performance of departments covering the quality of the policy development process as well as policy implementation. Accountability reviews or performance assessment produced by a totally independent body such as the NAO or as an extension of the capability reviews could provide the substance of a (say) triennial public hearing. That hearing could be the responsibility of the appropriate select committee to avoid over-burdening the PAC. It might also involve not just the permanent secretary but perhaps also at least the deputy secretaries, to whom accounting officer status could also be extended. For the first time, as a result, we could have senior civil servants being held publicly accountable for their stewardship of their department.

Some will see this accountability solely in terms of delivery and policy implementation rather than policy. That would be a mistake. The redefinition of ministerial responsibility will have reinforced ministers' primary accountability for policy and strategy. Nonetheless the service remains responsible for ensuring that there is in place a process which ensures that policy is developed in a way which offers the best chance of delivering a successful outcome. That means using evidence where available or capable of being obtained, involving stakeholders with relevant knowledge, researching international experience and making considered choices between policy alternatives. Too often in the past, officials' failings in the management of this policy process have gone unreckoned because of its proximity to ministers. It is possible and necessary on occasions to criticise the process. This kind of accountability should enable better judgements to be made about whether undesirable outcomes derive from poor policy, poor policy development and advice or poor implementation.

Independent boards

At the time of writing a great deal has been made of the Chancellor's stated intention to establish an independent NHS board and to devolve services away from the centre. The Conservative Party has been considering a similar proposal. The implication of the first, in particular, is that freeing the civil service from political control and importing independent professionals to manage will somehow lead to improved performance. But the challenge described in this chapter is more complex. It is to find a way to confirm, not take away, ministerial responsibility for policy and strategic decisions, because they frequently involve making judgements about competing priorities which are not straightforward and for which the democratic mandate alone provides some form of authority.

The second challenge is to hold officials more explicitly accountable for delivery than is currently possible. If the result of any change was to distance politicians from policy and strategy and to do nothing to hold the professionals more explicitly to account, it would in many ways achieve the worst of all possible worlds. Of course, the establishment of a board for the NHS need not result in that happening, but before structural changes are made the objectives need to be clearly thought through. The kind of model described earlier would provide a framework within which the idea of a board could be developed, not just for the NHS but for other major service areas.

The question of whether civil servants need greater independence in the management of public services is not new. The radical reform of the service in the early 1990s to establish executive or next-step agencies was and remains a vehicle to provide some greater autonomy to managers of operational units. Those managers needed, it was argued, to have greater freedom to devise, for example, HR and reward systems appropriate to the needs of their business rather than the wider department of which they were a part. One of the problems encountered by the agency concept was in drawing a line between policy and operations, which the redefinition suggested above would go some way to address. But there were other problems, not least the distaste felt by the centre of departments at the loss of power and control. Gradually, therefore, agencies have been 'reined in' and the true potential of the concept never entirely realised. The arguments for devolving more operational responsibility to officials, coupled, of course, with greater accountability, remain strong but they need always to be exercised within the framework of political control. For that reason refreshing agencies may have more in its favour than establishing independence boards, which could, as Julian Le Grand argues, slow down the pace of reform by acting as a 'veto player'. It may be that the natural desire of any new government or Prime Minister to introduce new concepts such as independent boards should on this occasion be exercised with caution. What is clear is that structural reform of central government institutions will not of itself be sufficient. It may well make sense to create new institutions of economic decision making. It may help with the problem of joining up government touched on below. But reforming structures rarely changes the behaviour of those working within the structures and that is the most pressing need.

Joining up

A major criticism of government and the civil service has long been its inability to join up policy and implementation. Departments are too often seen to work in isolation when the major social and economic problems of the day have no regard to bureaucratic boundaries. New Labour's first three terms have seen genuine attempts being made to address this with cross-cutting reviews, ministerial champions, shared budgets and action plans, Cabinet committees and central policy and delivery units. In spite of these initiatives the consumers of government – not least local authorities and the voluntary and community sectors – continue to complain loudly that central government too often behaves in ways which are fragmented and non-corporate. They may sometimes over-state the case but it is hard to deny that the dominant culture of government (and Whitehall) remains departmental. As a result it can look rigid and ill equipped to cope with the interconnected problems of the day.

For many of the same reasons little real progress has been made in developing a longer-term strategic focus. Indeed this has been an issue during most of the post-war period with various high-profile attempts being made to resolve it. This government has recognised the problem but has found it difficult to deliver convincing solutions, with the strategic report in 2002 a further worthy but unsuccessful initiative. The importance of joined-up government and the need to develop a strategic perspective are made greater by the fact that many of the key issues now exercising the public are usually cross-cutting and long term and seem unlikely to be tackled successfully by a fragmented departmental approach to government. The big issues of tomorrow are climate change, terrorism, ageing, anti-social behaviour, consumer and public expectations, community relations and demographic change. These demand connected government like never before. Any new administration will need to produce radical new approaches if it is to convince voters that it is capable of addressing such complex problems. The civil service will need to work in very different ways if it is to convince the government that it is fit for purpose.

That will require a shift in culture rather than merely additional ad hoc or structural initiatives. At the highest level it must involve permanent secretaries as a board taking more corporate responsibility for the national priorities. At least until the arrival of the current Cabinet Secretary, Gus O'Donnell, the 'Wednesday morning club' of permanent secretaries had set its face against doing what most local authority management teams had been doing for twenty years – working corporately to identify and then develop strategies jointly to address their community's most significant problems. It is inconceivable that the success of places such as Manchester, Newcastle, Birmingham and Leeds could have been achieved on the back of old-style professional departments with a town clerk acting as a *primus inter pares*. What has been achieved locally with effective chief executives chairing well-focused corporate management teams has to be replicated in central government. And that will only happen with clear Prime Ministerial support and an acceptance by ministers that government has more to gain from such a change than they have to lose personally. It will also require a clearer definition of the relationship between the Cabinet Secretary and permanent secretaries. The Cabinet Secretary should be the chief executive of the delivery machine, whether that machine is delivering policy advice or service improvement. It should be said that this has been the recent direction of travel but it needs to be made explicit and urgently delivered.

In addition Parliament could take a more direct interest in the development of a longer-term perspective by establishing a select committee of senior members focused on the future policy issues which the government should be addressing: a committee for tomorrow's generation. Their reports would be discussed by the Cabinet and the permanent secretaries at twice-yearly strategic meetings.

All these are necessary and vital changes if public sector reform is to be delivered in a fourth term. But they will not alone deliver the kind of civil and public service we need. Much more could and should be done to articulate more clearly the kind of civil/public servants we need for the twenty-first century, to develop the skills they need to succeed and to create an environment through leadership which produces rather than consumes energy and delivers outcomes. At the moment there are serious weaknesses in the civil service which need to be addressed. In addition to the lack of corporacy and the inability to join up policy and delivery already referred to, these weaknesses include the following:

- The culture of the service, which at best remains risk averse and counter-creative at a time when innovation and initiative are the keys to effective government. Today's complex fast-moving social problems need new answers but the service appears unable to build the kind of climate which encourages/supports creativity; it is not good at managing risk; it consumes rather than creates energy; it continues to protect the culture of the written word; and it opposes attempts to develop a more informal style less dominated by hierarchies and status.

* Poorly developed political skills, which are the root cause of the criticisms one hears regularly from ministers – at least when out of earshot of their permanent secretaries. Too many civil servants seem to me unsympathetic to the political process and to politicians, partly perhaps because they were not exposed to the political process early enough in their careers to feel comfortable with it. At an intellectual level they can recognise the political dimension of an issue but they do not seem to be able to progress beyond that and fully appreciate the political implications of alternative handling strategies. They find it difficult to get inside the skin of their political masters – all of which actually inhibits their capacity when necessary to say 'no' in a way that commands respect. They take pride in their willingness to speak 'truth unto power' but some seem to do it too often and with evident glee.

* A continuing deficit of leadership, management and procurement skills, in spite of the increased level of external recruitment. In truth you cannot just import these skills. They need to be developed in house among existing staff and not solely via formal training and development programmes. A requirement a decade ago that all candidates for the senior civil service should have had real operational experience would have gone some way to ensuring that there were, for example, people at the centre of departments capable of setting stretching, achievable, outcome-focused, measurable targets. It might have ensured that we had more people capable of specifying and managing contracts. And front-line experience would also help develop a fit-for-purpose culture. Currently the search for perfection in all systems, procedures and processes leads to the creation of – to take one example – appraisal systems which have come close to bringing departments to their knees.

* A disconnection between Whitehall and the clients and communities who are the ultimate recipients of its policies and services. Local government has recognised more the importance of citizen engagement

and the futility of providing services that reflect neither citizen need nor citizen behaviour.

- A perceived reluctance to share information and knowledge with citizens which could and should be in the public domain and which sometimes seems to be withheld for the convenience of Whitehall rather than the public good. This in particular has contributed to the falling levels of public trust in government – not just the civil service machine.

No government which aspires to be progressive as well as effective can any longer ignore these long-standing weaknesses. They colour the public's view of the government itself. A fourth-term Labour government has the right to expect more and needs to play a positive role in developing a civil service fit for the twenty-first century. But the fact is that any government of whatever colour should be seeking the same. It should be seeking a service which addresses these weaknesses but which also meets these five criteria:

- **Greater accountability and transparency.** Tomorrow's civil servants cannot just tolerate more challenging assessments and greater freedom of information. They need instead to understand that these are central to a healthy modern democracy and potentially a major step towards regaining the trust of the public and media. They should expect material to be made freely available rather than assume that it is not, and they should develop through their training and experience a capacity to accept challenge and criticism as a route to self-improvement and service improvement. In other words, the long-standing tendency towards introspection and defensiveness needs to be addressed by the leaders of the service and by the expectations set by government itself. The service must be more self-critical and respond more constructively to challenge and criticism.
- **Commitment to personal responsibility.** The importance of teams is well recognised in Whitehall but team working should not dilute the need for individuals to take responsibility for success and failure. The problem with bureaucracies can be that they disguise that responsibility by the complexity of the processes and the numbers of individuals involved in making a decision or managing an initiative. But individuals need to have their achievements and successes recognised if they are to be motivated to deliver continued quality; furthermore, they should be prepared to accept responsibility for failures and to have that reflected in

pay and appraisals. These should be part of an official's set of values, developed from the very beginning of their Whitehall career.

- **Creativity, innovation and energy.** The civil service should be the most exciting of all the creative industries, constantly producing ideas for policy and delivery innovation. To do that it will need, with the support of ministers, to confront the blockages to energy and creativity that still abound. The excessive number of over-long meetings; the production of reports which are too lengthy and which aspire to perfection rather than being fit for purpose; the dysfunctions which are conveniently ignored rather than confronted; the individuals who are ineffective but continue to occupy senior well-paid positions; and the procedures which are excessive or unnecessary. To work as I did with a blind secretary of state is to understand how 'liberating' it can be to dispense with so many of these blockages because there is no alternative. But the rest of Whitehall could learn the lessons of that experience. In addition the leaders, whether political or official, need to understand the contribution they must make to developing an energised, creative government. They need to demonstrate a passion for the service and disown the sarcasm that is so prevalent and which destroys creativity. They need to provide positive responses to new ideas and indicate their distaste for status and hierarchies, which make many officials feel as if a contribution is only valued if it is made by someone at Grade 2 or 3 (just below the permanent secretaries). Ministers, in particular, should insist on even more new people being recruited because they bring new ideas and new approaches. They should encourage people not to see the civil service necessarily as a lifetime career. Ministers should demand evidence that departments are genuinely connected to clients, citizens and communities because without that connection policies will continue to lack nails and to misfire. The best leaders always see clients as a source of ideas and energy – ways of improving the service. The worst see them as an irritant, an inconvenience. And ministers and officials should understand that creativity only thrives where the risk which inevitably accompanies it is managed effectively – but not avoided – and where achievements are recognised and celebrated. Energy and creativity are essential to effective government – and that means they should engage the interest not just of the officials but of political leaders too.

It may well be that introducing some competition into the provision of policy and analytical advice to ministers has a part to play in enhancing creativity and showing policy officials that they, as well as service providers, can and will face competition.

- **Focus on value for money.** There is no 'silver bullet' and some progress has been made – but no public sector bureaucracy will naturally prioritise value for money as the private sector does. It needs to be constantly reminded how important it is to make the best use of limited resources, but the additional investment of recent years may have lessened the resolve. The increasingly confused signals surrounding contestability need to be clarified, not least so that the private sector knows whether it is in a market worth its investment. Procurement and commissioning skills need to be enhanced and then properly applied; the culture of aversion to outsourcing services needs to be confronted; the service should be held publicly and independently accountable for achieving the savings targets it has been set; and there needs to be more effective policing of some of the creative accounting currently being employed to suggest that savings have been achieved. There will be fewer resources for the public sector in the future. They need to be used efficiently.

- **Imaginative and effective use of IT.** The transformation of public services with limited resources requires the effective use of IT and therefore a civil service which is skilled in its deployment. There have been some successes but too many failures to give confidence that this is currently the case. To be successful an IT project needs to be business led in the sense that it resolves a perceived business problem; its design and development need to involve the operational staff who will use it to ensure that they will 'buy in' and that the project will be operationally credible; its specification needs to be contained, avoiding excessive complexity and continuous elaboration; and, of course, it needs to be managed effectively as a project. Too often one or more of these preconditions has been missing, with financial and reputational consequences for government. The lack of procurement skills, only partially remedied, has also played a part, IT providers regularly bemoaning the inability of Whitehall to engage with them in a professional way. I doubt that there is any way in which the public's expectations of modern public services can be met without the imaginative and effective application of ICT, and the lessons of the past need to be quickly learned.

Conclusion

It is always more difficult for a government or chief executive to resolve issues which have been unsatisfactorily or only partially addressed earlier in their term of office. That is now the case with civil service and public sector reform. Success will, therefore, prove difficult for a fourth-term Labour government. It is still possible; however, if it is to be achieved it must be on these conditions:

1. The leader, i.e. the Prime Minister, needs to believe that civil service reform is a necessary precondition to public service reform even though it will be painful and unlikely to win votes.

2. The leader and the government need to have sufficient public trust for people to believe that the issue is being tackled for reasons other than party-political gain. If the public believe that reform is purely political interference it will fail.

3. There needs to be complete agreement and trust between the Cabinet Secretary and the Prime Minister on the issue.

4. Incentives need to be provided to encourage reform. The appraisal and reward systems need to reinforce the kind of behaviours outlined in this chapter. Promotions need to take account not just of posts held and experience gained but what individuals have achieved, as well as the extent to which they have used their initiatives to, for example, improve the quality of services. In addition ministers and especially the Prime Minister need to do much more to show that they value the modernisers within the system.

5. It should be seen as a long-term project producing some short-term gains.

For all the difficulties, transforming governance and the civil service is a prize as great as the constitutional reform achieved by the first-term Labour government. It would be a clear signal that even in the fourth term the radical ambition remains. Without it much else the government wants to deliver will be lost.

9

Effective governance and the role of public service professionals

Charles Clarke

Over the last decade, one of the most potent rallying cries against New Labour reforms throughout the public service has been 'trust the professionals'. Innovations such as the literacy hour, NHS Direct and the Home Information Pack have all been attacked as undermining professional standards and weakening the professions. The government has been rebuked for 'telling teachers how to teach', for downgrading doctors' professional judgement and for undermining the integrity of professions such as law and accountancy.

At the same time some of the professional associations and trade unions have made themselves pretty obdurate opponents of change. They appear focused upon defence of their own short-term interests despite obvious consumer concerns and there have been some classic formalised stand-offs, the overall consequence of which has been demoralisation, which immobilises progressive reform.

The purpose of this chapter is not to set out the history of the last decade of these reforms, instructive and worthwhile though that is. It is to suggest an approach for reinvigorating reform and renewal in a way which engages the professions and draws upon their strength and creativity.

I believe that this approach should be based first upon defining 'modern professionals' within 'modern professions', and then upon outlining the structures which are necessary to support them. This will build public support for reform and for public services; as we do this we will find much to learn from the way in which other societies are addressing these same challenges.

For decades the professions have been the bedrock of English society and they still retain great respect and admiration for the work that they do. Doctors and nurses, police officers and lawyers, schoolteachers and university dons, accountants and civil servants are only a few examples of the range of professionals who, in every part of our lives, give us their expertise, help us with our judgements and enable us to sort out our problems. In general they are trusted and respected for the high quality of their work and the integrity with which they serve consumers of their services.

However, this model of the professional has been under increasing strain. This is not the consequence of the election of New Labour in 1997, still less of the views of any given individual or any particular event. The tension arises because each profession has had to face the strain of increasingly rapid change and many professionals, particularly the most senior, have found this difficult to address. The increased rarity of the 'job for life' is of particular concern to professionals who have committed themselves to a life-long vocation.

Let me give six examples of such change.

First, technological and scientific innovation has massive implications for the way teachers teach, as interactive whiteboards and distance learning become commonplace; or for the way in which doctors diagnose and understand how conditions of ill health develop in an individual; or for the way in which crimes can be solved, for example using DNA data or detailed intelligence analysis; or for the way in which legal agreements, such as house conveyancing or wills, can be easily standardised using a word processor. Such new techniques are not always easy to master, and this gives rise to controversy about the need for changes in professional methods.

Second, the relationship between professionals and the 'consumers' of their services has been transformed by the fact that most people are now better educated and better informed, notably through the internet. Traditional deference has disappeared and with it have gone traditional ways of working. In both education and health, for example, time-honoured discipline has given way to a framework of highly assertive, even aggressive, pupils, parents or patients whose powerful sense of their 'rights' pushes aside grateful appreciation. And, in an atmosphere which rightly emphasises the benefits of problem prevention, the task of the modern professional has changed to one more of leadership and inspiration to the consumer, for example to learn to live a healthier lifestyle, or to look after their children better. This happens on the basis of a more equal relationship between professional and consumer, which for instance requires first-class communication skills in place of assertion, instruction and sometimes impenetrable and obfuscating language.

A further consequence of this change is that consumers demand fuller and more accurate information about the availability and quality of professional services, on the basis of which they want to exercise greater choice. So parents want to know about school performance; patients want to know where best they can get medical work carried out and, in some cases, to challenge their doctors about the nature of their treatment; residents want to know the pattern of crime and detection in their locality; and so on. That is why various types of league table have evolved. They are often controversial, either because they can be over-simplistic, or because they challenge professionals in their conduct and practice, or both. But they result from increased consumer expectation rather than ideologically driven government.

Third, increased public debate about public services has highlighted the quality and performance of the professions, so that their ability to fulfil their traditional roles has come into serious question. If, for example, a significant proportion of eleven-year-old children cannot read and write properly, what is to be done? To what extent do the professional teachers bear responsibility, either individually or as a profession? The same is asked of the time endured before a hospital operation or interview with a consultant, and similarly in other professions. In short the level of questioning of professional standards from a wide range of angles has increased in a way which can push the professions into a defensive and sometimes consequently aggressive posture.

This concern inevitably and sharply raises issues of management and decision making which exacerbate tensions between professionals and managers, and challenge professionals to take full responsibility for the quality of all aspects of service delivery. More profoundly, this debate brings into the open important moral issues, such as euthanasia and health rationing, which were conventionally hidden under the cloak of professional judgement.

Fourth, actual working methods have changed very significantly over decades. Work generally has become more team based and flexible, less hierarchical and stratified. This has massive implications for professionals, as the 'school team', 'health team' or 'police team' becomes conventional. This in turn leads to a spectrum of responsibilities within the team and to the redistribution of tasks, so that nurses do some tasks which were traditionally done by doctors, teaching assistants supervise classes in some circumstances, police community support officers become a visible and responsive local police presence, civilian analytical staff do some traditional police detective work and so on. This widens the number of workers who have 'professional' responsibilities and challenges existing professional chains of command and pecking orders in a way which some see as threatening. The boundaries of professional work are changing (and will continue to change) and will lead to continuous redefinition of the role and character of 'the professional'.

This pressure is exacerbated by the move across society away from traditional nine-to-five working, for example in relation to Sunday trading. This affects public services. It means that health services are offered in the community (for example NHS Direct), education is offered for longer times (for example in breakfast and 'after-school' clubs), courts are asked to sit at weekends or overnight. The move to 24/7 provision of professional services becomes ever more powerful.

And in many, though not all, of these areas privately provided alternatives stand ready to fill the void if publicly provided professional services are not available. But if such private services are organised outside the context of general public provision, they may well be expensive and so become potentially socially divisive.

Fifth, all this, taken together with the other changes, has a major impact upon pay and conditions. The status of professionals over decades, taken with their near-monopoly control over key public services, has often led to these matters being settled through a 'pay review body' structure designed to promote stable industrial relations and so obviate the need for industrial action. But these processes have proved inflexible in dealing with the complex and interconnected work environment at a time of rapid change.

Finally, increased public concern about professional standards places greater scrutiny upon the capacity of the professions to regulate themselves. The very existence of a Harold Shipman in medicine or an Ian Huntley in education means that society is inevitably bound to be ruthlessly intolerant of any mistakes by those who should have our public confidence. At a less serious level there remains continuing public concern about the accountability of our professions for their actions. The very concept of professional self-regulation is on the defensive, which influences professionals to turn inwards.

Every profession is facing challenges of the type I have described and this is of course true throughout the world. The professions have addressed these changes in patchy and inconsistent ways. Innovation and initiative have been rare and defensiveness and introversion are too often the norm.

No government can stand aside from the issues raised by this process of change, if only because of the increasing public demand for higher quality in the services, which in general are paid for through taxes. The political significance of these issues is now immensely high – I would argue rightly so, and I suggest that such pressure is far more likely to increase than to diminish.

Moreover, this public demand is more significant for Labour, which positively believes in the provision of high-quality public services for reasons of both social justice and economic efficiency, than for the Thatcherite Conservatives, who were perfectly happy for the quality of public services to decline, so pushing consumers towards the private sector.

Nevertheless, any government has to face up to the need to improve the quality of public services, and successive governments have taken on that challenge. An important part of the answer has been money. Certainly in 1997 increased resources were desperately needed for a variety of purposes, including increasing the number of professionals, raising their pay to competitive levels, investing in new equipment and buildings and so on.

For many professionals this was enough. Their response could be summarised as 'give us the tools and we'll do the job'. They believed that the problem was simply lack of resources. They felt that scrutiny of the way in which the money was spent was unnecessary and sometimes unfair, and that government intervention in the way in which it was spent was often prejudiced and pernickety. The government should simply provide the money and then keep out of the professionals' hair.

But the government did not accept that – no government could. It doubted whether, left to their own devices, the professionals would spend the money in the best way to improve public service standards, or that they would be prepared to focus upon the requirements of those whose needs were greatest or where the challenges were greatest.

The relationship between the government and the professions has festered as a result of that mutual lack of confidence. And one of the government's errors has been to imply too often that professions are a conspiracy against the public. The truth is that within every profession there are progressive advocates of change and the aim of government should always be to work with them, and to strengthen their elbow, rather than condemning the profession as a whole.

These doubts and concerns have been aggravated by the existence of different and inconsistent models of reform. Unfortunately there has rarely been a consistent and coherent national model of change. National leadership – political, official and professional – has too often sounded an uncertain tone with too many running disputes about the best form of change and insufficient resolution of outstanding problems. And in addressing change and approaching reform there has been a significant division between those reformers whom I would describe as 'traditional Webbites' and those whom I would describe as 'social entrepreneurs'. This description has elements of caricature but it also contains truths which explain some of the policy divisions that have led to a lack of clarity in the promotion of reform.

The traditional Webbites essentially believe that the key to change driven from the centre is to establish the right framework of national law, administrative and professional practice and central leadership. They believe that fairness and equality can best be achieved by use of central regulation. They distrust local or professional initiative on the grounds that it is likely that those who are already better placed will use that advantage to reinforce their position and so those who most need support will fail to receive it. Many professional organisations and trade unions are more at ease with this approach, either because of its explicit ambition of social justice or because they are more comfortable with the various national frameworks which are already in place and fear challenges to them.

The social entrepreneurs in contrast see the mobilisation of energy as essential, whether at the level of the individual or the organisation, for example a school or hospital. They support policy changes which encourage such mobilisation and strong local leadership. They encourage a variety of incentives for success. And so they see institutions such as specialist schools and foundation hospitals as the means to positive change and doubt that this leads in practice to increasing inequalities for consumers of the service. The recent television series *Can Gerry Robinson Fix the NHS?*, in which Robinson, a businessman, ventured into hospital management, illustrates the case for the 'social entrepreneurship' model.

Uncertainty about the best model for reform has led to acute political debate about ideas such as foundation hospitals, trust schools, the role of police basic command units and the extent to which Parliament constrains judicial freedom in relation to particular crimes, for example through on-the-spot fines. These political examples are not isolated but are symptoms of a much deeper and wider malaise in the relationship between government and the professions. This has become so fraught that too often it has become a dialogue of the deaf.

In teaching, for example, government ministers point to increased numbers of teachers, all better paid, to more preparation time for teachers, far more support staff, better staff rooms and facilities, greater resources for in-service teacher training and vastly increased technology resources within large numbers of new school buildings. On the 'professional' side, important groups of teachers point to greater intervention in how teachers teach, continued use of league tables, a rather unsatisfactory introduction of performance-related pay, new assessment regimes (SATs) which they claim reduce teachers' professional independence, changes in school structure (such as specialist schools, academies and trust schools) which challenge existing practices, and a climate in which they feel that teachers have been under attack from government leaders. A similar list, on both sides of the discussion, could be set out in just about every public service arena and such a dysfunctional discourse characterises the relationship just about everywhere.

The best way to tackle this is for each public service to have the kind of clear and authoritative reform strategy which faces up to and resolves these issues, based upon partnership with the professions, which hasn't always existed. The establishment of a new relationship of confidence is a precondition both for the success of public sector reform and for the survival of respect for the professions in the modern era.

The fundamental basis of such a relationship of confidence has to be the establishment of a modern profession, staffed by modern professionals and capable of adapting and preparing itself for the changes in the world around us. Professionals need to take on the responsibilities of managing their public services and accepting the disciplines which go with that. That is principally a task for the professions themselves, but it is one where the government has to help and, if necessary, insist. The paradox for the professions is that the more they meet modern standards and needs, the less the government will want or need to intervene; but the less the government intervenes, the harder it will be to modernise and meet contemporary needs. The more the professions take up responsibility, the less tension there will be.

In many areas the elements of a modern profession are already in place, but they have to include responsibility for managing the modern public services. The professionals themselves need to be the agents of change, to take command of that process rather than being pressed into it.

The means of doing this can be summarised by reference to the six examples which I set out earlier:

- All professionals need the training which enables them to properly use the most modern methods and techniques, to build proper relations with the consumers of their services, and to be fully up to date with modern professional thinking. This may mean some redefinition of the modern professional.
- Professionals need to accept and welcome full and well-informed accountability to the public.

- The professions need to take full responsibility for the wider social impact of their work, including its quality and its ability to serve those with the greatest and most difficult needs. This includes establishing professional strategies focused upon problem prevention.

- The modern professions need to promote team working with full respect to all within the team and a readiness to redistribute responsibilities within the team. This has to include flexibility in working arrangements and incentives for success, including the promotion of co-operation rather than competition, both within and between professions.

- Payment systems for modern professionals should reward professional success and leadership of change, encourage self-improvement and training and seek stability.

- Professional self-regulation should include significant external moderation and demonstrate absolute intolerance of incompetence or corruption.

To the layperson, these six points may well seem self-evident. However, each has been subject to serious wrangles with different professions. And in each profession there remain serious gaps between the aspirations I summarise above and the reality of the profession today.

So I argue that the best way to establish a relationship of trust is for both government and profession to make a formal commitment to the creation of a modern profession, each characterised by something like the six points set out above. The government cannot impose the solution and if it tries it will fail. But the modern profession is needed and it must be owned by the modern professionals.

This is not dissimilar to the 'social partnership' approach in labour relations more generally and I now turn to examining the way in which the government and the profession can work towards a shared ambition of a modern profession on this basis.

Training and updating

Both initial professional education and comprehensive life-long development of skills have to emphasise flexibility and change to meet modern challenges. However, despite substantial resources, it is not clear in every profession whether the initial training does establish a proper modern professional foundation, whether existing in-service training models are at all effective, or whether individual professionals are themselves making sufficient commitment to update their own skills.

There is a very good case for an increased proportion of training to take place 'on the job' rather than in lecture theatres, in a way which encourages practical experience, including with 'consumers'. And once trained it ought to be a defining characteristic for a professional to make the commitment to personal professional renewal, but many seem still to regard this as a responsibility for the employer alone.

The quality of an agreed programme of initial and life-long education and training will determine the respect in which the modern profession is held.

Public accountability and information

In most areas the controversies about assessment, performance indicators, targets, league tables and the like remain divisive and diverting issues for the government–professional relationship. They are often seen as mechanisms to promote competition rather than as the provision of routine information to the citizen or consumer.

However, I believe that there is a basis for constructive agreement where the professions accept that the public and consumers have a right to data and information about professional practice, and that they themselves have a responsibility to improve their practice in vital areas, setting their own targets to do so in ways which are open to public scrutiny. For its part, the government should accept that consumer information should be comprehensive (which is possible on the internet) rather than a simple number, that national targets should be the result of the addition of local targets, rather than simply imposed from above, and that publication of information should be designed to promote improvement rather than to drive competition between schools, hospitals or whatever. Similarly the government should confine itself to regular and consistent assessment of outcomes, and eliminate its own demands for the management information which is now so easily available through information technology.

The government should be explicit in promoting co-operation, as for example the Excellence in Cities school improvement programme did. This can be done by sponsoring a variety of partnerships, including federations of schools, joint organisations across the criminal justice system and health and social services co-operation. Professionals in general want to co-operate and to work in a 'joined-up' way; there is a whole range of government legal, administrative and other hurdles that make this difficult in practice, but they could be changed.

Wider social impact

The elected government has the right and duty to set key social and professional priorities, since the vast bulk of the resources which pay for the professions come from the taxpayer. These priorities may be to attack social inequalities, for example in health or education; to promote sustainable solutions to particular problems; or explicitly to acknowledge the positive social benefits of co-operative working relationships between professionals.

A significant difficulty since 1997 has been the excessive focus on the use of 'pilots' to address these issues. Justified on the reasonable basis of discovering pragmatically 'what works', hundreds of often expensive pilot projects have been launched, in some cases as a means of targeting resources at social priority areas. These pilots have often operated apart from so-called 'mainline' provision with its own professional practices and operational methods. Though usually conceived as a way of testing more modern professional methods, with a view to then generalising and 'mainstreaming' their conclusions, the pilots have more often been in practice an end in themselves, which have too often left a great part of existing professional methods and practices unaffected.

There are many examples of such pilots. The inspirational Sure Start approach to support for pre-school children has yet to be mainstreamed into all children's services; neighbourhood warden schemes, which are massively popular for good reasons, have yet to transform the working practices of local authority employees in their communities; the justly lauded North Liverpool Community Justice Centre still has to change existing judicial practices across the country. The reason for the pilot schemes' failure to become more widespread is that they are still seen as somehow apart from regular public services, so the issue becomes finding funds to extend the pilot rather than turning the positive lessons learned from the pilot into regular professional practice throughout the country.

So the commitment from both government and the profession, in each area, should be to learn together the lesson of the pilots and then to apply it to transform professional practice so that every modern profession, supported by government, can meet the wider social obligations that it seeks to serve.

The professional team, leadership and flexibility

Support for the idea of team-based working is now almost universal across society. This means the erosion of hierarchies of all types, the promotion of collaborative thought, commitment to greater transferability of knowledge and skills and openness and shared goals in working methods. This approach is now commonplace because it delivers better results for consumers and better satisfaction for workers, usually at better value financially.

It is also spreading across professional public services, although not always as smoothly or as effectively as is desirable. The best working model has probably been the school workforce reform programme for teaching and learning, which has the capacity to transform schools for the better and would have moved faster had the National Union of Teachers not sought to prevent all progress, often on the basis of misrepresentation.

Leadership is essential, both to building successful teams and to constructing stronger local co-operation with other services. But it is also essential for general success. That is the basis of the case for devolving as much power and resources as possible to the very local level. It is an argument for three-year budgets for individual schools and for school governing bodies to control their own resources without reference elsewhere except for reasons of inspection and accountability. It is the basis of the case for encouraging local partnerships and co-funding where possible and for giving local leaders, such as headteachers, far greater ability to set pay and to hire and fire.

Such team working and strong leadership have to be central ambitions for both government and the professions.

Payment and rewards

The setting of pay and rewards has been at the centre of many battles around reform. Issues such as higher pay for greater responsibility or better measurable performance, requirements for life-long training and its funding, changes in working practices, acceptance of government priority targets and a range of others are all contested and influence the discussions about pay. These have sometimes led to sharp political controversy, for example regarding the contracts for GPs and consultants in the NHS, performance-related pay for teachers, or judicial pensions. And these arguments have hampered progress on professional reform.

A change of approach is needed from both government and the professions. We need four innovations:

- Longer-term pay settlements must be agreed, over at least three years and possibly five. This gives stability, allows changes to be phased in and removes a very damaging annual 'sword of Damocles' for the whole process of reform.

- The Treasury must stop insisting on a single across-the-board percentage pay increase, to be replaced with a fixed percentage change in the size of the overall pay bill, devolved to local centres, such as schools and hospitals. This greater pay flexibility would address market pressures, both geographical and skill based, and would raise the quality of leadership and management.

- The settlement must include more explicit reference to the responsibilities of both employee and employer to secure effective in-service training throughout life.

- The employers must issue an explicit statement of their ambitions in relation to team working, local leadership, performance improvement and accountability.

The management approach to these discussions has often been very weak and there need to be consistent and constructive working relations between the trade unions, staff associations and employers. The relevant pay review body should explicitly represent the conclusion of a process of negotiation and agreement and all sides should commit to this approach.

Regulation of the profession

Regulatory issues have been among the most vexed in recent years. Increased openness and transparency have strengthened the pressure for a high level of public confidence in professional behaviour. This extends to police and doctors' disciplinary procedures, the sex offenders register, the Criminal Records Bureau, measures to outlaw solicitors who exploit ignorance for financial gain, for example in immigration law, and a range of other measures.

There is now no public tolerance of professional misconduct, especially but not only in matters of sex abuse or sex discrimination.

It is better for these matters to be regulated by the professions themselves, but this can only be on the basis that the modern professions understand and accept them, and then act within the context of modern public concerns. Any vestigial tolerance of professional incompetence or misconduct has to be removed and modern professions must themselves ensure that abuse and bullying are outlawed, and that high-quality and objective public service are the watchwords for professional regulation.

Conclusion

The core of this chapter is the need to end the rather uneasy relationship between professions and government which now exists. Each side gives credit to the other for some positives but is deeply frustrated at the other's perceived failings. The process of public service reform is deeply damaged by this lack of trust.

Now is the time to put this relationship onto the right basis as a foundation for future stable reform and change.

My central message, which has to be embraced by both the professions and the government, is the need to create modern professions, peopled by modern professionals. By definition this means looking forward not back and by definition it means being outward-looking and confident.

The essence of these modern professions is that they

- are committed to world-class professional standards in initial education and training, and then renew and refresh that throughout life;
- are accountable and transparent in the way they work, and so committed to improved professional outcomes which can be publicly discussed;
- acknowledge their wider social impact and are ready to agree with government changes in their practice which address that impact;
- work in teams, with other professionals, and focus on the best outcome for the team, based on strong local leadership;
- commit to long-term agreements for pay and rewards which incentivise professional improvement;
- regulate themselves ruthlessly in ways which fully reflect modern public concerns.

The professions have to commit to that approach and so too does the government. To the extent that professions fail in this, the government has the right to insist that they commit, but we should acknowledge that whenever insistence is needed, the profession is damaged and so too is the government. And that truth is the fundamental common interest shared by the government and the professions. They both want public regard and respect and they will get it better by working together rather than in opposition.

10

Competition for social justice
Markets and contestability in public services

David Albury

Competition between providers of public services can, as in many walks of life, be a spur to quality improvement, value for money, innovation and responsiveness. But unfettered or so-called 'free' markets have undesirable social consequences: poor or limited service for those with few resources and constrained access to information; reduction of all activities to cost and economic value; elevation of individual above social goods. This may not matter too much for handkerchiefs but it is crucial for healthcare. Equally, managed monopolies (as in the traditional public sector) tend to operate more in the interests of providers than users; often lack dynamism, efficiency or innovation; and find it difficult to personalise their offerings to individual needs. Too often the framing of debates around public services is seen as a choice between centralised states and free markets. The challenge for progressive politics is to explore the rich terrain that lies between states and markets, and to evolve new models and organisational forms that can accommodate changing realities.

In this chapter I will argue that competitive pressure needs to be a central element for self-improving public services – systems less bureaucratic and less reliant on top-down target setting and intervention – and that these competitive pressures can and should be built up through three levels: robust and accessible comparative performance information for professionals, the public and politicians; contestability, opening up failing organisations to be taken over or replaced by better existing or new providers; a level playing field on which the best from all sectors – public, private and third – can contribute to the delivery and improvement of public services. If competition is regulated with the right values base and managed competently it can help us realise our progressive and social democratic aspirations to provide a higher quality of life for all, greater social justice, empowerment for individuals, families and communities, and an enhanced public realm. In this it is crucial that commissioning should be recognised as an intrinsically political activity and as such needs to be part of the public and democratically accountable public sector. Taken in its widest sense, it is how places are shaped and made. Hence – over time – local authorities should become the commissioners of all public services for their area.

A brief history of competition in public services

Competition and plurality in public services did not begin with New Labour in 1997 or even with Margaret Thatcher in the 1980s. Elderly care has for many decades been provided by a mix of council, private and voluntary organisations. The origins of the probation service lie in the activities of the London Police Court Mission, now known as the Rainer Foundation and a registered charity. And of course private healthcare and education have been available for centuries to those who could afford it.

The Conservative government of the 1980s and early 1990s sought, through compulsory competitive tendering (CCT) in local authorities and other services and the privatisation of utilities, to shift significant elements of public services into the private sector. While this had the benefits of introducing consideration of alternative providers and breaking up some stagnant and inefficient monopolies (few would wish to return to the Post Office-run telephone service of the 1970s), it was driven by an ideological belief in 'private sector good, public sector bad' and a determination to reduce the power of public sector unions and the costs of public service provision. The result was some increases in efficiency but often at the expense of quality of services and worsening terms and conditions for public service workers.

In 1999 the New Labour government introduced the more balanced Best Value regime, which retained the notions of challenge and competition from CCT but gave greater emphasis to issues of quality as well as cost. And, through a series of steps culminating in the 2005 Warwick agreement with the trade unions, it safeguarded the salaries and job security of public service workers and prevented the development of a 'two-tier workforce'.[1]

Alongside these developments the government has made extensive use of the private finance initiative (PFI) and public–private partnerships in undertaking the largest-ever programme of hospital, GP surgery and school building and refurbishment, such that by the middle of the next decade most of the core infrastructure of public services will have been renewed. The National Audit Office and other studies have confirmed that PFI projects have, in general, a much better track record than traditionally procured projects in coming in on time and to budget.

Against the backdrop of these wide-ranging frameworks – Best Value and the PFI – the government's development of markets and competition in public services over the last ten years could be described most generously as a learning journey or most critically as sporadic and inconsistent. To take education for example, in nursery provision we have a mixed economy and subsidised choice; in higher education subsidised choice but mainly public institutions; for adult skills training the Leitch review is recommending a system that is more led by demand (from employers and learners) and contestable, as elaborated in Chapter 20; and for schools a debate still rages about the merits or otherwise of parental choice.[2]

There is not scope within this chapter to provide a fully comprehensive analysis of how areas of public services have fared when greater levels of competitive pressure have been introduced, but some key learning can be extracted and summarised:

- Commissioning capability is critical to success. The relevant skills, including those of procuring and contracting, are both relatively sophisticated and in short supply. Hence markets which have been developed through national commissioning (such as intervention in failing local education authorities) have in general been more effective than those that have relied on the necessarily more variable quality of local commissioning (such as primary care). It may well be that new markets need to be made and developed nationally, but when relatively matured the responsibility for commissioning can transfer to local organisations.[3]

- The regulatory framework is a crucial determinant of the outcomes produced – good or bad – by the operation of competition. Elderly care is an almost textbook case of what can happen in (public service) markets where price is unregulated and quality is set at minimum thresholds with little or no incentive for improvement: excess profiteering, dumping of difficult or demanding clients, poor matching of supply to demand, and gravitation to worsening conditions of service and low-cost residential areas. Especially in the early days, when the

Conservatives developed the market by requiring each local authority to spend 85 per cent of their residential care expenditure in the private and third sectors, one set of poorly funded providers was replaced by another in an adversarial market with purchasing often based on short-term individual requirements rather than a strategic assessment of local needs.

• For markets and competition to function effectively there have to be robust failure regimes. The potential benefits of competition will not be realised – and individuals and communities will be poorly served – if under-performing organisations are constantly bolstered and supported through traditional performance management approaches. Childcare illustrates this. The private and third sectors have enabled the government to extend entitlements and choice considerably. Quality, judged by Ofsted reports, is 'satisfactory' (though not outstanding) but serious questions remain of affordability for less well-off parents and carers. The market is dominated by a host of micro-businesses (nurseries and childminders) with even the biggest providers having only 1 or 2 per cent of the market. This type of market has the major benefit of providing local business and employment opportunities, particularly for women, but almost invariably has high churn of providers (up to 40 per cent per annum in some areas) and volatility of services, with consequent lack of continuity of care. The government's response to this has been to provide more business support. This has the effect of turning marginally unviable organisations into marginally viable ones, but impedes the expansion of providers of higher quality or lower cost.

The above three important, but relatively managerialist or technocratic, sets of considerations are accompanied by a fourth of greater political salience. The higher the level of interdependency between organisations within a sector, or with organisations in other sectors, the more difficult it is to establish an effectively functioning market, particularly one which will achieve social as well as individual outcomes. Hence prisons are easier to work with than schools, elective care than primary care, public parks than public spaces. As will be discussed further below, this becomes of greater importance the more we wish to move to integrated, seamless, joined-up provision.

What are the implications of this learning for the place and management of competition in the next decade of public service reform? Can markets and contestability not only enable and empower the realisation of individual aspirations, especially for the poorest and least advantaged, but help achieve social, collective and public outcomes? And are competitive mechanisms useful in addressing more complex, seemingly intractable social problems? But the abstract questions of whether and where markets and contestability should be used are no more important than the real and practical ones of how and under what conditions they should be used.

Three levels of competition

Hours of debate and acres of print have been consumed in trying to divine the principles whereby we can decide in which public services it is appropriate or effective to introduce more competitive pressures. Few free-marketeers, let alone social democrats, claim that core provision of policing or defence – services which, though they protect individual security and rights, are collectively consumed – should be handed over to the private or third sectors or subject to user choice. And there are major differences in how competition and choice might be introduced in services which are basically transactional – for example, benefit payments – and those which are intrinsically relational, such as health and education. But beyond this it has proved difficult to articulate criteria. One of the most powerful arguments against introducing choice and competition into public services has been that of 'information asymmetries'; that is, members of the public have insufficient knowledge to exercise informed choice ('buyer beware' is an unreasonable injunction) and, because of professionals' possession of specialist knowledge, any market created will be dominated by provider rather than public interests. Leaving aside the intrinsic merits or otherwise of these views, they do establish the correct base line for how policy on competition in public services should be developed.

Comparative performance information

Most public service professionals – doctors, nurses, teachers, police officers, managers and so on – want to do a good job, to serve their pupils, patients and the public as best they can. Few want to be seen to be performing less well than comparable organisations or colleagues. Since the early 1990s there has been a steady increase in the availability of information comparing the performance of different organisations within particular services. First introduced for schools and then local education authorities (LEAs) by the establishment of Ofsted, extended to local authorities through the work of the Audit Commission, and more recently available for hospitals and police forces, there is little doubt that the publication of comparative information and 'league tables' and the ranking of organisations as 'excellent', 'weak' and so on, accompanied in some cases by rewards for good and sanctions for poor results, has sharply focused attention on and driven up overall performance.

The introduction of such tables to any new sector or profession is greeted with protests about the crudeness and inadequacy of the data. Over time and through healthy debate, however, the measures become more robust and sophisticated, and the media and public learn to use the information to exercise choice and exert pressure, on top of peer challenge, for improvement. For those who are still sceptical, listen in to the conversations among parents waiting after school for their children on the day when the media publish school league tables. And, it should be noted, most of these tables induce competition within the public sector: competition can be effective even when there is no use of the private or third sectors.[4]

This is not just a managerial or technocratic exercise. The intent to collect and publish data on comparative performance forces discussion which is intensely political: what are the measures by which we should judge our public services – our schools, our GPs, our local authorities? But such comparative performance information is intensely political in another way. It helps to shift the balance of power; it empowers citizens and the public.

League tables are here to stay. They need extending in four ways. Firstly, there are still areas of public services where there are few or no clear performance criteria and little or no readily and publicly accessible data on comparative performance based on these criteria. This needs to be remedied.

Secondly, there needs to be a better balance of measures to reflect the importance of the user experience/satisfaction and value for money as well as the outcomes. For example, in hospitals, while clinical and health outcomes are clearly important, there is a wealth of evidence that patient satisfaction is more driven by whether they are treated with respect and dignity and have appropriate privacy. The quality of the experience and the nature of the relationship are critical and need to be reflected in the performance measures.

Thirdly, we need to stimulate the increased sophistication of measures. We need to ensure that like is being compared with like. In parallel with more robust case-mix adjustments[5] in health, London Challenge, a partnership between central and local government and schools, has pioneered the use of 'families of schools' data – schools which share basic socio-demographic and ethos characteristics. And we need to explore whether and where it is appropriate to compare performance of organisations, teams within organisations or individual professionals. If you have just had a stroke, or are designing a strategy for stroke services, in south-east London, what matters is not whether King's College or Queen Mary's Sidcup is overall the better hospital but how good the stroke teams are.

Fourthly, we need to encourage the development of information 'brokers': those who process data into forms which help professionals, the public and politicians. This will include those organisations which are finding ever-smarter ways, generally using the internet, to garner and focus user views of particular providers (such as Patient Opinion).

Contestability

The availability and accessibility of comparative performance data is the foundation for developing competently managed, values-based competition in public services. However, it inevitably raises the question of what should be done about under-performing or failing organisations. The New Labour government cannot be criticised for lack of initiatives in relation to this. Some have involved a clean break: new buildings, new management, new ethos. Others have sought to harness the goodwill or energy of the relevant sector – peer-to-peer support, 'buddying', mentoring – or provided strong support or intervention. And others have relied on contestability: lowering the entry barriers to new providers, consonant with maintaining quality standards, and lowering the exit barriers to existing ones, ensuring individuals and communities do not suffer from inadequate public services. Indeed the problem may be inconsistency of approach rather than lack of effort. While different approaches may be appropriate for different services, there is always a danger that combining them (see the childcare example discussed earlier in this chapter) can reduce the potential positive effects of any single approach. All too often we have talked of using market and competitive pressures, where failing providers would be taken over by more successful or new ones, but in practice have used intervention and support measures to prop up failing organisations and thus maintain the status quo ante.

We certainly need to make clear that contestability does not mean the removal of the services in question but the provision of services by better and different means. This is not to minimise the difficulties of dealing with under-performing schools or surgeries, or of health service reconfiguration involving closure of local units. People have strong emotional attachment to their schools, GPs and midwifery provision: to them they have entrusted their lives and life-chances, and those of their children. Any alteration of such cherished services needs to be handled with managerial competence, political conviction and emotional sensitivity.

But there is little doubt that contestability in the event of failure works. Whether it be in LEAs or prisons,[6] not only has the performance of the replaced failing provider improved – and some new models of improvement and innovations in staffing and staff deployment been made available – but the threat of contestability has induced improvement throughout the sector, particularly on those who might otherwise have been in danger of 'failing'. But contestability in the event of failure has its limitations. New providers are unlikely to invest in a market where the only points of entry are through the replacement or, even more inhibiting, takeover of weak providers. And since the desire is to move provision from, in Michael Barber's phrase, 'awful to adequate' – an entirely sensible and worthwhile endeavour – contracts are often written to ensure that standard elements of best practice are followed, thus inhibiting radical innovation.

So although both comparative performance information and contestability can stimulate significant improvements in public services, the full benefits of competitive pressures can only be realised if a true level playing field is established. Conversely, it is very difficult, if not impossible, to introduce effective and appropriately managed competition between sectors without the foundation of comparative performance data or more particularly agreed criteria as to the aspects of performance which are judged politically and by the public to be important. One of the reasons that the introduction of competition into the National Offender Management Service has proved so difficult is precisely the absence of such agreed criteria and data.

Level playing field

While incremental improvement is always welcome, more is required from the reform of public services: plurality and diversity of provision to respond to the varying needs of different individuals (personalisation) and communities, especially disadvantaged and deprived ones; step changes in productivity and efficiency to square the circle of ever-rising demand and tight financial resources; radical innovation for new forms of provision which keep pace with changes in lifestyle, expectations and technology. Competently managed values-based competition is key to all this, enabling the full experience, expertise and excellence of professionals and providers in all sectors – public, private, third – to be harnessed in pursuit of improved outcomes, user experience, efficiency and social justice.

There are four central elements in establishing a level playing field: the role of government, regulation, commissioning and user choice. The last of these, and its resulting potential tensions and trade-offs, are discussed fully in Chapter 5, hence the following discussion is confined to the first three.

The role of government
Markets, competition and contestability – carefully developed and intelligently regulated – can be key elements of self-improving systems in public services. But crucial responsibilities remain with government:

- Clearly articulating national objectives and (the relative balance between) priorities. This would build on the introduction and evolution of public service agreements and would provide the basis for shaping developing markets and judging their efficacy or otherwise.
- Setting down and periodically raising national thresholds and minimum standards, with advice from professional experts and in the light of international benchmarking: social democrats should be clear about the need for continuous improvement.
- Determining the resource envelope within which a particular service sector will need to work or which will be available to address a specific issue.
- Ensuring that providers from different sectors are not advantaged or disadvantaged by particular fiscal rules or tax or capital financing regimes, and that there are fair and transparent procedures for commissioning and procurement.
- Initial market making. Some markets can be made or stimulated locally but many will require decisive national intervention, including senior official and political-level dialogue with potential providers and national procurement to kickstart them.
- Putting in place the necessary frameworks and arrangements for regulation and commissioning (including appropriate separation from providers).

A relentless focus on improving outcomes, increasing the quality of the experience of public services, equitable access and social justice is, combined with the inspired leadership of the requisite change, the essential role for government.

Regulation

All too often over the last decade, markets have been opened up in public services without sufficient or early enough consideration of the necessary regulatory framework. Neither has there been enough consideration of the overall shape or nature of the market required to achieve the desired social and political aims. As such frameworks are crucial to the management of competition, there have unsurprisingly been adverse consequences (such as cream skimming and emerging monopolies) which could have been avoided.

A primary function of the regulatory arrangements in any particular service area is to decide who and which organisations are fit to practice; that is, to approve or license providers which do or will meet or exceed national minimum standards. While this is, to a considerable extent, common practice already, two issues arise when markets are created: what to do about incumbent providers who do not meet these standards (discussed above in the context of contestability), and whether a regulator should have regard to the number and size of providers in the relevant service area (pursued below in relation to scale).

To assure itself, and more importantly the public, that providers continue to meet the required standards and to create public and peer pressure for continuous improvement, a regulator needs to collect and communicate accessible, robust comparative performance information. Clear performance criteria and good-quality performance information are key prerequisites for a well-functioning market. Indeed such information, as was discussed earlier in this chapter, is a stimulus to competition and improvement even in the absence of formal markets. This form of quality regulation is now common-place across most public services, and there has been a gradual but welcome shift from burdensome top-down inspection and monitoring to a lighter touch of self-assessment, with appropriate audit sampling as a check on accuracy. Less well developed has been the economic or market regulation of public service markets.

There has been a substantial debate about whether, given the inevitable political considerations and sensitivities, economic regulatory functions should be undertaken by the government (particularly in the early stages of market development) or whether they should be entrusted to an independent body. While the former situation provides the government with the advantage of adapting to circumstances as they arise, it runs the risk of allowing the government to fiddle with arrangements and disguise a lack of clarity over the social and political objectives of market development. And the latter raises the question of whether there should be a single economic and quality regulator or two distinct bodies. Experience nationally and internationally, from public services and utilities, suggests that on balance a single regulator encompassing both quality and economic functions is the best arrangement.

This same experience highlights two other issues of political importance concerning the regulation of public services. The first is that price-regulated competition (for example, as in the national tariffs being introduced into the NHS), when fully embedded, tilts the focus of providers towards quality, as opposed to cost reduction, and that concentrated but non-monopolistic markets, that is those with relatively few providers, appear to show the most improvement in quality. Within this generalisation, however, the design of the funding incentives and financial flows is critical. Over the last decade incentives have been put in place for public service organisations to increase their volume of activity: to do more (for example, funding following pupils in schools, 'payment by results'[7] for hospitals). To ensure equity and access, further consideration needs to be given to additional weightings for hard-to-reach and disadvantaged groups, and for individuals with complex needs.[8] Incentivising higher quality (doing things better) and transformation (doing things differently) requires funding streams which reward an organisation's improvement in performance.[9] Such a stream would place the greatest incentive on poorly performing organisations, those who need it most.

Delivering better outcomes for more money can prove very good value, especially if poorer performers are removed from the market. Currently in many parts of public services there is still too severe a separation between revenue and capital funding, with capitation formulae (formulae, generally weighted, which calculate funding on the basis of the numbers and types of user in the population served) often only paying for operating costs. In order to incentivise good providers to expand and new providers to invest, and to lessen the need for centralised capacity planning, capital costs should be included in such regimes.

These funding matters are a sub-set of wider considerations. There is much to learn (but not copy) from the privatisation and subsequent regulation of utilities and from regulators of other areas (for example both FSAs: the Food

Standards Agency and the Financial Services Authority). Since the 1970s a veritable art or even science of regulation has developed, understanding how to translate the objectives of market development in a particular sector into the appropriate design of that market and the trade-offs between efficiency and innovation, cost reduction and quality improvement, short- and long-term aims.[10] And in this lies the possibility of a sharper and more workable distinction between the responsibilities of the government and those of an independent regulator. As outlined earlier, the government should set the objectives and priorities, determine the public expenditure resources available and then hand over to the independent regulator the task of designing and implementing the appropriate rules of competition.

This design task includes some sense of the required overall market shape. If, for example, personalisation and innovation – new forms of delivery – are high priorities then what is needed is a relatively small core of large providers, each with significant market share, to take innovations to scale and to provide the bedrock of routinised operations or platforms on which personalised services can be developed, and a large periphery of suppliers and start-ups to continually generate innovative products and services. Arguably the lack of providers at the appropriate scale and of new start-ups has been a major factor inhibiting innovation and its diffusion in public services.[11]

The function of the regulator is, through regulating entry and exit, mergers and acquisitions, including the prevention or breaking up of emerging monopolies and cartels, and establishing the financial rules of the game, to develop and maintain a dynamic market of a shape and structure which ensure that there are sufficient providers of the right scale and quality to replace under-performers and which will achieve the objectives laid down by the government: public value and public values, but harnessing the best from all sectors.

Commissioning

So, if the government sets the objectives, priorities and public funding available for public services, and regulators design the best rules of competition, what is the role of commissioners? To put it at its simplest, and to borrow the phrase from Sir Michael Lyons, it's 'place shaping'. Despite the stream of pamphlets and guides to good practice on commissioning, the political importance of commissioning has tended to be obscured. Although commissioning requires high-level capabilities (in needs assessment, procurement, contract management etc.) it is a profoundly political activity, shaping and raising aspirations for learning and education, health and healthcare, safety and policing in particular places. So while the regulator ensures that providers are fit to practise and that there is appropriate competition at a national level, it is up to commissioners to put in place the right plurality of provision, providers, packages and pathways to meet the needs of, and provide choice for, local individuals and communities; to support the social and economic well-being and development of the area; and to manage the tensions which can arise between increased personalisation and responsiveness on the one hand and developing community cohesion and solidarity on the other.

Three consequences follow from this view of commissioning and its enhanced political role. First, commissioning is the site for democratic accountability, the set of processes by which the public through votes and voices (petitions, deliberative juries, consultations or 'community calls for action' as envisaged in the 2006 local government White Paper) can shape and own the values and priorities of services, facilities and activities in their area. This is where voice as public and citizens should be exercised and communities, not just individuals, empowered. As the NHS Confederation and other organisations have begun to argue, how providers engage with the public should be different from how commissioners engage. Except where providers are community owned, it is not democratic accountability they require – they are held to account through contracts with commissioners – but responsiveness to their users.

The second consequence of accepting the role of commissioning as place shaping, combined with the oft-stated need for more seamless and joined-up services, is that, over time, local authorities and groupings thereof where appropriate (for example, sub-regional groupings for skills or transport) should be the commissioners of all public services for their area. I say 'over time' because, though political, commissioning involves a highly skilled set of activities and nearly all local authorities are struggling with sophisticated commissioning of services for which they currently have responsibility, let alone taking on the immensity and complexity of, for instance, health services. The development of local authority/primary care trust joint commissioning, strategic assessments of need, local area agreements, local strategic partnerships and increased scrutiny of health services are steps towards this. But the direction of travel should be explicit, and capacity building and devolution of powers should be aligned with this long-term aim, while recognising that until there is sufficient capability for all localities, some commissioning will need to take place at a higher spatial level than is ideal.

The third consequence is that individuals within an area should not have a choice of commissioner. Though some authors in this book, and others elsewhere, have identified benefits of competition among commissioners, if the primacy of commissioning lies in place shaping, individuals cannot opt out of it for their area. There must be mechanisms for removal or replacement of inefficient or under-performing commissioners and supportive technical functions should, where appropriate, be outsourced. But decisions about the assessment of need, the ranking and resolving of conflicting priorities, and the consequent allocation of resources are inherently and rightly political decisions.

However, discussion about its role and organisational location does not exhaust the difficult issues which need to be confronted if commissioning is to drive improvement and modernisation of public services. Most commissioning has focused on contracting with organisations to undertake a set and volume of activities to a particular standard at a fixed price. Especially when organisations and government departments are new to commissioning (for example early LEA outsourcing), they have tended in the procurement process to be over-prescriptive on inputs and processes and in order to try to minimise risk have tended towards short-term contracting, particularly with third-sector organisations. Over-prescription and short-termism combine to severely limit investment and innovation. Longer-term contracting and more assured deal flow would help[12] but a more decisive shift in commissioning is required: from contracting with organisations for activities to commissioning pathways, often networks of organisations, for outcomes – commissioning the total care of the cancer sufferer rather than separating the commissioning of the treatment and the aftercare. Without this there is a real danger of fragmentation of provision and the risks of cost shunting and compartmentalisation which resulted from the Conservatives' botched privatisation of the railways.

This shift towards pathways and outcomes would also enable local commissioners to stimulate co-production (see Chapter 7); to engage third-sector organisations, social enterprises and community interest companies more thoroughly and effectively; and to encourage community-owned mutual organisations to run facilities such as children's centres and parks and take over the management and maintenance of estates.

Conclusion

Competition and contestability are not ends in themselves but can, if properly managed and regulated, be deployed in the service of social and political objectives. Through commissioning for pathways and outcomes, competition need not stand in opposition to but can foster collaboration, partnership and alliances between organisations – within and across sectors, or perhaps even a new, emerging 'fourth sector' – and encourage the development of more seamless and integrated services.

With the right financial and other incentives and appropriate regulation, competition can both mitigate the potential domination by producer interests and empower professionals to innovate, develop new relationships with the public and deliver higher-quality services. Competition is an essential element of self-improving systems, enabling a significant reduction in reliance on targets.

As more and more public services operate across borders within Europe,[13] and as the world demand for healthcare and education expands, the development of competitive public services in the UK enhances the potential for global trading to the economic and social benefit of the British public: world-class public services.

Developing markets, contestability and competition in areas of public services is a complex and challenging set of tasks involving difficult political considerations and demanding managerial skills. One of the failings of the past decade is insufficient transfer of learning – about failures and pitfalls, as well as successes and potentials – from one area of market making and management to another. The Office of Government Commerce has spearheaded cross-departmental learning for procurement, contracting and project management and both the NAO and the Audit Commission have produced valuable studies. Market making has worked best when appropriately skilled and experienced market makers have worked closely with politicians and senior officials. But more could be done to create better learning processes within government as to how to get value out of the private and third sectors when it is decided to use them.

11

Economic inequality and public services

John Hutton

Introduction

New Labour's commitment to tackling social and economic disadvantage has been strong and wide-ranging and stands comparison with that of any previous Labour government. Our commitment to eradicate child poverty and the progress we have made towards it, our record on full employment, together with our aim to reduce the numbers on incapacity benefit by a million over the next decade, bear ample testimony to this. Despite the progress that we have made over the past decade in tackling poverty and disadvantage, if we are to entrench our ambition to create a strong economy and a cohesive society, we must be more explicit about reducing the high levels of economic inequality that still persist in the UK today.

This ambition should not be regarded as some token gesture towards the past, but as a sign of confidence in the future. For progressives, economic inequality rightly offends our sense of morality and social justice. Reducing high levels of economic inequality, however, is ultimately an argument that goes beyond values or morality. It is equally a hard-headed recognition that unless we succeed in this endeavour we will inflict long-term and potentially unsustainable costs on the criminal justice system, social services, health and welfare.

Economic stability, tax credits, active welfare and reformed public services have all contributed towards a major reversal of the growth in income inequality that occurred during the 1980s. Despite this progress it is also clear that there is more we need to do. There is persistent income inequality and weak income mobility across society. There continue to be strong correlations between poverty and parental education, worklessness, qualifications, geography, family structure, disability and ethnicity.

Making substantial medium- to long-term reductions in poverty will depend upon radically reconfiguring the design of key public services such as health, education and welfare, as well as a clear strategy to reduce the absolute levels of poverty in the short term. Our ambition to reduce economic inequality must be capable of being sustained over the long term. It must be done in a way that does not create unacceptable tax and spending burdens on the vital wealth-creating sectors of our economy. New Labour has always striven for the lowest possible level of taxation commensurate with our social democratic ambitions, whether on businesses or individuals. If we want to maintain the broad coalition that has kept us in office for the last decade we must be clear that there is no scope for achieving further poverty reduction by imposing ever-higher tax burdens on those who aspire to become better off in order to fund public service reform.

The prospect of more intense global competition, fewer low-skilled jobs and the growth of mass transient migration are critical economic factors that will affect the UK's ability to make further progress in the decade ahead. The increasingly polarised growth in asset wealth has the potential to accentuate the difference in economic inequality even further.

Reformed public services can make a decisive contribution towards a sustained reduction in economic inequality. For this contribution to be effective, resources will need to be increasingly directed towards prevention and early intervention rather than cure. Public service institutions must be funded and rewarded more transparently and explicitly for their ability to overcome structural disadvantages and social immobility. Our priority now and in the future must be to weight investment and reform towards those areas which have a critical bearing on whether someone is likely to stay or become poor, such as health, disability, education, skills and employability. Local institutions must be increasingly incentivised to tackle the systemic barriers to economic and social inequality. However, this sharing of responsibility must come with a price: a greater emphasis on excellence, stronger forms of accountability and an intolerance of poor performance.

Tackling economic inequality and social immobility will depend upon forging a new relationship between the state and the individual. New Labour must not get 'bored' with the goal of configuring public services around the needs of individuals. Our sustainable approach must have at its core a commitment to redistributing aspiration and opportunity across society. We must renew the contract of rights and responsibilities, enabling individuals to make choices about their future. We must get rid of the remaining vestiges of a dependency culture in welfare. We must ask more of individuals and families in return. Eradicating child poverty, raising educational attainment and reducing health inequalities will only come about through a partnership between state, patient and parent.

New Labour and inequality

The discrediting of the goal of economic equality by the neo-liberal right in the late 1970s and the collapse of communism a dozen years later made the centre-left uncertain how it should both talk about and tackle entrenched poverty and social immobility. The Labour Party's inability to connect with the newly mobile aspirant working-class voter left us out of power and detached from the mainstream. After Tony Blair's election as leader of the party in 1994, there was a huge amount of ground to make up. In particular we had not only to admit our past failures, but to demonstrate that we were a party that believed in enterprise, in fairness, in people getting on and making the most of their lives. Our three successive general election victories are in part a testimony to the validity of such an approach.

It would, however, be fair to say that as a consequence New Labour has been tentative about the language it uses to describe its poverty and inequality objectives. If ministers talk about it at all it is often through the language of meritocracy and equality of opportunity. The tentativeness in New Labour's language has led to a fashionable and often lazy critique from many on the left, who suggest that New Labour has neither the stomach nor the heart to do what is necessary to tackle economic inequality. In the Labour Party's irreducible core lies the notion that no one should be denied the opportunity to lead a fulfilled life by accident of birth. The reality of a decade in office proves that this notion continues to shine brightly in New Labour. Across a range of indices there is clear evidence that the tremendous growth in income inequality experienced during the Thatcher years has been checked.

During the 1980s and early 1990s the country experienced two of its worst recessions since the Second World War. Unemployment reached more than three million on two separate occasions. An increasing demand for skilled labour combined with the Thatcher government's assault on trade unions and refusal to countenance a national minimum wage polarised the pay gap between no-earner and two-earner households. The uprating of benefits in line with the retail price index during a period of mass unemployment combined with no active labour market policies contributed to a widening income inequality gap.[1]

By contrast, the government's decision to let the Bank of England set interest rates and its new rules to control fiscal policy have delivered the longest sustained period of economic growth in over 200 years. The creation of the New Deal, a system of active labour market support for the long-term unemployed, has made a significant contribution to the performance of the UK labour market, which is now one of the best in the OECD. The UK has the highest employment rate of the G7 countries, standing at 74.3 per cent.[2] Employment has increased by 2.5 million since 1997; a million lone parents are in work for the first time. After a trebling of the number of people on incapacity benefit during the Thatcher and Major eras, New Labour's reforms have started to bring about the first reduction in this number for twenty years.

The introduction of tax credits (benefiting around six million families and ten million children), the minimum wage (at one of the highest values of any OECD country) and changes to the benefit system have made work pay for millions of individuals and families and significantly raised the incomes of the poor. Families with children are on average £1,550 a year better off in real terms since 1997. The poorest fifth are on average £3,450 a year better off.[3]

Change on this scale doesn't happen by accident. A re-elected Conservative government in 1997 would never have introduced these measures. It took a progressive government with progressive values to make it happen. Neither would a Conservative government have announced, as Blair did in 1998, that the country should put an end to the scandal of child poverty within a generation. During the Thatcher years child poverty trebled. Setting a target to eradicate child poverty within a generation was and continues to be the most ambitious economic and social policy objective of any government in the last century. The decision to use the internationally accepted definition of poverty (60 per cent of median household income) was clear and explicit evidence of the government's commitment to reducing relative poverty and income inequality.

The cumulative impact of the government's drive to eradicate child poverty shows that the gains made between 1998/9 and 2005/6 (the latest data available) have begun to reverse the growth in inequality that occurred under Margaret Thatcher. By 2005/6 there were 600,000 fewer children living in relative poverty in the UK.[4]

Overall, in stark contrast with the Thatcher era, income growth under New Labour has been broadly similar across the population. It rose 2.2 per cent over the period for the poorest quintile (the poorest fifth of the population) and 2 per cent for the richest quintile. This contrasts strongly with the period 1979–97, when the poorest quintile gained just a 0.8 per cent rise in income while the richest quintile rose by 2.5 per cent.[5]

The latest Gini coefficient data shows that compared with the period 1979–97, when inequality rose steeply from 25 to 34 on the index, in the period 1997–2005 the index stabilised.[6] This is particularly impressive during a period of economic prosperity when, in the past, such periods have been associated with significant increases in economic inequality. By way of comparison, the Institute for Fiscal Studies predicted that had the tax and benefit system remained the same since 1996, the Gini coefficient would have increased considerably.

Despite the progress in tackling child poverty, the constantly shifting nature of the target (as incomes rise, the relative poverty line shifts) means that the government fell short of its interim 2005 target by approximately 200,000 (although the target was reached in Scotland). It is now clear that meeting the interim 2010 target to halve child poverty will be extremely challenging. Furthermore, despite the government's progress in halting the steep rise in income inequality, it remains higher than that in many of our neighbouring European countries, as well as Japan and Canada.[7]

There continues to be a strong statistical correlation between poverty and lone parenthood, disability, worklessness or membership of an ethnic minority. And despite the economists' view that the UK is enjoying full employment, nearly four million people of working age remain economically inactive, of whom some 2.6 million are on incapacity benefit. It is clear that the entrenched nature of poverty and the continued weakness of social mobility in the UK pose the most pressing challenges for the decade ahead.

The government has invested £2 billion in creating a national network of Jobcentre Plus offices, one of the most effective public sector labour market agencies in the world. It places a million people in jobs each year and distributes five million benefit payments each week. However, scratch below the surface and you see the structural poverty and inequality that remain. Seventy per cent of Jobcentre Plus clients are repeat claimants within a three-year period.[8] No fewer than 100,000 jobseeker's allowance claimants have been on benefit for six out of the last seven years, and 250,000 have been on benefit for eighteen months out of the last two years. Twice as many lone parents as non-lone parents exit the labour market within a year of finding work, revealing a welfare state that despite its progress is still not able to respond effectively in an integrated way to the individual needs of a critical client group.[9]

Income mobility data provides evidence of the generally weak nature of social mobility in the UK.[10] Academic research reveals that although 50 per cent of the poorest tenth in any one year are not in the poorest tenth in the next year, approximately half of these people only move up to the second decile group.[11] The Department for Work and Pensions commissioned research on income mobility between 1991 and 2003, which found that the majority of individuals in 2003 had the same income position as they did twelve years earlier.[12]

Some have argued that the level of mobility in the UK is low by international standards and that it has fallen over the past forty years to the point where 'children born to poor families are now less likely to break free of their background and fulfil their potential than they were in the past'. Much of this has been attributed to the fact that 'the expansion in higher education benefited those from richer backgrounds far more than those from poorer backgrounds'.[13] Data emphasises the wide gulf that continues to exist in the difference in higher education performance between children whose parents were in the poorest and richest income brackets. By the late 1990s only 9 per cent of children from the poorest quintile at age sixteen had completed their degree by the time they were twenty-three whereas the equivalent figure for the richest quintile was 37 per cent.[14]

The cross-generational probability of experiencing a similar income to that of your parents remains high. In the UK, one quarter of a child's income can be explained by that of their parents, whereas only around 15 per cent can be explained in Denmark, Sweden, Finland, Norway and Canada.[15] Children of parents with unskilled manual backgrounds had a 20 per cent probability of getting five GCSEs or equivalent at grades A* to C, compared with a 69 per cent probability for children whose parents had professional managerial backgrounds.[16] Despite considerable and welcome additional government expenditure on benefit transfers, tax credits and child tax credits, children of poor parents are still four times less likely to end up in the highest income bracket.

The weakness in social mobility is increasingly compounded by the growth in asset wealth. The latest figures (2001) show that the wealthiest 1 per cent of the population own 23 per cent of the wealth within the UK, that the wealthiest 25 per cent own 75 per cent of the wealth and the wealthiest 50 per cent own 95 per cent.[17] Although these figures have changed markedly since

1911, when 1 per cent of the population owned 70 per cent of the wealth, there has been little change in the past twenty-five years. Housing asset wealth (with owner occupation having risen to 70 per cent[18] but first-time buyers increasingly reliant upon family networks to help secure a deposit on a mortgage) and pensions assets (with at least seven million people estimated to not be saving at all or enough for their retirement)[19] are just two factors that threaten to exacerbate income inequality over the next twenty years.

During the next decade, the UK faces an increase in the pace and scope of economic change. This provokes fear as much as hope in people. A complex and interdependent global economy, accelerated by the rise of the new industrialised economies of India, China and Brazil, has the potential to polarise opportunity and aspiration yet further. No one is exempt from its impact. The relatively secure middle classes in many developed economies now find their relatively high-skilled, educated professional jobs being lost to overseas providers and the poor find their labour market value threatened by mass transient migration. No fewer than 550,000 migrants from eastern Europe came to the UK between May 2004 and December 2006 and found work.

If education and skills are to be important tools for making further inroads into entrenched poverty and income immobility, then, as the recent report by Lord Leitch makes clear, the importance of addressing the inadequate skills base of millions of working-age adults over the next decade cannot be over-stated. The correlation between income and education continues to be strong. A degree is estimated to give a gross financial return to an individual of 25 per cent, A-levels 15 per cent and GCSEs 25 per cent.[20] As the demand for unskilled labour in the UK continues to decline, it was still the case that in 2004, 33 per cent of the working-age population were estimated to have no formal qualifications equivalent to Level 2 or above, equivalent to five good GCSEs. In 2005, 13 per cent of the working-age population had no qualifications at all (although this was down from 21 per cent in 1994 – demonstrating the impact of education reforms since 1997). More than six million adults do not have the literacy levels expected of an eleven-year-old and an astonishing seventeen million adults (46 per cent of the working-age population) lack the numeric ability expected at the same age.

These statistics reflect decades of under-investment and lack of reform in the education system before we came to office in 1997. It is not surprising therefore, that the UK ranks eighteenth out of thirty in the OECD for the proportion of its working-age population with lower level qualifications. However, with 70 per cent of the 2020 labour force having already left formal education, we must be equally focused on how we improve the skills of the existing workforce if we want to make further progress in tackling income inequality over the coming decade.

Given the scale of the economic challenge before us, it is tempting for some to want to believe that we can continue tackling inequality in the future only by turning inwards and shutting ourselves off from the outside world. The answer of course is not for the centre-left to retreat and look inward, embrace economic protectionism and turn its back on the policies of free trade. This might help save a few jobs today, but only at the expense of many more in the future. There is much to be gained at home and abroad for a fair system of traded goods and services across the globe. The question for public services in the UK is whether, in the face and pace of this economic and social challenge, they are able to respond in new ways that are equal to the ambition of a radical reduction in entrenched forms of poverty and social immobility.

As we look towards the next decade we need to recognise the limitations of existing patterns of social mobility, the deficiencies in the machinery of the state for tackling them and the external threats that drive the potential for a greater polarisation of inequality, opportunity and aspiration.

How must public services respond to this challenge?

At their best, public services can be a powerful collective instrument for realising individual aspiration and opportunity. Too often, however, even with sustained and significant investment over time, they appear unable to make the breakthrough in life-chances that a progressive society demands. The question for social democrats is whether we still believe that public services can be the vehicle through which it is possible to make significant progress in tackling entrenched poverty and social immobility.

If public services are to be effective at this in the course of the next decade, they will need to

- promote more effective early intervention and prevention in areas such as health and education;
- redistribute power and aspiration through a radical extension of choice;
- incentivise more ambitious, responsive and integrated support through increasing the use of payment-by-results funding systems;
- ensure a renewed contract of rights and responsibilities between individuals and public agencies.

These themes should become the basic design principles of public service delivery, and each is considered in more detail below.

Early intervention and prevention
The government can claim success in better institutionalising more evidence-based policy making. The more we understand about the causes of income inequality and immobility, the more we realise that early, deeper and more integrated intervention is critical to tackling inequality and disadvantage.

The government's recent social exclusion report[21] was a stark reminder nine years into office that deeply entrenched structural forms of poverty and inequality will be overcome only through an approach that focuses coherently and consistently on the person and their family as a whole. The report revealed that 3.7 million adults in the UK were still suffering from five or more disadvantages (such as low educational attainment, drug abuse, mental health conditions, poor housing, contact with the police). It highlighted the importance of early intervention, asserting that there is now 'powerful evidence that poor attachment, stress during pregnancy, post-natal depression, harsh parenting styles and low levels of stimulation are strongly associated with negative outcomes later in life, including anti-social behaviour and offending during adolescence'.

In recent years more evidence has come to light regarding early educational attainment as a predictor of outcomes in later life. Significant differences in life-chances are becoming increasingly apparent even before children enter the education system. Research has shown that performance in tests at the age of twenty-two and forty-two months is a strong predicator of later educational outcomes.[22] Children in the bottom quartile at the earlier age are significantly less likely to get any qualifications than those in the top quartile. Three times as many of those in the top quartile at forty-two months as those in the bottom quartile go on to get A-level qualifications or higher.

Significant public and private investment in the NHS has yielded real benefits for patients in terms of reduced waiting times, and improvements in cancer treatments and heart disease. But there has been no real narrowing of the gap in life expectancy between social classes over the past thirty years. Male life expectancy among the professional class increased by seven years (from 72 to 79) between 1972–6 and 1997–9 compared with an increase of six years for unskilled manual workers over the same period (from 69 to 75).[23] Although there has been a small fall in health inequalities, the gap remains stark between different parts of the country. A man born in Glasgow is still likely to die twelve years earlier than a man born in Kensington & Chelsea.[24] What we do know today, though, is that the latest scientific estimates of death rates attribute 50 per cent of the difference between men in the top and bottom social classes to whether they smoke.[25]

Infant mortality rates and the incidence of childhood mental illness are higher in unskilled and lower-income households. More than 20 per cent of boys aged between five and fifteen whose household income is lower than £100 per week experience mental disorders compared with 10 per cent of boys and 5 per cent of girls from households whose income is greater than £770 per week.[26] Despite the more challenging circumstances of raising a child within a low-income household, basic early intervention services provided by the NHS (such as health visitors in the immediate aftermath of a child's birth) are far more likely to be accessed by wealthier households than poor ones.[27]

The government is right to have recently announced strengthened support for the parents of newly born children from low-income families. More intensive engagement, one to one as well as in groups, to provide advice on health, eating, safety and well-being will be a critical investment in our future. For lone parents (40 per cent of whom do not have any formal qualifications), we should consider outreach support that will encourage skills acquisition early on so that they can return (or in some cases, go for the first time) to work.

Health and education systems must shift their resources, human, technical and financial, to become increasingly focused on early intervention and preventative measures. The system of healthcare needs to reward primary care trusts and GPs more effectively for working with other public agencies locally, if they are to intervene in this way. For example, someone in their early forties going to their GP with lower back pain is more likely to be given a sick note or, worse, become eligible for incapacity benefit than to receive a clear, prioritised course of treatment to get them back into work. Failure to intervene early, to resource and prescribe a clear recovery process for that individual, is likely to lead to a longer-term disconnection from the labour market. This in turn can trigger mild mental health conditions and a further downward spiral of the individual's state of health. The downstream human cost to the individual and their family (as well as the financial cost to the state) can become colossal. The Department of Health's decision to review its entire healthcare expenditure has the potential to bring about a fundamental shift in focus of our healthcare resources, so that we tackle the entrenched poverty that is the direct by-product of poor health.

In education, the government has invested significantly in early-years support, providing for the first time in the UK an integrated health and early leaning service within deprived communities. The commitment to create 3,500 Sure Start children's centres by 2010 is a critical part of a base line infrastructure that needs to be in place to support children in their early years. Fifteen hours per week of free learning and childcare will be available for all three- and four-year-olds from 2010. However, it is likely that we will need to go much further in the decade ahead.

The demands of a modern labour market and the increasing economic liberation of women to participate in the workforce means that full- or part-time work for people of working age should become the norm. That in turn will place an unparalleled emphasis on the quality and not just the quantity of early-years provision. All too often childcare provision is regarded as a 'Cinderella' public service, with high levels of staff turnover, paid at or barely above the minimum wage with little career structure. There is clearly a case for stronger, more effective regulation of the childcare market to improve the quality of public and private sector provision but no amount of regulation can compensate for the fact that as a country we still spend a smaller proportion of our GDP on childcare provision than France, Germany and the Scandinavian countries.[28] This is one of the most important investments the country can make in its future.

Redistributing power and aspiration
Income inequality and weak social mobility partly reflect an uneven distribution of power and aspiration across society. President Clinton once said, 'Intelligence is equally distributed, but the opportunity to succeed in life is not.' The same could be said of aspiration. If you are educated, surrounded by family or peer role models who expect to achieve, it is likely that you will be motivated to achieve. You will likely acquire the skills and confidence necessary to navigate the public bureaucracy to access what you need. When people have the knowledge and confidence to get what they want from public services or their income is sufficient to allow them to exit the service and find an alternative provider, they feel empowered.

For many people trapped in a cycle of poverty and under-achievement, the scale of ambition for themselves and their families is equally low. Public services are currently ill equipped to help foster aspiration and the confidence that flows from it. If you lack these attributes, then the relationship between you and the service can still too often be a passive one, where poor outcomes become accepted as all that can be reasonably expected in the circumstances.

That is why progressives must put a radical extension of choice in public service provision firmly at the heart of the challenge to redistribute power and aspiration across society and tackle inequality. Exercising choice over the provider or programme can be a powerful way of restoring within people that basic impulse that government should never seek to supplant: that they have the primary responsibility to make the most of their lives.

Choice in public service provision can never be absolute for obvious, practical reasons. Sometimes there are genuine capacity constraints. We can't all send our children to Great Ormond Street Hospital, for example. In other cases it is simply unrealistic. People in Manchester are unlikely to choose Devon and Cornwall Police to investigate local car crime. Choice of provider should not always be regarded as the primary goal. Nor, in certain circumstances, is choice of provider compatible with maximising value for the taxpayer. Rather choice, whether of provider or programme, time of appointment or type of treatment, should always be regarded as the default in public service delivery, because choice can promote equity as well as improve quality. The challenge for New Labour in the decade ahead is to create systems of public service delivery that embed a re-balance of power between the individual and the state rather than allowing vocal producer interests to determine whether and what kind of choice should be available to consumers of these services. It is easy to forget how many consumers in society make regular choices in their lives. With the exercise of these and other choices comes a cumulative level of control and empowerment.

While recognising that the effectiveness of many public services is increasingly dependent upon the user engaging as an equal partner in delivery, we should not use the diverse nature of the customers in public services as an excuse to deny them the opportunity of empowerment through choice. At its simplest, a radical extension of choice is still about getting the very basics of a service culture right within the public sector, or it's about a choice of channels to use in accessing services or booking a next-day appointment with your GP. At its most complex, choice is about a deliberative process of engagement with a school about your child's education.

Greater choice should also be seen in some parts of public service delivery as a 'privilege', particularly where there is a stronger emphasis on the responsibilities of citizens to engage alongside associated rights. So in welfare, for example, we should move to a position where choice of either provider or programme is available to people in the early stages of their claim. However, the longer their claim continues, the fewer choices should be available and the more prescriptive the intervention should be.

For those that play by the rules and do not abuse the system, redistributing power and aspiration should not just be about a radical extension of choice in the delivery of public services. It must also be about a major extension of rights of access, service and redress.

Incentivising more ambitious, responsive and integrated support

The creation of a universal welfare state free at the point of need and a national system of social insurance to support people in times of hardship was a progressive ideal. However, over time, the increasingly literal interpretation of this progressive ideal created a sometimes cumbersome and inflexible rules-based structure of public service delivery, and led to uniformity and prescription becoming barriers to greater equality.

A Bangladeshi lone parent with three children under the age of five, without formal qualifications, suffering poor social housing, anti-social behaviour and racism, and facing cultural barriers to entering the workplace poses a formidable set of challenges. A progressive society has a responsibility to engage with her, not turn away. She in turn has a responsibility to herself and her children to engage with that support. However, the complexity of the challenge and the limited extent to which our collective ambitions are translated into practical integrated support for her bring the inadequacy of our existing systems into sharp relief.

For years, the collective abandonment of nearly three million people on incapacity benefit, many of whom relied upon state benefit support as their primary source of income, created a culture of dependency, depression and low aspiration. Society has a responsibility to provide support but it also has the right to expect in return that people will do everything possible to help themselves and their families by finding work if at all possible. But their success will be limited if we do not create a public service delivery system that is sensitive to and responsive to the needs of those 2.7 million individuals and their dependants.

We need systems of public service delivery that can more intelligently discriminate between different circumstances and individual complexity. There is plenty of variation in existing public service performance but little is intentional. It is unlikely that intelligent discrimination could ever be achieved without a major extension of devolution and empowerment to communities, institutions and individuals within the system of delivery. Such an approach will inevitably produce challenges and tensions given the UK's highly centralised system of public service delivery and welfare support.

So strategies that are adaptive and sensitive to the needs of millions have to be based upon strengthened forms of local accountability. At the heart of this new approach must be a more transparent system of funding that incentivises outcome-based performance by recognising the additional resources needed to tackle structural inequality and social immobility. Whether funding secondary school education or welfare-to-work provision, we should move towards a system of payment by results. Funding should be increasingly allocated and schools rewarded on the basis of the value-added results they generate for each pupil. Welfare providers should be rewarded for helping people stay in employment and progress through the labour market.

A more transparent system of payment by results would significantly improve performance accountability and help generate a greater intolerance of failure in the system, at the level either of the individual employee or of the institution. Too often we have given the benefit of the doubt where more swift and conclusive action should have been taken. There has been a considerable improvement in educational attainment over the past ten years, but disadvantaged communities still suffer from too many poorly performing primary and secondary schools. The tolerance threshold for tackling poor performance is still too generous.

A renewed contract of rights and responsibilities
Originally the welfare state was founded on two core principles: that public goods should be available on the basis of need, not ability to pay, and that there would be a 'something for something' approach to benefit entitlements. During the 1960s and 1970s this link between benefit entitlement and the responsibility to engage was broken. The corrosive impact of that legacy was all too clear. New Labour remade that link and during the next decade we will need to modernise it still further.

The government's pensions White Paper of May 2006[29] modernised the contributory principle by recognising for the purposes of the state pension entitlement the non-financial contribution made by many (such as bringing up children or caring for relatives). These changes to the state pension system, together with the new personal accounts saving scheme from 2012, will create a modern framework of rights and responsibilities that should significantly reduce pensioner poverty in years to come. It's a framework built around modern New Labour principles and values. Rather than compelling people to save, we will automatically enrol people into a private pension but give them the choice to opt out. Rather than compelling employers to contribute to an individual's private pension, we will first insist on a matching contribution from individuals. Rather than investing in a new version of the national insurance fund, where assets are owned by the state, people will own their savings.

Tackling economic inequality and promoting social mobility can only happen if we strike a new deal between the citizen and the state. If the state invests and provides personalised, integrated and tailored support, and creates the right financial incentives to make work pay, then it is right to expect that individuals will take steps to lift themselves and their families out of poverty. During the next decade we will need a process equivalent in scale and seriousness to the Pensions Commission to stimulate and address the long-term challenges that the country faces in dealing with the costs of care in old age, where millions of older people could see the assets they have built up over their lifetime disappear in order to pay for a few years of residential care.

The route to redistributing aspiration and power across society is to demand more, not less, of people. So if we are serious about a sustainable approach to tackling child poverty based around the value of education, work and progression through the labour market, then we must offer more support and demand more engagement.

The mistake is to believe that state action can or should do it all. Over the next decade, the partnership between the state, the individual and their families must be rebalanced. In health it is right that we should begin a national debate about the priority taxpayers afford to your healthcare if you are not able to prioritise healthy living for yourself. The renewed contract needs to have consequences for those who don't fulfil their obligations.

Conclusion

For too long the centre-left believed that tackling entrenched poverty and social immobility could be achieved only by penalising the wealthy. There was an obsession with lowering the ceiling as much as there ever was in raising the floor.

Ultimately, debates about regulating the incomes of the wealthy are a distraction. The hard grind of tackling income inequality through an assault on social immobility should always be more pressing. The fact that FTSE-100 directors are disproportionately more likely to have been educated privately rather than in the state system should be the focus of our energy, rather than rhetorical debates about the difference between chief executive and average staff salaries within organisations. Senior executive remuneration must ultimately be a matter for shareholders to exercise their scrutiny and judgement upon. It should not become a candidate for crude and impractical government regulation. The Labour Party should never forget the critical political dimension to this debate: if we were to fracture the coalition of high and low earners that has underpinned our electoral success, then we would inevitably drift back to being a party detached from aspiration and financial success.

New Labour has a strong record on tackling income inequality and poverty. We need to speak proudly about what we have achieved. The creation of city academies has been one of the clearest examples of our commitment to tackling educational inequality in poor, deprived parts of the UK. These schools have received capital investment programmes significantly higher than the average secondary school rebuilding programme. And yet many Labour Party activists remain deeply sceptical about their impact and potential social divisiveness.

Many social democrats have referred to the 'electoral dilemma' facing the centre-left: the challenge of building and maintaining an electoral coalition, based as it must be on a need to secure the support of an ever-increasing middle class, with the objective of explicit and implicit redistribution.[30] The question in part is whether it is possible to redistribute without unacceptably high taxes or limited personal freedom. It is critical that New Labour continues to maintain and deepen its electoral coalition, governing in the national interest and communicating the compelling desire we all share to overcome poverty and low aspiration across society.

In a short chapter of this kind I can touch on only a small number of ways in which public service renewal can help tackle income inequality. Of equal importance over the coming decade is the continued expansion of social rights (gender, race, religion, sexuality) as well as strategies to tackle the growing problem of asset inequality (everything from adequate child trust funds to helping young people into their first homes). In all of these areas too, New Labour has forged the instruments of future progress.

The challenge for politicians and policy makers is considerable. Can we speak more confidently and openly about the role of public services in tackling inequality? Can we build a consensus for both the ends and the means to these goals? Are we open to new approaches?

We must be confident about using a language that reflects our values and aspirations for society. Too often, debates in the UK are consumed by the technicalities of means not ends and we become even further disconnected from the public. If we want to maintain the coalition of support for the radical changes that are necessary in the future to tackle entrenched poverty and social immobility, the public need to understand what we are trying to achieve and the values that are driving that ambition.

There is no doubt that new approaches will be needed in the coming decade if we are to continue to make real progress on eradicating the causes as well as the effects of poverty on our society. The importance of tackling relative poverty is as great now as it has ever been. Yet we need to resist the temptation to be satisfied with just getting people 'across the line' of poverty. Instead our ambition should be a sustainable route out. This will be built on often unglamorous, under-reported, work. It will not happen overnight. It is truly generational, based on reforming institutions – the grind of changing processes, people, systems, financial incentives. The challenge for the Labour Party is whether we can build the nationwide commitment, patience and courage to see it through.

12

Innovation, improvement and the empowered user in public services

Geoff Mulgan

We lump many very different things under the loose term 'public services'. All at their best embody an ideal of selfless service, but while some, such as postal services or benefits payments, are large-scale retail and distribution industries with many close parallels in the private sector, others, such as policing or public health, are radically different, operating at the intersection of public behaviour, strong professions and profound asymmetries of power and knowledge. In some services the public's primary concern for reliability is best delivered by high levels of integration and co-ordination (for example, in crisis management or transport, where planning continues to be the decisive, and often missing, factor), while in others improvement is most likely where there is decentralisation and user empowerment. As James Q. Wilson pointed out in his classic book *Bureaucracy*,[1] the essential qualities needed to run a good prison are very different from those needed in an excellent school or an excellent hospital. Generalisations mislead, and it's no coincidence that researchers have repeatedly found that generalist managers tend to perform less well than managers with deep experience of the area in which they are working.

In this chapter I look at how in very varied public services governments can give more meaning to the idea of service, both by embedding a capacity for continual self-improvement into the big systems that they oversee – health, policing, education and welfare – and by encouraging more radical innovation to drive up performance, productivity and public satisfaction in the long run. I argue that although in some services there is still more scope to empower consumers, in many we are moving into a post-consumerist era, when many of the biggest challenges involve encouraging changes to public behaviour and a spirit of shared responsibility between state and citizens: obesity, fitness, smoking, carbon use, welfare, recycling and education are all obvious examples. This new agenda is reasonably well understood in some parts of the world (including Scandinavia and Australasia) but has yet to move centre stage in the UK. Everywhere, however, it poses major challenges to existing agencies as well as raising fundamental questions about the role of the state and politics.

Relearning our history

Many of today's debates have long histories behind them, and one figure more than any other connects the arguments of the 2000s to Labour's past efforts to improve public services. Michael Young was Labour's head of research during the 1940s and author of its 1945 manifesto. Labour defined itself as the party of public services, and at the time the ideal social democratic service was national, equitable and run by professionals. However, by the end of that decade Young was having second thoughts about the risks of top-down monoliths in which the state held a monopoly, and during the 1950s and 1960s he mapped out a series of ideas about how public services could be reformed, which are still in some respects ahead of the contemporary debate.

First, he argued for consumerism: greater choice and consumer power in public services as well as private ones, extending to people of all incomes the choices that were commonplace for the wealthy. That meant new channels, such as the Open University, which made higher education accessible to people of all classes and ages; much more information for users (one of the organisations he tried to set up was a society for parents and learners, a public version of his earlier organisation the Consumers' Association); and much greater pluralism in supply.

Second, he argued for empowerment: greater citizen power in the design and delivery of services. Passive consumerism was not enough. Instead, he argued for what we now talk about as co-production, co-decision making and co-creation, setting up a range of new organisations and initiatives, such as Healthline (the forerunner to NHS Direct) and the College of Health (one of the precursors to the NHS Expert Patients Programme), as well as new ways of involving tenants in running housing estates, and ideas on how to run user networks in innovation. Informing many of these initiatives was a strong belief in mutualism and responsibility – without these a consumer society would risk degenerating to a shallow selfishness.

Third, he argued for community: although the public sector could provide strong infrastructures or platforms (to use today's terminology), public services needed to be grounded in local and specialised needs: policing, for example, needed to be tailored to individual neighbourhoods with some direct accountability at that scale; housing policy needed to take note of family ties. Excessive standardisation would tend to crush the informal social networks and family commitments that are crucial to making public services work – particularly in health and education.

These ideas have never gone away, and some have become much more prominent over the last fifteen years, partly as debates around co-production have become more mainstream, and partly because Young's ideas offered some insights into how upward pressures on spending could be contained without reductions in service quality. Yet for the past thirty years – at least since the oil crisis of the early 1970s – most of the reforms introduced into public services in the English-speaking world have never made it beyond consumerism. The dominant ideas have been premised on a narrow idea of consumer and user power drawn from mainstream economics; they have promoted privatisation, the use of markets and quasi-markets, passive consumer choice and top-down performance management to mimic some of the effects of the market. In their milder versions some of these ideas have helped to improve public services – making them more focused and more responsive. But their results have fallen short of their promise. A recent survey of international comparisons of performance by Christopher Hood found that the countries which had done most to follow these routes remained generally poor performers. The UK, he noted, is 'in a position mostly in the middle to lower third of the top dozen or so developed countries'. The United States comes last in his survey – ironically given its continuing influence in UK policy debates.

Those countries which went furthest in marketisation now stand out as warnings to the rest. New Zealand's government long ago disowned its more radical market-based reforms of the 1980s and 1990s. Britain has had more than its fair share of very visible failures that derived directly from ill-conceived pro-market ideas, ranging from the botched rail privatisation to the significant proportion of private finance initiatives, which now look like poor value for money because of their high transaction costs and their failure to transfer risk. More extreme examples include Russia's shock marketisation therapy (which achieved an unprecedented 50 per cent cut in GDP), the remarkable collapse of China's once impressive health system, which came about when market principles replaced collective provision, and Latin America's profoundly flawed privatisations and pensions reforms in the 1990s and 2000s, whose failures paved the way for the recent sharp swing to the left.

360-degree models of improvement

Some of these failures were predictable. The neo-liberal reforms so enthusiastically promoted by organisations such as the World Bank and by many eminent academics were largely informed by theory rather than evidence or experience, let alone the views of users. By contrast, the evidence on the world's best public services – whether measured by outcomes or user satisfaction – points to a fairly consistent set of conditions that are rather different from those suggested by economic theory. These include:

- stable and generous funding;
- strong professional ethos;
- political pressure for results and reform;
- intelligent and demanding users;
- policy stability;
- structures and cultures that favour improvement and innovation;
- mixed economies of provision.

All of these can be found to different degrees in the very successful models of care provided in Denmark, in the first-class e-government programmes of Singapore and Canada, and in the radical alternatives to prison pursued in Scandinavia, as well as in the excellent universities of the UK and the United States. These models do not have a single explanatory factor. For example, money has only a weak correlation with service performance; nor is there any clear link between market structure or organisational form and outputs, contrary to the claims of several generations of advocates on both left and right (and contrary to the assumptions of the many UK policy makers who have tried to design the perfect market structure).

However, in most of the best systems it is possible to find a combination of pressures and supports, some from above, some from the side and some from below. In the UK this simple empirical observation contributed to the shift away from a one-dimensional over-reliance on top-down targets or quasi-markets which had become fashionable in the 1990s. Instead, government started to promote what is coming to be called a '360 degree' approach to improvement, and to take more seriously the roles of users as choosers, shapers and makers of public service. The essence of the emerging approach, drawing on UK and international experience, is that the best way to drive up quality and embed a capacity for self-improvement in public services is through a combination of

- top-down pressure and support (via targets, funding etc);
- horizontal pressure and support (through contestability, collaborative learning etc); and
- bottom-up pressure and support (through user choice and voice as well as personal and collective responsibility).

This three-dimensional approach to change does not solve some of the fundamental tensions that can be found in any public service: the basic choices that have to be made between universal and targeted provision, and between provision on the basis of entitlement and provision on the basis of need; the balance between market dynamics and equity. Nor does it answer what should be funded through general taxation or charges. Moreover its application is bound to vary between different services, depending on how much patterns of need and demand vary, economies of scale and scope in planning and provision, and the place of expert knowledge. But this framework provides a much clearer way of understanding reform proposals, and of considering the key gaps in each public service area – and when combined with a strong political commitment to empowerment it provides a possible basis for a new wave of reform. In what follows I sketch out what it means in practice.

Bottom up

The starting point for all reformers in the 2000s must be a presumption in favour of passing power downwards: all public services that wish truly to serve the public should seek ways to share power with their users. This is important from a moral and political perspective as well as from a pragmatic one, since user power is likely to be an important driver of performance and satisfaction. As I've argued elsewhere, too, the best governments have always embedded a sense of service deep in their DNA.[2] Here I summarise the half-dozen or so building blocks of strategies for empowerment in public services.

At a first level empowerment simply means services that treat people as if they have power – with cultures of responsiveness, respect and care. The best do this almost instinctively. But many services in both the private and public sectors are poor on the details: unresponsive, hiding behind the grim options of modern telephone technology; unable to apologise when things go wrong. In some fields the norms of rapid responsive service in the private sector clearly outperform those of public organisations. Yet the depth of care provided by many public services is unmatched except by the most expensive private services. Many of the biggest private firms – such as the retail banks or cable companies, which operate in relatively oligopolistic markets – provide often dire standards of service that would be unacceptable in the public sector (I'm certainly not alone in having received far worse service from my own bank and cable service provider, to give just two examples, than I've ever received from public organisations). Even the better ones are still essentially applying manufacturing principles (of automation, modularisation and standardisation) to services rather than the intensely personal care demanded at the high end of the market.[3]

Instilling a culture of service involves action on many fronts, including training, coaching, import from other sectors and user power. In some cases it can be reinforced by targets. For example, every service, and any ruling party, can consider whether loose commitments should be hardened up into formal guarantees of national or local standards of service delivery (for example, all patients to be treated within x months; every school or pupil to achieve at least y exam performance), which can then be used by citizens. In some cases there may even be advantage in putting these into legislation as part of the rights available to citizens – one means of making advances irreversible (so that, for example, rights to healthcare would become as fundamental as rights to due process in the law). In some cases service cultures can be strengthened by rights to redress or compensation. This can bring with it risks – of empowering lawyers, or benefiting one group of users at the expense of others. But some kinds of mechanism for righting wrongs, and apologising to the public when things go wrong, are a vital part of modern public service.

A second level of empowerment is choice, whether for schools, hospitals or social housing (as in choice-based letting schemes), extending to everyone the options that are already available to the higher end of the middle class. Choice can sometimes be helped by new tools such as electronic patient records (subject, of course, to strong protection for privacy); it can be helped by easily accessible information and advice, by funding regimes in which money follows the user, by helping people make use of rights to choose (for example through patient care advisers), or by formalised dialogue between providers and users over the pattern of provision (curriculum choice, care pathway, treatment type). As the very extensive literature on choice shows, however, it is far from being a panacea. The details are all-important: some expansions of choice can harm significant groups of users; some kinds of choice can be hard to use; and some can simply create confusion. However, with careful design greater choice can improve both quality and equity.

A third level of empowerment is voice. One of the oddities of many of the most important public services is that there is so little room for public debate and accountability. In health, for example, accountability really only operates at the national level, which has made it impossible for individual towns, cities or counties to consider the strategic choices between maintaining big hospitals and more decentralised models of health based on primary care. In policing it is notoriously hard to pin down accountability, although very recent steps to give neighbourhoods more say over policing priorities, and more feedback, have paid off. Some similar moves to give the public greater voice in health will be an essential complement to any future reforms.

Accountability and voice can of course be helped in many different ways. Accountability can be helped by mandated regular reporting of performance, or easily accessible real-time data, and in some cases through direct election (or the negative power of 'democratic contestability', in which user communities have a backstop power to sack unelected quangos).[4] Equally, voice can be helped when the decision makers open themselves up to a wide dialogue over what is possible and the trade-offs between options. Where this has been tried – for example with pensions or transport – it has often made difficult decisions much easier to follow through.

An important field now emerging where voice and choice can reinforce each other is that of systems allowing direct feedback to providers and opportunities for parents, patients and residents to discuss their own experiences. This is the model pioneered by Paul Hodgkin's Patient Opinion and being developed in William Heath's project on feedback with the Young Foundation, which would enable 'Amazon-style' reviews of schools alongside league tables and Ofsted reports.

The fourth level of empowerment is resource power, passing real monetary power to users in ways that go beyond vouchers for already specified packages of service. In one era the vital resources included housing – the right to a council house, or later the right to buy. Increasingly, human capital occupies a similar space – this was the insight of the American GI Bill in 1944, which provided for college or vocational education for returning World War II veterans, and of new rights to places at university and in further education. Other types of resource that may become increasingly important include financial assets (such as the child trust funds) or rights to packages of time off and money for parents.

A good example of direct empowerment in public services is the direct payments model. Introduced despite the scepticism of many ministers, it has shown how much scope there is for citizens themselves to decide on the right mix of cash and professional and informal support, and is now being extended to other areas of social care. The In Control project has shown how these principles can be extended.[5] An equally radical model that has been promoted by the Young Foundation would give groups of patients – for example suffering from multiple sclerosis or diabetes – rights to control budgets and service configurations through 'care pools'.

In each of these cases responsibility as well as power is being shared – and citizens may have to live with the consequences of bad decisions. How far this is acceptable will depend on the specifics of the situation – the capacities of the user themselves, the social implications of poor choices, and the presence of competent intermediaries (such as the personal advisers in Jobcentre Plus) – but this broader issue of personal responsibility or co-production is already central in many areas of policy, particularly in welfare to work, public health and home school contracts.[6]

Later in this chapter I spell out in more detail some of the emerging ideas around co-production. At this stage I want to emphasise that the appropriate balance between choice, voice and personal responsibility is bound to differ in each service. For example, the maximum benefits of choice depend on good information for the user, spare capacity and some mitigation of the unequal power to make use of choice. Where these are missing, choice in public services can have very inequitable results. Direct democratic control over individual services, by contrast, is likely to work best where everyone uses or is affected by the service, and where there are different needs in different areas. In some fields it could be very damaging – particularly if there aren't adequate media to engage the public in thinking through the implications of their choices. The greatest scope for more direct voice in the UK context is at the very local level – for example around neighbourhoods' management of public spaces and play areas, where citizens currently have to navigate the often obscure arrangements of local authorities that typically represent hundreds of thousands of people (on average, England's lowest tier of governance is divided into areas roughly ten times the size of those in other western countries).

Horizontal

These bottom-up pressures are crucial for democratising public services – and turning their attention to end users rather than upwards to politicians and bureaucrats. The next set of design issues concerns the horizontal pressures and supports that impact on the units delivering public services – schools, command units in the police, hospitals, primary care trusts and GP practices in health. Some of these are essential for making choice and voice meaningful, including fostering a more diverse supply side based on contestability backed by freer entry and exit of providers (such as private and non-profit providers of employment services or social care, private and public prisons and probation), which depend in turn on capital funds to cover new entry costs; introducing funding rules that remove the protection of existing suppliers; and actively licensing new suppliers. Some are softer and more about promoting quick learning and collaboration, through more real-time performance information that is discussed by the main providers (as with New York's Comstat crime statistics system), and through collaborations to formally assist mutual learning. In recent years a fair amount of experience has built up of using better performers to coach and mentor weaker ones (while recognising the risks of diluting what made them good in the first place).

The importance of horizontal relationships is coming to the fore in many fields. In some sectors chains of public service providers may be better placed than very small units to promote innovation, offer a wider choice, manage under-performing providers and exploit the benefits of scale in back-office functions and common processes (for example school federations under common management, or networks of correctional service providers). In others the best results rely on strong partnerships that bring together more specialised agencies to address the same individuals, communities or problems. In these cases success depends not only on good cultures of co-operation but also on lean structures that ensure clear accountability for results, and wherever possible oversight of outcome-focused funding to incentivise collaboration.

In some fields the strongest horizontal pressures may come from empowering communities to take over or reconfigure services. For example in rural areas there may be substantial efficiency gains from using community interest companies to take over transport services and sub-post offices, combining formal paid work and volunteer commitments in ways that are simply impossible for public agencies, let alone private companies.

Top down

Finally, central government, as the provider of the bulk of funding for public services (and state or provincial governments in some nations), is bound to retain overall responsibility for performance. Full laissez-faire can be as inefficient as full central control. Equity has to remain a concern of national governments, and it has to be supported through the design of funding and entitlements. But central governments' capacity to understand the day-to-day realities in front-line services is bound to be limited, and its interventions are bound to be blunt. There are nonetheless important roles which nevertheless need to be managed from the centre and which can contribute to self-improving systems.

One is to mandate extensive and transparent performance information, giving all stakeholders standardised and trusted data to assess performance (real-time crime data, monthly individual pupil progress reports, extensive school value-added data, risk-adjusted success rates for hospitals and so on), and avoiding some of the more obvious pitfalls of league tables and scoring systems. In some fields where national government has a clear mandate it can play an important role in setting targets, in consultation with those who will act on them, which will often mean setting floor standards rather than averages. Where these standards are not met, governments need some in-house or arm's-length capacity for swifter and more decisive intervention to replace service providers or managers (for example more rapid change of management in schools, hospitals or social services if performance is below standard; swifter takeover of under-performing institutions by successful providers, including new chains).

Central government is also likely to be implicated in the design of the 'DNA' of public services, the underlying patterns of finance, pay, qualifications and so on. These design principles can reward improvement – or cut against it. For example, many current funding systems do not support improvement (most are based on deprivation, which provides some perverse incentives for local agencies, mixed in with political horse trading and the accidents of history). Alternative options that enable multiple providers (through simpler formulae, or funding that follows the user) or that reward performance improvements (some school funding linked to value added) are more likely to drive greater quality. A good rule of thumb is that wherever possible, financial responsibility should be better aligned with professional decision-making (for example, sentencing guidance linked to resource requirements); another is that wherever possible multiple funding sources should be integrated into a single funding stream before reaching the delivery unit, and ideally there should be a 'single conversation' with those responsible for delivery.

The balance between top-down, horizontal and bottom-up pressures and supports is never easy to strike. In recent British history the top-down has tended to triumph; in other countries by contrast there have been substantial shifts of power to regions and localities. These different arrangements in turn shape how nations negotiate changes to the overall boundaries of political settlements – for example over the balance of collective responsibility for care of the elderly versus individual or family responsibility.

Even in the more centralised systems such as the UK's, this model of 360-degree pressure and support has radical implications for how central government is organised. It implies a leaner set of top-level agencies, less engaged in micro-management and more in assurance. It implies a sharp cutback in the scale and intensity of inspection, which would be shaped much more by risk (so that intensive inspection is reserved for weak performers) and data validation, and inspection agencies reformed as innovation and improvement agencies. It implies smaller central departments, focused on strategy, setting minimum quality standards, taking allocation decisions that cannot be taken at a lower level, articulating the overall mission of the system rather than direct involvement through funding or directives. And it implies a different model for the civil service – operating much more through cross-cutting teams, bringing strategy, policy and delivery together on issues that are not easily solved by individual agencies (as happened in the UK with rough sleeping, street crime and handling of crises).

Much of this package is at heart about two overlapping deals which may provide the basis for the next phase of reform: one is a deal with the public in which central government promises high minimum standards, greater reliability, greater personalisation, stronger choice and more say in exchange for a steady level of taxation and some greater personal responsibility for funding and behaviour. The other is a deal with staff and managers, offering more freedom, more challenging workforce roles, greater career opportunities and support, and improvements in pay and status in exchange for greater accountability for performance, transparent information, universal performance management and stronger citizen power. With these deals in place continuous improvement is more feasible; it's certainly more likely than against the familiar background of swings between feast and famine in spending (which in some respects have become even more marked under

Labour) and the rapid swings of ideological fashion that have characterised British post-war history.

However, these models of improvement are not enough to answer the changing needs of the British public – nor are they enough to address the areas where public services are most clearly not working well at the moment, such as in relation to recidivism, the management of chronic disease or the cultivation of the non-cognitive skills most demanded by employers. To address these we need to turn to the question of innovation, which is still a relatively new topic in the public service field.[7]

Public service innovation systems

In the 1960s Britain's Labour government created a radically new kind of university. Where all existing universities were based in a physical place, this one would be virtual – making full use of television and the telephone. Where existing universities aimed to teach people who had just left school, this one would be open to anyone at any age.

Most people in existing universities scoffed at the idea. There would be no demand; it wouldn't work; standards would be too low. Yet the government went ahead and today the Open University is the UK's largest provider of higher education and an acknowledged world leader in distance education. In a survey in 2006 it also scored the highest marks of any higher education institution in terms of student satisfaction. It has massively expanded participation in higher education through bringing in new students – in particular adult, not necessarily prequalified, part-time students. And it made full use of new communications technologies as they came along – from satellites to the Web – as well as new ways of using time, including summer schools.

Thirty years later another Labour government introduced another radical innovation that was equally opposed by vested interests. This was a phone- and Web-based medical service which the public could call on for diagnoses – even at 3 a.m. NHS Direct combined three existing elements in a new way: the telephone, nurses and computers with diagnostic software. Within a few years it was receiving more than a million calls each month and evaluations showed that its diagnoses were as reliable as those given by doctors meeting patients face to face.

Both of these models originated outside the public sector (and both were pioneered by Michael Young). Their prototypes began as non-profit organisations before being absorbed into the state. Both took more than a decade to move from early prototype to mainstream public service. And both serve as reminders that good government isn't just about doing things well, or more efficiently. It also involves expanding the realm of options – the possibilities for a society.

The word 'innovation' is used to refer to new ideas that work: some will be modest and incremental, some much more radical and even systemic. For any society the importance of innovation will vary. In stable sectors that are working well, innovation will be less of a priority. It is likely to be most important

* where existing programmes work poorly;
* where underlying problems are worsening;
* where costs are rising;
* where new possibilities arise, for example because of technological change.

In the current UK context, obvious areas where some of these conditions can be found include ex-offenders and crime reduction, NEETs (people not engaged in employment, education or training), chronic disease management and the care needs of the elderly, achieving carbon reductions, and providing real-time feedback to public service providers. Active promotion of innovation is also likely to be most important in fields where the barriers to innovation are most evident:

* cross-cutting needs, where it is generally harder to secure resources and political will for action than within silos;
* capital-intensive projects;
* fields without strong outside stakeholders with an interest in innovation (third sector, business, user groups etc.)

There is a widespread assumption that public sectors are inherently uncreative. Reasons for this include the lack of competition in the sector and 'Baumol's disease', where gains in labour efficiency tend to lag behind gains in capital efficiency (the public sector is disproportionately subject to this due to the inherently labour-intensive nature of many of its tasks). Other factors include conservatism, and a workforce which is unresponsive and unwilling to change.

However, history shows that public sectors have often been highly innovative. Indeed, over the last 200 years public organisations have generally been more creative than businesses, devising novel solutions to law, governance, public health, unemployment and crime. Their ability to achieve dramatic improvements in public health, to supply vast armies on the move or to educate millions depended on innovation and imagination as well as good administrative skills. In technology the most radical innovations of the current era have come from public institutions, including the internet (from the American Defense Advanced Research Projects Agency) and the World Wide Web (from CERN). Public organisations have often been much poorer at translating these into useful products and services, but the idea that there is an inherent lack of creativity in the public sector simply doesn't stand up to analysis.

Innovation in the public sector has to pass through one of two main routes. One is politics: politicians and political activists promote new ideas partly to promote their beliefs and partly to gain an edge in political competition – more public support and more chance of winning and retaining power. They campaign through party structures, newspaper articles, meetings and lobbies to get their ideas into party programmes and manifestos, ministerial speeches and broadcasts, and then into legislation or spending programmes. So for example, campaigns for tougher building regulations requiring energy-efficient materials, support for community bus services and foyers for homeless teenagers all focused on politics as the best route to achieve change, even if the services were then run by NGOs. Some political leaders are natural innovators: Jaime Lerner, former mayor of Curitiba in Brazil, was over several decades an outstanding example, who completely refashioned his city's transport system, rebuilt parks, libraries and schools, and experimented with lateral solutions, such as paying slum children who brought rubbish out of the slums with vouchers for transport. Some political leaders take pride in being on the cutting edge of cultural and social change: the City of San Francisco, for example, pays for sex change operations as a result of politics, while in the 1980s Ken Livingstone's London pioneered radical models of equal opportunity, appropriate technology and social inclusion (and more recently pioneered congestion charging, which national government saw as far too risky).

Bureaucracies can also mobilise and deliver innovations. The motivation is usually to address a compelling problem or to cut costs. Here the experience of officials themselves, consultations and contestable markets can be key to taking innovations from ideas into reality. Promising ideas may be tested through incubators (such as Singapore's for e-government ideas), zones (such as the UK's Employment Zones), pathfinders or pilots, with formal assessment and evaluation methods to prove their efficacy. Scaling up is then achieved through new structures and spending programmes. A good example of encouraging public innovation is the partnership between the state and the city of New York to support the Centre for Court Innovation, which helps develop, test and appraise new approaches to courts and crime reduction – for example drug courts and domestic violence courts.[8]

However, there are real barriers in the way of lateral creative thinking in public organisations – risk aversion, political and media scrutiny, lack of competition. In all processes of innovation new ideas face the problem that the new model is likely at first to be less efficient than the existing model, which has had many decades to optimise itself. The first cars were much less efficient and reliable than horses. Other barriers include vested interests, lack of leadership, lack of institutional backing and perceived political and organisational risks.

In the face of these barriers, however, there are many ways to accelerate the process of innovation. Some are about generating more options. The public sector's most striking innovation of the last century was arguably the moon landing in 1969. The particular type of spacecraft used arose from competition within NASA to design it (without competing teams a single spacecraft might have been used). Some of the best processes for innovation start with outcomes and objectives (such as travelling to the moon) and help teams to work backwards from them rather than forwards from existing programmes. There is now plenty of experience of the practical methods that can be used in these processes, though they remain much less widely known than the techniques of performance management and improvement. They include

- user engagement and empowerment, and the mobilisation of user networks (as in the NHS Expert Patient Programme);
- different funding models, such as the Invest to Save Budget, innovation funds and competitions;
- removing rules and restrictions, as in Employment Zones;
- market structures and contestability.

One of the key lessons from experience is that many different factors need to be in alignment for innovation to happen.[9] For example, it used to be thought that contestability alone would generate innovation. However, the more contestable public sector markets have not turned out to be especially innovative. One reason is that the most innovative private industries often rely on substantial public subsidy (typically between 1 per cent and 2 per cent of GDP) and key institutions to promote innovation in particular sectors (such as the Pentagon, the NHS, the BBC or Sitra, the Finnish national fund for research and development). So long as contestable markets rely solely on contracts for services delivered, whether outputs or outcomes, without any overt funding for higher-risk R&D, innovation is likely to be modest. The prisons field offers a good example of this in the UK: the advent of competing suppliers has generated disappointingly few new ideas, even though some of the private operators have brought in new approaches. The dozens of highly innovative projects which do exist in and around the prisons system tend to be in the voluntary sector, operating on a very small scale. Their problem is that no one – whether in the private or the public sector – has responsibility for supporting and nurturing innovation of new practices that could become mainstream in ten or fifteen years' time.

The UK's other problem has been scant ministerial engagement with innovation. There has been top-down promotion of reforms – but usually of unproven ideas. At worst there has been a tendency to proclaim every pilot a success. But so far there has been very little of what is taken for granted in science and technology – deliberate support for a portfolio of options offering varying patterns of risk and reward, some of which will fail and some of which will succeed.

The classic example of this is health. The NHS has experienced a series of reforms, some wise, some less so, that have been imposed top down, often at great cost, with a mix of resounding successes and glaring failures. Yet there has been much less use of experimental models of innovation, and where there has been large-scale activity to promote innovation it has been divorced from users and their needs. The government spends nearly £1 billion each year on R&D in health – but nearly all of this goes in subsidies to the pharmaceuticals industry and very little to innovation in services, despite abundant evidence that the pharmaceuticals industry has delivered diminishing health gains in return for its subsidies.

Health exemplifies a broader problem. In government Labour has followed the traditional model of science-based innovation, handing control of large sums to peer-reviewed science in accordance with the traditional 'funnel view' of how new ideas emerge – the principle that a greater body of research will lead in time to a flow of new products and then to greater prosperity. Although this approach is popular with scientists, the academic study of innovation long ago called this into question – and showed that demand and users (and the nature of the networks that link them) are just as important as supply.

For the UK the weakness of the traditional approach is particularly striking since our economy is much more based on services than hardware (no public R&D support goes to services). Government has belatedly started to recognise that private services and industries such as finance are places of innovation as important as manufacturing – but the policy shift is only just beginning. A similar shift is even further behind in public services, which is doubly ironic given that the largest sector in the UK economy is now health; within a generation it is quite possible that the three biggest sectors will all be 'social': health, education and care will be larger than financial services, cars, telecoms or IT.

Fortunately there is now a cluster of countries – mainly north European (Denmark, Finland, Sweden) – experimenting with more systematic innovation. Their governments are the ones which tend to come out top in rankings of effectiveness,[10] and all now recognise the need for new models that bridge the worlds of R&D and innovation on the one hand, and public service reform on the other. Within the UK, local government and the devolved administrations have been quicker to understand the importance of innovation than Whitehall, which remains wedded to the traditions of diktat and command, rather than experiment and learning.

The user revolution and co-production

A common factor in all the countries that are doing most to innovate is a growing interest in user power and its role in innovation. The words 'user', 'citizen' and 'consumer' overlap in public services, but users are also often themselves producers and much of the history of public services is a history of users taking the initiative to meet their own needs – parents setting up schools, poor citizens clubbing together to provide welfare.

Over the last forty years the idea of public services as a co-creation has increasingly challenged the dominant philosophies of professionals, bureaucrats and business. There are many reasons for this: deep cultural shifts towards autonomy and self-governance, the faster spread of ideas, dwindling deference towards professions and big institutions, and above all growing recognition that desirable outcomes in fields such as health and learning depend as much on the labour put in by the citizen as they do on the labour put in by professionals. Seen through this lens, relatively few of the things that matter can be simply 'delivered' by one group of people to another. Instead they depend much more on the quality of relationships between teachers and pupils, doctors and patients, or between citizens and other citizens. This has led among other things to the rise of home schooling, the proliferation of self-help groups in health, and the return of micro-credit and mutual finance. Similar ideas have spread on the edges of the big mainstream services. The work of the Primary Care Collaborative is a particularly good example and has achieved good results. The ideas floated by the RED team at the Design Council, and by EMUDE and other such design networks around Europe, have hinted at what could be achieved by new alliances of users, designers and public services. All are in a sense rediscovering the vital traditions of user empowerment that have thrived on the margins of healthcare over the last thirty years, inspired by figures such as Ivan Illich and by much older mutualist traditions, and which have informed much of the day-to-day practice of individual doctors, nurses and public health practitioners.

A growing toolkit of methods for influencing behaviour is taking shape: these include laws (such as smoking bans), incentives (such as carbon taxes), provision (for example of condoms), social marketing (of the kind used to drive down car traffic in some cities), visible leadership, advertising (of the kind used for drink-driving), mobilising endorsers and celebrities, new roles to promote change (such as street wardens or personal advisers), contracts such as those used to persuade parents to read to their children. In some countries these are becoming fairly mainstream, and psychologists and sociologists are gaining as much weight within government as economists.

However, there are large swathes of policy making which remain largely oblivious, and the UK, which was at one time a leader in public service reform, has rather fallen back. The different approaches can be seen most clearly in relation to technology. Many services are still implementing consumerist policies, which provide for better contact centres, websites and so on for consumers. These still look outwards from the public agencies towards consumers (just as is the case for big private companies). But the cutting edge of technology goes far beyond these to empower users both individually and in groups to reshape services to meet their needs. Projects such as the mySociety site Neighbourhood Fix-it, Patient Opinion and the BBC's Action Network (or even the Directionlessgov website, which notoriously performed better at accessing relevant government data than the official Directgov site) point to a very different future, in which users themselves do some of the joining up for government, and the government services become more like infrastructures and platforms. NHS Direct is a good example of this – in its first phases it has been a service provider for the public, but increasingly it is also becoming a platform directing the public to trusted sources of information and advice. These models have more in common with YouTube and MySpace than with the previous generation of technologies. At their best they promote behaviour change in a spirit of partnership between the state and citizens.

To get the full benefit of these new approaches, however, the government needs to change some of its own instincts. One is the love of bigness. Early this year the NHS decided to copy the approach pioneered by Patient Opinion and others – yet its tender went only to very big established organisations, virtually guaranteeing higher long-term costs and poorer results (just imagine if the newcomers such as YouTube and Google had been excluded from the IT industry). A second is the sin of pride. Governments around the world have spent and are continuing to spend billions on portals to access their services. Yet most of these portals are neither very effective nor very attractive. As a result the public have tended to rely on simpler tools, such as Google. A third is the error of trying to control and restrict data. A great deal of public sector data has been either kept unnecessarily secret or treated as a commercial resource. Yet far more can be achieved by making it freely available for citizens to match, mine and reconfigure.

The idea that public services are a shared enterprise, a co-production, between state and citizens has profound implications. It represents an alternative both to traditional bureaucracy and to narrow consumerism. It offers the prospect of better results, particularly in fields such as health. And it fits better with a more open, reciprocal view of how politics should be done. This view does not imply that the user or customer is always right; instead, like so much of modern politics, it implies that a good society depends not just on service to the public but also on working with the public to shift patterns of behaviour, rewarding pro-social actions and discouraging anti-social, whether in relation to waste, smoking or violence.

A state that can learn self-restraint and habits of co-operation is more likely to instil similar habits among the public. This is the deeper meaning of co-production and of seeing public services as a shared enterprise between the state and public.

This all matters because we are not in a period when very major changes in public sector shares of GDP are likely (with the partial exception of care for the elderly); nor are radical changes to charging as likely as they appeared a decade ago (partly because charges have turned out to be a lot more politically painful than many expected — relatively invisible taxes have at least some virtues). Instead the greatest challenges for public services will lie more in how they engage users in improvement and innovation and how they share power and responsibility.

13

Governance of place
Shaping a new localism

Dermot Finch

Introduction

This chapter highlights the strong link between public service delivery and local governance. The effective delivery of many essential services has so far been hampered by an over-centralised and excessively uniform approach. This degree of centralisation is no longer tenable. In order to deliver a step change improvement in public service outcomes, we need significant new empowerment of individuals and local agencies, more differentiation and innovation in local methods of delivery, and more place-sensitive governance.

This chapter sets out a new direction for local government reform in England, and places particular emphasis on economic development. It argues for the following:

- The empowerment of local government, especially at the sub-regional level. This would help our cities and towns to improve outcomes in key services such as transport and housing.
- Stronger local leadership. This would help to rebuild trust with the centre, unlock greater devolution, re-engage the electorate and deliver better-quality services. Closer collaboration among local authorities would also support economic development objectives.
- Financial devolution. Local government needs more revenue options – with greater scope to raise its own revenues, borrow more flexibly and decide on mainstream spending.

The story so far

After ten years in power, New Labour remains undecided on the future shape of local government reform in England. This reflects a rather muted and inconclusive debate within the government and the Labour Party. Local government reform is not a top priority. And as is argued in Chapter 1 of this book, the role of local government has largely been ignored in relation to public service reform.

Over the past decade, decentralised government has been realised in Scotland, Wales and Northern Ireland. But in England, with the notable exception of London, progress on devolution has been very limited: 'The recent story of devolution in England is one of what might have been . . . The current system of government in England is complex and spatially inconsistent.'[1] We have heard arguments in favour of a stronger regional dimension, the emergence of a new focus on city regions and continued support for the empowerment of neighbourhoods and local communities. But we have seen only haphazard and faltering steps towards the genuine empowerment of local government.

The emphatic 'no' vote in the 2004 North-East elected assembly referendum ended any realistic early prospect of elected regional government in England. Since then, local government coalitions have emerged at the sub-regional level – most notably in Greater Manchester – pressing for devolved powers over planning, transport and other economic development activities. And at the local level, a small number of towns and cities, such as Hartlepool and Middlesbrough, have elected their own mayors.

The net result has been one of confusion and inertia. The local government debate has become bogged down in narrow discussions about structures and financing mechanisms. On the ground, 'partnership fatigue' has emerged alongside institutional proliferation. In Whitehall, the rhetoric around devolution is not matched by reality. Centrist tendencies still predominate. Real devolution has yet to materialise.

We are now at a critical point in the evolution of local government in England. The centre–local relationship is at a crossroads. The 2006 local government White Paper set the stage,[2] with its vision of rolling back central control and allowing more local freedoms and flexibilities. The triple set of major independent reviews in the same year – Eddington, Barker and Leitch – all hinted at the need for changes to sub-national governance. And early in 2007 the Lyons report set out a range of options for enhancing the role of local government, and reforming the system of local government finance. Looking ahead, the new Prime Minister's first 100 days are likely to include a strong element of constitutional reform. And the comprehensive spending review in the autumn will require local government to do more with less. It will also include a review of sub-national economic development and regeneration, which will decide on the appropriate spatial scale (regional, sub-regional, local) for key functions such as transport, housing and skills. Meanwhile, the other main political parties are fully on board the devolution bandwagon. Their message is clear: if Labour doesn't devolve, they will.

Barriers to devolution

So the time is ripe for the next wave of local government reform. But there are some real barriers that threaten to limit its reach and radicalism. For example:

- **Whitehall.** Ministers now say that Whitehall is the biggest barrier to devolution and needs to 'let go'. But this isn't realistic. The centrist tendencies of governing parties, and those of the civil service, are likely to continue. And, in reality, there will always be a pivotal role for central government across a range of core services. We should be wary of the gap between rhetoric and reality.
- **Party politics.** Real tensions exist within the Labour Party, at national and local level, regarding the shape and scale of local government reform. This has led to slow progress over the emergence of directly elected mayors, for example. More widely, we should be cautious of the ability of incumbent politicians to lead the charge for devolution.
- **Public disconnect.** The public would like a greater voice in how their services and local councils are run, but they are totally switched off by the local government debate – which is largely confined to think tanks, columnists and councillors. Politicians need to reconnect with voters on this and make the devolution debate more accessible and meaningful to them.

There are also a number of practical difficulties in the way of local government reform:

- The multiple layers of institutions and agencies, from neighbourhood to regional level, are going to be very difficult to rationalise. Government is very good at raising institutions. It is less good at weeding them out.

- Local government is still mistrusted by Whitehall, despite a decade of markedly improved performance. Civil servants worry about local government's relative lack of capacity, and draw on that as a reason not to devolve.

- Increasing local financial power is a risky business. The Treasury is concerned that local revenue-raising powers, for example, would compromise the overall fiscal picture – and could backfire in a downturn.

- There is a strong tendency, including within the Labour Party, to insist on uniform treatment for all areas across England – and to resist differential devolution, which is criticised for generating 'postcode lotteries'.

Concerns about equity and equality in particular have acted as a major barrier to local government reform, as expressed, for example, by David Walker: 'The pursuit of equality makes a strong centre necessary. If the history of the Labour Party in the twentieth century has a lesson, it is that relying on local government to deliver is both fiscally impossible and involves unacceptable sacrifices of equal opportunity.'[3]

There will always be a role for the centre. But the current degree of centralisation makes it difficult to deliver equal outcomes and opportunity across the country. We already have postcode lotteries, in the NHS and elsewhere. Fairness in outcome is not always best achieved by uniform delivery mechanisms. Indeed, a more devolved approach – utilising local networks and knowledge – would be more effective at tackling inequalities locally. And a more powerful local political system would be better able to drive up standards in local public services.

This chapter argues for a model of devolution that is consistent with equity and equality goals. In particular, equity can best be achieved not through a command-and-control system of centralisation, but through a devolved approach in which different areas benefit from their own mix of locally tailored interventions. To maximise growth in our towns and cities, we cannot adopt a 'one size fits all' approach. We need different strategies in different places.

For public services such as health, education and welfare, central government should set national standards but allow local providers to innovate with methods of delivery. For economic development, equity is best achieved by adopting strategies that build on indigenous local assets and address local weaknesses – by nurturing growth in and around key regional cities, and then spreading the benefits to less vibrant areas through transport, the labour market and other supply-side interventions. Simply spreading resources thinly and evenly across all regions is not the right way forward.

Centralism versus new localism

Centralism

England is one of the most centralised countries in the developed world – and its cities and towns lack financial power. Major decisions affecting localities are taken by Whitehall and by regional institutions. Only London has a measure of control over its own economic development policies and spending. And yet, as Gerry Stoker argues in Chapter 3, citizens see the state as not just a source of interference or control, but as a benign provider of public goods. This helps to explain why the British public has tolerated our centralised system for so long.

On balance, this excessive centralisation is holding our towns and cities back. Local councils do not have the flexibility or autonomy they need for local service delivery, community leadership and economic management. And they are placed in a rather passive role, waiting for the next central government initiative to come along. Local government has been scaled back and boxed in over several decades – partly by dint of its own patchy performance, but also by too much direction from the centre. Town halls no longer attract the best people. There is a lack of trust between local authorities and business. Voters don't understand what local government does. Less than half of us turn out for local government elections.

This situation cannot continue. A growing consensus is now emerging: we can only get so far with such a centralised approach. As even the Treasury now admits, Whitehall is the problem: 'Whitehall centralism is the biggest obstacle to progress. The real challenge is to devolve more power, policy decisions and resources from Whitehall to the regions, and to the local level.'[4]

The current Labour government has played its part in this centralisation story. It has been characterised by a very strong central drive to improve public services, through centrally set public service agreement targets. Centralised command and control has delivered public service improvements, but there is a limit to its effectiveness. The scope for local policy innovation has been limited, and the ability of localities to adapt programmes to their own conditions has been constrained.

Ministers such as Ruth Kelly and Ed Balls have conceded that the degree of early centralisation was necessary but excessive. They say that the government had to push through many of its flagship early reforms from the centre – programmes such as the New Deal and improving school standards. Ministers also now acknowledge that many of its early policies were not sufficiently 'place sensitive', and that excessive centralisation had the effect of damaging public engagement.

More recently, this excessive centralisation has given way to a minimalist version of devolution – or 'steering centralism', where the centre steers and facilitates rather than commands and controls.[5] This approach has included the concept of 'earned autonomy', with additional freedoms and flexibilities for those councils that are deemed to provide better services. All this is a step in the right direction, but it does not go far enough. The centre is still calling the shots, and the associated performance management arrangements can become unduly onerous.

So the top-down, centralist approach to public service delivery has proved ineffective. Public service delivery is complex; it requires different approaches in different places, and depends on local knowledge and networks. A more local approach, including closer consultation and involvement of the public, would also help to re-engage local government with its electorate.

New localism

New localism envisages a much more fundamental rebalancing of the central–local relationship in England. It came into its own early in Labour's second term, arising in response to the fundamental tension at the heart of government between centralisation and devolution.

New localism, unlike many previous arguments for devolution, focuses on ways to empower local government as a provider and deliverer of services, while acknowledging that central government will continue to play an important steering role. The concept proposes

- replacing command-and-control government with a more positive steering and enabling function at the centre;
- entrusting local government with the power and resources required to deliver effective public services;
- acknowledging the complexity of local governance, including the need for partnerships and networks;
- encouraging the direct participation of local communities in service delivery and oversight.

As Dan Corry and Gerry Stoker put it:

> The argument, here, is not for an independent local government as a good thing in itself…rather that if the governing system of our country is going to deliver the public services and benefits we want, it needs to have a strong local dimension to its operation to match a new role for the centre.[6]

At its heart, new localism is about outcomes, rather than structures. Though it is supportive of broad-based devolution to local government, the principal goal is to ensure that key services such as education and health are delivered. At the same time, however, new localism also provides supporters of devolution with a formula to overcome the centre's ambiguous approach to local government reform. As Stoker has argued, Labour has exhibited a 'lack of coherent and consistent faith in localism' over the years.[7] The party has frequently been pulled in different directions, with some urging continued central decision making,[8] while others have become convinced that greater devolution and decentralisation is needed.[9]

New localism correctly argues that there is a limit to what the centre can do. It should focus on safeguarding minimum standards and spreading best practice. The local level, meanwhile, should be empowered to make its own decisions on the design and delivery of local services, and be relied upon to achieve improved outcomes.

Influenced by the philosophy of new localism, the government has begun to transfer power to local institutions such as schools, hospital trusts, housing bodies and community regeneration partnerships. These transfers did deliver more local control over key services, but generally took place outside the traditional channels of local government. As a result, a range of partnerships, trusts, boards and forums has emerged in cities and towns across England.

New localist thinking has had a substantial impact on the reform of local service delivery. But it has not delivered a radical shift of power from the centre to localities – especially for key functions such as economic development, transport and skills, where cities and towns are vocal about the need for reform.

Opportunity for reform

The 2007 comprehensive spending review offers a critical opportunity to advance the devolution agenda. Here we focus on the sub-regional level, and the powers and funding streams surrounding economic development.

Local government White Paper

The 2006 local government White Paper promised to advance the devolution agenda. Announcing it, the Secretary of State for Communities and Local Government, Ruth Kelly, said:

> We propose a new settlement with local government, communities and citizens. We will give local authorities a stronger role in leading their communities and bringing services together. Central government . . . will play its part in guaranteeing minimum standards and setting overall national goals, but we will step back and allow more freedom and flexibility at the local level.[10]

The 2006 White Paper called for local authorities to play an enhanced role in shaping and leading their communities. Its vision was based around strong community leadership and closer engagement with citizens. The Lyons report has made proposals to reinforce this leadership and 'place-shaping' role still further.

The White Paper included the following key proposals:

* Rebalancing the central–local relationship, including a radical reduction in the number of national performance indicators and targets. This would reduce the current range of between 600 and 1,200 national indicators to around 200.
* Local government as strategic leader and place shaper, through vehicles such as local area agreements and local strategic partnerships – with a new duty for local authorities and other partners to co-operate.
* Stronger and more stable local leadership, with three leadership models for local authorities: a directly elected mayor, a directly elected executive of councillors, or a leader elected by councillors with a clear four-year mandate.

Kelly hinted in the White Paper that the directly elected models would be rewarded with greater powers: 'The greater the powers being devolved, the greater the premium on clear, transparent and accountable leadership.' But given its positioning ahead of the comprehensive spending review and the Lyons inquiry, the White Paper fell short on specifics. It was only able to set out a broad, high-level vision. And it was notably silent on the highly sensitive issues of sub-national governance and local government finance.

Sub-national review
The Labour government has placed regions at the heart of its devolution strategy in England. Regional development agencies (RDAs) and other regional entities now take some key decisions on transport infrastructure, strategic planning and economic development. Going forward, the government intends to devolve further to the regions, and from there to local government. However, there are two key problems with a regional approach – both highlighted by a recent OECD review of the North-East region,[11] which was very critical of regional governance structures.

1. **Spatial focus.** Economic development does not respect the administrative boundaries of local or regional government. There is now a growing consensus that regions are too big a scale at which to conduct most economic planning, and local authorities are too small. A more appropriate spatial scale for most devolved functions such as transport and skills would in fact be the sub-region, which is not represented in current governance arrangements.

   RDAs have an important role to play, but need to be more responsive to their own regional economic geography.[12] For example, Greater Manchester should contract with the Northwest Regional Development Agency (NWDA) and other regional agencies to gain more control over economic development resources. Multi-area agreements would be an appropriate vehicle for this. This need not threaten the legitimacy of the NWDA, which would retain oversight of the whole North-West region.

2. **Accountability.** Regional agencies are not sufficiently democratic or accountable. Ed Balls, one of the architects of regional development agencies, conceded this in a recent report for the New Local Government Network: 'The mechanisms for holding to account regional bodies have not proved effective.'[13] The 'no' vote in the North-East devolution referendum of November 2004 put an end to the immediate prospect of directly accountable regional government in England. Indeed, we are unlikely to see directly elected regional assemblies for at least a decade, if ever. This limits the scope for further significant devolution to the regional level.

   In their report, Balls and his co-authors proposed various options for improving the accountability of regional agencies, including a set of select committees to monitor the regions and hold the agencies to account. These are interesting proposals, but ultimately they will not fill the democratic deficit at the regional level. As Balls et al. say, 'RDAs will always be plagued with questions about their legitimacy and accountability.'

We need to build accountability from the bottom up. Sub-regions, with local authorities as their building blocks, offer a useful way forward. The review of sub-national economic development (jointly carried out by HM Treasury, the Department for Communities and Local Government and the Department of Trade and Industry, and part of the 2007 comprehensive spending review) is looking at the spatial distribution of powers, accountability and incentives across a wide range of government functions.

Up until now, government interventions in local areas have occurred at many different spatial levels – national, interregional, regional, sub-regional, local, neighbourhood. Institutions and partnerships have proliferated at every level, leading to a confusing array of programmes, initiatives and agencies; and an inefficient dispersal of functions and funding up and down the governance ladder. As Gerry Stoker says: 'Central government has been quite promiscuous in its chosen range of partners at the local level.'[14]

While some degree of fragmentation is inevitable, current governance arrangements are far too complex. The sub-national review aims to address this institutional proliferation, by working out what functions are best delivered at what level. It also aims to rationalise and improve the effectiveness of existing sub-national arrangements for economic development and regeneration.

So far, the review has revealed a series of structural problems with the current approach to economic development and regeneration, for example: too much centralisation; too many strategies, bodies and funding streams; a lack of regional accountability; spatial inconsistencies in decision making; and weak local growth incentives. It is likely to recommend a more devolved approach, with a stronger focus on sub-regions, increased powers for local authorities, streamlined decision making, closer collaboration between areas, a differential approach and stronger accountability.

On funding, we need to see a cascade of resources from the centre to other spatial levels for appropriate functions. RDAs are here to stay – at least under a Labour government – but they should pass more funding down to sub-regions, and below, where appropriate. Economic development – including regeneration, transport and skills – would best be delivered at the sub-regional level, since sub-regions are the closest match to real, functioning economic areas.

Unfinished business

We now face a real opportunity for more radical change. So what remains to be done? The local government reform strategy implemented by New Labour has made some notable advances, and the performance of local councils has undeniably improved. We have seen an increase in the quality of local service delivery, more effective partnership working and new executive structures that have enhanced local capacity.

Nevertheless, local government reform has so far been faltering and piecemeal. It is still unfinished business. Progress has so far been limited – compromised by internal tensions within the Labour Party itself, a lack of commitment to localism and a lack of real trust in local government. For example, New Labour has been unable to reach a consistent, united position on directly elected executive mayors. The local government White Paper put forward the options of directly elected mayors and council executives, but in reality most authorities will stick with the current model of indirectly elected leaders – not because it is necessarily the best, but because it is the least disruptive.

The mayoral story outside London has so far been one of missed opportunity. Mayors are not a panacea, but they should be given more encouragement. Instead, the mayoral initiative has effectively been blocked by narrow party concerns about local political control. Despite the clear success of the Greater London Authority model, incumbents in other big cities have dug in and defended their vested interests.

Meanwhile, unelected quangos such as RDAs and regional learning and skills councils continue to take major decisions affecting localities, effectively bypassing elected local councils. This has added to the disengagement of the public from local decision making, who remain largely uninterested in local government and the reform debate. This has allowed ministers to take the easiest option available to them – a minimalist, gradualist approach to devolution in England.

Next stage of local government reform

Local government must become a much more significant player in our political system. The reform agenda should not just be about rearranging administrative responsibilities or institutional structures. It must go beyond a narrow focus on local service provision, instead aiming to provide stronger local leadership and promote local economic development. This will require more co-ordination around, and devolution to, the sub-regional level.

Leadership

Stronger local leadership must be a top priority. Local government should be empowered so that it can make a real difference to people's lives. Currently, it lacks the resources and tools required for effective leadership. Ministers call for strong leadership but deny local leaders the means to achieve it. We need to break through this impasse, with a clear set of financial incentives and freedoms for local councils, to encourage them to grow their own economies. Stronger leadership and stronger economies go hand in hand.

Michael Lyons has given expression to this next wave of reform, with his concept of place shaping. The Lyons Inquiry into Local Government found that over-centralisation is a key constraint on local government, and called for a step change in the centre–local relationship – with fewer central government targets and mandates, and simpler performance management and reporting systems. Lyons also concluded that local government must raise its game substantially and make better use of its existing powers.

Economic development

Local councils could do a lot more to develop their own local economies. But they do not currently have the financial freedoms they need to do so effectively. Recent evidence, including our own,[15] strongly suggests that local authorities should be able to raise more of their own income. That is why Lyons proposed not just greater local flexibility on spending and borrowing, but also new local revenue-raising powers such as supplementary business rates. These incentives are essential if Lyons's concept of place shaping is to become reality. Ministers, local authorities and business leaders now need to reach agreement on reforming local government finance, so that our cities and towns can play a bigger part in promoting their own economic prosperity.

Sub-regional level

This focus on economic development has led many to consider local authorities within the context of economic geography. Since administrative boundaries do not match economic areas, a growing consensus has emerged around the need for local authorities to collaborate more closely across political boundaries on functions such as transport, housing, planning and skills. This opens up a new front for the further development of localism.

Recent research over the past year has underlined the importance of city-regions. The report *A Framework for City-Regions* provides a useful definition of city-regions, and explains why they are so important: 'The city-regional scale reflects the "geography of everyday life" rather than administrative boundaries . . . The city-region is a functional entity within which business and services operate. City-regional economies play a strong role in driving forward the economies of their regions.'[16]

The Treasury published an important paper on cities and sub-regions to coincide with the 2006 Budget, titled *Meeting the Regional Economic Challenge: The Importance of Cities to Regional Growth.*[17] It set out a clear rationale for targeting economic development at the sub-regional level. Sub-regions are the right level for strategic leadership of economic development across a conurbation – including transport, skills, regeneration, housing and planning. They offer significant added economic value and improved co-ordination efficiencies.

Transport is a good example of why councils need to work together across political boundaries, for transport routes clearly cross local authority lines. The Eddington transport study underlined this, recommending a review of the sub-national governance arrangements for transport.[18] Skills are another suitable function for the sub-regional level. The emerging city-regional employment and skills boards, in places such as Manchester and Nottingham, are a very useful model that should be pursued in other conurbations.

Conclusion

The centre is currently doing too much. Local government can do some things better than the centre. As new localists have argued for years, local government is much better placed than central to detect and respond to new needs, and to involve local people in shaping policies and services.

We need a new central–local settlement. But rather than a lofty, idealistic

manifesto for change, we need pragmatic and achievable measures that
devolve power – especially for economic development purposes. Looking
forward, three measures are essential:

1. A new partnership between local and central government, based on
   (a) stronger and more independent local authorities, (b) greater
   accountability to and engagement with the electorate, and (c) more
   coherent public service delivery. This could involve a new division of
   responsibility between central and local government, with a light-touch
   centre and more autonomous localities. Central government would
   retain its lead role in core services such as education and health. Here,
   local government would contract with central government and deliver
   services to a central remit, funded principally by central government.

   Over time, responsibility for other services such as planning, housing
   and transport would be pushed down to the sub-regional level. Here,
   local government would be much more independent and locally
   accountable, delivering tailored local services and funding them much
   more through local taxation and charges. This would involve a major
   shift in the balance of funding, away from the centre and towards the
   local level.

2. Stronger local leadership, including more directly elected mayors and
   executives – and the universal extension of unitary councils. We should
   give further consideration to the case for unitary government across
   England – with sensible boundary revisions that enable cost-effective
   service delivery. Unitaries could help to bring about greater sub-regional
   collaboration and stronger leadership, particularly for economic
   development purposes such as transport and skills. Multi-area
   agreements offer a useful way forward here, as do specific issue-based
   vehicles such as employment and skills boards.

3. Greater local revenue-raising capacity. This is absolutely critical to
   enhancing the role of local government. In particular, local councils
   should be given greater freedom to borrow money on the market against
   future revenue streams from housing or transport, for example. Local
   authorities should be able to raise their own local tax revenues for capital
   infrastructure projects. More locally based revenue-raising measures
   would also incentivise councils to promote local economic development. In the short term, marginal tax powers or shared taxes offer a
   sensible way forward.

So far, progress on each of these three fronts has been patchy. The government has been unable to pursue a clear strategy, due to a range of factors – persistent centrist tendencies within Whitehall, disagreements over elected mayors, sensitivities over the regional versus the sub-regional agendas, and caution inside the Treasury over the extent of financial devolution.

We need to see much more progress on all these fronts. After a decade of incremental local government reform, New Labour must now be bolder in transferring power downwards to the local and sub-regional levels. We must also engage much more effectively with voters on this agenda, and make clear that empowered local government can help to deliver improved outcomes for individuals and communities. Public service reform and devolution go hand in hand, and will help all our towns and cities rise to the major economic challenges of the decade ahead.

Part IV

Tailoring reform to public service challenges

14

Better outcomes, better value

Geoffrey Filkin

The ability of the state to get better outcomes and better value for the citizens from whom it takes taxation is fundamental if the public are to retain their belief in public services. But this contract is problematic, for while over the last decade many improvements have been made to public services in Britain, people have not experienced as much improvement and value as they had hoped, given the significant increase in public expenditure. As a consequence, there is an impression of failure and waste in some aspects of the reform process.

This matters too because Labour has not been able to improve people's lives as much as had been hoped. It matters politically because if people no longer trust that state-funded activity can deliver good outcomes and value, continuing support for publicly funded services will wither. So being able to achieve better outcomes in the future is crucial to the mission of progressives. And this will be a more fundamental challenge for the next few years, not least because there will be much less new finance than in the last ten. To secure improvements will need change, not new money.

Against such a background, this chapter seeks to explore four problems that are central to improving public services:

- How do we get better outcomes in practice?
- How should the central state change to this end?
- How do we shift from top-down to local drivers for improvement?
- How might we implement such major changes?

Getting better outcomes

The challenges

A fundamentally important political issue is how public services can in practice help bring about better outcomes for the public. It is only the outcomes that count with the public. This will be a sharper one now without increased resources.

The context is more challenging. Expectations of services are rising but the public are not willing to support a larger state. So the pressure is on social democrats to show that a progressive state can deliver better value from the public services it funds. To improve public services without increasing the proportion of GDP taken in tax is then the political challenge for the rest of this parliament and beyond. This also defines the electoral challenge – to convince the public that they have got value from existing expenditure and that Labour is well able to get more. The Tories will fight the next election claiming that for the same taxation they will deliver better public services and that over time there will be no need for further tax increases. So a clear vision of how to improve public services and the outcomes the public desire and how to get more value from existing public expenditure is essential.

Why better outcomes matter

In the past decade public services in Britain have achieved considerable increases in both inputs and outputs, but this has not persuaded the public that their experiences of them are better. This is partly because we have failed to involve the public in the delivery of their outcomes. Outputs can be controlled by a service. They can be planned and monitored and improved within the service. Outcomes, a better life and greater well-being all intrinsically involve the public in their creation as well as inputs from public services.

The government needs to recognise much more that it is the outcomes that matter to the public and to achieve them requires the public to have more involvement. This suggests that the state must focus on where it is best able to deliver value, to work to get better value from what it does focus on, and to recognise that the contributions that the individual and communities make are critical to achieving the outcomes that are the goals of public service polices. Better outcomes cannot be achieved by a top-down central state acting alone.

Being able to improve public services obviously matters in human terms. Sub-optimal results from existing expenditure fail those who need them most. Research by the Social Exclusion Unit has shown the shocking fact that those in greatest need often get the poorest public services; and in health Julian Tudor Hart's famous inverse care law, where the people who need the services the most get the least, still has an impact. It is essential to get better results from current resources if those who are most reliant on public services are to have a better chance. Better value now is what they want.

Better value and better outcomes matter for a further reason, economic competitiveness. For an economy open to global competition to be competitive, its productivity overall has to improve, and public sector productivity matters as much as that of the private sector. If private sector productivity is rising by 5 per cent per annum but public sector productivity is zero then the net effect is an overall productivity increase of only 3 per cent. In those regions of the country where the public sector represents more than half the economy this drag on productivity is even more serious.

The failure to increase public sector productivity when private sector productivity is rising will in the long term lead to a belief that the public sector cannot improve its value. Furthermore, poor public sector productivity limits the investment that can be made in new public services. So progressives should see public sector productivity as a major political issue, as it is in part the means to deliver better outcomes for the public.

A new political focus

There is a need, therefore, to refocus the political agenda on this different context – concentrating on how to increase public value and improve outcomes. To date there has been insufficient political attention to getting better outcomes and better value; too often these are defined as managerial issues.

There are structural problems in achieving much better outcomes. Central government lacks systemic incentives to raise its effectiveness and efficiency. It responds to ministerial demands but its tradition and style is not to initiate. If ministers do not challenge obsolete programmes, or promote performance and productivity issues as massively important, civil servants will not do so. And the mass of central expenditure and programmes will tend to accumulate. Whitehall has focused primarily on meeting annual efficiency targets rather than on re-engineering its processes to improve the value these inputs generate by much larger amounts. If value is to increase significantly over a period of years, then services must be fundamentally reviewed, questioned, transformed or stopped.

But the difficult jobs of challenging existing policies and programmes, devolving functions and transforming services will not be addressed unless there is strong and collective ministerial pressure to do so. Officials will tend to avoid this without ministerial leadership.

Under its new leadership, the government will need to develop a collective commitment to the new reality: improving public services without expecting significant resource growth. This requires major shifts in attitude, behaviour and attention by ministers and officials.

Challenge all policies and programmes
It will be necessary to devise a system to give a much stronger political challenge and to question the value of all existing policies and programmes in four ways:
- What value is this programme creating? Is it worth the cost?
- In the light of this, should the function be continued or stopped?
- Could we get better outcomes if the function was devolved?
- If it cannot be devolved or scrapped, how can its value be improved?

Implicit in all this is the question: Could an alternative unfunded programme give better value for the resources? This is an issue for all ministers and departments, not just the Treasury, and should be seen as the collective responsibility of the government, not something that the Treasury alone owns.

The period covered by the 2007 comprehensive spending review (CSR) will offer a great opportunity for the government to prove that it understands the importance of improving value in public service and can do so. However, it is necessary first to recognise that the outcomes currently delivered are not good enough, that there is too much social waste, too little value from the inputs and too little emphasis on delivering the experiences the public want. In the summer of 2007 there will be a new Prime Minister, a new Cabinet and a new spending settlement that will run to March 2011. The combination of these three events gives a great opportunity to redefine the political strategy for the next five years.

A central state more fit for purpose

A key issue then is how the state is to be able to deliver the improved outcomes that the public want. It is not good enough to invest, to develop programmes, to produce White Papers, to legislate, regulate, direct and recruit. All that matters to the public is that the outcomes should be more effectively produced; that levels of reoffending, anti-social behaviour, drug taking and deaths from heart disease and cancer should fall; that transport systems should improve.

The central state should focus on what it alone can do. It needs a rigorous process to identify which functions these are, as above. It should concentrate on strategy, limited national-level functions, system design, standards and the performance of the overall government and delivery system. It should delegate wherever possible to other tiers of government and to other delivery systems. It should externalise delivery when it cannot delegate and devolve it. It should move from delivering services to paying for outcomes.

In short, we need a smaller, more strategic, central state.

Why should the central state be redesigned?

Realism about what the state can do

The state has to escape from the impossible position that it is responsible for everything and able to solve everything. Some of that thinking comes from within the state and some is projected onto it by an anxious public. In fact there is not much it can do at all without the consent of the public and the active involvement of civil society.

The limits to top-down

One of the major areas of service improvement over the last decade has been the development of a set of powerful top-down pressures and incentives. They have yielded results such as improved reading skills, reduced street crime and shorter waiting lists. But there are disadvantages to a command-and-control model. It can lead to game playing, it can disempower those to whom it is applied and it is not sustainable long term, relying on the energy of a limited number of central actors. So we have to devise better ways to improve public services and to motivate those who manage them.

Co-production

To get better outcomes it is necessary to involve the public themselves in actions beyond the public service. The prime health outcome is a longer healthier life and this involves people and their behaviour, not just the public services. An education outcome is not simply a better exam result but involves improved life-chances for the person with that result. Successful outcomes must involve the public themselves in taking actions.

Public services need much more to work with the public, to engage and support them to work for the outcomes they desire. The old model, where the state took individuals' income and 'delivered' to them as passive and grateful recipients a one-size-fits-all set of services is not sustainable. The public must be involved in delivering the outcomes they want, so that they feel that the improved service outputs are relevant to them and willingly support their funding and provision.

It is implausible that such relationships can be developed primarily from the national level. They have to operate at a more intimate level, hence the need for devolution and delegation.

Behaviour change
Many of the challenges facing society require shifts in behaviour – to address health, global warming, congestion, better education and skills. Understanding how to change behaviour is a crucial but neglected public policy question. Behavioural change can be partly motivated by the central state but will often require local action and always the participation of the public.

Promotion of democratic choices
The dilemma of meeting rising demands with limited resources requires a more active debate with the public about choices and trade-offs. It is essential that there should be more direct public understanding and involvement in these choices, and this is often done most effectively through local democratic debate and processes. So the choices of what should be done and how will have to be made much more often at local level in the future.

Stronger accountability and responsibility
A real problem with excessive centralism is that it makes the central state responsible even when it should not be. And this weakens the accountability and responsibility of others. So we have to redesign the state to locate accountability and responsibility at the regional and local level, as the corollary of empowering local government, local delivery units and local managers.

How should the state be redesigned?

To focus on commissioning
The state, whether at central or local level, should focus on a strategy for securing better outcomes, not the direct provision of services. This will require it to move wherever possible to procure the best services rather than

being distracted by production management from its more important roles. To that end it will need to develop a much better understanding of what good commissioning involves.

To pay for outcomes

As we have seen, what the state and the public want are outcomes. Yet conventionally, public services are delivered by paying for inputs. The state must develop new forms of procurement where it pays organisations or suppliers for outcomes, not inputs. A start on this has been made with foundation hospitals, which are paid for the operations they perform rather than given money to pay for premises and salaries.

Such a system should be extended as rapidly as practicable to all suppliers, whether public sector, private or voluntary; it is not as simple as it sounds, though, and further work is required to make it happen. Schools would be rewarded for the added educational value they generated. Integrated offender management services would be rewarded according to the reduction in reoffending they achieved. Under such a system organisations that failed to generate value would lose funding and would go bankrupt or be taken over by a more competent provider. There would as a consequence be a much more powerful set of incentives to achieve the outcomes desired. Take-overs (or other intervention mechanisms, if a take-over was not appropriate) could be triggered by the public or promoted by the local commissioners.

To devolve

Local government has been seen as the problem, not the solution, for most of the last decade. So some roles and functions have been delegated to it, but within a very strict accountability framework and with tight reporting systems, targets, inspections and sanctions. Local government has been seen essentially as an agent of the central state rather than a partner in governance with its own rights and roles.

Yet the centre cannot do it all. Localities have to be motivated and supported to own and manage their own challenges. And therefore the central state has to reduce its obligatory demands, to allow more choice by localities over priorities – owning the funding consequences that go with their decisions, as Chapter 13 suggests. Functions should be devolved from the centre wherever there is a need for more local nuancing, and whenever it is likely to lead to better integration across public sector agencies and better motivation and outcomes. The default assumption of progressives should be to devolve.

To empower managers

It is crucial to empower and motivate public service managers who run institutions, in all sectors, to get better outcomes. Public service reform has been too bureaucratic. Public service managers and their delivery units – hospitals, schools, police basic command units – need to be freed to deliver better outcomes: give them three-year budgets; demand that they look for radical ways to improve outcomes, reduce input controls and regulations and promote much more innovation and enterprise; hold them to account and fund them through results – the outcomes that they achieve. Success should be much better rewarded and failure less tolerated than in the past. To liberate managers of public services in this way will require big shifts in behaviour and commissioning by both central and local government and all who commission services.

To reshape local government and local governance

All of this has profound implications for how local government and governance would need to work in the future. We are not proposing to recreate the local bureaucratic state, the world that some aspire to restore where the local authority owned the means of production in everything from electricity supply to public baths. The local state should focus on market making and effective outsourcing. It should promote and develop the voluntary and community sector. It should oversee the performance of stand-alone public service delivery functions, to stimulate change and to close them when they fail to improve.

Above all the local state would govern in a very different way, with the public rather than dictating to them, seeking to co-produce and to stimulate and support them in the solutions to their needs, whether as individuals or as local neighbourhoods. It would seek to lead change, to 'place-make' and to combine the actions of the public themselves – but would also initiate voluntary effort and the actions of all other local agencies when collaboration was necessary to address a locality's needs and get better outcomes. This is nothing like the way some local authorities currently operate.

This is a radical set of changes to both the central and the local state – to create new delivery organisations that are far more accountable by the outcomes they generate for the resources they consume, and to change the nature of the relationships between public actors and citizens. If, as we believe, these are the right prescriptions, how would one move from a top-down set of drivers to more local ones and how in practice should such a set of changes be implemented?

From top-down to local drivers

Devolving power and reducing top-down pressures will not automatically result in better outcomes and a better relationship between the public and publicly funded services. It would be possible to get the worst of all worlds – an increase in taxation and cost at local level and a reduction in performance and accountability – if the centre let go of all performance demands, expenditure controls and accountability systems. This would do little for the credibility of public services. It is why New Labour was so distrustful of much of local government for so long.

Better comparative information about the cost and quality of local publicly funded services may help, but will not be sufficient. Improvements will require stronger incentives to stimulate devolved managers and political leaders, which is why we have argued for changing the funding of all delivery organisations over time to pay them according to the outcomes they achieve rather than for the inputs they consume.

Also, changing the relationship between the citizen and the state is necessary to reshape delivery structures so that they become far more consumer centred. The real drive for improvement comes best from the public – empowering them is the best way of developing an improvement culture. The only way to ensure that this happens is wherever possible to give the public the right to get their service from somewhere else. Only a few public services have been so re-engineered to date. This requires a far more radical approach to system and service redesign, along with the use of technology to make transactional services more accessible and less costly, as has happened in other sectors.

A new local government
We have sketched out here a new model for local government. Implicit in this model would be that local government had greater revenue sources and was free to set the level of its own taxation. Local government has argued for this for twenty years or more. Again it is not simple; the Treasury, for example, will be concerned about losing control of the aggregate level of taxation.

Politicians and the public will worry that without the disciplines provided by constrained resources, local government performance will decline. It is often easier to raise taxes rather than face the difficult challenges of getting more value from existing resources and axing those policies and programmes that deliver poor value. So how can local government itself be refashioned to create value and get better outcomes?

Moving to the commissioning model helps, since it is easier to be tough with others' performance than with our own. Second, local authorities need a new system of accountability, both to the public and to central government, for the outcomes they generate. Local strategic partnerships are moving this way. Greater electoral competition is necessary, and so proportional representation should be introduced in local government elections.

The process of change

Not all government expenditure gives value. Some interventions fail. Some mechanisms are poor. We set out earlier the need for a root-and-branch process to review all government policies and programmes, assessing what value they offer and whether they should be continued, devolved or scrapped altogether. This was meant to have happened as part of the CSR process but did not take place. A key task from the summer of 2007 onwards must be for all departments to carry out such a review, with external support to increase the challenge function. The expectation should be that they will identify significant functions to be devolved and significant functions to be stopped, and from this a sizeable amount of money to be invested in improving those services which are to be retained centrally but need to be transformed.

As part of this process there is a need to increase the systemic incentives within central government for reform. This requires a culture where delivery is valued above 'policy' and where a minister, civil servant or delivery chief will resign or be asked to leave if delivery targets for which he or she is responsible are not met. He or she also needs to be much better rewarded if successful.

The process of transformation will require looking at a service not within a series of institutions but from the public's perspective. A service needs to be considered holistically; we need to look at what we might call the pathway of the service. Patients do not suffer from disease in the abstract. They have specific diseases or conditions – diabetes, for example. And diabetics are not interested in the distinction between primary and secondary care – they are interested in a seamless pathway of care that they can access at different times. Until recently, the way in which we organised that care failed to construct those pathways. Too many diabetics found themselves suffering crises and having to go to hospital as emergency admissions. This is awful for them and, as it turns out, very expensive for the NHS.

We needed an incentive system that would encourage those who commission healthcare to construct a service that would help diabetics to stay out of hospital. This was best achieved by putting the budget in the hands of local GPs, who know their diabetics and can recognise where a little extra spent on primary care, which can help people manage their own condition, will save considerable resources in hospital. This creates better outcomes for the diabetic and better value for the taxpayer.

However, these resources are only saved if the hospital beds that would have been used by the diabetics are closed because they are no longer needed. The money can then be used for investment in prevention or earlier remedial interventions, but it bears repeating that it can be found only by scrapping policies or delivery systems that are failing to get good outcomes from it.

Ministers will know that the resources allocated to them from the 2007 CSR settlement define what their department will have until March 2011. They need to carry out fundamental reviews of their department's expenditure, activities and efficacy so that they can identify which of their current policies and programmes need to be radically changed or abandoned. But not all politicians are experienced and skilled at leading such processes of radical review, challenge and change. Organisations do not easily let go of power. There is an embedded tradition that believes that improvement in public services and in value must require increased expenditure. So there is a need to encourage ministers to challenge their department's base expenditure, to assess whether value is being obtained, to look for much more innovative ways to get desired outcomes and to recognise that some expenditure should stop as it is wasteful. Ministers have to see this as their collective commitment, as against the current approach of seeking to defend their department's budget and programmes from changes.

Three reform blueprints

Over the next two years, three further changes need to be planned in preparation for co-ordinated implementation in a fourth term.
- **A blueprint for devolution** – the functions that will be devolved over the fourth term to local government and the supports, incentives and accountabilities to go with this.
- **A blueprint for stand-alone delivery units**. Delivery should generally be through commissioned contracts for services from private,

voluntary or public sector organisations wherever possible. Where this is not possible, public services should be delivered by stand-alone organisations, whether they be trusts, charities or public sector units. These stand-alone units should get their funding from the outputs or outcomes they deliver. All hospitals, schools and offender management organisations would be so rewarded by the work they do. Similar stand-alone delivery units should be established for most other public sector delivery functions when it is not possible to buy them from the market.

These units would have to operate on a profit-and-loss basis. In some cases they would get their funding rewards for their outcomes or outputs from public sector procurers, in others they would be rewarded when the public chose to use them rather than their competitors. They would therefore be strongly incentivised to be imaginative and committed to improving outcomes. We should progressively move away from the past tradition that we fund inputs and hope to get some outcomes.

Such a system would mean that those which could not rise to the challenge would have to close or merge or be taken over by other deliverers. The system should allow this to happen albeit with clear protocols to ensure continuity of service to the public.

Over the next two years a blueprint for implementing such a system should be developed across central and local government and throughout the National Health Service.

- **A blueprint for a smarter central state.** Finally, over the next two years a blueprint should be developed for how a more strategic central state would operate, focusing on the key functions of assessing system performance and amending system design where needed, as Patrick Diamond elaborates in Chapter 1.

Summary

- Commit in the general election manifesto to a major programme of reforms that will empower individuals and communities to define and solve their problems and needs.
- Develop a collective political commitment to increase the value obtained from public expenditure by improving outcome achievement.
- Promote a similar commitment to getting more value in all services –

police forces, primary care trusts, foundation hospitals, local authorities and the professions.

- Review the outcome and cost-effectiveness of all programmes – to decide on priorities for devolution, reform or closure.
- Concentrate government on strategic leadership and minimum standards, not production management, and so radically slim down departments.
- Focus government's role as a better commissioner – to secure better outcomes, not to provide services. Develop a better understanding of what good commissioning involves.
- Pay for outcomes – Seek to pay organisations for outcomes, not inputs, whether they are publicly or privately run. Research how to develop such contractual forms, to make such markets and to commission such supplies.
- Devolve and decentralise to localities, so that they can manage their own challenges. Reduce the central state's obligatory demands; allow more choice by localities over priorities, giving them the funding consequences that go with their decisions.
- Develop co-production, as an essential new way of engaging the citizen in designing and delivering solutions to their needs, as suggested in Chapter 7.
- Develop strategies for prevention and early intervention – late interventions by the state after things have gone wrong dominate public expenditure; research earlier intervention and prevention models.
- Empower public service managers – give them the authority to deliver; stop micro-managing them; free up input controls and regulations; promote innovation and radical change; give them three-year budgets. Hold them to account by results; reward success much better; be less tolerant of failure.

15

Governing effectively[1]

Robert Hill

Introduction

Mario Cuomo, the former governor of New York, famously talked about campaigning in poetry and governing in prose. He was describing the hard grind faced by governments in turning the pictures politicians paint during election campaigns into changed outcomes in everyday life. He could have been referring, to put it in New Labour speak, to the challenge the Blair government has had in translating pledges and manifesto commitments into effective delivery – particularly when it comes to improving and reforming public services.

This chapter charts the different phases of the Labour government's approach towards public service reform, though not as an end in itself. My purpose is to highlight the learning and to distil what we now know about using the levers of central government to effect change as we think about the future changes and improvements we want to make.

The risk is always when writing about the state, particularly if you write from a left-of-centre perspective, that you are immediately pigeonholed as some sort of latter day Soviet-style centralist. That is to miss the point. Whether you want to decentralise, marketise, privatise or prioritise, whether your focus is innovative or preventative, consumer driven or environment focused (or both), you need to understand how systems work, how to incentivise change, how to take people with you and, above all, how to combine interventions to achieve the outcomes you want.

That does not mean that all change and all reform must or will come from central government – far from it. Charles Leadbeater and Hilary Cottam, for example, write persuasively in Chapter 7 on the power of individuals and communities to devise their own solutions and write their own futures. But we also need to look at how change and reform can be made scalable. As

Professor Michael Barber has argued, we need to avoid confusing the role of government in policy development and performance management with the separate notion of command and control. You can govern strongly and make policy effectively without being centralist.

The notion of effective governance is important to Labour for another reason. Incompetence erodes trust not just in political parties (as we saw with John Major's government) but in institutions and in the role of government as a force for good. The enabling state needs to be an effective state. And to be effective means grappling with the seven challenges I pose in this chapter.

Some history

The Conservative legacy
Context and history are always important in understanding change. The reforms that the present government is attempting need to be seen against the background of developments in public services management over the past thirty or so years. Dating the start of modern public service reform is not an exact science. You might go back to the Plowden committee of 1959 or the Fulton report of 1967. What is certain is that it did not begin with Labour's election on 1 May 1997.

During the 1980s and 1990s the Conservatives, as Table 15.1 shows, developed a number of approaches for reforming public services. The managerial initiatives towards the top of the table came earlier and the moves towards devolution, contestability and citizen empowerment somewhat later during their period in office. Their market-based reforms brought innovation and some gains in efficiency but, because they were driven by an overly ideological approach, were divisive. They set school against school, GP against GP and fostered a very adversarial relationship between reluctant public service commissioners and private sector providers. The reforms were undermined by a lack of investment in services or any strategic or systemic approach to improving user outcomes, with the result that, so far as ordinary people were concerned, they did not deliver. They did not, for example, seem to make any difference to how long one had to wait to get an operation on the NHS.

Table 15.1: Conservative public service reforms 1979–97

Nature of reform	*Examples of policies and initiatives*
Managerial reform	Management information for ministers
	Financial management initiative
	Creation of next-step agencies
	Fundamental expenditure reviews
Stronger central accountability	Council tax capping
	Introduction of the national curriculum for schools
	Establishment of Audit Commission
	Her Majesty's Inspectorate restructured as Ofsted
	Development of performance indicator regimes
Contestability	Prior options and privatisation
	Market testing and compulsory competitive tendering
	Mandating 85 per cent of social care spend in the private sector
	NHS internal market
Devolution to the front line	GP fundholding
	Local management of schools
	Grant-maintained schools
Citizen/consumer empowerment	Start of direct payments to users to purchase services
	Citizen's Charter
	Vouchers for nursery education

Labour's first term

Having been out of power for eighteen years, Labour kicked off with lots of enthusiasm and ideas for improving public services but with no consistent strategy. Frustrated by a lack of performance data for some services (the Department of Health famously could not tell the then Secretary of State for Health, Frank Dobson, how many hospitals there were in England) and by a postcode lottery of provision for others, the government introduced national standards in key areas along with targets for improved performance. Ring-fenced funds were applied to ensure that specific policy objectives such as higher literacy and numeracy standards were prioritised for funding. Independent inspection was brought into areas such as the NHS for the first time. A lack of trust in local government as a delivery partner led to the creation of purpose-specific agencies such as Sure Start, drug action teams and the Youth Justice Board. The principle of intervention in proportion to success was used to justify closing and replacing failing schools.

What was seen as a dogmatic market approach was abandoned and the internal market abolished but Best Value, a big extension of the private finance initiative and a substantial increase in the delegation of powers and budgets to schools and primary care groups ensured that devolution continued as part of the reform programme. The first steps towards opening up public services to new types of provision were also made – parents, for example, could choose to exercise the new entitlement to free nursery education in the private and voluntary sectors as well as in maintained schools. A concordat was signed with NHS private healthcare providers. Contestability was used to help set up new services such as Connexions and NHS Direct.

And Labour ventured into areas of reform that the Conservatives had not really tackled. In particular, the new Labour government invested heavily in building up the capacity of the public sector to deliver improved services through supply-side measures such as using 'golden hellos' to attract graduates into teaching, supporting the development of professional leadership, promoting collaborative best-practice groupings of front-line NHS staff and expanding new types of public sector roles such as teaching assistants and nurse consultants.

Labour's first term also saw the first tentative steps towards providing increased choice over where you could get NHS treatment.

Labour's second term
As the Labour government moved into a new century and its second term its public service reform programme still lacked coherence. The need to synthesise the various initiatives grew more urgent as the government committed itself to a big increase in investment in the infrastructure and capacity of the public services. A month after being re-elected in June 2001, the Prime Minister made a speech where he described the three pillars of public service reform as being 'national standards, local innovation and more and better-rewarded staff'. But by March 2002 that rather crude formulation had developed into a more sophisticated articulation of the government's public service reform strategy with the publication of *Reforming Public Services: Principles into Practice* by the Office of Public Services Reform. There were now four public service reform principles, with choice and markets taking a more prominent role in the government's thinking:

- national standards within a framework of clear accountability;
- devolution and delegation to the front line;
- flexibility and incentives (particularly around workforce reform);
- expanding choice for customers.

These principles are as good a description as any of Labour's approach to public services during its second term. National standards were developed through the development of public service agreements, which linked extra investment to improved targets for performance. Devolution involved a politically contentious battle to introduce foundation hospitals and increase the number of academies and foundation schools. The growth of flexibility was reflected in agreements that reshaped the way that school and NHS staff, including family doctors, worked and were rewarded. Community support officers became a feature of local police teams. Choice for consumers was, for example, developed through making it easier for popular schools to expand, by introducing choice-based lettings for tenants, by the roll-out of new independently run centres to cut waiting times for treatment and by giving patients the right to go to another hospital if the waiting time for an operation at their local hospital exceeded set targets.

The establishment of the Prime Minister's Delivery Unit not only provided a dedicated central resource to support the implementation of this reform programme but was itself symbolic of a new focus on delivery across government.

The third-term agenda

The result of this strategy was that by the time of the election in 2005, public services were on an upward trajectory – as measured by improvements in test and exam marks, waiting times and survival rates and levels of crime. But Labour's public service language and message, both during and in the aftermath of the 2005 election, were far from triumphalist. This was for the following reasons:

- There was still a long way to go to get public services up to the standards people wanted. Maximum waiting times for hospital in-patient treatments may have fallen from eighteen months to six months, but six months can still be a long time to wait.
- Public expectations were rising as the digital age heralded a revolution in patterns of consumption and the government recognised the need for public services to offer a much more personalised service approach to service delivery.
- The poorest and most deprived were still being failed by key public services. For example, although schools with deprived intakes improved at a faster rate than the average, the gap between the attainment of children from lower- and higher-income families had not narrowed.
- Mistakes had been made on the way. Although the emphasis on targets

had galvanised performance in some sectors, there had been too many of them and too many of the targets had focused on process instead of outcomes. Ring-fenced funding and service-specific agencies had also brought a 'silo' mentality in areas where a cross-cutting approach was needed. Many professionals and front-line managers felt disempowered.

The Prime Minister emerged from the 2005 election determined that reform should be much more self-generating and self-sustaining: much more driven from the bottom up rather than imposed top down by government – a move away from what he characterised in a speech to the Labour Party conference in September 2005 as 'command public services'. He saw the choice agenda as the way to achieve this.

So the expansion of choice came from being one of the four principles of reform to being presented as *the* instrument of change. Choice was seen as the way for those failed by public services to have the same rights and access as those who could buy their way to decent service. Choice was the route to personalisation. And market diversity and competition linked to consumer power would provide the self-sustaining energy to drive forward the public services revolution. The vision was most clearly articulated in a speech made by Tony Blair on the eve of the publication of the education White Paper in October 2005 – which for a time resulted in schools reform becoming the political battleground for the future direction of public services.

Partly because the Prime Minister over-reached himself politically, partly because the policy was an over-simplistic representation of the government's strategy and partly because the strategy had little to offer some public services, this approach was adapted and, in June 2006, the government published a more rounded public service reform philosophy based on four main elements:

- top-down performance management (pressure from government);
- the introduction of greater competition and contestability in the provision of public services;
- the introduction of greater pressure from citizens including through choice and voice;
- measures to strengthen the capability and capacity of civil and public servants and of central and local government to deliver improved services.

The government has been looking to develop these four dimensions (as shown in Figure 15.1) to create a self-improving system. The approach was essentially based on a taxonomy of interventions, with the four dimensions being applied differently to different services.

Figure 15.1: The government's model of public service reform

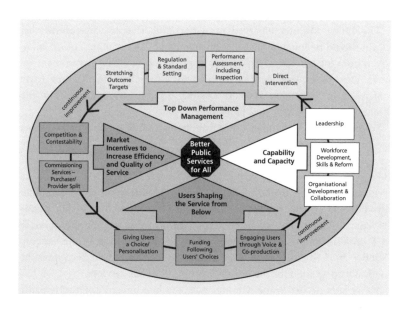

Source: *The UK Government's Approach to Public Service Reform* (Prime Minister's Strategy Unit, 2006).

Challenges for the government

The recognition of the need for a range of levers or change drivers was sensible and more in tune with previous thinking. But by itself it only starts to deal with the first layer of complexity in thinking about how to manage public service reform. The approach developed by the Prime Minister's Strategy Unit raises a number of big questions:

- How should policy makers and managers select the levers to effect change in a service and achieve service improvements and desired policy or political outcomes? Are some levers intrinsically more suited for some services and circumstances than others?

- How can policy makers move to a more mature use of policy levers?
- How can policy makers better combine policy levers to deliver a coherent workable system for a service?
- How can a strong role for central government be squared with an empowering approach for local authorities, front-line managers, local innovators and community engagement?
- How quickly should change be made—what are the merits of a 'big bang' approach as against a more incrementalist style of reform?
- How can the energy and commitment of public service professionals be engaged in devising and implementing reform programmes?
- How can a more sophisticated approach towards public service reform be communicated to the public and the media?

Challenge 1: Selecting the right levers for the right circumstances
The government has rightly argued that a monolithic approach towards public service is way past its best-before date. The corollary of that is that public service reform must also recognise and celebrate difference. Public services come in all shapes and sizes, as Table 15.2 highlights. If the one-size-fits-all era is dead so far as the consumer is concerned, then we should not be looking to adopt an identical reform programme for each service. Because reforms are right for one service does not automatically make them appropriate for another. Because something works well in the NHS does not mean that it will necessarily work in schools, can be transferred to children's services, or is relevant to policing or applicable to offender management.

If recognising differences between services is, therefore, the first principle in selecting the right lever to use, then understanding their application to different types of service is the second. Figure 15.2 shows that the levers for influencing the delivery of universally provided services will be different from those where we consume services on an individual or transactional basis.

Universal services are much more likely to be commissioned on our behalf by, for example, a primary care trust (PCT) or a local authority. We would expect these local agencies to work within a national framework but to be able to respond flexibly to the needs of our area. We would want them to select the best and most efficient provider (as David Albury describes in Chapter 10) and we would also look to independent inspection to tell us whether we are getting value for money – whether, for example, our local waste collection service is more expensive or recycles less than in a comparable area.

Table 15.2: The varying nature of public services

Type of service	Examples
Some public services are universal and are 'bought' and organised on our behalf, i.e. we use them as citizens. This particularly applies to regulatory or infrastructural services	Street cleaning, refuse collection, emergency healthcare, road maintenance, as well as regulatory services such as policing, environmental health
Some public services are organised universally but structured to provide a degree of choice – the state cannot afford unlimited supply but theoretically organises sufficient or surplus capacity to provide some consumer preference	Schools is a classic example, GP registration would be another
Some public services enable consumers to choose from a wide but approved list of state-funded providers	Free nursery entitlement, direct payments for recipients of social care, university places and, increasingly, hospital elective care
Some services combine a number of the above features	Hospital care is an example – choice can be applied to elective surgery but is less applicable to emergency care, which requires a more universal approach

Increasingly, given how we experience other consumer goods and services, we would also want the PCT or council to consult us on the sort of service we should receive, to be responsive and swift in dealing with complaints and to enable us to force changes if services are not up to scratch. In other words with universal services it is, as the government is increasingly doing, using *voice* that empowers groups of users or a neighbourhood to influence services and to get collective redress if they feel that local policing, health or council services are not meeting local needs, and gives them opportunities to run and organise local facilities.

However, for transactional or personal services *choice* (in terms of being able to choose between providers on a personal basis) is much more likely to be an appropriate and powerful agent of change. Entitlements, vouchers and direct payments can be, as Liam Byrne and Anne Rossiter discuss in Chapter 5, popular, enabling and effective levers for those services where needs and preferences are very individual, such as when we arrange childcare, have a hospital operation or need social care support.

Figure 15.2: Using different interventions for different types of service

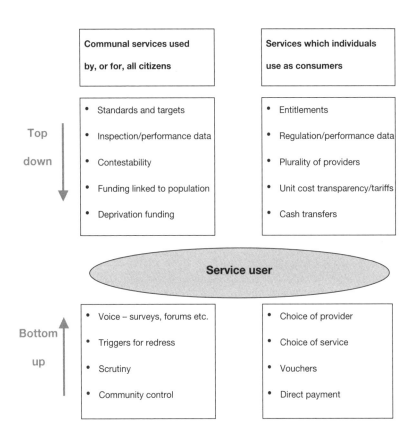

Table 15.3: Commissioner-driven and patient-driven commissioning in the NHS

	How does this work to improve quality, patient experience and value for money?	*When is it most suitable?*
Patient-driven (choice, voice and competition)	Because of choice, providers will have to take more notice of patient views about services. Patients will know much more about the quality and outcomes of care between different providers.	Patient voice will be important for all services. Choice and competition are likely to be appropriate to services where real choice of provider is possible and good information is available to support patient choice. The quality and responsiveness of elective care; maternity care; primary, community and intermediate care; health prevention; and large elements of mental health services could all be improved by this approach.
Commissioner-driven (contracting, contestability and service redesign)	GPs and PCTs will understand the immediate and long-term needs of the patients they serve. They will translate this understanding into robust contracts as well as patient-focused clinical pathways. Poor performance will be contested.	Likely to be appropriate where choice of provider is limited or local competition is not possible, but where services can still be effectively commissioned at a local level. Urgent and emergency care, and emergency mental health services could benefit from elements of this approach.
Nationally driven (national standards, targets, agencies and regulatory approaches)	Wherever you live, wherever you go for care, you can be assured of receiving care under a national health service.	All services need to be provided within a regulatory environment that guarantees core standards of safety and quality.

Source: *Health Reform in England: Update and Commissioning Framework* (Department of Health, 2006)

This in turn means developing and regulating a mix of providers rather than just picking the most effective. Similarly targets will be expressed as entitlements for individuals rather than as goals for organisational improvement. Inspection and performance statistics will be bent more towards giving consumers clear up-to-date data on different providers so they can make an informed choice. A patient deciding which hospital to be treated at will, for example, need to know about comparative waiting times, the incidence of hospital-acquired infection and survival rates for the procedure they will undergo.

Table 15.4: Strengths and weaknesses of different types of public service reform lever

Lever	Strengths	Weaknesses	Point to note	Example
Targets	Provides clear focus for action and measurable performance	Too many targets can distort priorities. Gaming, if targets not owned at front line	Outcome targets or targets agreed between commissioner and provider work best	Child poverty
Financial incentives	Can galvanise performance	Can lead to gaming and distortion of priorities as providers chase funding	Need to be well designed and tested	Flu immunisation jabs
Cost transparency via tariffs or money following the user	Allows benchmarking. Forces public bodies to address real costs and inefficiencies	Can be bureaucratic. Can result in cost shuffling	How far to allow for regional variation in labour costs?	Unit funding per learner per subject post-16
Inspection	Provides objective report for users and elected representatives. Exposes bad performance	Can be too focused on process and not outcomes. Can get over-professionalised	Cumulative inspection burden needs watching as joint reviews and 'single conversations' increase	New school self-evaluation inspection model
Choice	Empowers the consumer and makes providers more responsive	Can lead to service fragmentation as providers 'compete' for custom	Much more applicable to services used or consumed individually	'Choice' system for bringing down waiting times for heart operations

The Department of Health's description of its commissioning framework (see Table 15.3) provides a good practical example of how different approaches are applicable to different types of services.

This analysis also informs the way we are likely to organise funding for services. With universally organised services, funding is much more likely to be linked to the population or user base, with funding formulae being used to recognise differing needs and characteristics including deprivation. If services are going to be offered on an individual basis or if there is to be a level playing field to support the development of a market then you need to have very transparent unit costs, develop tariffs or introduce direct payments or vouchers. Issues of equity and deprivation in an individual system will be dealt with through cash transfers – i.e. giving the least advantaged a bigger personal budget. The childcare element of working tax credits is one example of how the government does this, by providing extra support to enable poorer parents to afford more childcare.

Challenge 2: Moving to a more mature use of policy levers
My argument thus far has been that the nature of a service to an extent dictates the type of policy intervention that is most likely to make for effective delivery. But this is only part of the story. Major policy levers can, as Table 15.4 illustrates, be used in a variety of ways, with each of these levers having its strengths and weaknesses. As we develop our agenda for the future we will move to using these levers in a more mature and informed way.

Take targets, as an example. It is fashionable to deride the use of targets. They have been over-used and can distort priorities. But to conclude from this that governments and public policy formulation should abandon their use is as daft as saying that athletes should not set themselves goals to improve their personal performance, public companies should abandon growth or turnover targets, or students should not have goals for what they want to achieve in their exams. How else can a society or a government create focus for action to deal with childhood poverty or obesity unless it formulates a target for improvement? The problem is not the targets, but the way they are used. Targets need to be

- prioritised so that they are strictly limited to the major objectives that the government is trying to achieve;
- focused on outcomes – most process and input targets can and should be scrapped;
- driven and formulated much more by the front-line perspectives of the public and the analysis of local partnerships;
- set on a multi-agency basis where the outcome demands cross-cutting action;
- tested and then monitored to reduce and squeeze out gaming (the fact

that there is gaming is not in itself an indication that targets as a lever of policy are flawed. All systems from financial markets to sports require policing).

Inspection can be a strong force for improvement but it can also be bureaucratic, costly and demoralising. The reorganisation of the school inspection system to focus on a school's self-evaluation of its performance and its own action plan potentially provides the model for a much more intelligent form of accountability in the future – particularly if the frequency and intensity of inspection is related to how well organisations are doing.

Financial incentives – whether in the form of money following the user, reward grants or standard tariffs for services – are potentially the strongest drivers of change. They illustrate why effective government is necessary if you want to make change happen. Financial incentives can mobilise individuals and institutions to deliver outcomes, expose inefficiency, stimulate innovation, incentivise action to tackle disadvantage and encourage partnership. Crucially they can also provide the level playing field that is necessary to support competition. But if inappropriately designed or implemented, financial incentives can cause havoc by undermining collaboration, destabilising a service and incentivising the wrong or unintended outcome. So their design and application needs to be tailored to the specific circumstances of a service. The arrangements for incentivising GPs are, for example, rightly very different from those for developing aspiration and achievement in schools. We have learnt that good financial incentive schemes have these attributes:

- They are based on an accurate analysis of the cost of providing different aspects of a service – for example, some operations are more costly to carry out than others and some subjects are more expensive to teach than others.
- Their designers understand the culture of a service and draw them up in consultation with front-line practitioners.
- They are aligned to the service outcomes that the government wants to see incentivised – particularly if there is a reward element involved. Local agencies and providers will 'chase the cash' and, although it seems obvious, central government does not always think through the priorities and ends it wants to see achieved.
- They learn from the lessons of other services and countries. The experience and false start of the New Zealand government in introducing loans and fees into its higher education system provided

useful pointers when the new funding system for universities in this country was developed.

- They balance transparency and a level playing field with provision (where justified) to allow for some local discretion to reflect local needs and labour costs.
- They model the implications of changes, assess and simulate the range of behavioural responses (which was clearly not done sufficiently when designing the new GP contract) and trial the proposed regime before rolling it out nationwide.
- They have built-in rules to promote equity, safeguard collaboration and minimise gaming.
- They assess the cumulative impact of changes, phase implementation, monitor the impact systematically and adjust the regime in the light of events.

Essentially the argument is this: public policy levers need to be seen as precision tools rather than as blunt instruments. They need to be customised for the particular service and the particular circumstances and challenges to which they are being applied.

Challenge 3: Combining interventions to deliver a coherent system-wide programme of reform

This leads on to the next challenge: ensuring that interventions are mutually reinforcing and that the combination of levers provides a coherent strategy. Arguably this is the most important and the most demanding challenge. Professor Michael Barber has suggested that a major factor in considering which levers to apply to a service should be the overall state and performance of a service at a particular point in time (see Table 15.5). If a service is in freefall it may well require interventionist measures organised from the centre to establish basic standards. But if the objective is to move to greater personalisation then, echoing the analysis above, incentivising a mix of providers and using markets becomes more appropriate.

In Chapter 16 of this book, Simon Stevens has a good example of how interventions can be combined. He charts how the development, and the threat of development, of alternative suppliers of elective surgery was aligned with the target for reducing waiting times to create momentum and rapid progress. He might also have added that the policy was reinforced by the way funding was allocated and performance management organised.

Table 15.5: Choosing between the options

	Command and control	Devolution and transparency	Quasi-markets	Combination
Circumstances	• Where service is awful • For very high priorities which are urgent • To drive programmes designed to tackle poverty (e.g. Sure Start)	• Where individual choice is not appropriate (e.g. policing or criminal justice) • To get from adequate to good or good to great	• Where individuals can choose (e.g. schools, hospitals) • Where a range of providers can be developed • Where diversity is desirable • During transitions	• During transitions • Where variation of performance within a service is wide • Where market pressures are weak
Key advice	• Do it excellently	• Combines well with contestability (e.g. prisons) • Transparency is crucial	• Equality needs to be built in	• Needs sophisticated strategic direction

Source: Michael Barber, 'Success – It's All in the Execution', in Robert Hill (ed.), *The Matter of How: Change and Reform in 21st Century Public Services* (London: Solace Foundation, 2006).

Aligning levers and interventions so that they are mutually reinforcing is not always easy, but it is an essential task. Where it is not achieved it will hold back progress. Take one thorny issue in education as an example. A key plank of the government's education strategy is strong autonomous schools focusing on raising standards. At the same time, the government is saying that schools should work together on behaviour issues, that the education of looked-after children should be taken much more seriously and that no one school should be expected to accept a disproportionate share of disruptive pupils. In other words inclusion as well as achievement is a priority.

The problem is that on the first objective, schools know they will be judged by performance tables so they are often reluctant to accept pupils who may depress their results. Or if they are forced to accept them, it has been known for some schools to effectively acquiesce in allowing some pupils to drop out of education in Year 11 so that they don't disrupt the others. The two objectives – improved results and inclusion – are in tension. Using protocols and innovative partnerships, local authorities and headteachers have managed to resolve some of these tensions at a local level. But the system needs to be better designed to support both priorities: by, for example, having funding incentives for schools to accept a more balanced intake of students or ensuring that money more clearly follows students with particular needs. Accountability systems could also be changed to assess schools' performance as a group as well as individually.

Aligning levers is more likely to be achieved if there is a description of how reform is meant to work across a service. It is surprising how many White Papers and government strategies are descriptions of initiatives or interventions which in themselves make sense but which then fail to set out how the system as a whole will work. The Department of Health, perhaps somewhat belatedly, has developed and keeps reusing a model of how the drivers for change in the NHS fit together (see Figure 15.3). Leaving aside whether the interaction of the interventions is the right one, it is using an overarching model to explain its thinking to those responsible for delivering change and it is continually relating planning, reform and operational targets to each dimension of the strategy.

Figure 15.3: Description of the government's NHS reform model

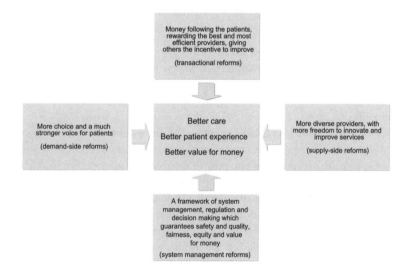

Source: Department of Health, *Health Reform in England: Update and Next Steps,* Cm 6268, 2005.

Aligning interventions is also more likely to be effective if the other challenges described below are addressed.

Challenge 4: Defining clearly the respective roles of the centre and the locality
The whole of the post-war settlement of public services and particularly the intensive reform period of the last twenty years have been bedevilled by arguments about the relative roles of central and local government. As the Local Government Association has put it, 'There is a real tension between on the one hand any government's need to ensure some form of national/ minimum standards and on the other local choice and diversity driven by the desire of local people to shape their priorities according to local needs.'[2] In Chapter 13 Dermot Finch explores this dilemma in depth; in terms of designing public policy Labour's period in office has taught us that central government works most effectively when it

- has clear policy objectives but involves local practitioners and consumers in formulating change;
- sets the policy framework but also encourages and incentivises local innovation;
- defines clear outcomes but stays out of specifying process as far as possible;
- takes action to make new markets (using a combination of legislative, economic and political measures) but devolves to local agencies as markets develop and mature;
- builds capacity to implement reform but learns from front-line practitioners;
- aligns financial regimes to policy objectives but enables localities to use money flexibly;
- co-ordinates and publishes comparative performance but avoids target overload and perverse incentives;
- explains and communicates policy constantly but listens to feedback.

One of the ways this mutual understanding and dependency between the centre and localities is increasingly being expressed is through 'contracts' – most notably local area agreements (LAAs) between local partnerships and central government. Negotiating and agreeing a limited number of core outcomes and then giving localities the freedom, backed by incentives, to deliver is a promising way to get the relationship between government and localities on to a collaborative and sustainable basis – instead of the adversarial and dependent relationship that has characterised the past forty years of public service delivery. LAAs also have the potential to allow for real flexibility and diversity – both within services and within areas – while maintaining a national framework of entitlements for key priorities.

Challenge 5: Implementing reform at a pace that will deliver improvements as quickly as possible but in a sustainable way

There is no right answer about how quickly to implement reform. As Table 15.6 shows, there are pros and cons in going for rapid big-bang change versus an incremental change programme. The decision on what is right for a particular service will depend on a range of factors: the scale of the current problems, the extent of the change proposed, the degree of political priority attached to the issue, the availability of legislative time and financial resources, and the capacity of the service to make the change. But faster and more radical change programmes have greater need for these elements:

- Strong performance management – even, or especially, with policies designed to promote local choice and diversity. Agreed implementation plans which identify milestones, 'traffic light' systems which track progress or lack of it and feedback loops that enable learning and adjustment in the light of experience are becoming the norm in most Whitehall departments. However, the capacity of ministers and officials to stick with an implementation plan and follow it through varies enormously. All too often – sometimes for understandable political reasons or media pressure – they move on to the next change before the last one has taken root properly. The NHS has at times seemed to be one continual merry-go-round of structural reorganisation. Policy continuity is an under-rated but big prize.
- More rigorous risk assessment of what could go wrong at each stage of the delivery chain and at different points in a change programme. Officials compile risk registers whenever new policies are developed but these are often nominal rather than real factors in considering the rate and perils of change. I am not arguing against taking risks (that would stifle innovation and creativity) but government should promote managed risk.
- Support to help make the change happen – central government consistently over-estimates the capacity of organisations to deliver policy changes.[3] Investing in capacity building, skill development and collaborative networks may not be politically sexy but it is essential if

grand ideas are not to be tarnished by scathing reports on failed implementation. At times the government has recognised this. The London Challenge programme for struggling secondary schools, the National Remodelling Team, which helped primary schools introduce workforce reform, and the national collaboratives in the NHS are good examples of capacity building initiated by central government. But at other times the government seems to think that new structures alone will somehow magically resolve complex issues. In terms of bangs per buck, investing in capacity building offers the most effective route to sustained change.

Table 15.6: Pros and cons of different rates of change

	Pros	*Cons*
Big-bang change	• Challenges inertia • Can generate enthusiasm, momentum and innovation • Gets to the root of problems • Avoids the uncertainty of protracted change programmes • Can bring long-term service improvements	• Is costly to implement • May generate public and political rows • Normal business and service may suffer during period of change • Good and experienced staff walk away from the service
Incremental change	• Avoids stumbling into untested disasters • Facilitates learning as you go • Enables responses to be made to changing circumstances • Allows time for staff development • Service quality maintained during change	• May fail to generate change momentum • Inertia can set in • Staff become demoralised by uncertainty of process • Risk of fundamental problems not being addressed

Challenge 6: Harnessing the energy and commitment of public services professionals
The lack of systematic and sustained engagement with executive leaders is symptomatic of a wider problem. In his seminal book *Motivation, Agency and Public Policy*,[4] Julian Le Grand described public service professionals as either knights (public-spirited altruists) or knaves (self-interested egoists). The government has tended to talk as though professionals were knights, making much of devolving power to front-line professional leaders such as headteachers, police commanders and GPs. But it has tended to act as though

they were knaves. Performance management regimes have been onerous and the room for local discretion circumscribed; initiatives such as such as the NHS national service frameworks, the guidelines on prescribing by the National Institute for Health and Clinical Excellence, the literacy and numeracy strategies and the inspection regimes say to professionals: 'We don't trust your professional judgement and practice to get the improvements and results in public services that we want to see.' And that has been the central problem: public service reform has operated in a low-trust rather than a high-trust environment. Chief executives and headteachers have not been enabled or felt empowered to moderate and adapt national priorities to fit local circumstances.

The fault has not all been on the government's side. Standards of professional practice had not been as rigorous or challenging as they should have been – as the inquiry into child deaths at Bristol Royal Infirmary showed. As Charles Clarke highlights in Chapter 9, professional resistance to transparent accountability and performance regimes ran counter to the public's demand to know and to choose rather than just to trust what the professionals told them. Professions had become too rigid and it needed government action to modernise and enhance the role of nurses, teaching assistants and other para-professionals. Left to their own devices, professions are unlikely to have had the capacity to address either cross-agency failures such as child abuse management or the cross-cutting social exclusion agenda. And there is a limit to how far any government can sit back and let diversity for its own sake and professional autonomy flourish when it knows full well that certain ways of working are both more effective and more efficient.

However, public service reform in 2006 is not where it was in 1997. The government's reform programme needs to recognise that what brings public servants into their job and sustains them in their vocation is moral purpose: a commitment to make society a better place by making people well, keeping them safe or giving them the best start in life. The government should adjust its strategy and presume that professionals and public servants are knights until their actions make it impossible to maintain that policy. In other words it should move to a mode of working with much higher levels of trust.

The formulation of the first NHS five-year plan in 2000 showed that it was possible to do this and secure professional ownership of radical change and big service improvements. The schools' workforce agreement provides another example. The relatively new self-evaluation-based inspection regimes are also predicated on a much higher-trust model of inspection. Performance regimes with fewer targets based on outcomes would be another good move.

Of all the challenges the government faces with public service reform, the high-trust model is most demanding but it offers the biggest prize. If ministers can find ways of involving professions and their leaders in developing policy, and recognise and use the motivation that drives public servants, they might find this provides the elusive accelerator to faster reform.

Challenge 7: Communicating a more sophisticated approach towards public service reform

Whenever front-line managers complain to me about the latest government initiative to affect them I am sympathetic but explain that it is incredibly difficult for an existing or new minister to stand up and announce: 'Just keep up the good work. Continue doing what you are doing. I have no new initiatives to announce today.' The nature of today's media and society is that more of the same does not make news and does not satisfy a public that is used to seeing new brands, new lines, new offers and relaunches on a daily basis.

So those who believe there should be a more sophisticated and more consistent approach to public service reform need to acknowledge the communication challenge this gives ministers. However, the answer to this dilemma is not to make the case for reform, as ministers have been prone to do, by constantly highlighting the shortcomings of the current system or resort to initiative overload. That only feeds demoralisation within public services, undermines what has been achieved and throws doubt on whether increased public investment in public services is worth the candle. Politicians should not of course gloss over service weaknesses; rather they should move to a communication model that assumes that progress is based on learning.

It's not that we are expecting mistakes or cock-ups (indeed, as I have argued, policy making should be proactive so as to identify and reduce them) but that learning is integral to policy and service improvement – and will become all the more so as we increasingly use the market, devolve to localities, empower individuals and sponsor innovation. We need to move to a culture where continuous improvement is accepted as the norm and we are less defensive about having to make policy adjustments. If the evaluation of Sure Start showed, as it did, that the early impact was not as great as had been hoped, that did not invalidate the rationale for the project. Rather the research pinpointed the need for more discipline in using the approaches with parents and children that were shown to be most effective. The evaluation was seen as a setback for the government because (understandably, given the widespread local enthusiasm for the initiative) it had prematurely over-claimed on Sure Start's impact.

Communication based on a learning model does not solve every problem, since the nature of the media is to focus on difficulties rather than celebrate success. But a narrative that does not pretend that government is perfect or can solve every problem with an announcement will, over time, result in a better appreciation of what a government is trying to do – particularly if it is allied with independently assessed and published statistics on the performance of services.

Conclusion

The Labour Party was born against the background of a struggle between two conflicting approaches towards how best to achieve greater social justice. On one side were the syndicalists or – to use the language of Charles Clarke in Chapter 9 – social entrepreneurs, who believed in radical local action and innovation. And on the other were the Fabians, who favoured a more incrementalist and statist approach to reform. As Charles observes, that tension is, in a different form, still with us today and we need to combine both approaches to make progress – in other words, we need to govern more effectively to take advantage of what both approaches have to offer.

16

A healthy future?

Simon Stevens

This chapter considers some of the key challenges for health and health services over the coming decade. To what extent is the NHS as currently configured fit for the future? What are the wider influences that will shape the health debate? And what are some of the key changes now needed to embed a progressive approach to the people's health?

Future trends

What then are some of the main environmental forces that will shape British healthcare over the coming decade?

Social attitudes and lifestyle choices will have significant impacts on both the demand and supply of care. Half of deaths globally are caused by chronic conditions that are driven by lifestyle decisions concerning diet, exercise and smoking. And an ageing population means the availability of informal care from friends and family for older people is likely to diminish. This will be a major driver of cost in the formal health and social care system since the economic value of this largely invisible activity currently exceeds what is spent on NHS hospital care. Yet as the baby boomers age, the NHS will face much more assertive older patients than the World War II generation it has been used to supporting. They will expect – and demand – choices tailored to their distinctive needs and preferences.[1] This trend will be reinforced by the explosion in health information, which will alter the informational 'terms of trade' between patient and professional. But it will also place an increasing premium on synthesis and interpretation. (Enter 'breast cancer' as a search term in Google and you get 54 million links.) Attitudes will affect supply and demand in other ways too. Trust in science will shape the climate for medical research (will people be supportive, as they have been of stem cell research, or suspicious, as they were about the MMR vaccine?) and their subsequent uptake (will people demand the latest new medicine or resort to various forms of complementary 'faith healing'?).

Underpinning this attitudinal superstructure lies healthcare's economic and technological base. The UK's overall economic performance will be the principal driver of total healthcare spending, as the best predictor of what a country will spend on healthcare is how well its economy performs. Increases in individuals' discretionary spending on health and well-being services, broadly defined, are also likely.[2] Technology will drive changes in the geographical distribution of health services to a greater extent than planning decisions. The capital intensity of healthcare is likely to increase – the question is whether that is matched by increasing miniaturisation. If so, there will be more near-patient diagnosis and therapy in community settings. If not, high fixed costs will drive hospital regionalisation. Electronic health records will allow continuity of care even as NHS care is increasingly delivered by a range of providers. Telemonitoring will improve the economics of home-based care. And the extent to which new drugs are available over the counter from chemists without a prescription will help reshape the boundary between informal and self-funded care on the one hand, and formal tax-funded care on the other.

More broadly, globalisation will increasingly mean that it is no longer the case that 'all healthcare is local' – a slogan which has essentially captured reality for the last forty centuries or so. There are, of course, good grounds for scepticism about the prospects for early convergence in entitlement or rationing decisions between EU member countries. Even putting aside questions about the constitutional and political desirability of this approach, with the expansion of the EU to twenty-seven countries the spending differences between western Europe and the accession states is just too great. A harmonised healthcare 'benefits package' that would be acceptable in Germany is unaffordable in Slovakia, and what is affordable in Slovakia would be unacceptable in Germany.[3] However, globalisation will play out on a number of dimensions highly relevant to healthcare. Diseases (such as SARS and bird flu), drug treatments (across the European single market), health professionals (thanks to free movement of labour within most of the expanded EU), care providers (with the gradual inclusion of more health services within the scope of the European procurement and single market rules), health policies (evident in heightened media interest in international comparisons of health systems' performance and in recent NHS policies that borrow heavily from continental Europe on foundation trusts and patient choice)[4] and of course patients (with an activist European Court of Justice now affirming that patients have the legal right to choose publicly funded treatment abroad) will all migrate with increasing ease across national boundaries.

Current realities

If these are some of the challenges of the coming decade, just how future-proof is our actually existing model? How do these challenges compare with the issues the NHS has been grappling with over the past decade? And in leading this process, what has distinguished the Blair government from its post-war predecessors on health?

First, this was a government uniquely willing to confront the fact that the NHS had been significantly under-funded for decades, and to put taxes up to fund it.[5] Second, it was a government that understood that in the name of solidarity the NHS has to support aspiration; that it needs to win the support of each new generation, meaning that responsiveness to users and taxpayers has for the first time to be valued in its own right alongside the traditional public policy goals of efficiency and equity. And therefore third, it was a government willing to unleash high-octane reforms, often in the face of opposition from quite powerful defenders of the status quo.

What are the fruits of these labours? Cancer and heart disease deaths are down, at least partly through better NHS care. Waiting times are shorter than at any time since records began, with the maximum wait for NHS treatment set to fall from eighteen months in 1997 to just eighteen weeks in 2008. NHS staff shortages have been tackled: medical school places are up by 57 per cent and between 2000 and 2005 the NHS recruited an additional 128,000 full-time equivalent staff over and above the historic staffing trend growth.[6] There is greater transparency about the enormous variation in clinical quality and safety. And at least for the time being, the argument has been won about funding the NHS through tax – all the main parties now profess to believe this. There is bipartisan agreement on the need for an independent quality inspectorate and for the National Institute for Health and Clinical Excellence (NICE). And there is now similar agreement on service personalisation as an explicit policy objective with a tariff system, patient choice and provider plurality as drivers to deliver it. Indeed most of the important health reforms of the past decade have initially been greeted with hostility before within a year or two being absorbed into mainstream political opinion. It is therefore tempting to look back and wonder what all the noise was about.

Yet noise there was. That in turn partly explains why – as Table 16.1 shows – there has been a steady process of health policy adaptation over the course of a decade. It has proved politically necessary to sequence the reforms, using successive waves of 'burning platforms' to generate the requisite sense of urgency to overcome the weight of institutional inertia. This evolving process has also allowed the emphasis placed on individual policy mechanisms to shift over time, in the light of prior successes and failures, newly emerging policy risks, and insights from other countries' health reforms.[7]

Table 16.1: The English health policy journey 1997–2008 and beyond

Main perceived problem 1997–2000: underfunding and capacity shortages; variable quality of care

Policy response: +2.4% of GDP for the NHS; NICE, a healthcare inspectorate, national care 'blueprints' &

targets

Emerging risk 2002 onwards: input price inflation

Policy response: fixed unit output prices, contestable elective supply, patient choice

Emerging risk 2005 onwards: 'misshapen' output growth

Required policy response: stronger commissioning and refined incentives

2008–12: enhanced responsiveness, technical and allocative efficiency?

Many commentators have argued, however, that the NHS would have performed better if it had received steady real growth of, say, 4.5 per cent per annum over the last decade, rather than the famine/feast funding swings it was subject to in the 1990s and the 2000s, when real annual growth ranged from zero to more than 7 per cent. Indeed it was this prolonged under-funding – well into the new government's first term – that produced huge pent-up demand for new treatments, infrastructure updating through the private finance initiative and wage increases,[8] and which in turn meant that large funding increases matched by large pay rises were in practice politically unavoidable.[9]

To compound matters, the NHS would have been better able productively to absorb the sharp increase in investment it then received had the government managed to frontload implementation of the reform programme set out in the 2000 NHS Plan and more particularly the 2002 White Paper *Delivering the*

NHS Plan. While this would inevitably have generated yet more criticism from opponents of reform, it would probably have enabled a faster return on investment and a speedier transition from target-driven to incentive-driven improvement. (At a time when NHS deficits and hospital closures are again topical, it is also worth pointing out that it is not the English health reforms per se that are causing them: NHS over-spending was proportionately as large in Wales as in England, and hospital closures are as prevalent in Scotland as in England, despite both countries having deliberately rejected most of the English reforms – at least until very recently, when they have begun grudgingly to accept the real-world impact of patient choice and contestable supply on reducing NHS waiting times. It is also worth remembering that the NHS has been closing hospital beds pretty much continually since the day it was created: down from 480,000 in 1948 to around 170,000 now. In fact the rate of bed reductions has slowed markedly in recent years by comparison with the decade to 1997/8, when new treatment techniques meant 43,000 general and acute beds disappeared - equivalent to eighty-six district general hospitals.)

Challenges ahead

So, given the reform trajectory of the past decade, and the challenges of the coming one, what are some of the key debates and important next steps that progressives should be contemplating for the NHS in the coming period? Here we consider five of them, by no means an exhaustive list: how a rejuvenated NHS can contribute to broader social policy goals; the interconnectedness of lifestyles, health and inequalities; how to pay for healthcare; improved productivity as a route to NHS sustainability; and whether NHS 'independence' is either feasible or attractive.

How can the NHS make a wider contribution to national well-being?
Health is clearly valued in its own right. And as GDP per capita increases, societies reveal a preference for higher healthcare spending as a share of national income. However, unlike education spending, there is a tendency to regard healthcare spending exclusively as current consumption rather than partly as social investment. A related phenomenon is the tendency to under-play the positive economic consequences of a high-performing healthcare system. For progressives interested in giving life to the idea of a 'social investment state', the challenge is therefore to strengthen the positive

relationship between health and economic success. Over the coming decade, that should happen in three broad ways.

First, we should recognise the contribution healthcare can make to labour productivity across the economy as a whole. For current workers, sick leave generates significant costs to employers and employees. For potential workers, avoidable ill health excludes them from the labour market, creating poverty, social dislocation and the need for transfer payments and other fiscal burdens. The NHS should therefore be required to play a far wider role through timely and proactive rehabilitation in supporting people on incapacity benefit to re-enter the labour market. And as Richard Layard has argued, it should take more seriously its role in mental health, depression and anxiety-related disorders.

Second, we should consider the economic multiplier effects of well-targeted healthcare spending. Healthcare systems produce economic effects not just by drawing in financial resources and producing healthcare outputs, but also by procuring inputs in product and labour markets, meaning that healthcare systems' buying power can be used to advance social objectives such as environmentally friendly production, as well as developing biomedical R&D partnerships to boost knowledge-intensive sectors of the economy.

Third, we should deploy healthcare interventions in support of wider public policy objectives: for example, expanding the availability of NHS treatment for people with drug and alcohol addictions. This is not only the right thing to do for the individuals and their families; it also produces positive knock-ons for local communities in terms of reduced crime and reoffending. And we should become more evidence based in the deployment of community nursing and child psychology resources to support children's development and the 'production of future citizens' – for example through redesigned Sure Start and school-based programmes.

Lifestyle, health and inequalities
When it comes to future health risks, obesity is the new smoking. Children may be 20 per cent of our population but – as the slogan goes – they are 100 per cent of our future. The Department of Health believes that by 2010 1.7 million of them will be obese. The downstream result will be diabetes, cardiovascular disease, osteoarthritis and cancer. Some have suggested this coming generation could therefore live shorter lives than their parents. The problem is that tackling this issue will be incredibly hard. No country has ever managed sustained reductions in obesity other than in times of war or

famine.[10] And many commonsense propositions – for example exercise programmes for young children – often turn out not to work.[11] The gap between rhetoric and reality, between ends and means, between generalised anxiety and concretely effective action, is probably greater in the case of public health than almost any other aspect of public policy.

Of course important work has been done over the past decade on the broader determinants of health inequalities (cutting long-term unemployment, poverty and social exclusion) and on the social context for lifestyle decisions (banning tobacco advertising, smoke-free workplaces and, belatedly, action to control children's access to junk food). Impressive gains have continued to be made in the major causes of avoidable death and illness (cancer, cardiovascular disease, mental health problems). However, a large part of the problem is that it is also necessary to influence those groups often least interested in their health-related behaviour. And underlying this challenge is the traditional ideological split on health inequalities. On the one hand is the 'pull yourself together, Carruthers' school of thought. Eat apples, go jogging and get a grip. Adherents of this view legitimately point out that up to half of the class difference in life expectancy is now explained simply by differential smoking rates. On the other hand, there is the belief (still lurking in the odd university faculty of public health) that nothing less than the overthrow of advanced industrial capitalism will suffice. Anything else is sordid compromise. Oddly enough, both polemics have therefore been profoundly disabling in the sense that if it's all just down to individuals the answer is presumably just to let them get on with it, or if it's all on hold until the Trotskyite revolution then anything short of manning the barricades is a pointless diversion.

Where do the public stand on this debate? One answer is provided by the NICE Citizens Council. They are a group of thirty people drawn from all walks of life, including an electrician from Widnes, a singer from Bristol, a fitness instructor from Derby, a Birmingham shop assistant, a scaffolder, a stay-at-home parent, a football referee and two unemployed people. In their report on health inequalities they debate the trade-offs between improving the health of the whole population versus concentrating resources on the most disadvantaged to try and narrow the health gap, even if overall population health is then lower than it would have been.[12] While they did not reach a clear-cut answer, their views probably accurately reflect important strands of public opinion. They variously considered that:

- 'The gap between advantaged and disadvantaged is society's problem and too big for the NHS.'

- 'We should help the disadvantaged now because having to do so at some future point will be less cost effective.'
- 'The NHS is there to serve, not to restructure society.'
- 'There's no point in pouring resources into groups that make bad choices.'
- 'Targeting social group five or ethnic groups may mean fewer resources for broader public health measures with a greater dividend.'
- 'Disadvantage is a social and political problem, not an NHS or health one – improving the health of the disadvantaged is better done through employment, economic regeneration etc.'
- 'It's better to encourage people to improve than imposing it on them.'

One point of agreement was on the importance of the co-production of health by patients as active participants. And this represents a critical insight about what needs to change in healthcare. But to have any real-world impact it needs to be matched by a tangible set of processes that bring that insight to bear. Alongside the more assertive use of regulatory and fiscal instruments and the selective testing of targeted conditionality, probably the most important challenge facing health policy makers over the coming decade is therefore systematically to import and adopt insights from other social sectors and consumer-orientated businesses on how to stimulate and support individual health-related behaviour change. It will mean incentivising healthcare providers differently, and holding NHS commissioners – the primary care trusts (PCTs) – to account for their population's stock of health risk, not just the annual flow of healthcare consumption.

Even then the NHS is not off the hook. Arguably its single greatest failure in respect of health inequalities lies in its failure to ensure good quality primary care in the poorest communities. As a result poorer NHS patients have greater difficulty finding a GP, getting in to see him or her,[13] and even when they do they are more likely to have major health conditions under-diagnosed and inadequately treated (see Figure 16.1). So as one academic has calculated, a 1 per cent improvement in GP care will do more to improve the health of the British population than a 50 per cent improvement in teaching hospital care.[14]

How has this situation been allowed to persist? Here are four reasons. First, because the average quality of general practice in this country is very high, it has been allowed to obscure – or even excuse – an entrenched minority of poor performers. Second, and relatedly, only in the last few years, through prescribing quality markers, the Quality and Outcomes Framework (QOF) and other emerging measures, has it been possible to get inside the 'black box' that is quality of primary care. Third, partly because of this lack of transparency, patient expectations in poorer areas have often been too low. And fourth, the absence of alternative potential providers in poorer areas has meant that the local NHS has been worried about upsetting the apple cart – almost regardless of the quality of the apples.

Figure 16.1: Quality of primary care for patients with diabetes by levels of deprivation.

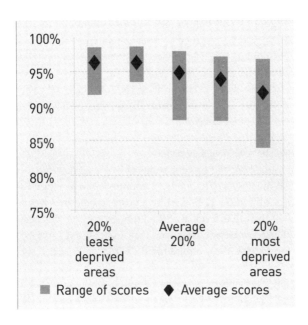

Note: The chart shows the range of GP practices' quality scores for diabetes on the Quality and Outcomes Framework, by deprivation quintile. The diamond shows the average (median) score. The bar shows how the scores vary between the 10 per cent of practices scoring highest and the 10 per cent of practices scoring lowest for each type of area.
Source: *State of Healthcare 2006* (London: Healthcare Commission, 2006)

'In South Shields . . . there were 4,100 persons per doctor, in Bath 1,590; in Dartford nearly 3,000 and in Bromley 1,620. That distribution of general practitioners throughout the country is most hurtful to the health of our people.' So declared Aneurin Bevan in 1946. And yet sixty years later it remains the case today that some PCTs have only half the number of GPs per needs-weighted unit population than others. In these areas, the existing small-business model of general practice has persistently failed to ensure uniformly high standard of care, with appalling consequences for health inequalities. And, adding insult to injury, a 20 per cent increase in the number of GPs between 1985 and 2003 did not lead to a more equal distribution.[15] So what is now needed is the same energy shown in transforming elective surgery to be deployed in bringing in new high-quality providers of primary care, particularly in poorer communities, and on an 'industrial' scale. It is time to insist that every practice vacancy is openly tendered; that the systematic contractual and funding biases in favour of poorly performing incumbents is translated into a level playing field; and that the barriers to entry for new providers of free, list-based NHS primary care are removed. The time for pilots and case studies is long since past; the poorest people in England are paying the price for past hesitation.

Paying for healthcare: how should we do it?

The richer a country is, the more it wants to – and in fact does – spend on healthcare. But there is no 'free lunch'. A country has to pay for its healthcare, however it raises the money. In western European countries this is mostly a collective rather than an individual choice, though it is true that the UK raises a slightly higher proportion collectively than most. From this risk pool, the healthy pay for the sick, the young support the old, and the rich subsidise the poor.

Risk-pooling mechanisms in western Europe mostly comprise two alternatives: general taxation ('Beveridge' countries) and mandatory employer-based social insurance ('Bismarckian' systems). Although the government chose to use an increase in social insurance – employers' national insurance – as its preferred route for raising NHS spending in 2002, it remains an article of faith in Britain that a tax-based system is preferable. The irony for the left is that had a version of Lloyd George's 1911 social insurance system continued, the French and German examples suggest that our post-war public spending on healthcare would have been several percentage points of GDP higher, producing more free healthcare and greater responsiveness to patients. However, looking ahead twenty years to a time when the dependency ratio will be increasing and self-employment may be on the rise, there seem few attractions to the UK of increasing the share of health expenditure levied as a payroll deduction. And in an era when British employers are struggling to meet their pension obligations it seems implausible that they would want to shoulder new financing responsibilities for their employees' healthcare, equivalent to perhaps 4–5 per cent of GDP.

There are, however, two features of (some versions of) social insurance that arguably offer policy advantages. Healthcare funding levels are more transparent to individuals, in that social insurance is a form of hypothecation. And in a number of countries, individuals also have a choice of social insurer, which potentially has a double benefit: it allows citizens to choose different types of benefit level, and it generates consumer pressure on the 'commissioners' or purchasers of care to raise their game. The new Dutch social insurance system is perhaps the best example of this high-equity, high-responsiveness model, in which individuals get to choose between competing social health insurers.

Could these features be incorporated in a tax-based NHS, creating the best of both worlds? Here are three future reforms of how we pay for healthcare that would get us some of the way towards that synthesis.

First, it is possible to envisage a system in which the NHS moved to a notionally funded rather than 'pay as you go' basis, with a set of independent trustees who reported to Parliament annually on the extent to which the 'contribution rate' from taxpayers was actuarially sufficient to meet likely future funding requirements. The Medicare Trustees in the United States provide one example of how this could work. A new fiscal rule could be added to the current Treasury set requiring the government to account for net healthcare liabilities on its balance sheet, in rather the same way that firms are now required to do for their pensions liabilities. While by no means a watertight solution, in the real world it might make it politically harder for future governments over extended periods surreptitiously to under-fund future healthcare liabilities without a proper national debate about the consequences.

Second, there is no reason in principle why a tax-funded NHS cannot be combined with a system in which patients choose their 'commissioner' (PCT). The potential advantages are obvious in terms of offering citizens with different needs and preferences choice of alternative combinations of health benefits. As importantly, in principle this could serve as a dynamic mechanism driving all commissioners to raise their game, and over time allowing the best commissioners to play an expanding role on behalf of their growing number of NHS patient 'members' – potentially a far more effective route to spreading best practice than the current system of monopoly PCTs, even when coupled with periodic reorganisations used as a crude and demonstrably unsuccessful mechanism for trying to weed out under-performers.

Traditionally the main policy question about this approach has been whether it is possible to 'risk adjust' the commissioners' budgets to fairly reflect the underlying health needs of their members, without on the one hand under-compensating commissioners with sicker patients, or on the other hand over-rewarding them for having failed to improve those same patients' health. However there are encouraging signs that the science behind risk adjustment has now improved to such a point that the potential efficiency gains from competing commissioners outweigh these possible efficiency losses. More to the point, we now have a real-world experiment from which we can apply lessons as they emerge, in the form of the Dutch health reforms that since 1 January 2006 have gone down this route. If that and other examples turn out to be positive, the NHS in England should consider a similar approach.[16]

Third, in the meantime it is crucial that the NHS demand-side commissioning function is strengthened relative to the newly liberalised provider supply side. This should now be done by periodically franchising the management of individual PCTs (which would nevertheless remain statutory NHS entities accountable to the Health Secretary). They would be responsible for structuring devolved commissioning budgets to those groups of GPs both interested and competent to take on these responsibilities, and of course for commissioning primary care itself. Since the franchising approach covers defined populations, it overcomes any issue with patient risk selection, while allowing more successful commissioning teams and organisations to take on a bigger role on behalf of NHS patients. Over time networks or chains of NHS commissioning management organisations would probably develop, thereby also overcoming the current 'talent trap' problem and inability to scale.

In the meantime, no major political party is arguing that the NHS needs more money or different ways of raising money. Which, since they are all apparently (re)committed to tax-funded healthcare, is just as well, given the hard economic fact that there is very limited headroom for more tax funding immediately after 2008. So through a combination of conviction and necessity, there is now a consensus that the immediate challenge is to generate more value out of the large budgetary increases the NHS has already received. How might that be achieved?

Getting more healthcare bangs for our buck: the coming productivity challenge
First, let's clarify terms. As well as 'technical efficiency' – that is the costs of producing a given output – we are also concerned with 'allocative efficiency' – that is getting the right mix of outputs so as to maximise health gain. And too often the claim that NHS productivity is falling is misunderstood to mean that NHS output is not rising despite the extra cash. That claim is untrue. What is at issue is whether output is expanding faster than the new cash, and the answer is that it is probably not. Of course there are real problems with the definition of NHS productivity: a new drug that reduces emergency hospital admissions would conventionally be deemed to have caused a reduction in measured output per unit cost and hence a productivity decrement. However, even taking account of these concerns, the latest refinements to the NHS productivity measure added a mere 0.8 per cent uplift.[17] So there is a real issue.

Indeed, the productivity of the NHS will increasingly affect the productivity of the UK economy as a whole. As healthcare heads towards 10 per cent of GDP, sub-optimal productivity in the health sector will have a bigger impact on overall standards of living and crowd out other valued social programmes and/or personal spending. This point is underlined by an analysis produced by Cabinet Office and Treasury officials (see Table 16.2), which suggested that by 2023 total health spending might range from 9.9 per cent of GDP to 14.5 per cent. But it also calculated that this will be overwhelmingly driven by the extent to which the NHS can raise its productivity as against lifestyle and public health changes. Specifically, the study calculated that if levels of healthy lifestyles in the population were 'low' as against 'high' that would merely add 0.9 per cent of GDP to total health spending by 2023, whereas flat NHS productivity gains of 2 per cent a year would add a whopping 3.7 per cent of GDP to healthcare costs by 2023.[18]

Yet it is not obvious for example that the pay reforms of the last few years have succeeded in stimulating labour productivity.[19] In part this is because of a reluctance to acknowledge one of the shared insights of socialism and neo-liberalism: that healthcare workers have interests as workers, and that, notwithstanding staff's generally principled motivations, these interests will influence attitudes and behaviour. So how might labour productivity be improved? The NHS tariff system will help, as NHS hospitals will no longer be able to pass on excess labour cost inflation to their purchasers.[20] That in turn means hospitals need more flexibility to decide pay rates, at the regional if not the 'plant' level. Indeed part of the problem historically is that the NHS – on the back of both national pay negotiations and the review bodies – has tended to under-pay nurses and other staff at the peak of the labour market cycle and in more expensive parts of the country, and over-pay in the opposite circumstances. The answer is not therefore to impose crude central pay caps. Instead, NHS foundation trusts should club together to determine pay regionally or sub-regionally, as they are legally empowered to do; hospitals should begin to experiment innovatively with QOF-type arrangements for their clinicians; and PCTs should simply periodically recontract for primary care services at the local competitive market rate.

Table 16.2: The impact of different productivity and health scenarios on predicted healthcare spending as a share of GDP in 2023

Unit cost productivity growth % p.a.	Level of health-seeking behaviours, self-care and lifestyle responsibility		
	Low	Medium	High
0	14.5	13.8	13.2
1.0	12.5	11.9	11.4
1.5	11.5	11.1	10.6
2.0	10.8	10.3	9.9

Source: *Health Strategy Review: Analytical Report* (Cabinet Office Strategy Unit, 2002), p. 78.

But better aligning staff incentives within NHS-provided care is only part of the story. What is also needed is a broader use of more sophisticated financial and non-financial incentives, to supplement reliance on traditional collegial and hierarchical approaches. This is an approach which appears to be paying off well in those areas where it has so far been tried – namely to help drive reductions in NHS waiting times. There is good reason to believe that it is the introduction – or more precisely, the promise to introduce – patient choice, a tariff system and new surgical providers that has been responsible for the major falls in NHS waiting times (see Figure 16.2). This is because the effect has been greatest where the threat of competition has been most concrete (for example, witness the stimulus to new working practices in diagnostics). This hypothesis is also consistent with the international experience, as reported in Scandinavia and in a wide-ranging OECD study, of why some countries have short waits.[21] And in practice this combination of new policies had the effect of inverting the incentive on hospitals so that short waits were financially rewarded – where previously long waits had served as their 'order book', had comprised an implicit bid for more funding, and had signalled to patients the benefits of paying privately.

Figure 16.2: Number of patients waiting more than 6 months for inpatient treatment, England

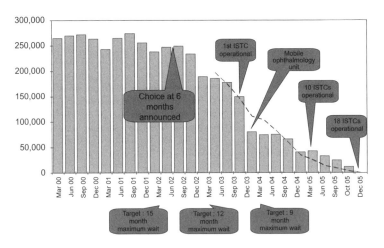

Source: Department of Health, July 2006

Of course right-wing ideologues depict the NHS as the healthcare version of the North Korean planned economy. Left-wing romantics – and those trying to appeal to them – (pre)tend to agree, delighting in the idea of the NHS as an autarkic peninsula in a raging sea of capitalism, where workers' motivations are pure and markets have no dominion. But the reality is different. NHS care is produced by employing staff in labour markets, and buying goods and services – such as GP services, drug treatments and some surgical operations – in product markets. According to the Office of National Statistics, the NHS currently spends 46 per cent of its funding in labour markets and a further 52 per cent in product markets. So the demotic 'anti-marketisation' slogan unwinds into a fairly prosaic argument about the balance of inputs to be sourced in labour markets versus product markets. Certainly as far as the labour market is concerned, no one seems to be arguing for the non-market alternative, namely forced labour and NHS conscription. And in the actually existing NHS, inputs sourced in labour markets as against product markets correspond to no obvious ideological distinction – certainly not the often favoured 'clinical' versus 'non-clinical' categorisation. Take primary care as an example – typically regarded by patients as the core of what the NHS is and does. As a Labour MP put it in a Commons debate recently:

> Most patients go to their GP – in the vast majority of cases a private partnership, are given a prescription that they take to their local high street pharmacy – a private business, and are then given a drug from a private drug company. That is accessed free at the point of delivery, funded by the public purse, but provided by a range of providers – so I am not quite sure what [the] argument is.[22]

The public agree. A 2006 *Guardian*/ICM poll found that 70 per cent of the public – and even more interestingly, 73 per cent of Labour supporters – believe private companies should be able to provide care for NHS patients. What's more, support for this policy is remarkably consistent across social classes and throughout the country.[23] So in place of crude targets and central instruction, we need a system in which patients exercising a meaningful degree of choice are actively supported in their role as co-producers of their own health, and in which providers can innovate and clinicians can lead. The point is not that co-operation and contestability are opposites; it is that the degree of contestability of supply influences the terms on which co-operation will occur. Without that stimulus, progressives in practice resign themselves to the status quo, lacking a meaningful account of power inside our major public institutions and how it might be redistributed in favour of citizens and consumers.

An independent NHS?

Does the notion of an NHS independent from Whitehall offer a route map for achieving that redistribution of power? Let us immediately dispense with one objection to the 'independence' idea: the claim that (a) because in a tax-funded system the NHS and politics are at some deep level inseparable, (b) the status quo is inevitable. Well, (a) is correct but (b) isn't. Certainly anyone who thinks a sector that constitutes nearly a tenth of the British economy, let alone one so interconnected with the eternal debate on taxation levels, can be entirely insulated from politics is living in cloud cuckoo land. But the real question is: just because some things are bound to be party political (tax funding levels), does it mean everything has to be (individual dropped bedpans)? Or can we reframe the set of health policy issues over which the political process plays out? Can we, in other words, insert some circuit breakers between politicians and care delivery, so that we nudge the NHS a bit further along the politicised–depoliticised spectrum?

And at a time when NHS 'independence' is being debated somewhat hazily, it is worth recalling that numerous functions traditionally overseen by health ministers are already now undertaken at arm's length from the Department of Health: independent quality inspection is carried out by the Healthcare Commission, rationing decisions by NICE, foundation trust governance by Monitor, board appointments by the Appointments Commission and pay negotiations by the NHS Confederation.[24] NHS foundation trusts[25] – said on their creation to herald the end of the NHS – have quietly got on with improving patient care; they now have more 'citizen members' than any of the national political parties.

However, what we do not need is NHS 'independence' understood as an attempt to convert it into some sort of arm's-length hospital national management board – a 1970s British Leyland-style nationalised industry or a stereotyped version of the BBC.[26] The de facto creation of an inward-looking and unresponsive provider monopoly, even accompanied by the inevitable but gimmicky appointment of a few business types to an NHS 'supervisory board', would be an act of recentralisation masquerading as the granting of freedom. By itself it would remove accountability to politicians without adding any to patients. It would therefore produce more inflation, a return to longer waiting times, services organised around the most powerful vested interests, a strictly limited regard for patients' preferences and a progressively disillusioned public. Nor, based on the international evidence, should we be too optimistic about an alternative model that passes responsibility for commissioning health services to local government while continuing to locate responsibility for revenue raising with central government. Australia, Canada and the United States all demonstrate the confused political accountabilities, cost shifting and buck passing that such split federal/provincial health systems tend to engender.

Instead, the right way to generate the trust and transparency that independence is designed to achieve is through a three-fold strategy. First, depoliticise key aspects of regulation, so that key functions such as rationing, inspection, foundation trust regulation, tariff setting, and pro-competitive provider cartel-busting are all conducted at arm's length from the executive. Second, strengthen the commissioning in the manner described above. And third, grant NHS hospitals local operational independence simply by converting them into foundation trusts – immune from Whitehall tinkering.[27]

This in turn needs to be supplemented by a genuinely level playing field in which any willing provider that can meet NHS standards and supply at the NHS rate is empowered to do so.

In short, the reason for the confusion over NHS independence is its elastic meaning. The answer is to think of a more, rather than a fully, independent NHS, and to think of independence as an attribute not of some sort of monolithic nationalised industry but instead of key national regulatory functions (perhaps accompanied by a new 'constitution' framing their roles and accountabilities to Parliament), the commissioning process and the operation of a plural supply side.

And finally...

What might all this mean for the NHS as an institution? Indeed what is the NHS? It has variously been described as a religion, a garage, a brand or a set of values, and a post-war compromise between capital and labour. Nor is the NHS the third biggest employer in the world, after the Chinese army and Indian Railways (as I was taught on starting work for the NHS two decades ago). Wal-Mart is far bigger. Major oil companies have larger revenues. And the biggest tax-funded health system is in fact Medicare in the United States. So no, the NHS is not uniquely complex or unreformable. And as this chapter has sought to argue, the next stage of those reforms needs – among other things – to emphasise the wider economic contribution the NHS can make to national well-being; to get serious about patients as co-producers of their own health; to inject new sophistication into the commissioning function; to open up primary care as a way of tackling entrenched health inequalities; to incentivise productivity in new ways; and to enact a new institutional settlement for the NHS.

But the NHS is clearly about more than health or indeed healthcare. It is a psychological compact with the British people. It produces not just health services but reassurance: reassurance that care will be available when you and your family need it. That in turn requires the NHS in all it does to embody the attributes of timeliness, reliability, compassion and respect. Rather than believing that the health sector can be inoculated against the changing expectations of society, while continuing to embody paternalism masquerading as solidarity, it has to recognise that a tax-funded system exists only with the consent of the people, and that in turn requires a new premium on institutional listening, adapting and learning. It is still the case, ten years into a major reform programme, that too many services are organised around the convenience of the institution rather than the individual. In respect of the 'cradle', women still lack meaningful choices and control over childbirth. In respect of the 'grave', four fifths of terminally ill patients still die in hospital when half want to die at home. These, then, will continue to be the touchstones against which to judge whether NHS reform is succeeding. Because progressives always lose when citizens are forced to choose between solidarity and responsiveness. To succeed, the NHS has to offer both.

17

Education, education, education
The next decade

Robert Hill

Young people today are doing better at school and achieving more than any of their predecessors. Those who hark back to an illusory golden age of learning conveniently overlook that it was only a generation or so ago that a full education was the preserve of a privileged few. In the early 1960s less than a fifth of pupils took O-levels and just 5 per cent of eighteen-year-olds went into higher education. Today's education story is truly one of progress and advance.

But alongside that progress there are also big challenges which come from continuing weaknesses within the education system, from the changing nature of society and technology, from rising expectations of schooling and from the growing competition of a global economy. This chapter argues that to meet these challenges we have to redesign our school and college system from top to bottom to meet the particular and individual needs of each pupil. This will involve making fundamental changes to the curriculum, to the way we conceive of teaching and learning, to the role of school leadership, to our approach to school improvement and to accountability and funding arrangements. Even these will not by themselves be enough. Success will also require us fully to harness the energy and commitment of students and the contribution of parents and employers.

How much progress has been made?

'Education, education, education' was Tony Blair's rallying cry. And ten years on his government has made a substantial difference, most significantly in educational outcomes but also to just about every aspect of our school and college system.[1] In terms of outcomes, as Table 17.1 shows, during Labour's period in government pupils have made sustained improvements in core subjects at both age eleven and age fourteen. The literacy and numeracy strategies have helped to raise standards of attainment.

Table 17.1: Key Stage 2 and 3 tests, 1997 and 2006

	% of pupils achieving level 4 English at KS2	% of pupils achieving level 4 maths at KS2	% of pupils achieving level 4 science at KS2	% of pupils achieving level 5 English at KS3	% of pupils achieving level 5 maths at KS3	% of pupils achieving level 5 science at KS3
1997	63	62	68	67	60	60
2006	79	75	87	72	77	72

Note: At the end of each Key Stage the government assesses and tracks the performance of all pupils in English, maths and science. At Key Stage 1 (age 7), 2 (age 11) and 3 (age 14) an expected level of performance is defined for each of the subjects: at KS1 it is level 2, at KS2 it is level 4, and at KS3 it is level 5. Study in pre-school settings and in reception classes is covered by the Early Years Foundation Stage.

Source: Office of National Statistics/Department for Education and Skills

The proportion of fifteen-year-olds gaining five good GCSEs has risen from 46.3 per cent to 59 per cent since 1997 and the percentage of pupils whose five A★–C grades include English and maths is also up, by more than 9 points since 1997. There are now around only sixty schools out of around 3,500 where fewer than a quarter of pupils have achieved five or more A★–C grades – down from more than 600 in 1997.

Significantly for a Labour government, there has also been some narrowing of the attainment gap between the most deprived and least deprived.[2] For example, since 1999 the proportion of pupils in the most deprived schools obtaining five or more good GCSEs and equivalents has increased by 23 percentage points compared to 4 percentage points in the least deprived. At Key Stage 2 the attainment gap between the most and least deprived schools in terms of the numbers achieving level 4 has decreased by 10 percentage points in English and 7 points in maths.

Improvements in educational outcomes may be the ultimate test of a system but there has also been progress in other areas as well. The introduction of free nursery education for three- and four-year-olds has been a success in terms of the education value it has added.[3] And at the other end of the school age range there has also been progress with tackling one of the UK's most intractable educational problems – participation rates in education and training post-sixteen. In 1998, among OECD countries, only Mexico and Turkey had a lower proportion of their 15–19-year-olds enrolled in education than the UK. However, by 2004 participation in this country had moved close to the OECD average[4] and since then the introduction of education maintenance allowances for sixteen-year-olds has seen further improvements.

Teaching has once again been turned into a high-value profession with a reformed career structure which includes innovative routes in, such as the Graduate Teacher Programme and Teach First. Workforce reform has freed teachers from a wide range of bureaucratic tasks, enabling them to focus more on lesson planning and the quality of teaching. The huge growth in teaching assistants and other support staff such as ICT specialists, sports coaches and learning mentors has resulted in pupils getting more support either in small groups or on a one-to-one basis. The creation of the National College for School Leadership and the introduction of the National Professional Qualification for Headship have helped drive improvements in the quality of school leadership. Thousands of schools have been repaired or rebuilt (it is easy to forget the state to which decades of under-investment had reduced them by 1997) and with the Building Schools for the Future scheme the government has embarked on the most ambitious secondary school renovation and redevelopment programme that has been seen anywhere in the world.

Another area where Britain is a world leader is in information and communication technology (ICT). In 2004 Ofsted reported that ICT resources were at record levels, 'comparing very well with other countries'.[5] And a combination of increasing access to personal computers in the classroom combined with laptops for teachers and broadband connections in all schools has seen 'the competence of staff in ICT increase dramatically' since 1997 with commensurate 'improvements in pupils' achievements'. More recently, interactive whiteboards have become 'prevalent in schools and colleges', enabling teachers to harness the resources of the internet for subject teaching.[6]

Perhaps the most under-sold achievement has been the creation of a more diverse secondary school system. The 'bog standard' comprehensive, if it ever existed, is largely no more. Three quarters of secondary schools now have specialist status – which has made a substantial difference to the ethos, the performance and the quality of teaching and learning in these schools.[7] Around a third of all secondary schools, through having foundation or aided status, now own their land, mange their assets and employ their own staff. The growth of federations and partnerships of schools is bringing new dynamism and variety to school organisation. Academies are bringing aspiration and progress to areas which for generations have been written off in educational terms, and the introduction of trust schools will add yet more diversity to the system.

It is important to chronicle this progress since 1997. Big challenges remain and further reforms are needed. But it is inaccurate – not to say demoralising for teachers and students – to characterise the education system as failing. The progress that has been made is widely admired in many parts of the world.

Significant problems remain

But despite the improvements there are still a range of significant problems to address:

- Progress in raising attainment in some areas has stalled – at Key Stage 2 the proportion of pupils achieving level 4 or above in 2006 has risen over the past two years by just 1 percentage point in English and by 2 percentage points in maths. At Key Stage 3 the percentage of pupils achieving level 5 or above in reading, writing and maths combined is at the same level as in 2005.
- There is a big gender gap in the relative achievement of boys and girls. Sixty-three per cent of girls are gaining five good GCSEs compared with just 53 per cent of boys. And at age fourteen there is a gap in all the core subjects but it is particularly acute when it comes to reading and writing skills, as Table 17.2 shows. And behind the headline figures lies another disturbing fact: white working-class boys are doing particularly poorly. In 2003 just over one third of white boys on free school meals achieved the expected level 5 at Key Stage 3 – around half the number for white boys not receiving free school meals.[8]
- There are substantial disparities between the achievements of pupils from ethnic minority backgrounds and white pupils, although progress is starting to be made in closing the attainment gap among some minority groups. Slightly less than 56 per cent of white pupils achieved five good GCSEs in 2005 compared with just 42 per cent of black Caribbean students. In the same year the proportion of Pakistani pupils achieving level 4 in English at Key Stage 2 was more than 12 percentage points behind white pupils.

Table 17.2: Percentage of pupils achieving level 5 or above in Key Stage 3 tests in 2006

	Boys	Girls
English	65	80
Reading	59	74
Writing	69	83
Maths	76	77
Science	71	73

Source: National Statistics/Department for Education and Skills

- Pupils receiving free school meals (which acts as a proxy measure for deprivation) are falling further behind other pupils at age fifteen.[9] This trend applies to both the most deprived and the least deprived schools. So although many of the most deprived schools are doing better overall, they are not yet successfully equipping those students who most need help from the education system to get the start in life they deserve.

- There are differential rates of improvement in different parts of the country. Some local authorities are working with their schools much more effectively than others to raise attainment. Between 1997 and 2005 the proportion of pupils in Tower Hamlets achieving the expected level in English at Key Stage 3 rose by 34 percentage points to 67 per cent. Over the same period the corresponding figure in Cornwall only rose by 15 points to 65 per cent. There was also a 12-point gap in the rate of improvement for maths.

- Children in care are let down badly by the education and care system. In 2005 only 11 per cent of children in care obtained five good GCSEs, compared with 56 per cent overall.

- There is still a significant tail of schools that are failing their pupils. At the end of August 2006, 208 schools were in 'special measures' – the most serious category of under-achievement. A further 446 were classified by Ofsted as requiring 'significant improvement', having 'serious weaknesses', 'under-achieving' or having 'inadequate sixth forms'.

- Student participation in subjects important to the economic competitiveness of the country is worryingly low. In the first year that modern foreign languages ceased to be compulsory at Key Stage 4, participation in language learning fell by 15 per cent. There has been a steady long-term decline in the numbers studying physics and chemistry at A-level. The fall in A-level entries for maths has been reversed but, as with languages and science, there is still a severe shortage of specialist subject teachers. The Smith inquiry estimated in 2004 that there was a shortfall of around 3,400 specialist maths teachers in maintained secondary schools in England.[10]

- There is a huge gulf to bridge if the government is to build on the improvement in post-sixteen participation and prepare a system that can cater for all sixteen- and seventeen-year-olds being in education and training – which is its declared intention.

- School leadership is not as strong as it needs to be and recruitment remains a major concern, particularly in the light of the impending demographic downturn. During 2005/6 one in four primary schools and a fifth of secondary schools in England failed to appoint heads after advertising vacancies. And behind those statistics lie even more worrying figures about the ageing profile of headteachers and the low number of applicants for posts. There are also serious concerns about the calibre of school leaders in the primary sector. Many of them have struggled to adjust to workforce reform and there are growing doubts about their capacity to take forward the curriculum and standards agenda alongside the challenges they face in relation to implementing big changes in early-years education, childcare and extended schools.

Underlying weaknesses

Underlying these specific problems are some bigger and more fundamental weaknesses which the education system is not yet properly or fully addressing.

Schools are not geared up to meet the future education and skills needs of the country
Lord Leitch's review on the skills challenge facing the UK looked ahead to the education and skills levels the country would require in 2020.[11] It highlighted how India and China together produced around four million graduates each year, compared with 600,000 in the UK, and argued that while growth in emerging economies does not come at the expense of growth in developed countries, 'the UK must ensure it is a world leader in skills or risk not reaping the full benefits of high value-added industries or new technologies'. Moreover highly qualified students from China and India are not just coming through in large volumes but are motivated and inclined towards creativity

and entrepreneurship.

As well as a need to increase the proportion of the population with high-level skills, the report also charted the polarised nature of the country's qualifications profile. More than a quarter of the population now has a high-level qualification of some kind, but at the other end of the scale 35 per cent have either low-level qualifications or none at all – more than double the figure in Japan, Sweden and Canada. And despite the massive expansion in university places, those from the top three social classes are almost three times as likely to enter higher education as those from the bottom three. In large part this is due to what the OECD has described as the UK's 'high excellence, low equity' schools system. Others pinpoint the academic/vocational divide as the underlying cause of the problem – a problem that has its roots in the Butler Education Act of 1944.

The scale of the challenge is reflected in the fact that by 2014 two thirds of jobs will be filled by those with at least intermediate skills and by 2020 more than 40 per cent of jobs may be filled by graduates. These projections present our schools and colleges with an urgent wake-up call. The standards and aspirations to which we have been working may seem demanding but over the next decade we must raise them further if as a nation we are to be competitive economically. We have to address these issues now. The children starting school today will be those that will be going into higher education or the labour market in 2020.

Employers are not getting the skilled workforce they require
Educationalists get impatient when employers say that school leavers are coming to them without the right skills – their response is that employers should do more to develop their workforce. There is some truth in that criticism but the views of employers cannot be dismissed so easily. A survey undertaken for the Department for Education and Skills by the CBI showed that just under a third of employers encounter problems with literacy among new non-graduate recruits either 'frequently' or 'almost always'.[12] For numeracy the corresponding figure was over a quarter. These results accord very closely with findings from the Learning and Skills Council (LSC)'s national employers' skills survey in 2005.

It is important to understand what employers are looking for: a grasp of grammar and spelling, legible handwriting, and abilities in understanding quantitative data in tables, doing mental arithmetic, calculating percentages without resorting to a calculator and spotting rogue figures. The government is introducing functional maths and English tests but at present fewer than half of all pupils are achieving a functional level 2 qualification in these subjects at fifteen.

Employers' problems are not limited to a lack of basic skills among school leavers. The LSC's work on vacancies and skills shortages shows that as well as technical and job-specific skills, employers are identifying problems with more generic skills covering areas such as oral communication, customer handling, team working and problem solving. As Sir Mike Tomlinson observed in his report, the school system is not doing enough to equip young people with what he called the 'common knowledge, skills and attributes' necessary to succeed in higher education and the workplace.[13] A balanced education has to both impart knowledge and develop the learner's skills. The school system is currently too oriented towards the former at the expense of the latter.

Students are bored
The need to redress the balance between performance-oriented and learning-oriented education is a view shared by young people themselves. But the system is not listening to what young people themselves think about the curriculum, what they find interesting and relevant, what they think about how subjects are taught and what motivates them to learn. Survey after survey shows that from age eleven onwards pupils are being turned off learning for the following reasons:[14]

- A perception that the curriculum is unengaging and disconnected from pupils' lives and concerns. Teachers are insufficiently relating what they are teaching to the world of work, the environment, health, citizenship or business.
- Lack of enjoyment – boring lessons. Beneath that headline lies a dissatisfaction with lessons that involve excessive copying of material which are based round 'teacher-centred content transmission' as one survey put it or, as another more bluntly described it, 'teachers talking too much'. Teachers and their style of teaching is a key determinant of a pupil's interest in a subject. Pupils value the subject-based knowledge of their teachers but are looking for lessons and styles of learning that are more interactive and practical – particularly in science and maths.[15]
- Lack of curriculum choice – more pupils, for example, are likely to continue with a modern language at age fourteen if they are offered a choice of languages to learn. They are looking for 'more responsibility, autonomy and personal choice in learning'. Pupils want to be more

involved and empowered in their own assessment of how they are progressing – particularly in subjects which they find 'difficult'.

None of this should surprise us. Young people are growing up in a more consumerist media-dominated society where information is presented in short, digestible, glossy packages, where the media invites you to phone in, vote out a contestant or press the red button, where access to the internet means that you can control your own news and learning environment, where MP3 players enable you to choose and construct your own music station and where video games can be more demanding in terms of non-verbal reasoning skills than much of what goes on in schools. Pupils are more independent: growing up faster and starting sexual relations earlier. They spend more time on their own listening to music, using their computer and maintaining constant contact with friends through talking and texting on mobiles.

The curriculum is too restrictive

The frustration that young people themselves often feel is shared by many teachers. Two thirds of them believe the national curriculum is too restrictive and almost the same number say it contributes to them preparing pupils for exams at the expense of deeper learning.[16] Teachers feel they are the victims of 'a content-dominated and overloaded curriculum'. There is a 'lack of scope for in-depth knowledge and critical analysis, driven by the need for teaching and learning to focus on broad coverage across the whole of each subject curriculum; and lack of time and curriculum "space" for learners to explore specific areas of the subject in more depth.'[17] The result is a focus on getting through the curriculum rather than providing a stimulating learning experience. The best schools and teachers manage to do both but this is despite rather than because of the demands of the system. The system does not encourage schools to be creative and to innovate.

The basic problem is that the national curriculum is predicated on a concept that is way beyond its sell-by date. As currently constructed it sets out for each subject statutory attainment targets for the particular key stage, programmes of study and non-statutory guidelines. The programmes of study are all couched in the language of 'students should be taught to . . .'. Pupils are conceived as passive recipients to whom knowledge must be imparted. The framework classically specifies inputs when it ought to be focusing on educational outcomes. The national curriculum in this form may have been introduced by the last Conservative government but it is command-and-control of the worst kind and it is high time that Labour moved to a more enabling model. The problem has been made worse by ministers under successive governments throwing more things – such as ICT, citizenship, personal, social and health education and enterprise education – into the national curriculum pot as time has gone by.

The assessment system is flawed

The problems with the curriculum are compounded by the nature of the assessment and accountability system. If the curriculum gives teachers too little room to breathe then the assessment and accountability system places them in a straitjacket. In part the problem is the number of tests and exams: the assessment system is overloaded. Among the criticisms identified by Sir Mike Tomlinson and his working party in their interim report on the 14–19 curriculum were 'excessive burdens on learners, teachers/tutors, institutions and awarding bodies, from the number of examinations which many young people now take, the increasing number of examination entries and the administrative and other arrangements which support the examinations system'.[18]

Since then the government has acted to reduce some of the assessment burden – particularly at AS-level and in terms of coursework. But as Ken Boston, chief executive of the Qualifications and Curriculum Authority (QCA), has commented, 'no other country devotes as much time and expertise to developing measures of pupil progress'.[19] A report for the QCA by PricewaterhouseCoopers estimated that the cost of running the examination system in England in 2003/4 was £610 million.[20]

But the problem is deeper than volume and cost. The five-A*–C regime, while understandable and laudable in its aim and focus, is to a degree distorting outcomes. Pupils assessed by their teachers as being just below a C grade are being been hot-housed to get them up to a grade C, at the expense sometimes of real and sustained learning, the progress of other pupils and deep-seated teaching and learning problems that the school needs to address. Subjects which are deemed harder to pass are downplayed as options – this in part helps to explain the drop in language and science applicants at GCSE. At age eighteen there are a growing number of qualifications that are outside the points scoring system that is used to compare schools and colleges.

The problem is not limited to post-14. The Key Stage 2 and 3 tests, undertaken by pupils at age eleven and fourteen respectively, are groaning under the weight of being asked to do four things:

- report on the performance of the whole pupil cohort and therefore the progress over time of the overall school system;
- provide the basis for assessing, comparing and holding to account the performance of each school;
- contribute to the performance assessment of teachers;
- assess the performance and help with the development of each individual pupil.

As the government has now recognised, the tests have been good at performing the first two tasks but far less effective in delivering the fourth objective. The universal set-piece tests in their current format are not supporting moves towards a more personalised approach in schooling.

The reform model is tired

When Labour came to power it brought focus and energy to school improvement with what has been described as a 'high challenge, high support system'.[21] The strategy was driven hard by central government and involved – in its early stages – a fair amount of prescription. The strategy can reasonably be said to have played a large part in the improvements and achievements of the English education system described earlier in this chapter. But one more heave on literacy and numeracy is not now the answer. As Professor Michael Barber, the architect of much of the strategy, recognises and advocates, you need to adapt your strategy according to how a service is progressing – particularly as the returns from a particular approach diminish over time. The art of good management is to be on to the next driver of progress before reaching the top of the bell curve of improvement resulting from the last strategy.

As results in some areas have plateaued, the government has adjusted its strategy. It has moved its focus from standards to structures. The 2005 education White Paper and the Education Act 2006 give schools greater independence, incentivise the creation of new types of school and then support parental choice as a spur to competition – and hence improvement – between schools. Essentially it is a market-based solution: independent state schools competing for pupils, though in 'a market with rules' and 'a market in the sense of consumer choice not a market based on private purchasing power'.[22]

The upside of this is that, as noted earlier, the school system is becoming more diverse and pluralistic and this is helping to bring innovation and energy to the school system – particularly in the secondary sector. It should also bring much-needed investment, aspiration and greater choice for parents, particularly in areas that have been neglected for far too long, and is, therefore, of especial value in highly urbanised areas such as London where there has been an historic lack of good secondary school places. However, as experience in the United States tends to show, market reforms will not by themselves bring the system-wide improvements that are needed.[23] For a start a competitive choice-driven model does not offer significant additional value to either the primary sector, where parental preference is already strong, or to rural or semi-rural areas of England, where there is effectively only one local secondary school. Part of the limitation of a market-based approach lies in seeing schools as a series of individual institutions rather than as parts of an interconnected and interdependent system. The 14–19 diploma reforms, behaviour issues, extended school policies and admission of so-called 'hard to place' pupils all require schools to act together to share responsibility.

Even more importantly, we need a system where all the schools in a town or a city – not just some – are progressing and raising their standards. We have to move away from a high-excellence, low-equity model to one which continues to put a premium on achievement while ensuring that no school is left behind. And if momentum in educational improvements is to be sustained we need to move to a school reform model that is driven more from the bottom up than imposed from the top down: a model where attainment rises because a culture of continuous improvement is all-pervasive rather than because particular improvement strategies are commanded from on high.

A lack of support for parental engagement

Parents are the first teachers that children have. The benefits of parents being involved in their children's education is overwhelming and the power of parents as co-educators is profound. The work of Professor Charles Desforges[24] among others has shown that what parents do with their children at home is far more important to their achievement than their social class or level of education. He argues that if the parenting practices of most working-class parents could be raised to the level of the best, very significant advances in school achievement could be achieved. As another academic, Professor David Reynolds, has neatly put it: 'Significant educational reform is more likely to occur when school and home are jointly addressed.'[25]

But the extent to which we use and engage parents in their children's schooling is very hit and miss. In the early years and primary schools parental support is welcomed – with reading, number-work and playing. But even then schools do not involve parents on a systematic basis in their child's learning: they do not explain how they are being taught and what they can do to help. Those schools that take this role seriously are the exception rather than the rule. Open evenings are for telling how your child is progressing rather than for recruiting and guiding co-educators in a common endeavour.

By the time pupils reach secondary school contact is less frequent, with subject material starting to move beyond a parent's level of understanding. There are schools that have excellent systems of pastoral contact with parents and intranets where parents can view their child's assignments and progress but again they are far from being the norm.

The government's strategy for parents has concentrated on parental choice of schools and giving them a say in running the schools through parents' councils. Supporting them as co-educators has been at best a second-order issue. Yet the millions parents spend on books and private tuition, the huge use of the BBC education website and the role of community schools are all testimony to the desire and willingness of most parents to support their children's education.

School funding is inchoate

The government has steadily increased funding for schools since the turn of the century. Per-pupil funding has increased by nearly 50 per cent, as Figure 17.1 shows. However, the process by which schools are funded is Byzantine – and that is insulting to the Ottoman Empire. Most of the money for schools is now separated out from the rest of local government spending and ring-fenced by the government in a dedicated schools grant (DSG), which is paid to schools via local authorities. Prior to the introduction of the DSG the sum each local authority received was based on a formula that took account of the number of pupils and factors relating to deprivation, sparsity, area costs and various other standard factors used in grant distribution formulae. But the DSG funds a local authority on the basis of its funding in 2005 – and uprates this for inflation and some ad hoc adjustments agreed by ministers.

Local authorities have the duty of passing on the money to schools. As the government's formula operates at the level of the local authority, each authority has its own formula for distributing the money to schools – having regard to government regulations. But they have discretion on how to weight the local formula for deprivation or special needs, for example. This means that

Figure 17.1: Real terms public funding (£) per school pupil, England, 1999/2000 to 2007/8

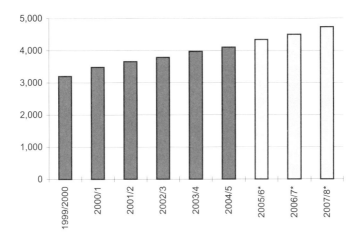

Source: DfES. *=budgeted rather than outturn figures

schools with similar profiles and needs in different parts of the country could end up with very differing funding levels per pupil. A joint Treasury/DfES review found that 'total funding per pupil in primary schools where 35 per cent of children receive free school meals (FSM) varies by around £400 after area costs are removed, and for schools at the 50 per cent FSM level the variation is much greater'.[26] This basic allocation is not related to how schools perform.

In addition to their basic allocation schools will receive via their local authority funding for specific purposes – the main one being the school development grant along with relatively small sums earmarked for extra support for ethnic minority pupils, school music and improving school meals. Each of these grants has its own separate distribution formula. Specialist schools and colleges receive a per-pupil top-up for each specialism for which they are accredited.

There is then a separate school standards grant – sometimes referred to as 'Brown' money as the allocations are announced in the Budget – paid via local authorities direct to schools but with a formula set nationally for how much each school receives. Describing and understanding the formula for this stream of funding is an art form in its own right. And on top of that schools receive funding since the 2006 Budget for personalisation distributed via a new (and entirely separate) formula which has some positive and very progressive features. In addition the government is about to trail the payment of a progression premium, payable to schools depending on whether they exceed a target for the proportion of pupils who make two levels of national curriculum progress between each of the key stages. As with the personalisation funding this is an innovative and interesting concept but these proposals have been added and overlaid on to an already incredibly complex system.

And just in case you think you have mastered this system, there is an entirely different one for pupils aged over sixteen, operated by the Learning and Skills Council.

This complexity and lack of transparency matters because it is undermining both the government's objectives and its structural reforms. Funding is not properly reflecting deprivation and disadvantage at school or pupil level. And the system is undercutting educational efficiency by

- making it hard for schools to understand and plan their budgets;
- failing to ensure that funding sufficiently follows the pupil – which in a more pluralistic system should be helping to expose weaker and less popular schools and acting as an incentive for successful ones;
- providing little incentive for schools to meet the government's objectives of adding educational value and admitting under-performing pupils and so educate a balanced, mixed intake of pupils.

Five big reforms

What then to do about these underlying and systemic weaknesses? We first need to build on what is working, drawing on the good and innovative practice of many schools – we should not engage in change for the sake of the change. We also need to think carefully about the pace of change and not attempt too many reforms at the same time. But where there are blockages in the system we have to be bold and be prepared to address them. Reform should be focused on five areas, which are discussed below.

Empowering students
As we have seen, the government is interpreting choice in education as being

choice for parents – particularly in terms of widening the range of options available to parents when their child goes to secondary school. But that is only one part of the choice-and-empowerment equation. An education system that does not listen to what young people think, respond to the individual needs of pupils or stimulate and empower them to learn will never get past first base in moving attainment on to a new level.

The government has recognised the need to address this agenda and in the report prepared by Christine Gilbert, the chief inspector of Ofsted,[27] it has begun to shift the education system towards a more personalised way of working. Personalisation is essential. As Charles Leadbeater has written:

> Children come into education from different starting points with different resources and expectations. They often learn in different ways, at different paces and styles. As they get older they forge different ambitions for the kind of person they want to be: not just the career they might follow but what interests and expresses their sense of identity. A differentiated education service should meet the needs of learners: differentiated provision for different need.[28]

But if we are to take this agenda seriously it will require a radical reorganisation of education as we know it. It will mean providing students with much more choice over what they learn as they progress through secondary schooling. That does not mean allowing pupils to opt out of acquiring basic English and maths skills but it does mean, for example in language learning, providing greater choice over which languages students can study and to what level. Survey research shows that many students who may not want to study a language to an academic level would nonetheless be motivated and want to acquire a working knowledge and fluent conversational ability in that language. The new 14–19 diplomas will also widen choice. And at Key Stage 3 the ablest students should have the option of completing it in two rather than three years, so providing them with extra flexibility and choice to decide how to use the extra year to try out new subjects or study some subjects in greater depth.

This agenda will also mean embedding a more interactive style of learning which in a systematic way focuses on deep learning: on how well students understand an issue and are acquiring skills demanded by the subject. In some schools, as part of adopting an assessment-for-learning strategy, it is now routine for pupils to assess their own learning achievements online at the end of each day or week and feed back to their teacher how helpful they found the teacher-led part of their learning and how far they themselves are realising the learning objectives that have been agreed with the teacher. This is a style of learning that does not necessarily follow the standard model of a 45- or 50-minute subject period but rethinks the timetable so that it can provide for in-depth engagement with an issue or a topic for a particular portion of a school year or school week. It may use a gifted and specialist maths or physics teacher to teach a complex concept to a class of fifty or sixty pupils but then follows the learning through on an individual basis with small-group work and personal tutorials. It uses older students – whether from higher education or from further up the school – as co-educators and mentors. It integrates all aspects of school life –assembly, lunchtime, outside play, school performances, after-school and sports activities, outside visits, work experience – into the learning process. It will introduce intensive support and learning for students struggling to make up lost ground – as happens with the Knowledge is Power Program (KIPP) in the United States (see box).

The KIPP approach

KIPP schools are free, open-enrolment, college-preparatory public schools where under-served students develop the knowledge, skills and character traits needed to succeed in top-quality high schools, colleges and the competitive world beyond.

KIPP schools share a core set of operating principles known as the 'five pillars': high expectations, choice and commitment, more time, power to lead, and focus on results.

One of the five pillars is **more time**. KIPP students are in school learning 60 per cent more than average public school students, typically from 7.30 a.m. until 5.00 p.m. on weekdays, every other Saturday, and for three weeks during the summer. Rigorous college-preparatory instruction is balanced with extracurricular activities, experiential field lessons and character development. In spite of the long hours, average daily attendance at KIPP schools is 96 per cent.[29]

Another change will involve tracking the progress of each pupil on a consistent basis throughout their school life, particularly as they move school or into a new phase of learning. There is now a wealth of data available to schools and teachers on the performance of each child. A school knows the level of attainment when a pupil enters and it knows the progress it would expect them to make. This provides the basis for setting learning objectives on a termly or half-termly basis with a pupil and sharing them with parents. It provides the framework for identifying problems early and providing extra support if pupils are struggling with a subject or more stretching work if they are coping easily with the set tasks. It's what most schools do for most pupils but it's particularly essential that students from a deprived or disadvantaged background are tracked and supported in this way.

Schools need to use ICT more imaginatively and extensively to support pupils' own sense of discovery and learning and to increase the range of subjects on offer. Why is open learning confined to the further and higher education sectors? Why should a pupil's studies be limited to the knowledge of the staff on a particular site when ICT provides the basis for learning on a much broader basis? The first online initiatives, which allow pupils to choose from thirty languages for their GCSEs – even if no one else in the school wants to study them and there is no one to teach them – are now underway. But this is just the start of a trend that will revolutionise learning in schools and the home. ICT also has a huge potential to help with mentoring, careers advice and raising the aspiration of students.[30]

The new agenda will involve linking the world of learning to the wider world more systematically so that young people can better relate what they are studying to the challenges, issues and opportunities they will encounter. This is partly about developing work experience and business enterprise for students. But it is also about schools having an open engagement with a wide range of local employers – public and private sector – and with other civic agencies, community organisations and voluntary societies. It's an area of work with which school governors can often help but it needs a member of the school leadership team to co-ordinate and orchestrate. It will also involve giving teachers, who have often been through the rather narrow school-university-school cycle, the chances to broaden their outlook and have tasters of other jobs and environments. And it will present a big challenge to business to deliver sufficient employers to support this agenda.

The all-round needs of each individual pupil will need to be addressed. The 'Every Child Matters' agenda is rightly encouraging schools to pay more attention to a child's overall development – to their emotional, physical and economic well-being, alongside their learning development. Smaller schools, schools within schools or house systems can be one way of helping to achieve this. The development of non-teaching pastoral staff, the introduction of children's centres and extended schools and basing services such as education welfare, psychology, careers and youth services in schools are other approaches that will enable schools to become more oriented around the needs of the young people in their charge.

Pupils will be more generally involved in the life of the school. In part this is about the traditional role that senior pupils have played in helping to run after-school activities and organise events for parents and the wider community. But it is also about using pupils as co-assessors and observers of teaching, involving them in interviews for leadership and teaching posts, and empowering and encouraging school councils to help shape the school's policies on behaviour, bullying, drug prevention, equal opportunities and cohesion, as well as consulting them on curriculum developments. The new agenda will also incentivise pupils and reward them for their efforts within school. A number of local authorities have developed the concept of 'opportunity cards', which will provide young people with access to a range of discounts on things to do and places to go and in the high street. Potentially such cards could be topped up by parents or by local authorities wishing to provide incentives for young people to volunteer or achieve in their education, but there is no reason why schools should not also be able to support such top-ups. The top-ups could to be spent on young people's choice of sports and other constructive activities.

Those who argue that student empowerment and personalisation are soft options pandering to the latest fashion ignore a strong evidence base. An international study of pupil motivation identified the following as the top issues that needed addressing:

- improving the personal and vocational relevance of the curriculum;
- giving greater choice and flexibility in the curriculum – including broadening the range of qualifications and courses available;
- emphasising differentiation and support for each pupil and encouraging gifted and talented learners;
- enhancing pupils' involvement and say in their learning;
- assessing learning in an appropriate way and improving understanding of learning styles and preferences.[31]

Overhauling the curriculum and assessment frameworks
Student empowerment and personalisation are not possible without major changes in the way the curriculum is structured and assessed. The government has accepted the need to change the way understanding and knowledge of the

national curriculum is assessed at each key stage. But it needs to go further and strip down the content of the national curriculum so that it focuses much more on what pupils need to know and the skills they should have by a given age, rather than on the detail of what they need to be taught or how they should be taught it. It's the framework within which the charter schools in the United States, much lauded by the government, operate.

A review by the QCA of Key Stage 3 is attempting to do just that and it is important that the government holds its nerve and does not put elements back into the curriculum just because a particular group lobbies powerfully for its favoured cause. It may be right for the government to prescribe that in history pupils should have to know about elements of the nation's past or in English that they be familiar with key authors but the prescription should as far as possible be related to outcomes and skills. As long as a school is delivering high outcomes (as demonstrated through a strong and effective performance management system) government needs to extricate itself from the process. The school system is not where it was in 1997. Where a school is failing or under-performing then of course the government will want to know that action is in hand to address the problem but even then being prescriptive on process is not going to be the answer. Good leadership backed by targeted support and help from high-performing schools with teaching and learning methods are what is needed.

A national curriculum up to the age of 14 based on knowledge and skills required at key points also provides the basis for a reformed assessment system. Already Key Stage 1 has moved away from external testing to teacher assessment over a period of weeks, based partly on banks of tests provided by the QCA and partly on a teacher's own judgement. Now the government is proposing to trial a series of changes for the other key stages, with the following effects:

- Teachers will be able to enter pupils for an externally based assessment when they think they have mastered a national curriculum level rather than waiting until the end of each key stage to make an overall assessment. In other words, pupils are to be assessed when they are ready rather than at a fixed point in time – so enabling a more personalised approach to progression. More frequent assessment would also, it is argued, help parents and the school to be clear about how each pupil was progressing in each year of their schooling.
- The targets framework will measure the proportion of pupils who progress by two national curriculum levels during each key stage. This

would provide a more intelligent incentive for schools to concern themselves with the progress of every pupil and not just with those capable of reaching a certain performance threshold.

The rationale behind these changes is absolutely right and chimes with a more personalised approach. There should be less of an incentive to 'teach to the test' and more of an incentive to improve the learning and attainment of each student. But the changes will result in more rather than less external assessment. A combination of online testing (particularly for Key Stage 3) and school-based assessment of tasks and tests – subject to either external moderation on a random basis or oversight by chartered assessors within the school (senior staff externally accredited to carry out internal assessment to external standards) – might help to alleviate this problem.

It also remains doubtful whether a single assessment system can provide an adequate mechanism for judging the performance of schools overall, holding individual schools to account and supporting the individual progression of each child. The government should adopt the approach advocated by Ken Boston of the QCA and assess how the education system as a whole was doing in absolute terms entirely separately, by using surveys or tests in a small representative sample of schools. This is broadly how progress was measured across the system until 1990 and it is how the OECD assesses and compares reading and numeracy skills of pupils in different countries. Schools selected to participate in the sample surveys would vary from year to year and schools would be given little notice of being included. This would enable ministers, Parliament and the public to assess how well education was progressing overall.

Such an approach would then leave the redesign of the national curriculum assessment to focus on the performance and progress of the individual child. The tests and assessment towards the end of primary school might even be expanded to cover cognitive abilities, an approach which many secondary schools already use for new pupils in order to help determine learning needs and setting arrangements. This could help to make for a more personalised transition at age eleven, each child leaving primary school with a personal learning statement summarising their achievements and their main learning development needs.

These changes should be accompanied by a move away from league tables as a way of publicly comparing schools to school profiles: an online system for parents and the wider community that compares in a standard but more rounded format a school's attainment, activities and achievements with other similar schools. And the profile, in keeping with the government's changes, could be developed to show more clearly the value added by each school for each pupil.

Even more fundamental reform is needed post-fourteen. The new vocational diplomas are an important step in the right direction but still perpetuate the academic/vocational divide. The diplomas could also potentially lock pupils into lines of learning at an early point in their life when they are still trying out new areas of interest and finding out what they are good at and what they enjoy. What is needed is a diploma or baccalaureate system that is much closer to the Tomlinson proposals – a diploma that

- includes a certain prescribed core of subjects – including functional English, maths, ICT and science. It might provide for students to reach a set stage on the 'languages ladder' in order to gain a certain level of diploma. Those wanting to acquire a diploma at the highest level could be required to continue maths and English beyond the current GCSE level;
- incorporates development of personal, learning and thinking skills including communication, presentation, team working and problem-solving skills as an integral part of the diploma;
- provides for academic and vocational pathways – and for the two pathways to be combined;
- uses a credit accumulation and qualifications system that is consistent with that applying to learning post-nineteen and so is better integrated with the world of work;
- facilitates pupils' ability to shift the emphasis of their learning as they develop their interests, knowledge and skills;
- leads to 'graduation' at different levels – foundation, intermediate and advanced – with the requirements of the advanced-level diploma being designed in collaboration with higher education to ensure that it meets the needs of universities for admissions purposes.

In the short term the diploma could incorporate GCSEs and A-levels, as is happening in Wales. In the longer term the diploma would include a mixture of public examinations (the reformed A-levels, for example) and accreditation of skills. The presumption would be, however, that GCSEs as a set of qualifications in their own right would over time disappear and all young people would continue to be involved in some form of education and learning up to age eighteen with the diploma not being awarded until that age at the earliest. Making it compulsory for young people to stay in some form of education or training until the age of eighteen would reinforce this approach, but prescription by itself is not the answer. That approach will only work if there is a flexible and attractive range of ways for young people to be able to combine work and study and if development and training in the workplace counts as being 'in training' and contributes towards a diploma.

A reform on these lines has been fudged for far too long. Tiptoeing round the problem is just making things worse. We are in danger of ending up with post-sixteen exam confusion – with the existing and highly rated BTECs, the new diplomas (at the higher level), the Pre-U assessment being developed by Cambridge University, the expansion in the use of the International Baccalaureate and the reformed A-level all jockeying for the position of being the definitive arbiter of standards and achievement at eighteen. A progressive government needs to go for radical reform if it wants an education system that both meets the needs of young people, universities and employers and provides the country with the skills base it needs.

Enabling schools and teachers to lead

Parents want their child's school to be a great school. But society needs every school to be a great school. The ambition must be an education system that is not just good in parts but uniformly good across the country.

School leaders increasingly share that moral vision and purpose. The government has failed to understand the power of its own reforms in developing leaders of specialist schools with a passion not just for making improvement in their own schools or even in their locality but for developing specialist excellence across the country. Why, they say, does the government invent initiative after initiative instead of using us to get the improvement they want?

The challenge is how to release this pent-up energy to drive the system forward. The answer lies in rebalancing the system towards schools leading reform and in developing system leaders with the capacity to lead that reform. In the secondary sector we need to foster system leadership by these means:

- We need to make school and college leaders responsible not just for pupils in their own school but for all the pupils in their area. In many areas they are effectively doing this already. Such a duty provides the basis for schools working together to tackle behaviour problems, the delivery of the 14–19 or wider diploma agenda, careers advice and extended school services. It also provides the basis for sharing curriculum support and a framework for executive leadership from a successful school or college for a failing or under-performing institution.

- We need to channel school development and other improvement funding via school partnerships, federations and trusts to give them extra leverage in providing or buying in support to tackle the deepest-rooted problems.
- We need to apply the school sport partnership model, praised by Ofsted and led by specialist sports colleges, to other specialisms and subjects. The model organises sports colleges across the country to provide structured support for PE and school sports to other secondary and primary schools in an area. It is a great example of schools leading schools and could be developed to apply to science, engineering, languages and maths specialist colleges.

We need to expand the number and use of training schools to train and develop teachers, particularly as teaching and learning methods adapt to meet a more interactive and pupil-centred style of learning.

- We need to keep faith with the revamped school and college inspection, which has proved a powerful catalyst of change by combining a school's self-evaluation of its performance and development needs with more frequent but shorter no-notice inspections.
- We need to start leadership development much earlier in a teacher's career as pioneered in the Fast Track programme.
- We should expect headteachers and college principals to see investment in the assessment and continuing development of their teaching and non-teaching staff as a priority. This will provide the basis for offering pupils as much one-to-one or small-group learning and support as possible. The bulk of this will come from qualified staff but other staff – teaching assistants, learning mentors, science technicians, specialists in PE, ICT or languages – will contribute as well. Pupil:teacher ratios, if not obsolete, will increasingly need to be seen alongside adult:pupil ratios. And we must empower school leaders to address performance management issues, particularly in relation to variations in performance between and within departments in a school.
- We need to expand the current National Leaders of Education (NLE) initiative, which enables able and experienced school leaders to work with and support schools that have big challenges or are under-performing. The government should also use NLEs much more to help make and test policy ideas – as it did when it asked Sir Alan Steer to

advise on behaviour policy in schools.

- Local authorities should be developed as a support resource for school leaders so that, as in the successful London Challenge model,[32] they can provide a wide range of support and challenge to individual schools and local partnerships to fit their precise needs – particularly in relation to schools that are struggling.

In the primary sector there is less strength in depth in terms of strategic leadership and so the priority is to provide financial incentives, as the Dutch have done, for schools to cluster together and appoint what the Dutch refer to as 'a non-school head': a strategic leader who works with, challenges and supports the schools and helps them to develop and implement an improvement strategy. These clusters, which are already beginning to emerge in the UK, could also provide the basis for sharing subject expertise, business support, ICT support and wider children's services. In the longer term they may also provide the basis for shared governance, whether through a federation or a trust, but, given the role that primary schools play in their local community, it will be important to involve local people and parents in the change. In some cases primary schools might join with secondary schools to form 3–18 through schools or cross-phase clusters, particularly in areas where a secondary school has a close relationship with its feeder primary schools.

Enabling and encouraging schools to lead reform and improvement will also entail changes to the accountability system. Working in partnership should not dilute a school's responsibility to be accountable for its own performance – accountability does need to remain specific. But as partnership becomes an essential feature of the school and college system it is perverse for at least some of the accountability not to be shared. Where federations, trusts or education improvement partnerships take on responsibility for a function or an objective or are allocated money on a group basis they should be held to account on that basis. That would help prevent what might be termed 'awkward sod' syndrome, where one head won't play ball in collaboratively tackling tough local issues such as hard-to-place pupils and exclusions.

Involving parents as co-educators

In the past some schools have seen themselves as – and have been – a safe haven from the problems and stresses that may exist in the home or the community. Today that separation is not sustainable. If there are ethnic tensions in the neighbourhood they are very likely to spill over into the school. If there is domestic upheaval or a lack of discipline and order at home it will affect a child's performance at school. If there is a sense of alienation and a lack of economic aspiration in the local community this will impact on pupils' learning and ambition. If parents are unable to speak English fluently this will reduce their ability to support their child's education. If the diet at home is chips, burgers, pies and beans then the best school dinners in the world will only make a small impact on reducing childhood obesity. Effective education has always been a partnership between school, home and the wider community. Schools in the twenty-first century need to redefine that partnership and make it work for today's challenges.

Involving and engaging parents in schooling starts from the premise that

Figure 17.2: The different dimensions of parental engagement

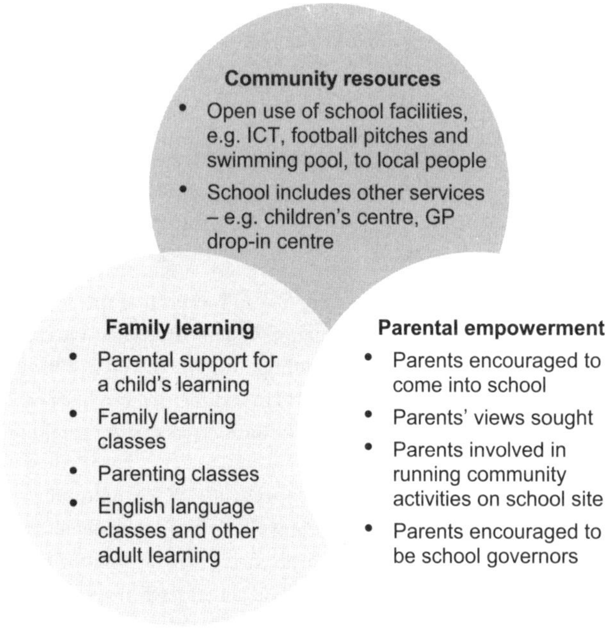

Community resources

- Open use of school facilities, e.g. ICT, football pitches and swimming pool, to local people
- School includes other services – e.g. children's centre, GP drop-in centre

Family learning

- Parental support for a child's learning
- Family learning classes
- Parenting classes
- English language classes and other adult learning

Parental empowerment

- Parents encouraged to come into school
- Parents' views sought
- Parents involved in running community activities on school site
- Parents encouraged to be school governors

With acknowledgement to the National College for School Leadership's project on community leadership in networks and to the Association for School and College Lecturers for permission to reproduce this from *Leadership that Lasts; Sustainable School Leadership in the 21st Century* (2006).

parents are not just customers of schools but co-producers of their child's education. So although parental preference and choice are important, parental engagement also needs to operate at a much deeper level, embracing the breadth of activities described in Figure 17.2. They include everything from parental involvement in knowing how they can best support their child to learn, through to developing a parent's own knowledge and skills and on to supporting the life of the school. For some families it will also mean schools working with other services and agencies to tackle a complex mix of problems that may be contributing to a child's behaviour or lack of attendance.

Not every school will need or be able to undertake the full range of these activities but the development of children's centres and the extended school services offer a great opportunity for schools (sometimes together and sometimes on their own) to forge a different kind of relationship with parents. A growing number of schools are increasing opportunities for parental engagement by having websites accessible to parents that show whether their child has been in school, what they are studying and how they are doing. Others are looking to building on home–school contracts and, as with the KIPP schools in the United States, are asking parents – along with students and teachers – to commit to a programme for raising attainment.

Reforming school funding

As we saw earlier, funding per pupil has risen rapidly since 2000. Some critics argue that the spending increases have not been sufficiently matched by improvements in results. It is too early for the full impact of the increases to have worked their way through the education system. But what we can say is that without the increases in education funding, schools would not have been able to develop their leading position in ICT, reduce the teacher:pupil and adult:pupil ratios, attract and retain sufficient numbers of quality teaching staff or refurbish school premises.

The critics also overlook the fact that, as the OECD has pointed out, the UK was starting from a low funding base and has in large part been 'catching up'. In addition private spending on education is rising at a faster rate than public spending.[33] But if further public increases in education spending are to command public support then the allocation system needs to be fundamentally reformed. Funding has to be shown to be fair and transparent; it needs to be seen to reward success and incentivise innovation.

The government has been consulting on changes to the system. What it proposes would deal with some of the worst anomalies highlighted earlier but would fail to grasp the nettle of funding schools directly. We do not need to look far to find the basis for a reform framework. The Learning and Skills Council already operates a national funding system for post-sixteen learning that is based on a formula which gives schools and colleges a direct allocation dependent on

- the number of students;[34]
- the number and range of qualifications being taught, including different weightings for different qualifications;
- adjustments to reflect disadvantage (using the school's free school meal index) and the labour costs of the area in which the school or college is situated;
- the school or college's success rate in retaining students and gaining qualifications.

A system along these lines could be applied to the whole of the secondary sector by making three adjustments:

- Reducing, though perhaps not entirely eliminating, the activity-based costing element (i.e. the different levels of funding for teaching different types of qualification), since at least for Key Stage 3 schools will broadly be undertaking a similar range of activities.
- Adding an element that reflects pupils' prior attainment. This would incentivise a more balanced intake at age eleven as schools would receive more money for those pupils with higher educational needs. A similar system has incentivised universities to increase the number of students from non-traditional backgrounds requiring more intensive support during their degree course. This approach, rather than admission by lottery or quotas, would provide a quicker, surer and less contentious route to schools becoming more mixed and less monocultured in their social and ethnic make-up.
- Making part of a school's funding relate to achievement by reference to the value a school had added to pupils' performance at fourteen, sixteen or eighteen. The government's proposals for progression premium are designed to do just this but, as noted earlier, as a complicated add-on rather than as an essential and integral feature of the system.

In the primary sector, given the very small numbers in some schools, a system based on these principles would work better if it were applied to clusters of primary schools rather than to an individual school.

It's important to stress why a reform of this magnitude is necessary. It supports equity both by treating schools in similar situations in broadly the same way and by targeting funding more precisely at need. It incentivises educational efficiency as well as greater social cohesion. A reformed system also provides the basis for doing away with many of the separate funding pots. It has the power to be as transformational as the tariff system introduced into hospitals has been and continues to be for the NHS.

It is also essential if the government's supply-side reforms are to have any bite: funding has to follow the pupil in a more transparent way, as the experience of charter schools in the United States has demonstrated.[35] There is a case for merging the existing office of schools adjudicator (which deals with appeals on plans for school expansions) with that of the new schools commissioner (which has been established to promote greater local choice for parents) to create a single and more powerful office for regulating and ensuring the diversity of supply of school places in each area. But there is little point in doing this until there is a level playing field in terms of funding per place to support fair competition.

There is also the potential, which the government has begun to develop, of paying supplements or vouchers direct to 'gifted' or 'under-performing' pupils and their parents to enable them to access extra personalised teaching and support. The evidence from the United States of the impact of full choice and voucher programmes in terms of raising attainment seems mixed but is most positive in terms of the motivation (and satisfaction) that parents gain from being involved in their child's education.[36] Introducing these learning vouchers or entitlements is certainly worth trialling but, as with the Treasury-led personalisation grants, adding these supplements to the existing creaking system would just compound complexity, unfairness and inefficiency and fail to deal with the root causes of the problem.

Critics will argue that it would be hugely disruptive and costly to move to a national funding system of this sort. That to a degree is true – though less disruptive now that there is a dedicated schools grant. But the trick will be to do it gradually over a number of years and to build in safety nets to ensure that schools that might 'lose' from the process have time to plan for budget adjustments. Moreover, the government's stated intention is to continue to increase spending on schools with a view to closing the gap relative to the spend per pupil in the independent sector. Direct funding of schools should therefore be taking place against a background of budgets rising rather than falling in real terms.

Conclusion

The English education system has come a long way in the last ten years. There is much to celebrate in the progress and achievements being made by young people, teachers and schools. However, the fact that this chapter has argued for a radical series of student-centred reforms shows the scale of what is still left to be achieved.

In taking forward this agenda we need to be mindful of some of the other arguments made in this book. For example, none of the five big reforms I have argued for will on their own be sufficient to deliver the improvements we need. The hardest part of the challenge lies in combining reforms into a sustained and sustainable programme of educational change. The key to achieving that, I believe, lies in forging a strong partnership between policy makers nationally and progressive and entrepreneurial school, college and community leaders locally. Much of what has been argued for goes with the grain of what many school leaders are wanting and thinking. So our plans for the future should harness their support and leadership to take our schools, colleges and students through the next decade of education, education, education.

18

Narrowing the gap
How early investment will tackle new inequalities

Patrick Diamond

The just society empowers its citizens 'from cradle to grave', as the architect of the post-war welfare state, William Beveridge, wrote in the 1940s. Equality of life-chances requires equal access to basic social goods for all. From the early years to adult literacy, the role of public services in improving life-chances has been a key focus of Labour's agenda over the last decade.

Britain still suffers from inequalities that are damaging to individuals and the country as a whole. The test of public service reform is not just to secure higher standards, but to help the most disadvantaged to improve their lives. Public services must be configured to remove specific clusters of social exclusion throughout life.

The argument of this chapter is that the goal of empowerment requires a radically different model of the progressive state, drawing on the Sure Start experiment. Centre-left governments need to institutionalise equal chances at the pre-school age – while continuing to redistribute opportunity throughout the life-cycle. This approach insists that social renewal should be built from the bottom up. The individuals who actually experience hardship and adversity should be directly involved in programmes of action – instead of absorbing public services from a class of professionals. This ethos was embodied in Sure Start at the outset, marking a reconnection with the early twentieth-century traditions of mutualism and community empowerment.

Public service reform needs to capture the original localist and participatory principles of the Sure Start approach. This requires the development of what I term an intermediate state: independent public institutions should deliver collective goods within a plural framework of central standards and devolved delivery. The evolution of self-sustaining institutions that empower individual citizens should be a defining mission for progressive politics.

Before considering children's services and the specific example of the 'Sure Start' initiative in greater detail, it is worth noting that the reform of public services has been impeded by a double paradox at the heart of the traditional social democratic model of the state. Both paradoxes have deep roots in Labour's statecraft, epitomised most heroically by the 1945–51 Attlee government. It remains an *idée fixe* of British social democracy that capturing the commanding heights of the British state alone will secure social change. This particular model has gradually emerged over the last sixty years. But it involves increasingly complex interventions in many aspects of economic and social life that, if ill conceived, are prone to failure.

The first paradox of social democracy is the presumption that the state is a neutral instrument that can be effortlessly redirected to serve progressive ends – the traditional model of state power is sufficient to alleviate poverty and hardship. Yet the existing machine has often been unresponsive to the kind of programme social democrats have sought to implement in post-war Britain. This has forced Labour governments to resort to the traditional command model based on the tried and tested procedures of the centralised state, thereby failing to encourage pluralist and decentralised solutions to public service delivery.[1] Yet the role of the state has to be reinterpreted in each generation as rising living standards, decreasing deference, greater social polarisation and new technology lead society to make ever greater demands on state-funded provision.

The second social democratic paradox is the view that volume rather than quality is the critical concern in the provision of public services. The sheer complexity of extreme deprivation requires us to focus not merely on the quantitative scale of delivery but also on the qualitative impact of policies that aim to release human potential. This is hardly a new insight, as Charles Leadbeater and Hilary Cottam suggest in Chapter 7, but one that has been forgotten in the rush to adopt centralised, target driven approaches to public service improvement and by extension social change.

This double paradox at the heart of the British social democratic tradition sets up profound contradictions and dilemmas in reforming public services. There is the familiar but enduring tension between centralisation and localism in public service delivery, for example. Another aspect is whether an emphasis on diversity, risk taking and local experiment is compatible with the central co-ordination of delivery and target setting. For progressives, empowerment through the 'new localism' embodied in Sure Start offers an approach that can resolve this enduring tension over the role of the state. The purpose is not to weaken the state but to make it an effective actor – a potent instrument for realising progressive ambitions. Public services that focus on how to empower citizens offer the most viable political and policy strategy for the centre-left.

It is no longer feasible to prescribe complex interventions from the centre. The dynamics of generational disadvantage vary starkly between localities. Every neighbourhood uniquely experiences the long-term effects of growing lone parenthood, teenage pregnancy and changing family structures – alongside neighbourhood deprivation and wider economic disadvantage. In the last fifty years, social and economic change has fragmented identities, broken down traditional occupational and geographical hierarchies, and created an ever-more complex distribution of spatial disadvantage.

The shape of British society is increasingly heterogeneous. London, for example, is one of the most ethnically diverse cities in the world. More than 300 languages are spoken and there are at least fifty non-indigenous communities with populations of 10,000 or more. Changes to household structures require the broadening of services for new 'types' of family, including lone parents, families with divorced parents, elderly independents and double-income families. The advantage of developing local institutions within a framework of central standards and funding is to ensure greater sensitivity to local conditions.

Politically, greater localism is also an important prerequisite of empowerment. Only through carefully defined but strengthened localism is it feasible to construct a deeper bond of allegiance between citizens and public services. If communities feel a stronger sense of ownership of public services, that should help to forge new coalitions of support for adequate levels of public expenditure. Giving individuals and communities a sense of control is also an empirically important factor in subjective well-being.

In the past, however, Labour governments struggled to realise their objectives because they could not entrench the commitment to public services in British society. Labour's failure was most dramatically symbolised by the events of the 1960s and 1970s, where several basic errors occurred. In the first instance, the Wilson governments pumped resources into the public sector immediately after election victory in 1964, 1966 and 1974. But they were soon forced into a humiliating retreat as the British economy entered into a familiar spiral of deflation and retrenchment. This perpetuated the debilitating pattern of 'stop–go' public investment.

At the same time, Labour had become closely associated with the incompetent and bureaucratic state, in both central and local government. Public services such as hospitals, schools and local authorities were increasingly perceived as insensitive to the individual needs of the citizen in an age of heightened consumer aspirations. Most tellingly of all, Labour was unable to build intrinsic support for public services. As the economic and political context became less favourable, public support quickly evaporated, permitting the Thatcherite firestorm after 1979. Intrinsic support for public services will be nurtured only if people and communities themselves are empowered as agents of change, working alongside decentralised public service institutions, not-for-profit groups and the private sector – instead of having distant Whitehall bodies determining the course of their lives.

At the heart of the debate is the appropriate division of responsibility between individual citizens, the community and the state. The citizens who benefit from public services should be able to shape the institutions that deliver them, instead of being passive recipients of central and local government. This reflects two fundamental principles of democratic empowerment. The first is that power should be widely spread. To make a reality of self-government, power should be diffused as widely as possible. The second principle is that the ideal of self-government entails a politics of pluralism, power sharing and negotiation. From the constitution to public services, power cannot be concentrated within an over-mighty central state.

The idea of giving local bodies and institutions greater influence in public policy has provoked widespread interest on the left. This marks an important reconnection with the historical traditions of ethical socialism explored in the writings of R. H. Tawney and G. D. H. Cole. Inevitably, there are also various criticisms that could be levelled at excessive localism. Britain is characterised by spatial and structural inequalities, and the central state is necessary to ensure a fairer distribution of resources.

The claim that uniformity ensures equity in public service delivery should be interrogated, however. The likelihood of a mother getting support from a health visitor rises with income,[2] for example, illustrating the weakness of traditional welfare state delivery models. Giving emphasis to localism in the management and delivery of children's services is not about rejecting the state, or substituting the state for the voluntary and private sector. There still needs to be fair funding and nationally agreed entitlements to access and equal treatment in public services.

But state intervention after 1945 still left a multitude of social and economic inequalities largely untouched. Class divisions were entrenched, while social mobility appeared to slow down in the 1970s. This was exacerbated by the Conservatives, but it long pre-dated the Thatcher governments.

The argument of this chapter is that it is not only the relationship between central and local institutions that should be revisited, but their relationship with citizens. In the model of the progressive 'intermediate' state, equalisation requires empowerment – not simply redistribution through the passive dispensing of state benefits and services. Users and stakeholders have to play an active role in the provision of public services. Participation helps to create pressure for organisations to perform well: that entails a new approach to public service reform.

Labour has to forgo its obsession with volume as the critical concern in public services, and instead focus ever more intensively on quality of outcome. But that will inevitably reduce the pace of change and the scale of delivery. This is problematic in an era where citizens are quick to express their frustration at poor performance. It will dramatically increase the long-term impact of Labour's policies, however, not least by promoting intrinsic support for public services. This should ensure that public service institutions endure, instead of being swept away by future governments.

Herbert Morrison, an architect of the Attlee government, argued that the left's achievements in office should be measured by a single test: how much private property organised and conducted for profit has been transferred to the community? But faith in the cure-all property of collective planning has long since evaporated, replaced by the fundamental belief in liberating human potential.

At the heart of the progressive agenda lies the insight that gaining the power to be free requires an enabling and empowering state. In contrast to neo-liberalism, this involves a positive view of freedom where individuals are able to control and govern their own lives. As well as redistributing income, progressives should redistribute power to the individual citizen. As Tawney put it, 'A society is free in so far as, within the limits set by nature, knowledge, and resources, its institutions and policies are such as to enable all members to grow to their full stature.'[3] In this chapter, I will explain what this implies in terms of practical policy.

But first, some general background is in order. As a response to the heightened inequalities of the Thatcher era, centre-left politicians have become especially astute at devising a coherent case for policies and investments that tackle early childhood disadvantage. In framing the debate about poverty, Labour began to talk specifically about child poverty, distinguishing between needy children and their potentially indolent parents. The emphasis on early investment and intervention was justified in several ways:

- Analytically, there was growing evidence that the effects of early experiences, from diet and parenting to cognitive development at school, have an enormous impact on subsequent achievements.
- There was also increasing emphasis on the externalities of poverty that are generated if children's problems are ignored or tackled incorrectly: the variety of ways in which higher crime, drug use, anti-social behaviour and family instability affect the more affluent in industrialised societies, not only the poor.
- Finally, the social policy debate was reframed by recognising the importance of maximising the human capital potential of the nation. It was claimed that reducing the waste of talent and potential while cutting the bills of social failure would raise the long-term growth rate of the British economy.

The research evidence also indicates that intervention in a child's early years is among the most effective means of improving educational performance and the likelihood of escaping social exclusion. The Sure Start programme was heavily influenced by American experience, though it does not conform to the tightly targeted strategies that prevail in the United States. The American example of Head Start puts particular emphasis on intensive cognitive development for the most disadvantaged children.

Since the late 1990s, public services along with modest redistribution have made a significant impact on developmental inequalities in the UK. There is evidence of real improvement in the life-chances of the most disadvantaged children. For example:

- The steady rise in income inequality that characterised the 1980s and most of the 1990s has been halted. Ninety-five per cent of the population have seen their incomes rise by 2 to 3 per cent a year. In the late 1980s, the incomes of the bottom 50 per cent grew by only 1 per cent per annum.
- As a result, relative child poverty has been reduced faster in the UK than any other European country as 2.5 million more people have found work, boosting the employment rate to more than 70 per cent.
- Since 1999, those primary schools with the highest proportion of pupils eligible for free school meals have seen the largest increases in the

percentage of pupils achieving level 4 at Key Stage 2. The proportion of pupils in the most deprived secondary schools obtaining five or more A★–C grade GCSEs has increased by 23 per cent. At level 4, the expected level of attainment at Key Stage 2, the attainment gap between the most and least deprived schools has decreased by 10 per cent in English and 7 per cent in maths.[4]

- Also in education, the gap between the most disadvantaged areas and the rest seems to be reducing. The difference between the percentage of pupils in the eighty-eight most deprived areas and others achieving five or more A★–C GCSEs narrowed from 10.2 to 8.1 points between 1997/8 and 2002/3.
- In tackling crime, the gap between the overall burglary rate in the eighty-eight most deprived areas and the England average reduced from 10.3 to 8.1 percentage points, helping to ensure safer neighbourhoods.

These improvements were achieved through a combination of stronger economic performance and higher employment, improved educational attainment across all age groups and increased welfare provision for the most vulnerable. They reflect important changes in conceiving how the state should act, with a multitude of innovations and novel initiatives for tackling childhood deprivation, social exclusion and family poverty. Labour historically has been cautious and conservative with regard to the state, but it is important to acknowledge where it has been bold on reform. For example, since 1997 the following measures have been taken:

- There has been less focus on a linear approach to policy making with endless Green and White Papers leading to more legislation from the centre. The government has placed greater emphasis on fine-tuning the process of implementation.
- Policy formulation within central government has been opened up to outside experts, for example, through the Social Exclusion Unit and the Social Exclusion Task Force in the Cabinet Office.
- Tighter performance management has been introduced to regulate service delivery and tackle under-performing local authorities.
- There has been much greater use of pilots and smaller initiatives to test what works and ensure that evidence better informs policy, for example through the New Deal and Sure Start.
- There have been real efforts to make policy design and implementation more holistic, for example in early-years provision.

- In addition, new professional roles have been created to provide more tailored packages of support, for example teaching assistants, Connexions advisers and learning mentors.
- Greater consideration has been given across government to the importance of early intervention and long-term prevention.[5]

Overall, however, progress in tackling developmental inequalities over the life-cycle has been slow, patchy and inconsistent. The challenge facing a progressive government in Britain is greater because children's life-chances have become more sharply polarised during the last two decades.

Other research evidence suggests that the socio-economic gap between children is getting wider. There are numerous examples of absolute improvements in well-being and achievement, but the fundamental challenge lies in the relative differences between socio-economic groups. In fact, strong overall performance in public services such as schools can disguise serious underachievement among a minority. For example both trend and snapshot data show the following:

- Pupils receiving free school meals (FSM) as a proxy for deprivation are falling further behind non-FSM pupils at age fifteen. This is occurring in both the most and the least deprived schools. More affluent schools are pulling ahead at higher levels of performance. At Key Stage 2, schools with the least deprived intakes are making most progress at level 5+.
- Not surprisingly, children from higher professional backgrounds are twice as likely as children with parents in unskilled or semi-skilled occupations to achieve five A★–C GCSEs.
- Since 1996/7, the rate of improvement in infant mortality has been three times faster for managerial and professional classes than for those in routine manual occupations. The chances of children surviving to their first birthday have become more unequal over this period.
- There are substantial disparities in ethnic minority achievement. Fifty-six per cent of white pupils achieved five good GCSEs in 2005 compared with just 42 per cent of black Caribbean pupils.[6]
- Families on the very lowest incomes have seen the lowest rates of income growth. The bottom 5 per cent of incomes increased by around 1 per cent a year in real terms between 1996/7 and 2004/5, compared with annual increases of between 2 and 3 per cent for the rest of the population.

- As many as 11 per cent of 16–18-year-olds are not in employment, education or training, and the figure has remained broadly static for the last ten years. For those with no qualifications, employment rates in the UK have fallen from 51.7 per cent in 1997 to 49.6 per cent in 2005.

The development of 'floor targets' was intended to raise achievement levels among those at the very bottom. But the evidence suggests that some children have still not been reached. There is little evidence that in the last decade the extent or impact of the gap in developmental progress has seriously diminished. The socio–economic position of parents affects children from an early age: as Figure 18.1 shows, even at twenty–two months there is a major gap.

Figure 18.1: The socio–economic position of parents affects children from a very early age

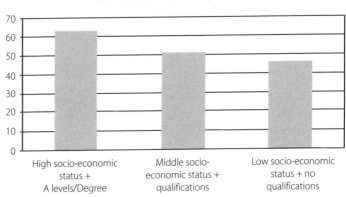

Age 22 months: average development ranking by mother's socio-economic status and qualification level

Source: Leon Feinstein, Birth Cohort Study (1999)

When children enter school, those from poorer backgrounds fall further behind those from higher income families. Leon Feinstein's analysis in Figure 18.2 shows that children from low-income backgrounds with a high developmental score at twenty-two months have fallen behind by age ten, in comparison with children from high-income backgrounds with a low developmental score at twenty-two months.

Figure 18.2: Children from poorer backgrounds fall behind those from higher-income families

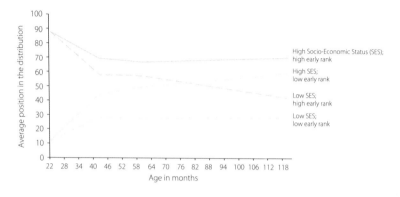

Source: Leon Feinstein, 'Inequality in the Early Cognitive Development of British Children in the 1970 Cohort', *Economica* (2003), vol. 70, no. 277, pp. 73–98.

The performance in tests at twenty-two and forty-two months is also a strong predictor of later educational outcomes. Feinstein's research shows that children in the bottom quartile at twenty-two months are significantly less likely to get any qualification at sixteen than those in the top quartile. Of those in the top quartile at age forty-two months, three times as many as in the bottom quartile go on to get basic educational qualifications or better. Significant differences in life-chances are apparent before children even enter the educational system.

Since the late 1990s, the sociologist Gøsta Esping-Andersen has observed 'ominous signs of rising welfare polarisation between income/work poor families on one side, and resource strong families on the other side'[7] across the industrialised world. The affluent consolidate their human capital by devising strategies to transmit it to their children. They do so financially by selecting schools or moving to better-off neighbourhoods. These families generate substantial levels of cultural capital that subsequently enforce the value of learning and the acquisition of formal qualifications.

The extent of inequality has grown worse as the redistributive capabilities of the welfare state and public services have diminished since the late 1970s. The virtuous circle between production and distribution, where strong growth allowed the financing of redistribution, which in turn supported consumption and finally growth, has weakened. Instead, an approach must be forged that reconnects with earlier phases of social democratic reform that focused on the empowerment of the citizen, guaranteeing real equality of opportunity. That requires radical reform in public services. I will set out what this entails with specific reference to the early-years agenda and the development of the government's flagship Sure Start programme.

The aim of Sure Start is to work with parents and children to promote the physical, intellectual and social development of pre-school children – particularly the disadvantaged – to ensure that they are ready to thrive when they go to school. When Sure Start was launched in July 1998, 200 local programmes were proposed, concentrated in areas of deprivation but not confined to poor families. These brought together core programmes of child and maternal health with early education and play, alongside family support for the under-fours.

At the outset, there were strong emphases in Sure Start on accessing hard-to-reach families and autonomy for local projects to add extra services such as benefits advice, IT classes, speech therapy, debt counselling and family literacy. Sure Start would be locally administered through partnerships between statutory agencies including local authorities, primary care trusts and the voluntary and private sectors. The relatively generous funding including an annual budget of £3.1 billion would be 'ring fenced' and sustained for at least ten years. The aim was resolutely child centred, focused on outcomes for children from disadvantaged backgrounds rather than childcare alone.

Sure Start was designed to build on knowledge that had accrued from previous research, but it differs fundamentally in several key respects.[8] First, it constitutes a universal area-based intervention for all families with children living in a designated area – limiting stigma that may affect those targeted. Second, the designated areas had high rates of deprivation, but there was considerable variation in the degree of disadvantage experienced by individual families, while some seriously deprived families were excluded because their area was not disadvantaged overall. Finally, Sure Start local programmes had no prescribed curriculum, avoiding the mechanised rigidity of highly specified initiatives.

The immediate impact of Sure Start was overwhelmingly positive. Those interviewed in twelve deprived neighbourhoods by the Centre for the Analysis of Social Exclusion at the London School of Economics and Political Science, for example, found a large degree of enthusiasm for the scheme. As one of the architects of Sure Start, Professor Norman Glass, concludes, however,[9] the initial localist and participatory premises were steadily emasculated as pressure to expand a successful experiment grew remorselessly at the end of the 1990s. This illustrates more generic weaknesses in the government's public service strategy – not least the tendency to elevate volume rather than quality as the critical priority.

It is important to distinguish these criticisms from exaggerated speculation that the Sure Start programme has allegedly failed. A recent study by researchers at Birkbeck College apparently showed very little evidence that Sure Start has achieved its goals.[10] It suggested that children from relatively disadvantaged families – teenage mothers, lone parents and workless households – were adversely affected by living in an area with a Sure Start programme.

It is clear, however, that the scheme was set unrealistically tough targets such as reducing the number of babies with low birth weight. Experts warned that effective results would come only when the same children had been followed for many years. The ambiguous results were also compounded by significant methodological problems. For example, poor areas have a high turnover of families: Enfield Sure Start, for example, had an 80 per cent turnover of under-fives so the evaluation missed children who had received help but moved away.

Indeed, complex social schemes do not fit into neat laboratory experiments. In the US Head Start programme, the results showed that every $1 spent on deprived under-fives saved $7 by the time the children were thirty. The sample committed fewer crimes, had a lower incidence of mental ill health, was less dependent on social security and gained better qualifications. But in its first phase, Head Start produced relatively little measurable effect.

The decision to expand Sure Start was controversial, though not because the schemes were failing. In July 2000, the government extended Sure Start to 550 local projects. But the projected number of Sure Start children's centres subsequently grew to 3,500 by April 2005. These centres would provide services on Sure Start principles, but would not be area bound and would be open to all. This aimed to tackle an endemic weakness in Sure Start that not all disadvantaged children live in deprived areas. At the same time, local authorities and health agencies had to deal with widely differing distributions of resources across similar neighbourhoods.

The strategic rationale for universalising Sure Start was robust. Public services exist to help every citizen. The aim of public provision is not only to redistribute resources and equalise life-chances, but to offer security and opportunity to all. In conceiving the modern welfare state, Beveridge understood that public services had to secure the allegiance of the middle class as well as the most deprived. This underpins the selective universalism of Labour's strategy since 1997.[11]

If the empowerment of individuals through the enabling state 'from cradle to grave' remains the central strategic ambition of progressive politics, there was nonetheless a fatal flaw in this approach. As Norman Glass observes, too many vital Sure Start principles were sacrificed as pressure grew to expand the scheme:

- Community development and participation are no longer central.[12] The programme was initially structured to allow local people, especially parents, to participate fully in the content and management of Sure Start, reflecting their own perceptions about what local areas needed. This is essential if policies are to take root, rather than be seen as yet another 'quick fix' in a long line of failed initiatives. Strict delivery timetables and national targets have inevitably relegated the goal of community participation, squeezing out local experiment and enterprise.

- Resources are spread too thinly across thousands of programmes. Labour has Scandinavian aspirations for universal childcare, but it will have to square the circle of rising fiscal pressures and rising societal expectations. The proportion of national income devoted to public expenditure in the UK, at 42.5 per cent in 2006/7, remains some way below the average of 49.4 per cent in the Scandinavian countries. Funding per head is now spread over 3,500 children's centres with an end to the ring-fencing of Sure Start resources.

- Sure Start has been captured by departments focusing on childcare and the employability of parents. The programme is run by a minister shared between the Department for Education and Skills and the Department for Work and Pensions, aiming to maximise maternal employment and women's participation in the labour market. Traditionally, NHS services have struggled to engage in cross-boundary and preventative working, and this looks set to be perpetuated by these arrangements.

- As a result, outcomes for disadvantaged children have been downgraded while the child-centred ethos of Sure Start has increasingly been lost. The hardest-to-reach groups may slip through the net more easily.

The argument so far goes as follows. The traditional architecture of the centralised command-and-control state in Britain has done too little to tackle inequality and deprivation. The preference for volume over quality of outcome does not get the most out of public services. Instead, social renewal is best pursued from the bottom up. Localities should be able to devise solutions that uniquely suit their needs and resources, shaping and developing their own public institutions within a central framework of standards and funding.

In this model there are no standard blueprints and users should have greater power to shape their own services. The new patterns of governance, as David Donnison argues, will need to combine an economic orientation that addresses jobs, skills and enterprise, an area focus bringing together the resources of different agencies and projects, with greater decentralisation drawing services and professionals together.[13] This is especially important in early years, parenting and family support. While the nature of the interaction between parent and child has a significant impact on later outcomes, there are no uniformly successful programmes that decisively improve parenting skills.

The prescription of highly complex interventions in economic and social life by the centralising state is prone to failure. The insistence on a uniform and regulated service squeezes out local enterprise and experiment. Indeed, public attitudes to state intervention within the family are generally negative. Historically, the state tends to limit its scrutiny to occasions when the deficiency is so great as to amount to child neglect. More effective parenting programmes will have to achieve buy-in from parents locally. That is why reclaiming the emphasis on localism and participation in Sure Start remains so important. This requires new patterns of governance and voluntary initiative in the delivery of children's services – giving the disadvantaged a voice in their neighbourhoods, making public service professionals directly accountable, and extending power to citizens both as a lever of improvement and to encourage civic participation.

There are several reasons why the case for greater use of local institutions and public involvement is gaining increasing prominence:

- Britain is an increasingly diverse country where needs and aspirations are not only different, but people are more confident that they have a right to an opinion about how they are treated. Policy needs to address specific risk factors that vary between neighbourhoods.
- The active welfare state is based on rights and responsibilities for the individual as well as the state. Much of what governments want to achieve requires the engagement of citizens. Public health, safer neigh-

bourhoods and a better start for disadvantaged children all depend on public services, but also on how citizens help themselves.

• There is increasing evidence that public services that go from improvement to transformation do so through concerted engagement with service users. Public services will help people to take up opportunities and feel more secure if they give confidence as well as care, empowerment as well as higher standards.

Since decisions over some public services, including children's services, cannot be devolved to individuals, they require collective choice and voice. There should be greater scope for local enterprise, as well as rights to hold public authorities to account. Local support is vital, building capacity and leadership. But this will occur only if communities are given resources and left to get on with it, forging their own autonomous institutions. The implications of the Sure Start model for children's services translate into several directions for future policy:

• The decentralisation of children's services into smaller, more accessible units from which teams of staff from different services operate, with greater commitment from the local community. This would enable citizens to define the service levels they expect from local service providers, and the responsibilities they will assume in return. Professionals who work with parents and children also need to better understand poverty dynamics.

• The creation of community-owned institutions that provide particular services, such as credit unions, nurseries and children's centres, and the extension of ownership co-operatives that have emerged in the social housing field.

• The development of social enterprises that provide facilities and services for children and families, producing and trading like other businesses, but using surpluses for the benefit of the community as a whole.

• Much greater focus on creating new forms of governance in children's services, linking providers and users of services, for example through neighbourhood councils. This should encourage a new ethos of co-creation in children's services.

• The encouragement of voluntary bodies that help to give voice to local people as advisers, advocates and pressure groups championing children and their needs. They should have stronger powers to petition local councils, forcing issues onto the local authority agenda.

- Devolving power, encouraging citizens to establish 'urban' parish councils that can levy and spend money on neighbourhood priorities such as children's services.
- Transferring the management and ownership of assets to communities through tenants' organisations and development trusts.

The general framework set out here is of a range of community-based suppliers providing children's services within a framework of centrally defined standards. This exemplifies the commitment to central standards and local autonomy elaborated by Stephen Bubb in Chapter 6, which embodies the approach to public service reform set out in this chapter in two main ways. First, it ensures that institutions enjoy significant freedoms from central government. Second, the notion of the public interest emphasises that they have to operate within a framework of central standards, upholding the principles of fair access and equity.

Diversity of provision recognises that no single form will be suitable across all contexts. Progressive politics has something to learn from the tradition of ethical and co-operative socialism, rooted in the commitment to solidarity and mutuality. Citizens freely form associations that are inclusive and egalitarian, and that operate in a co-operative spirit to meet shared needs. These principles are embodied in parent–baby schemes, self-help therapy groups, tenant co-operatives and credit unions. What makes mutuality attractive is that it emphasises self-help and solidarity, rather than setting the two against one another as simple state/market dichotomies imply: disadvantaged individuals are energised by forms of community self-help.

In fact, what any local programme requires is patience from politicians and government: 'transformation' is a long-term process of change that cannot be initiated from the centre alone. It means breaking with traditional approaches to state power – including the public sector audit-and-control culture, intolerant of risk and failure – giving priority to quality over volume in the delivery of public services.

There are inevitably, of course, tensions over volume and quality. One of the central challenges of social and public innovation is how to scale up promising experiments. That means creating systems where ideas and improvements are readily shared. Participative models of public services mean that solutions are spread by word of mouth or peer to peer, rather than mandated by central government. The dilemmas of scaling up are explored by Charles Leadbeater and Hilary Cottam in Chapter 7.

Conclusion

Social democratic governments in Britain in the last century were characterised by a deep paradox of purpose in relation to the state and public services. They have been torn, as David Marquand argues, between two alternative statecrafts, each a legacy of the past.[14] One is the tradition of mechanical reform that is essentially top down and dirigiste. This reflects the premise that national governments should seek to change social behaviour by regulation and manipulation from the centre. But central states do not have the authority or the capacity to engage successfully in complex social engineering.

The empowerment of individuals through the enabling state entails the revival of moral reform, as Peter Clarke describes it.[15] That means returning to the traditions of self-government advocated by G. D. H. Cole, Richard Crossman and Harold Laski, implying active engagement in the public sphere and the devolution of power and control in public services. That tradition is not about rejecting the state, nor does it insist that localism is a panacea for every social ill. It means trusting people, and people can be wrong – and, of course, localities can be small-minded, insular or even corrupt.

It is the relationship between local and central government, and ultimately the relationship between the state, the public service provider and the citizen, that needs to be transformed to achieve the goal of empowerment. Social democratic governments should draw a stronger connection between public service and constitutional reform – articulating a coherent conception of the public interest, not resorting to the arid language of technocratic management and markets. This model of the state implies equalisation through empowerment and public institutions, instead of the passive dispensing of state benefits and services.

The central challenge for progressive politics is to frame a model of the state that will combat new risks, new inequalities and new insecurities – not least the sharp polarisation in children's life-chances. This is a demanding task: all reforms inevitably set up contradictions and dilemmas. It is inevitable that in order to remain accountable, governments want to impose centralised targets in return for investment. But these incentives often conflict with bottom-up, peer-driven pressures to improve. The dominance of national targets and regulation in children's services will reduce the scope for local experiment and enterprise. That undermines the ability of programmes such as Sure Start to achieve enduring outcomes, especially among the hardest-to-reach groups.

Changing the form of the state and with it the nature of citizenship transforms the context in which public services are delivered. The great failing of social democratic governments has been to believe that they can achieve radical domestic reforms through the use of existing state machinery. It is precisely this form of state that frustrates progressive ambitions. The decentralised polity carries risks but also advantages – not least the flourishing of local initiatives such as Sure Start with firmer roots. If communities feel a stronger sense of ownership of public services, this will help to forge new coalitions of support, ensuring adequate levels of public investment.

Over the last decade, the old model of the traditional centralised state has been broken. But a new model is not yet in place that will genuinely empower the individual citizen. Beyond Sure Start and children's services, Britain needs to evolve what I have termed an intermediate state, where independent, decentralised public institutions become self-sustaining actors in the public sphere. Increasingly, progressives must connect the pluralist, decentralised polity with the delivery of better public services. That is the challenge for the future.

19

'Rebalancing' the criminal justice system

Ben Rogers

It is often said that Tony Blair's government has been a centralising one and it is sometimes said that this is particularly true where crime policy is concerned. Like most generalisations about New Labour, this is much too simple. The present Labour government has done much to decentralise crime policy and give local government and local people greater influence in directing police and other criminal justice agencies and holding them to account.[1]

Nevertheless, there is some truth in the centralisation claim. Before New Labour, Britain already had a very centralised criminal justice system. And since 1997 the Home Office has gained new powers over police, courts and probation services. As one government adviser put it to me, nicely capturing the essential point, 'Most people living in England or Wales today would not be able to name anyone, below the Home Secretary, responsible for criminal justice policy in the area where they live,' There are very few, if any, other liberal democracies where this is the case.

Yet there are good prima facie reasons for thinking that while central government has a vital role in funding and regulating police and correctional services – and running national-level agencies – these services work best where there is a strong element of local accountability and a sense of local ownership:

- Problems vary from place to place. The challenges facing a rural police service differ very profoundly from those facing an inner city one, but even neighbouring high-crime inner city neighbourhoods often vary quite dramatically.[2] Tailor-made approaches are needed.
- The criminal justice system, as is often pointed out, cannot do its job without active contributions from other services, including health, education and social care. Yet these services need to be co-ordinated at the local level.

- The criminal justice system cannot do its job without the trust and active engagement of the public. Criminal justice agencies need citizens willing to report crimes, give evidence, employ former offenders and do countless other things.

With these considerations in mind, this chapter lays out some of the ways that the criminal justice system needs to be and could be given a more devolved and participatory character. To emphasise, I am not arguing for an end to central government involvement in the criminal justice system, but merely for a significant shift in the distribution of power and responsibility in favour of localities. We need central government to monitor and control a little less, and we need local government to take on more of a leadership role, holding local criminal justice agencies to account, and being held to account itself, for reducing crime and reoffending.

First of all, however, I pinpoint five main challenges facing the criminal justice system.

The context of criminal justice reform: five challenges

High-crime harm
Overall, crime has fallen by more than 40 per cent since the early 1990s. Britain remains, however, by historical and international standards, a high-crime society. There has, moreover, been a rise in some categories of crime – including organised crime, gun crime and some forms of low-level crime or 'anti-social behaviour'. And the harm done by crime remains very inequitably distributed. People who end up in the hands of the criminal justice system are more likely to come from the disadvantaged 20 per cent in what Ben Lucas calls our '20/80 society',[3] but so are the victims of crime.[4]

High levels of concern about crime
The public believe that the crime rate has not fallen, or at least not in the way the statistics tell us it has – indeed, more people believe that crime is rising now than they did in 1997, according to MORI. Its polls show that crime remains a major public concern – indeed as concern about the economy has declined, so the public has become more worried about issues of security – encompassing terrorism and immigration, but also crime. And though 'fear of crime' has fallen along with the crime rate, it has fallen more slowly than the crime

rate. This is not a superficial thing. Concern about crime has a very severe impact on people – especially the less well off.[5] It also feeds punitive attitudes.

Rising severity of sentences
Despite falling crime levels, this government has presided over a dramatic increase in the number of prisoners. At 80,000, the prison population is, per capita, the highest in western Europe and more than 20,000 higher than when Labour came to power. Yet it is predicted to keep on growing, reaching 90,000 by the end of the decade. The number of child and women prisoners has risen especially sharply. But the number of people serving community sentences has also increased. The criminal justice system, in other words, has become a lot tougher under Labour.

High reoffending rates
The proportion of former male prisoners reoffending within two years of leaving prison has gone up from 55 per cent to 67 per cent in the past five years.

Low levels of confidence in the criminal justice system
Though confidence in the police and the criminal justice system CJS as measured by the British Crime Survey has edged up in the last few years, it remains relatively low. In the early 1980s, for example, over 90 per cent of the public thought the police did a good or very good job. That figure has fallen to less than 80 per cent today. The public are particularly dissatisfied with the criminal justice system's handling of low-level crime and disorder – vandalism, drug dealing, littering and the like.

These, then, are some of the issues that any reforms will need to address. But what contribution can a move towards a less centralised system make? And what would such a system look like? I begin with one general point before focusing on police and 'correctional services' in turn.

First, the challenges identified above can not be tackled through the criminal justice system alone. Social policy is key – in the form of reducing inequality, promoting social mobility and solidarity, and, in particular, redistributing resources to early-years support, as Patrick Diamond elaborates in Chapter 18. Indeed, we need a more evidenced-based and strategic approach to crime reduction, investing more in policies aimed at tackling the roots of crime, and less in the Sisyphean attempt to tackle its consequences. I return to this point below, but it is fundamental and needs emphasising here.

Police and police governance

Everyone now acknowledges that Margaret Thatcher, John Major and Tony Blair between them have presided over a substantial centralisation of power over the police, so upsetting the tripartite system of police governance put in place by the 1964 Police Act – the system that distributed power over the police equally between force leaders, local government in the form of police authorities and the Home Office.[6] To take just some leading examples, centrally run police agencies dealing with serious and organised crime have grown in size and power. Police forces have been amalgamated and those that remain have to meet nationally imposed targets, work within the constraints imposed by the government's national policing plan and subject themselves to regular evaluation by a small army of inspectorates. The Home Secretary has gained new powers to 'intervene' where performance is poor.[7]

These developments have not all been negative. Control has, at least in some cases, led to better governance and improved performance. Centrally imposed standards, targets and inspections have concentrated minds; top-down pressures have enabled introduction of a modest degree of workforce reform and other changes. And much of the pressure from the centre has been directed at promoting greater partnership working and community and stakeholder involvement.[8]

This said, it is hard to deny that recent changes have created an accountability system which is ill balanced and ill defined, with too much power invested at the centre and not enough at the locality. Below I distinguish between four levels at which the police are or can be governed – central, regional, local and neighbourhood – and lay out a broad agenda for reform at each level.[9] If realised, these reforms would represent a considerable devolution of power, with local government in particular coming to take on a much more important role in directing the police and holding them to account.

Central level
At this level – the level of Whitehall and Westminster (in the case of policing the Home Office), the Association of Chief Police Officers, HM Inspectorate of Constabulary (HMIC) – there are a number of shortcomings in the present arrangements.

One problem is that crime policy is simply insufficiently strategic. As already indicated, public spending on crime reduction has not always been used to best effect: too much, arguably, goes on remedial rather than preventive activity. The present government has begun to rectify this, asking hard questions about the value for money of different types of social investment, but there is a lot further to go. Few politicians, for instance, seem ready to explore in public the question of whether spending on more police officers is money well spent. On a more practical note, strengthening parliamentary select committees by giving them more resources and greater powers to call civil servants and not just ministers to account would help reduce the democratic deficit at the top of the criminal justice system.[10]

A second shortcoming of recent policy is that investment has not always been progressive, with the disadvantaged relatively neglected.[11] Again, the government has done much to address this, but government analysis, seen by the author, shows that the Home Office's funding formula, with 'floors' and 'ceilings' limiting the scope for redistribution, still favours better-off areas.

Perhaps the greatest concern here, however, is that the centre is simply doing too much, at the expense of localities. The challenges facing the police vary very significantly from locality to locality. But as things work currently, the Home Office sets priorities over very local issues: the national policing framework is too prescriptive, there are too many targets and they remain too focused on output.[12] Professor Mike Hough has argued persuasively that the very significant falls in confidence in the police in London over recent years – the percentage of Londoners thinking the police do a poor job doubled from 9 per cent in 1982 to 18 per cent in 2000 – have been due in large part to excessive centralisation, a managerial focus on reducing crime at the expense of a 'more subtle balance of policing goals', and the overbearing use of centrally imposed targets.[13]

But what would a less controlling centre look like? As far as targets are concerned, central government needs to shift from setting targets for the reduction in specific categories of crime, such as street robbery, to targets for reducing aggregate crime levels (what is sometimes called a 'basket of crimes' approach), to placing a greater weight on reducing inequality in the harm done by crime and to promoting public confidence in the police and perceptions of police fairness. (To its credit, the government has already introduced targets of this type,[14] but the next round of targets need to give greater weight to these.) This will enable police to refocus efforts on building community relations and earning trust, which are themselves vital to the long-term effectiveness of the police service – not least in combating terrorism.[15] At the same time, government should rely less on targets and develop other strategies. Perhaps most importantly, the Home Office and national policing organisations need to renew efforts to reform the police workforce and promote greater professionalisation on the part of the police and the larger policing family.[16] The centre has an important role in creating a more flexible and efficient police service, with greater movement in and out, better standards of project and performance management and more effective deployment of civilian and police staff.

Finally, the inspection system needs to be given greater punch. The current police inspections regime has none of the profile or the weight of Ofsted, comprehensive performance assessments or HM Inspectorate of Prisons' regime. There is in particular a dearth of well-publicised and legible performance data that would allow local government officials and local people to assess the performance of their police service.

Regional level

Since the 1964 Police Act, direction and oversight of Britain's forty-odd police forces has formally rested in the hands of police authorities, made up of local councillors from areas covered by the force, along with independent members. But whatever their qualities in the decades after the Act, police authorities are nowadays widely judged to be weak and ineffective. In particular:

- they have a very low public profile and weak conventions of public engagement;
- they are poorly resourced and supported;
- the 1964 Act's deliberate vagueness about the precise powers and responsibilities of police authorities allows police chiefs to resist demands or even effective scrutiny from police authorities – though authorities appoint senior officers and can remove them, they do a poor job managing their performance.
- elected members (councillors), though making up a bare majority on every authority, lack much punch – they tend to be backbenchers, each from a different local authority.[17]

There is a strong case, then, for giving police authorities more bite. But even if they were to be strengthened in this way, it is not clear that they could alone make good the deficit in local democratic accountability and responsiveness. Police authorities always were remote, but as the government has over the last thirty years gradually reduced the number of forces and increased the size of the area each covers, so they have become remoter still.

Rather then than expect police authorities to play the main sub-national accountability role, we should look to them to serve a more limited and managerial function, working with democratically accountable local government leaders in developing force strategies, and then managing force performance. In order to do this effectively, police authorities need, among other reforms, to be given proper resources (currently chief superintendents can determine how much funding an authority gets) and explicit powers to set force strategy and appraise and remunerate senior officers. The performance of police authorities should in turn become subject to external inspection.

Local level
Though local authorities help pay for the police through the police authority-levied precept, they have little direct say in the setting of the precept or in its expenditure, or more generally in governing the police. Basic command units (BCUs) are now almost all co-terminous with local authority borders, but they answer upwards to force headquarters, and through them to police authorities and central government, not outwards to democratically accountable local authorities. Perhaps the very substantial democratic deficit at the local level helps explain why poll after poll shows that the public are very dissatisfied with the way their towns and neighbourhoods are policed – and why the police have in the past been slow to respond to concerns about low-level crime and anti-social behaviour, or more generally to develop the sort of familiar and responsive 'community policing' the public want.

True, the government has sought to improve this situation. The 1999 Local Government Act gave local authorities responsibility for promoting public safety, and local strategic partnerships (LSPs) and crime and disorder reduction partnerships (CDRPs) provide local government with an opportunity to exercise a leadership role on community safety. But LSPs and CDRPs have low public profiles, are not always accorded primary importance by local authority leaders, and give democratically elected government only an indirect purchase on the police. Government research seen by the author has found that while around 60 per cent of unitary and district councils identify community safety as a key priority, few have community safety programmes 'that go beyond the usual low-level activity of CDRPs'.

Arguably, then, the single most important step that needs to be taken, where police governance is concerned, is making the police more accountable to democratically appointed local leaders and, through them, to local people themselves – though local authority leaders need in turn to step up to the plate and take responsibility for public safety. One approach, advocated by the right-of-centre Policy Exchange think tank, would be to give local government the power to appoint and remove local police chiefs or 'sheriffs', on the American model.[18] This deserves serious consideration, though it would entail a very fundamental recasting of the way the police have been organised in this country since 1964.[19]

A second, less radical option would be to give local authorities greater control over some of the funds currently raised through the local police precept. The majority of police budgets would continue to be passed from central government directly to police force headquarters. And police force heads – chief constables – would continue to appoint and line-manage the heads of local units. But local authorities could retain control over a proportion of the funding they are currently obliged to pass to the police through the police precept, which they could spend on local community safety or crime reduction work. This would encourage greater accountability and scrutiny of police funding, so ensuring that the local police are providing value for money. Giving local democratic leaders new powers and responsibilities over policing would ensure that public safety becomes a high-profile local government priority and encourage them to promote cross-cutting approaches to public safety. Money from this new, locally controlled community safety budget could be spent on non-police services (neighbourhood wardens, youth services, probation and resettlement, even pre-school care), so enhancing 'contestability'. Removing precepting powers from police authorities and giving them to local authorities could also exert downward pressures on council tax.[20]

It is important to recognise that reforms of this kind would involve a change to the role not only of local leaders but also of local police leaders, who would have to negotiate with, and answer to, council leaders as well as senior officers in force headquarters. This could cause problems where local priorities clash with force priorities. On the other hand, it would make local police leaders more sensitive to local priorities and demands. These reforms would also, of course, create a new role for police authorities. They would no longer be the main source for public accountability of the police. The way police authorities and local authorities would work together would depend on the precise allocation of powers and responsibilities, but there are plenty of international examples of locally accountable police forces working successfully with regional- and national-level forces and authorities.

Neighbourhood level

We know the public have long been particularly dissatisfied with the way their immediate environments have been policed. Polling shows that the public has become increasingly concerned about anti-social behaviour and related 'liveability' issues. At the same time, there is good evidence that high-profile, familiar and responsive local police services drive public confidence in the police and reduce concern about crime and demands for more punitive policies.[21] And it has been shown that while involving local people in tackling local problems can be very difficult,[22] it can also help create the familiar and responsive services the public want.[23] For these reasons, and very much in keeping with the government's own 'double devolution agenda', ways need to be found of promoting greater public involvement in directing and working with the police at the parish or neighbourhood level.[24]

Again, central and local government and the police themselves have taken steps to improve the way local communities are policed. Reassurance policing and community policing have been encouraged. Many police forces now consult very effectively with local communities and minority groups. The New Deal for Communities and neighbourhood renewal funds, among other things, have opened up new lines of communication between police and community groups in poor neighbourhoods. But these developments have been far from universal – some forces are doing much better than others. And police accountability to neighbourhoods remains largely informal.

What further, then, could be done to encourage greater accountability and public involvement at the neighbourhood, ward or parish level? The difficulty here is that neighbourhoods differ very widely. For this reason it is probably better not to impose a single accountability structure at this level, but instead rely on indirect pressures and the encouragement of local innovation and the promotion of best practice, as Geoff Mulgan makes clear in Chapter 5. Giving local government greater authority over the police should encourage them to become more outward-looking. Putting greater weight on confidence-centred targets could do the same. There are also opportunities for building an enhanced role for councillors in representing their neighbourhoods to the police and holding police to account for the quality of neighbourhood policing – along lines laid out in the recent local government White Paper, *Strong and Prosperous Communities*. It would be good, in particular, to see some large, high-crime cities experimenting with a Chicago-style approach, requiring the police to hold regular neighbourhood beat meetings, where local councillors, members of the public and the police air problems and agree on a plan of action[25] – this, in effect, would be an example, in the criminal justice area, of the sort of 'co-creation' of public services that Charles Leadbeater and Hilary Cottam explore in Chapter 7. Ensuring more publicly available and comprehensible information about the performance of local forces could also help boost neighbourhood accountability and engage the public in under-performing services.

Police accountability: conclusion

It is widely agreed that the tripartite system of police accountability is now either dead or nearly so. This is often followed by calls for its revival. But times have moved on and the tripartite system is no longer, if it ever was, 'fit for purpose'. Indeed some of the problems, I have argued, stem not from a lack of power invested at the police authority level but an excess, disempowering more local accountability. In so far as there is a historical precedent to guide reform, the pre-1964 arrangements are a better one. These gave local authorities, or at least urban local authorities, a real and direct accountability for funding the police, directing them and holding them to account.

Courts, prison and probation

As mentioned earlier, these services face two main challenges: reducing the severity of sentences and tackling reoffending. As with policing, reform is required on a number of fronts, but creating a less centralised and managerial set of services should be a priority.

Tackling sentencing inflation

I begin with a couple of preliminary points. First, it is important to establish that the increase in the number of people serving prison and community sentences cannot be explained by an increase in crime or in the seriousness of cases coming before magistrates and judges. Crime, as we have said, has fallen; there has been no increase in the number of cases coming before the courts, nor, apparently, in their seriousness.[26] Indeed, as Patrick Carter has pointed out in his official report on the correctional services, the proportion of prisoners who are first-time offenders has increased.[27] What we are dealing with here is 'sentencing inflation'.

Second, while some argue that the increase in the severity of sentencing should be welcomed because it reduces crime, by deterring would-be criminals and keeping others locked up, the evidence for this is poor. The number locked up, though high compared with other countries, is relatively small, and has a very moderate effect on the crime rate. Research suggests that in so far as criminals are deterred by anything, it is the perceived likelihood of being caught and found guilty, rather than the severity of the sentence.[28] Nor is the increase effective as a way of promoting reassurance or confidence in the criminal justice system. The public are not well informed about sentencing levels, and are anyway rather less punitive than is generally assumed – a point I return to below.

But it is not just that sentence inflation has not produced any benefits. It has been positively harmful. Prisons are particularly costly institutions. And the over-crowded, under-funded prisons we have are not at all effective at reducing reoffending. In fact almost everyone is agreed that we need to reduce the number of short sentences being handed down, which are particularly pointless.[29] But even community sentences don't come cheap – especially when compared to fines and pre-court diversions.

What then should be done to combat sentencing inflation and in particular the over-reliance on prison? Again government needs to work on a number of fronts at once. Modern governments are very fond of criminal justice legislation, and ten years of intense legislative activity has undoubtedly helped increase offender numbers. Too many people with drug and mental health problems, who would be more effectively treated by the NHS and drug programmes, are ending up in the criminal justice system.[30] The government should also look again at the very tough approach it now takes to offenders who breach the terms of a sentence. This is pushing up the number of those in prison. Probation services and judges need to be given more discretion in deciding when a failure to adhere to the terms of an order should be dealt with informally and when it should be treated as a breach necessitating a return to court and, possibly, a more severe sentence.

Yet the single most important factor driving up inflation is what is sometimes called 'the climate of opinion'. It is hard to say whether public opinion has become more punitive or not over the last few decades – but it certainly has not become less so. It is almost as if, as Nick Pearce has suggested, that as we have become more liberal in most respects, so we have become less tolerant of breaches in those rules that remain.[31] This in turn has worked to drive up sentencing, by encouraging law makers, sentencers and those in the prison and probation services to get ever tougher in the way they respond both to crime and to breaches of licence.[32] But what shapes the climate of opinion?

What we have here is a tragedy of misunderstanding. In fact, the public is not particularly punitive in its attitudes. Take a couple of recent findings. A Joseph Rowntree Foundation survey last year found that when it came to dealing with anti-social behaviour by teenagers, the public favoured investment in early-years intervention above investment in constructive activities for young people and tough action against perpetrators.[33] In a similar vein, a recent survey by SmartJustice and Victim Support found that two thirds of victims did not believe that prison discouraged reoffending. Seven out of ten victims also want to see more treatment programmes in the community for offenders suffering from mental health problems and for drug addicts to tackle the causes of non-violent crime.[34] The public, however, encouraged by the media and politicians themselves, consistently under-estimate the severity of the disposals being handed down. The view that the criminal justice system is soft on criminals, then, is fuelled less by a desire for it to be more punitive than it is than by a belief that it is less punitive than it is. At the same time, those responsible for sentencing take citizens to be more punitive than they are; they respond by issuing ever tougher sentences, though these in turn do very little to meet public concerns.

How can this spiral of failed communication be tackled? This is where the arguments for a more localised and participatory court and correctional services begin. True, there is much that the centre can do to reduce inflationary pressures on the system. Politicians should stop talking as much as they do, or in the way they do, about the need to get tougher on criminals or to 'rebalance the system in favour of victims'. The government needs to find ways of engaging the public in making criminal justice policy, to work hard to bust the myth that the system is soft on crime, and to provide people with a more realistic understanding of what courts, prison and probation actually do. But more visible, responsive and participatory courts, probation agencies and prisons have a vital role to play in answering public concerns that the system is 'soft' and unresponsive, and pushing the climate of opinion in a more progressive direction.

Three local participatory processes/institutions merit a special mention: restorative justice, community payback and community courts. Restorative justice has been shown to be extremely popular with victims and is generally at least as effective as prison in cutting reoffending, at least for less serious crimes. At the same time it is relatively cheap to administer. As such it has enormous potential as a compliment to or, where possible, an alternative to more expensive and 'tougher' disposals.[35] 'Community payback' or offender community service, whether involving prisoners or probationers, is similarly popular with the public, who like to see that justice is being done, and can help promote confidence in criminal justice services. It can also contribute to rehabilitation and resettlement.[36]

Finally, community courts and community justice panels – panels staffed by citizens – are perhaps best understood as institutions that pursue the sorts of approach I have been describing. Local institutions that work with other public services and the public more generally to promote a 'problem-solving' approach to crime make wide use of restorative justice and community payback. Starting with its flagship North Liverpool Community Justice Centre, the government is beginning to promote a more outward-looking, public-minded approach to sentencing and rehabilitation, but it could do more. The Institute for Public Policy Research has in the past suggested that the government pilot 'community justice panels' and is currently helping pilot a 'teen court' – a court run for teenagers by teenagers.[37] Given that most crime is committed by young men in their late teens and early twenties, perhaps we should also be exploring the possibility of peer courts for this age group. These sorts of problem-solving, restorative initiative have enormous potential to bring the justice system closer to the public it is meant to serve.

Bringing down reoffending

What about the second main subject of concern: high and rising rates of recidivism? As already said, severity of sentencing and its corollary, prison over-crowding, make a major contribution to reoffending and measures that bring down prison numbers should reduce it. Beyond this, there is a fairly broad consensus to what best practice involves when it comes to rehabilitation and resettlement, though even best practice is very far from failsafe. First, successful rehabilitation involves carefully worked-out and tailor-made programmes of support for offenders, and this in turn involves continuity of care between probation and prison. In this light, recent reforms to sentencing that promote personalised sentences aimed explicitly at addressing the problems that lead to reoffending (notably, the Criminal Justice Act 2003) and the creation of a unified prison and probation service, the National Offender Management Service (NOMS), directed at offering an 'end to end' service for offenders are clearly to be welcomed. Formal integration, however, will achieve little unless offenders are supported by able and committed staff dedicated to their welfare; rehabilitation depends on sustained personal relations – mentoring – and personalised support in developing moral and social skills (Raynor and Maguire 2006).[38] NOMS must not, in the rush for efficiency and cost savings, lose sight of this.

Even the best-integrated criminal justice system, moreover, can't do its job alone. Joined-up working between correctional agencies and other local services, including health, education and skills, employment and housing, is essential. As an influential social exclusion report found, stable housing can reduce reoffending by 20 percent, employment by between a third and a half.[39] Drug treatment, healthcare and family networks are also crucial. The government has gone some way to encouraging more joined-up working between all these services in caring for offenders: local area agreements, for instance, now offer a structure through which joined-up measures to reduce reoffending across different agencies can be delivered. But there is further to go. The police have taken a relatively active role in new local government partnership arrangements, ushered in by the Local Government Act 1997, courts and probation much less so.[40] And there is real concern that with the decision to structure NOMS regionally, and more or less to abolish probation boards in their traditional guise, prison and probation will become more rather than less remote from local services and local people.

What then could be done to increase the accountability and connectedness of these services? Measures such as local government representation on court boards might help – along with building capacity to look after offenders across services.[41] But ultimately, just as local authorities should be given some financial control over and responsibility for policing, so they should be given more control over and responsibility for the performance of courts, prisons and the community management of offenders. This will not only give the system a degree of local democratic accountability almost entirely lacking at the moment. Making local councils bear more of the costs of offending and reoffending will concentrate their minds on reducing these things.[42] There have been a number of experiments in the United States to give very local communities responsibility for money that is currently spent on offenders from those communities ('justice reinvestment') and the results look encouraging.[43] Smaller, more locally based prisons would also help cut reoffending, as Charles Clarke argued while Home Secretary.

Conclusion

The centre will always have a key role to play in the criminal justice system –
in setting and upholding standards, ensuring equity and in directly managing
national-level agencies. But we need greater localism to encourage joined-up
working, improve responsiveness to local concerns, and promote confidence
and legitimacy.

20

Drowning in alphabet soup?
Is there a case for simplifying skills policy?

David Coats, Laura Williams and
Alexandra Jones

Introduction

The chapters in this book seek to develop a new approach to public service reform. How can we embrace the notion of citizen-consumers? What can markets do that conventional models of public service cannot? How do we draw boundaries around what we mean by 'the public'?

While all these issues have been central to the debates of the last five years, they are in a significant sense a new departure for the left. Skills policy, on the other hand, is an old chestnut that has left policy makers perplexed and frustrated. The skills bureaucracy appears to have a life of its own. Institutions have come and gone with surprising rapidity. And despite this hyperactivity all governments have struggled to make any detectable impression on the underlying problems.

In this essay we return to first principles and offer some tentative but (we hope) compelling answers to the following core questions:[1]

- Are skills increasingly important to the UK's prosperity? And if this is so, can we be clear about the objectives of skills policy?
- Does the UK have a skills problem and, if so, how is this best described?
- How successful has government policy been since 1997? What are the major successes and disappointments?
- The Foster review, the Leitch review and the current Further Education and Training Bill are all designed to set a clear direction for policy.[2] But given our diagnosis, are these measures sufficient? Are they radical enough and, if not, what more needs to be done?

Our central case in this paper is that the skills debate must be widened to embrace social policy as well as economic policy goals. Three themes underpin the argument: improving the quality of the demand for skills, improving the quality and consistency of supply, and raising the aspirations of both employers and individuals.

The objectives of skills policy: what's the destination?

Consistent with our desire to return to first principles, we believe that a clear statement of policy objectives can help to inform our understanding of the problems that the UK faces and the solutions with the best chance of success. It might seem a little presumptuous to suggest that we have the answer when so many others have struggled and failed. We therefore present these ideas with a degree of caution and humility.

First, we argue that policy should aim to create a culture where both individuals and employers place a high value on learning. A core objective is to ensure that no group is left behind. The purpose must be to encourage aspiration, to facilitate development and allow people to make as much progress as they can in their lives and careers. In other words, we believe that policy should go beyond the Leitch review's notion of 'economically valuable skills'.

There must be a particular focus on those groups suffering from multiple disadvantage – especially those currently excluded from the labour market who would like to work if they could. We endorse the government's goal of reducing the number of people in receipt of incapacity benefit (IB) but believe that an integrated approach is essential, linking benefit reform (making work pay) to skills development, improvements in housing and community safety and the provision of proper support to those with mild to moderate mental health conditions. An increasing proportion of IB recipients are showing problems such as anxiety and depression; unless government recognises the roots of the problem and invests in mental health provision, then reducing the number of IB recipients will remain a noble aspiration rather than a practical reality.

Second, skills policy should be oriented to the promotion of innovation by individuals. The aim here must be to ensure that individuals have the wherewithal to think constructively about how they might do their jobs better, how they might contribute to continuous improvement and how skills development can enable a greater sense of fulfilment from work.

Third, the institutional architecture should encourage innovation by skills providers, allowing a multiplicity of organisations to test new approaches and offer learners new options in response to rapid change in the economy. This objective is consistent with the Leitch recommendation that the system should be demand led. It embraces the criticism that the existing planned system offers weak incentives to providers to respond to changing circumstances.

Fourth, while we would not suggest that the 'planned' system should continue, we do believe in the importance of ensuring that employers express their skill needs, based on the best information available, at the level of the sector. Our purpose here is to allow employers to collaborate and to develop a sophisticated understanding of the challenges that they face. Employers have to be aspirational too.

Fifth, we need more 'political staying power'. In the past, further education (FE) has been a rather low priority, viewed by politicians as less glamorous than higher education and less electorally important than schools. It is essential that the pressure for continuous improvement is maintained and that politicians recognise that continually tinkering with structures is not the best way to drive sustained change through the FE system. A higher level of political commitment is also essential if we are to create 'parity of esteem' between the academic and vocational routes. The idea that 'vocational is second best' remains deeply embedded in the UK's culture – and may have been exacerbated by the rapid expansion of higher education over the last decade. It is slightly disappointing that the government felt unable to endorse the more radical proposals of the Tomlinson review, which would have created a unified system, placing vocational and academic qualifications on an equal footing and allowing easy transfer from one path to another.

Finally, we need a clear vision of what FE is for. In the past this has been the 'everything else' sector, serving the needs of those aged sixteen to eighteen, participants in the government's active labour programmes, adults with basic skills problems and other adult learners pursuing vocational qualifications or seeking a stepping stone to higher education. Clarity about objectives can help to bring a greater measure of consistency to a very diverse portfolio of activities, knitting them together in a narrative about improving demand, improving supply and raising aspirations.

So what's the problem?

It is easy to offer a rather bleak diagnosis of the UK's skills problem. Employers claim that they are unable to find recruits with appropriate skills for the job; learners find the skills system bewildering and are confronted with options that are poorly understood; historic problems such as poor literacy and numeracy among those already at work have yet to be adequately addressed; and many people at work report that their skills are not being fully used by their employers. Most seriously perhaps, the quality of provision is variable and mediocrity is sometimes allowed to flourish unchallenged. Disadvantaged communities have been left behind despite many policy interventions. Employers have adopted 'coping strategies' to deal with workers' deficiencies in literacy, instead of addressing the problem at the root by investing in the basic skills of employees.

These hard realities seem somewhat distant from the government's vision of a high-skill, knowledge-driven economy. In straightforward terms, public policy has failed to adopt the long-term and consistent approach required for the government's objectives to be achieved. There have been too many initiatives, too much change and too little commitment to a strategy for skills development rooted in a political consensus. The status quo cannot continue if the UK is to achieve higher productivity overall and better life-chances for the most disadvantaged.

Of course, one might say that this is an overly pessimistic assessment, but anything less than a dispassionate critique can easily lead to complacency. These are problems of long standing with which governments of all political colours have wrestled. It is difficult to think of a period over the last forty years when government was not trying to stimulate a wide-ranging national conversation about the weaknesses of the UK's skills base or when the label 'under construction' could not have been attached to the UK's skills system.

Skills, qualifications and institutions

Economists tend to view employers' inability to match skills supply to skills demand as a simple market failure, but the reality is that inconsistency of policy combined with institutional confusion has produced an institutional failure too. One reason, for example, why the German skills system has generally been viewed as superior is not because it is mostly market led or characterised by more widespread contestability but because employers are well organised in trade associations, have a stake in the institutions and work closely with public agencies to ensure that the supply of skills meets their needs.

We might see this as an unavoidable difference between Germany's co-ordinated market economy (where institutions do a lot of the work) and the UK's liberal market economy (where markets are supposed to play the co-ordinating role).[3] One interpretation of this analysis is that there is little value in trying to build employer institutions in the UK when such initiatives have had little success in the past. Nevertheless, we are not necessarily the prisoners of history and it is possible with adequate time and patience to develop both formal and informal networks that facilitate a more sophisticated expression of employer demand. It is unlikely, for example, that the Leitch prescription will cure the patient without some effective intermediate institutions offering high-quality brokerage at sub-regional level. Moreover, the provisions in the Further Education and Training Bill to simplify the introduction of training levies suggest that the government also believes that institutional gaps need to be filled if the system is to work effectively.

Despite these acknowledged institutional failures, perhaps the central issue is that policy remains focused on qualifications rather than skills, although the terms are often used interchangeably. When employers complain about 'skills shortages' they are generally not complaining about a shortage of staff with the appropriate qualifications. According to the most recent National Employers Skills Survey there were only 159,000 skill shortage vacancies in England in 2004, representing 0.8 per cent of employment. Twenty per cent of organisations reported 'skills gaps', where existing employees were judged to possess insufficient skills to perform effectively, but even here only 7 per cent of the national workforce was affected.

This raises the inevitable question of whether employers are disgruntled without reason. From one perspective the persistent expression of employer dissatisfaction could be seen as little more than anecdote-driven moaning. But viewed slightly differently, employers may have more cause for complaint if their real concern is with communication skills, problem-solving skills, the ability to work in a team or the ability to undertake tasks without close super-vision. Some of these features are not skills per se, even if they can help to explain why employers complain that employees with the right characteristics are in short supply. We can be certain, however, that these attributes are not (and probably cannot) be guaranteed by the existing qualifications system.

Much ink has also been consumed by the economic analysis of the UK's skills deficit. Most recently, HM Treasury have published six special reports examining the productivity problem and identifying five policy areas where action must be taken if the UK is to close the 'productivity gap' with other major developed economies.[4] The pervasive influence of HM Treasury's economic analysis is confirmed by the Leitch review, which explicitly talks about world-class skills as a necessary response to the intensification of competition associated with globalisation. In our view a better approach is to accept the importance of this macro-economic argument and to make clear that widening access to skills is critical to the prospects of both the most disadvantaged in the community and the more affluent who want to 'get on'. Policy must rest on an understanding of two unavoidable facts: there is a class gradient in achievement levels; and investment in skills is essential for the achievement of conventional centre-left goals such as equality, social justice and social inclusion.

How far have we travelled . . . and what's wrong with where we are?

At this point it might be useful to summarise the implications of our story so far. First, what is needed more than anything else is a consensus about the nature of the skills 'problem'. Second, we need a better appreciation of the reasons for a trans-generational culture of low aspiration, where learning is either not valued or is seen as 'not for the likes of us'. Third, the brutal reality of spatial inequalities (that some regions, sub-regions and localities perform less well than others) must be at the heart of policy, suggesting that a differentiated strategy is needed, building on the idea that decisions about resources and priorities should be better matched to needs. However, it is important not to be too critical. Some progress has been made in the last ten years and sound foundations have been laid, enabling policy makers to address the deeper problems in the future.

For example, since 1997 there has been an improvement in staying-on rates post-sixteen (although they remain low by the standards of comparable countries). We have also witnessed better results at both GCSE and A-level. Initiatives such as Train to Gain have put skills back on the agenda for those employers who might have been inclined to avoid the issue in the past, especially among small and medium enterprises. The UK's higher education system generally works well and expansion has been a success. And public institutions (regional development authorities, local authorities, local learning and skills councils, Jobcentre Plus) have become slightly better at identifying likely structural change in the economy so that anticipatory action can be taken – although there is still scope for significant improvement and a generalisation of best practice across the country. A good example is the Rover Taskforce, which, while fairly effective at dealing with the closure of Longbridge, still left displaced unskilled workers in jobs which saw their pay fall by an average of £3,500 per year.[5]

Nevertheless, despite these modest advances, the Leitch criticisms of the 'plan and provide' model are well made. There is too much centralisation, too little flexibility built into the system and too many incentives for providers to do tomorrow precisely what they are doing today. Similarly, there are too many organisations in the skills field, undertaking overlapping functions, failing to collaborate effectively and confusing both employers and learners. It is the most disadvantaged communities and those labelled as 'failures' at the end of their school careers that have been left behind.

We might therefore set a straightforward test for the effectiveness of the Leitch recommendations: can we be confident that we are about to put in place a skills system that enables both employers and employees to articulate their needs and have them met in a policy context that is focused on the achievement of desirable social outcomes?

If we know where we want to go, then how will we get there?

The Leitch review proposes what is essentially an injection of market discipline into the provision of training. 'Plan and provide' is to be abandoned and the supply of training refocused on expressed employer and individual demand. Put simply, providers will stand or fall by their ability to offer courses that employers and learners find attractive. Revenue will follow customer preferences so that falling enrolments lead to falling revenue.

Even though this may look like a radical break from previous policy, there is a strong case for saying that the direction has been detectable for some time. For example, the Employer Training Pilots (ETPs, now rebranded as Train to Gain) are essentially rooted in this model. We can see that they are demand led because employers (and employees) are responsible for articulating their own demands. As with the Leitch proposals, the money follows the learner.

And despite some criticism of deadweight costs, there can be little doubt that the ETPs have been a success in improving the supply of and the demand for level 2 qualifications.[6] It is also welcome that the government is developing Train to Gain at level 3 with some co-payment by employers, since it is at this level that organisations can expect to reap significant productivity gains from skills development.

In this context, policy makers therefore have to answer two questions as they consider the implementation of the Leitch recommendations: What kind of market is needed for a demand-led system to be effective? And how should this market be regulated? Perhaps we should begin with some simple statements of principle: this is a market that should be configured to ensure

- effective competition between a range of providers;
- relative ease of entry to and exit from the sector;
- high-quality standards set by the regulator with a proper regime of inspection, although with a lighter touch than the present arrangements;
- reserve powers on intervention where it is clear that the market has failed.

Consistent with our earlier observations, it is essential that a demand-led system does not further exclude the most disadvantaged. We refer below to the need for a comprehensive approach that embraces more than skills policy. However, the regulator might also place a premium on encouraging providers who have a track record of innovation in meeting the needs of poor communities.

Competition

A natural consequence of the Leitch proposals is that providers who can spot gaps in existing provision or who can anticipate future demand will do well, whereas those with less market intelligence and creativity will suffer. Even a careful student of Leitch would be hard pressed to understand the full implications of the proposals. Indeed, the potential benefits of a market-based approach are implicit rather than explicit and the reader is left to draw their own conclusions.

It is not our intention to challenge the fundamental assumption that a demand-led system is needed to break the UK's institutional deadlock. However, we would say that the test of success should be straightforward and tough: contestability is working if it leads to higher demand for skills, quality and innovation in the provision of training and rising aspirations among both employers and individuals. Equally, and in line with our earlier observations, a market-based framework must be demonstrably better at delivering both economic and social policy objectives than the 'plan and provide' model that exists today. These are exacting standards, but it is important to be clear about what contestability can do, not least so as to have a robust argument against those who may be hostile to or sceptical about the effectiveness of a demand-led system.

Effective competition demands informed consumers. And insights from the economics of information show us that information asymmetries can lead to inefficient markets and unintended consequences.[7] In this context it is important to understand that the ETPs included a brokerage function to assist employers in identifying skill needs. It was assumed that employers, without information and guidance, would find it hard to identify the best options available. We would argue that this is a necessary condition for the successful implementation of Train to Gain as a national programme. Most importantly perhaps, properly brokered information must be available to minimise the risk of information asymmetries. This is not just a matter of publishing league tables, but also of monitoring the labour market destinies of students from individual institutions. There is a strong case for saying that the Learning and Skills Council (LSC) as regulator should take responsibility for funding these activities, setting appropriate standards for transparency, brokerage and the provision of individual advice and guidance.

Sector skills councils (SSCs) also have a critical role to play here. They will be scanning the horizon for new skills challenges – new markets, new technologies, new sources of competitive pressure – and adapting the qualifications system accordingly. This is a matter not only of responding to employer needs as currently expressed, but of anticipating change and, by engaging employers in the design of qualifications, raising the quality of demand. This means that SSCs must have the highest-quality staff and effective strategic leadership. They are the indispensable lubricant of the demand-led system.

While Leitch is fairly clear that a demand-led model will require strong contestability, the provisions of the Further Education and Training Bill seem to be pulling in the opposite direction. This apparent tension need not be fatal, particularly since we are recommending that the LSC have reserve intervention powers where the market is failing. Nonetheless, as Leitch is implemented, policy makers must be clear about where they expect the heavy lifting to be done. Are they really committed to allowing the market to do the job, or is there still a hankering after centrally directed improvement programmes sponsored by the LSC? Both are equally rational policy approaches, but the balance between them needs to be explicit otherwise, once again, the system will run the risk of becoming dysfunctional.

Ease of entry and exit

A demand-led model can offer new opportunities for significant improvements in the quality of provision by allowing new suppliers to enter the market, facilitating the 'exit' of the mediocre or failing and letting the high performers acquire or merge with under-performers. It is self-evident that in a demand-led system mediocre providers, or those that have failed to adapt to labour market change, will find that enrolments and revenue are falling. Encouraging positive merger and acquisition activity can lead to economies of scale, better use of assets and a transfer of knowledge and expertise from the excellent to the mediocre. One might also anticipate an improvement in the quality of management alongside improvements in the quality of teaching and learning. Inevitably there will be some consolidation across the sector, with providers running more than one institution and innovators finding that they have captured a large share of the market. But if the arrangements work well then we can be confident that the Leitch reforms will lead to a levelling up of standards.

From the point of view of both learners and employers it is essential that this process should happen with as little disruption as possible. If our goal here is to use the market to improve standards then all learners must have access to high-quality courses, preferably in their locality: we cannot have endless controversies about college closures or reductions in the range of courses on offer. Nor can the regulator allow 'cherry picking', with providers focusing on the most lucrative or 'easy to deliver' courses at the expense of more complex or less popular options. For learners and employers, turbulence in the provider market should not be translated into turbulence in the provision of training; transitions should be as seamless as possible, with learners and employers hardly noticing the process of restructuring beyond the fact that they are benefiting from improvements in quality.

Quality guarantees and inspection

A demand-led system cannot be a free-for-all and the regulator must continue to take responsibility for maintaining quality standards. However, we might anticipate a lighter-touch inspection regime simply because employers and learners will be 'voting with their feet'; bad institutions will see enrolments fall and they will either disappear from the market or be taken over by more effective institutions. Nevertheless, the LSC as regulator should still be setting some targets for institutions as a spur to continual improvement alongside the collection and dissemination of information about provider performance.

Moreover, it is essential in a demand-led system for funding to be linked to outcomes. And it is here that the government must be explicit when Leitch is fully implemented. In other words, money should be passed to providers on the basis of high-quality results. The quality standards need to be exacting and should be increased over time – just as employers will be required through sector skills agreements to meet demanding targets in raising the skills of the workforce.

A reserve power to deal with market failure
We have already seen that the market, if working efficiently, should ensure that under-performing institutions are taken over by more effective providers better able to respond to local demand. This reflects the 'market for corporate control' argument used to justify the efficiency of mergers and acquisitions in the private sector – it is said that capital markets are essentially making a judgement that the management team of the acquiring company will be able to improve the performance of the target organisation.

However, we also know that capital markets can fail. There is ample evidence to show that merger and acquisition activity does not always lead to greater efficiency or effectiveness.[8] And some companies are able to keep their shareholders and customers happy with mediocre performance for a prolonged period. We need to guard against the risk of a similar phenomenon emerging in a demand-led training system. In particular, there is a case for giving the regulator reserve powers to deal with those situations where the market is not adequately addressing under-performance.

We would emphasise that these are reserve powers and we expect them to be used sparingly. In other words, we are recommending a strong contestability regime, supervised by a regulator that understands markets, providing high-quality information to both employers and learners, with effective powers to intervene only if the market fails.

Skills in the context of wider policies to combat social disadvantage

Our wider account of skills policy objectives has already made clear the importance of social justice and social inclusion. In thinking about the journey that policy makers must take we would suggest that the focus must be on holistic policies that incorporate skills into a comprehensive framework to tackle social disadvantage. Improving skills alone cannot enhance the life-chances of the most excluded communities, since they are unlikely to be in work, looking for work or aware of what skills they might need to find work. Indeed, despite the relative success of the government's 'work first' policy, some communities have failed to benefit from rising prosperity and the 'more work in fewer households' story that began to emerge in the mid-1990s remains a persistent problem.[9]

For progress to be made, skills policy must be linked to Sure Start, the various new deals, policies to promote enterprise, community safety initiatives, public health programmes and housing improvement schemes. Achieving the government's target for the reduction of child poverty is also important in this context, as is the legitimate desire to get more IB recipients back into work.

Even though this may sound like common sense, it is a hugely ambitious undertaking demanding collaboration across many government departments. Nothing on the same scale has been attempted since the community development programmes of the 1970s. But the case for a radical policy initiative is compelling and a determined effort to improve the prospects of the poor demands nothing less.

Under-utilisation of skills

Even if we can get the demand-led system to work effectively and we can use an integrated approach to skills to tackle social exclusion, an improvement in the supply of skills does not necessarily mean that employers will deploy those skills effectively. The Working in Britain survey, sponsored by the Economic and Social Research Council, revealed some persuasive evidence of under-utilisation of skills.[10] Support for this analysis can be found in Leitch's discussion of the importance of management and leadership, where it is explicitly accepted that skills will be under-used unless managers achieve a high level of competence – and there is evidence that the UK is weak on this dimension, ranked behind the United States, Germany and France.

Leitch places a high value on the conclusion of new sector skills agreements with 'hard attainment targets for employers to deliver improvements in skills'. We would endorse this approach, but would add that 'hard' must mean 'hard' – employers must be challenged to improve their performance and accept their responsibilities. Nor should we under-estimate the importance of skills development for employee motivation and productivity. It is not just a matter of employers demonstrating their commitment to employees by investing in skills – important though that may be. The reality is that individuals who are engaged and sometimes challenged by their work are more likely to experience a sense of achievement, more likely to be committed to their employer's enterprise and more likely to develop an appetite for further learning and development. A culture of aspiration cannot be sustained in workplaces where employees are bored, disaffected and disconnected.

Conclusion

We believe that the approach set out here goes with the grain of current policy, but establishes a wider skills vision for the future. Social justice and social inclusion are central objectives of skills policy and it is insufficient to frame the discussion solely in terms of 'economically valuable' skills. Drawing a clear distinction between skills and qualifications is another important element in the mix – particularly when we are exploring the existence of alleged skills shortages. The Leitch review's proposals for a demand-led system can overcome the bureaucratic confusion of today's alphabet soup of institutions. It is our strong belief that a market-driven model has a much better chance of breaking out of the UK's low skills equilibrium than previous interventions, provided of course that the system meets our conditions for market effectiveness.

To restate the essence of our case: market efficiency depends on effective competition, ease of entry and exit, and the absence of information asymmetries. This means that both employers and individuals must make better choices about skills development using accurate, transparent and accessible information. Effective brokerage supported by individual advice and guidance is essential in improving the quality of both employer and employee demand. In those relatively rare cases where markets fail, the regulator must have appropriate powers to intervene and safeguard the public interest. Markets can be tremendously powerful tools, but they are servants, not masters.

It would be a major achievement if the implementation of a demand-led approach to skills policy was able to halt and indeed reverse more than a century of British under-performance, while achieving a more inclusive society with better life-chances for all; in other words, if the implementation of the Leitch review secured our three central objectives for UK skills policy – higher demand, higher-quality provision and higher aspirations.

About the contributors

David Albury is an independent policy and organisational consultant. Between 2002 and 2005 he was, for half his time, principal adviser in the Prime Minister's Strategy Unit, making major contributions to policy and strategy for health, education, devolved decision making and innovation in public services. As a consultant he has worked with professionals and politicians, managers and users in organisations across all sectors of public services and at all levels – national, regional and local – including leading the turnaround of a number of failing or under-performing organisations. Prior to becoming a consultant he held senior management positions in universities and in regeneration agencies. The thread of continuity through his career has been the inter-relationship between technological innovation, cultural development, organisational change, economic growth and social justice. David is a member of the governance group of PSRG.

Sir Michael Bichard has worked throughout his career in the public sector – twenty years in local government and nearly ten in central government. He was chief executive of Brent Borough Council and Gloucestershire County Council and in 1990 became chief executive of the government's Benefits Agency. In 1995 he was appointed permanent secretary at the Department of Employment and then the Department for Education and Employment. Michael received a knighthood in the 1999 Queen's Birthday Honours. In May 2001 he left the civil service and in September 2001 was appointed rector of the London Institute, the largest art and design institute in Europe, which in May 2004 became University of the Arts London. In January 2004 he was appointed by the Home Office to chair the Soham/Bichard inquiry and on 1 April 2005 he became chair of the Legal Services Commission.

Stephen Bubb is the chief executive of Acevo, the third-sector body representing 2,000 top leaders, and the secretary general of the newly established European Third Sector Leaders Network. He is also chair of the Adventure Capital Fund, which invests into community enterprises in

England. After Oxford, he held major national roles in the Transport and General Workers' Union, the National Union of Teachers and the Assistant Masters Association and was a founding director of the National Lottery Charities Board. He has also sat on many boards in the health service, education and the third sector and was a councillor in Lambeth. Much in demand as a speaker and commentator here and abroad, he advocates a radical role for the third sector in national life.

Liam Byrne has been member of Parliament for Birmingham Hodge Hill since 2004 and minister of state for nationality, citizenship and immigration at the Home Office since 2006. Previously, he spent a year as under-secretary of state for care services at the Department of Health. Liam began his career at Andersen Consulting and worked for N. M. Rothschild before starting a venture-backed technology company in 2000. He is the author of *Local Government Transformed* (1996), *Information Age Government: Delivering the Blair Revolution* (1998), *New Strategies for Full Employment* (2001) and *Britain in 2020* (2003). He was also co-editor of *Reinventing Government Again* (2004).

Charles Clarke is member of Parliament for Norwich South. He gained extensive experience of local government in the London Borough of Hackney, where he was chair of the Housing Committee and vice-chair of Economic Development between 1980 and 1986. He worked as a researcher and then as chief of staff to former Labour Party leader Neil Kinnock from 1981 to 1992. From 1992 to 1997 Charles was chief executive of Quality Public Affairs, a public affairs management consultancy, before his election to Parliament. He has been MP for Norwich South since 1997. Charles was made parliamentary under-secretary of state for school standards in July 1998. He was appointed minister of state at the Home Office on 29 July 1999 and became minister without portfolio and Labour Party chair in July 2001, Secretary of State for Education and Skills in October 2002 and Home Secretary in December 2004. He left the Home Office in May 2006.

David Coats joined the Work Foundation as associate director of policy in 2004, having previously been head of the Economic and Social Affairs Department at the TUC from 1999 to 2004. He was educated at University College London and the Inns of Court School of Law. From 2000 to 2004 David was a member of the Low Pay Commission. He was appointed a member of the Central Arbitration Committee in 2005.

Hilary Cottam is founding partner with Charles Leadbeater of Participle, the public service design agency. Hilary's previous projects include the design of preventative healthcare services, with the participation of service users; a new approach to school design; and a radical rethink of the prison system. She was previously director of the Design Council and founding director of School Works and the Do Tank. Prior to returning to the UK, she worked for the World Bank. In 2005 Hilary was named UK Designer of the Year and in 2006 she was nominated as a World Economic Forum Young Global Leader for her pioneering work on service design.

Patrick Diamond is a senior visiting fellow at the London School of Economics and Political Science and is the director of the international think tank Policy Network. He is also a fellow of the Royal Society of Arts, a visiting fellow at the University of Northumbria, and is on the board of several charitable organisations. He has written and published widely, including most recently co-editing *Global Europe, Social Europe* (with Anthony Giddens and Roger Liddle, 2006). He was formerly a special adviser in the Prime Minister's Policy Unit (2001–5) and at the Northern Ireland Office. He is a graduate of the University of Cambridge. Patrick is a member of the governance group of PSRG.

Geoffrey Filkin (Lord Filkin) has spent most of his working life in the public sector, rising through local government to become chief executive of Reading Borough Council and then chief executive of the Association of District Councils. In that role he worked with others to form the Local Government Association and to promote new policies for local government before the 1997 general election. In particular he led the creation of the policy of Best Value. He was appointed CBE in 1997. He then worked as a policy analyst and writer and helped form the New Local Government Network. He was appointed to the House of Lords in 1999 and in 2000 led the manifesto review programme for No. 10 on Labour's policies for local government, in particular the need for a new positive partnership, the New Localism. For four years from 2001 Geoffrey was a minister in the Home Office, the Department of Constitutional Affairs and the Department for Education and Skills with a wide range of ministerial responsibilities. He now chairs the PSRG, which he founded in 2005, as well as chairing the Merits Committee in the House of Lords and St Albans Cathedral Music Trust. He is also a non-executive director and adviser to various companies.

Dermot Finch is director of the Centre for Cities at the Institute of Public Policy Research, which is taking a fresh look at the economic drivers behind urban growth and change. Previously, he was a senior policy adviser at HM Treasury (1994–2005), including three years at the British embassy in Washington, DC (2001–4) and two years as a private secretary in both Kenneth Clarke's and Gordon Brown's ministerial teams (1996–7). His range of Treasury policy responsibilities included financial services, the euro, productivity, enterprise and cities.

Anthony Giddens (Lord Giddens) is the former director of the London School of Economics and Political Science. He is currently life fellow of King's College, Cambridge, and a member of the House of Lords. He is the author of *The Third Way* (1998), among many other books.

Robert Hill's early working life involved a wide experience of public services, politics and public policy. Following a period working for the Audit Commission, Robert was Tony Blair's adviser on health and local government during Labour's first term. In 2001 he was appointed as the Prime Minister's political secretary. When Charles Clarke became Education Secretary in late 2002 Robert joined him as his special adviser and continued to work with him at the Home Office until May 2005. Robert now works as an independent consultant with a range of organisations, helping them to think about and implement public policy. He also teaches and writes regularly.

John Hutton has been Secretary of State for Work and Pensions since 2005. He was previously minister of state with responsibility for social care, then health, at the Department of Health. From 1994 to 1999 he served on the Select Committee for Home Affairs, as parliamentary private secretary to Margaret Beckett, and was nominated parliamentary under-secretary of state for health and social care in October 1998. Before his election to Parliament he was a senior law lecturer at the University of Northumbria.

Alexandra Jones has been associate director of research at the Work Foundation since 2002. She is responsible for developing and running large-scale projects, working with a range of stakeholders across the public and private sector. Her key areas of expertise include cities, flexibility and work–life balance, diversity and public service reform. Alexandra previously worked as a private secretary for the permanent secretary at the Department for Education and Skills and as a researcher at the Institute for Public Policy Research. She has a degree in social and political science from the University of Cambridge.

Charles Leadbeater is a leading authority on innovation and creativity. He and Hilary Cottam are founding partners of Participle, the public service design agency. He has advised companies, cities and governments around the world on innovation strategy and drawn on that experience in writing his latest book *We-Think: The Power of Mass Creativity* (2006), which charts the rise of mass participative approaches to innovation, from science and open-source software to computer games and political campaigning.

Ben Lucas is a graduate of Liverpool University, and a former chair of Labour Students and of the modernising soft-left group the Labour Co-ordinating Committee. He was head of research and communications at the Union of Construction, Allied Trades and Technicians from 1987 to 1992, and became Jack Straw's political adviser during the mid-1990s. In 1997 he co-founded the political communications consultancy LLM Communications. He is also a founder and board member of the think tank the New Local Government Network. Ben is a member of the governance group of PSRG.

Geoff Mulgan is director of the Young Foundation, which was founded in 2005 from a merger of the Institute of Community Studies and the Mutual Aid Centre, bodies through which Michael Young created dozens of new organisations, from the Open University to Which?. Between 1997 and 2004 Geoff had various roles in the UK government including director of the government's Strategy Unit and head of policy in the Prime Minister's office. Before that he was the founder and director of the think tank Demos. He has been chief adviser to Gordon Brown MP, a consultant and lecturer in telecommunications and an investment executive. Geoff began his career in local government in London, where he pioneered policies to support creative industries that have been emulated all over the world. He has also been a reporter for BBC TV and radio and a columnist for national newspapers. He has lectured in more than thirty countries and is a visiting professor at the London School of Economics and Political Science, University College London and Melbourne University, and a visiting fellow at the Australia New Zealand School of Government. Geoff is a board member of the Work Foundation and the Design Council, chair of Involve (a charity bringing together practitioners in democracy and public engagement) and a member of the International Steering Committee of the Program of Innovations and Excellence in Chinese Local Governance. From late 2006 until 2008 he will be chairing the Carnegie inquiry into the future of civil society in the UK and Ireland.

Ben Rogers is an associate director of the Institute of Public Policy Research and head of the Democracy Team. He is the author of several acclaimed books, including *Beef and Liberty: Roast Beef, John Bull and the English Nation* (2003), and has written numerous articles and reports on public service and local government reform. A contributing editor of *Prospect* magazine, he has written features, comment pieces and reviews for a wide range of newspapers and magazines and has produced several radio series on history and philosophy.

Ann Rossiter is the director of the Social Market Foundation, an independent think tank that provides innovative economic and social policy ideas. Before joining this organisation in July 2003, Ann had built extensive experience in politics and policy making, working for four years as a director of Fishburn Hedges, the corporate communications consultancy, and for Lexington Communications. She also spent time in the BBC Political Research Unit, and worked in Parliament for John Denham MP and Glenda Jackson MP, on pensions and transport policy. Ann is a specialist in welfare reform and was involved in drawing up Labour Party policy on stakeholder pensions in the early 1990s. Other policy interests include employment and the operation of markets.

Simon Stevens is visiting professor at the London School of Economics and Political Science, chair of UnitedHealth Europe and a trustee of the King's Fund. He was the government's health adviser at 10 Downing Street and the Department of Health from 1997 to 2004.

Gerry Stoker is professor of governance at the University of Southampton, having held previous posts at Manchester, Strathclyde and Essex universities. Gerry's main research interests are in governance, democratic politics, local and regional governance, urban politics, public participation and public service reform. He has written or edited more than twenty books and published more than seventy refereed articles or chapters in books. Gerry was the founding chair of the New Local Government Network, which was the

Think Tank of the Year in 2004. His most recent book, *Why Politics Matters*, won the 2006 Political Book of the Year award from the Political Studies Association. Gerry is a member of the governance group of PSRG.

Laura Williams has been senior researcher at the Work Foundation since 2004, having previously worked in the Office of the Deputy Prime Minister. An experienced qualitative and quantitative researcher and analyst, her key areas of work include skills, cities, demographics and work–life balance. Laura holds a masters degree in sociology from the University of Edinburgh.

About the Public Service Reform Group

The Public Service Reform Group was established as an informal network immediately after the 2005 general election. Its aim is to advance rigorous debate about the future of public services in Britain. All of the participants have been involved as ministers, advisers and front-line professionals in the government's public service reform programme since 1997.

The group has met regularly since its formation and offers a forum to develop and test new ideas, to undertake general policy and political analysis, and to build the platform for future progressive governments. No other organisation inside or outside government provides a comparable function.

This book has been conceived by the PSRG at a time when the modernisation of public services is one of the central challenges facing the centre-left. *Public Matters* will aim to address these debates through clear, incisive, empirically rigorous and theoretically informed analysis from leading experts in the field.

About Policy Network

Policy Network is an international think tank dedicated to promoting progressive policies and the renewal of social democracy. Launched in December 2000, Policy Network facilitates the sharing of ideas and experiences among politicians, policy makers and experts on the centre-left.

Our common challenge
Progressive governments and parties in Europe are facing similar challenges. Perceived threats to economic, political and social security linked to globalisation, and the limitations of traditional policy prescriptions in the light of rapid social and technological change, increasingly demand that progressives work across national boundaries to find solutions. Insecurities associated with

increased immigration flows, terrorism, shifts in economic power and environmental change are increasingly driving the political agenda. Responses to these challenges must be located within an international framework of progressive thinking, rooted in social democratic values.

Our mission
Policy Network's objective is to develop and promote a progressive agenda based upon the ideas and experiences of social democratic modernisers. By working with politicians and thinkers across Europe and the world, Policy Network seeks to share the experiences of policy makers and experts in different national contexts, find innovative solutions to common problems and provide quality research on a wider range of policy areas.

Policy Network team

Director	Patrick Diamond
Executive assistant	Suzanne Verberne-Brennan
Head of research	Olaf Cramme
Accounts/office manager	Anna Bullegas
Events manager	Joanne Burton
Website manager	Matthew Carter
Policy researchers	Constance Motte, Chelsey Wickmark
Events assistant	Fatima Hassan
Publications officer	Lucy Greig
Media officer	Annie Bruzzone

Policy Network
Third Floor
11 Tufton Street
London
SW1P 3QB
United Kingdom
Tel: +44 (0) 20 7340 2200
Fax: +44 (0) 20 7340 2211
www.policy-network.net

Notes

Chapter 1

1. See 'Public Attitudes to Public Services', Ipsos MORI, December 2004.
2. Amartya Sen, *Development as Freedom* (Oxford: Oxford University Press, 1999), p. 75.
3. See Colin Crouch, *Commercialisation or Citizenship: Education Policy and the Future of Public Services* (London: Fabian Society, 2003); David Marquand, *The Decline of the Public: The Hollowing-Out of Citizenship* (Cambridge: Polity Press, 2004).
4. Stephen Gibbons, Stephen Machin and Olmo Silva, *Competition, Choice and Pupil Achievement* (London: Centre for Economic Performance, London School of Economics and Political Science, 2006).
5. 'The Role of the State', presentation by Ipsos MORI to the Prime Minister's Strategy Unit, 15 January 2007.
6. See Andrew Gamble and Tony Wright (eds), *Restating the State?* (Oxford: Blackwell, 2004).
7. John Maynard Keynes, *The End of Laissez-Faire* (London: Hogarth Press, 1926).
8. See Gamble and Wright, *Restating the State?*.
9. Albert Hirschmann, *Shifting Involvements: Private Interest and Public Action* (Oxford: Robertson, 1982).

Chapter 2

1. Ipsos MORI, Government Delivery Index, October 2006.
2. Ibid.
3. Jim Murphy (ed.), *Social Mobility and Public Service Reform* (London: Policy Network, 2006).
4. Morgan Johansson, 'Social Mobility: The Swedish Experience', in Murphy, *Social Mobility and Public Service Reform*.
5. Jørgen Abildgaard and Torben Vad, 'Can Vouchers Work for Health?: The Scandinavian Experience', *Progressive Politics* (2003), vol. 2, no. 1, 35–40.
6. R. H. Tawney, *'The Attack' and Other Papers* (London: George Allen & Unwin, 1953).
7. Amartya Sen, *Development as Freedom* (Oxford: Oxford University Press, 1999).
8. Robert Nozick, *Anarchy, State, and Utopia* (New York: Basic, 1974).
9. Ipsos MORI, February 2004.

Chapter 3

1. Colin Crouch, *Commercialisation or Citizenship: Education Policy and the Future of Public Services* (London: Fabian Society, 2003).
2. For a development of this argument see Gerry Stoker, *Why Politics Matters* (Basingstoke: Palgrave Macmillan, 2006).
3. 'Most People Expect More than NHS Can Ever Deliver', Ipsos MORI, 31 August 2006.
4. Figures quoted in Nils Pratley, 'The rise and rise – before the fall', *Guardian*, 4 October 2006.
5. David Wilson and Chris Game, *Local Government in the UK*, 4th ed. (Basingstoke: Palgrave Macmillan, 2006).
6. *Daily Telegraph*, 22 March 2005.
7. Andrew Gamble, *Politics and Fate* (Cambridge: Polity Press, 2000), p. 46.
8. Figures taken from Stoker, *Why Politics Matters*.
9. Harriet Sergeant, *Handle with Care: An Investigation into the Care System* (London: Centre for Young Policy Studies, 2006).
10. Robert D. Putnam, *Bowling Alone: The Collapse and Revival of American Community* (New York: Simon & Schuster, 2000).
11. J. Bendor, A. Glazer and T. Hammond, 'Theories of Delegation', *Annual Review of Political Science* (2001), vol. 4, p. 242.
12. Lester M. Salamon, *The Tools of Government: A Guide to the New Governance* (Oxford: Oxford University Press, 2002).
13. Frances Butler, *Rights for Real: Older People, Human Rights and the CEHR* (London: Age Concern England, 2006).
14. Sarah Kitchen, Juliet Michaelson, Natasha Wood and Peter John, *2005 Citizenship Survey: Cross-Cutting Themes* (Communities and Local Government, 2006).
15. John Hutton, 'Supporting Families: The Role of Welfare', speech at the Clapham Park Project, London, 15 September 2006.
16. Ibid.

Chapter 4

1. Sir Peter Gershon CBE, *Releasing Resources to the Front Line: Independent Review of Public Sector Efficiency* (Treasury, 2004).
2. Martyn Hart, 'The Gershon Report and the Value of Outsourcing', *eGov Monitor*, 22 March 2005, p. 1.
3. Peter Robinson, *How Do We Pay?: Funding Public Services in Europe* (London: Institute of Public Policy Research, 2004).
4. Ibid., pp. 21–2.
5. Ibid.
6. Julie Foley and Malcolm Fergusson, *Putting the Brakes on Climate Change* (London: Institute of Public Policy Research, 2003).
7. Commission on Taxation and Citizenship, *Paying for Progress: A New Politics of Tax for Public Spending* (London: Fabian Society, 2000).

Chapter 5

1. David Cameron MP, leader of the opposition, speech to the Power Inquiry, 6 May 2006.
2. David Miliband MP, Minister for the Cabinet Office, speech to the New Local Government Network annual conference, 19 January 2005.
3. L. T. Hobhouse, *Liberalism* (London: Oxford University Press, 1911).
4. C. A. R. Crosland, *The Future of Socialism*, (London: Jonathan Cape, 1956).
5. Roy Hattersley, *Choose Freedom: The Future for Democratic Socialism* (London: Michael Joseph, 1987).
6. Amartya Sen, *Commodities and Capabilities*, (Oxford: North-Holland, 1985).
7. The most notable areas in which choice has been introduced are choice of secondary school, choice of healthcare provider, choice of manager of social housing stock, the use of direct payments for social care (choice of social care provider) and choice-based lettings.
8. *Public–Private Partnerships* (Washington DC: International Monetary Fund, 2004). For an overview of the evidence, see David Hall and Emanuele Lobina, *The Relative Efficiency of Public and Private Sector Water* (London: Public Services International Research Unit, University of Greenwich, 2005).
9. Tony Blair, 'Choice, Excellence and Equality in Public Services', speech at St Thomas' Hospital, London, 23 June 2004.
10. See Chapter 12.
11. *Patient Choice at the Point of GP Referral*, report by Controller and Audit General, Session 2004/05, HC 180.
12. Charles Leadbeater, *Learning about Personalisation* (London: Demos, 2004).
13. Results based on internal evaluation by the Department of Health. An independent evaluation is also being carried out by a team of researchers from the National Primary Care Research and Development Centre, based at the University of Manchester and the University of York.
14. Angela Coulter, Naomi Le Maistre and Lorna Henderson, *Patients' Experience of Choosing Where to Undergo Surgical Treatment: Evaluation of London Patient Choice Scheme* (Oxford: Picker Institute Europe, 2005).
15. David Chater and Julian Le Grand, *Looked After or Overlooked?: Good Parenting and School Choice for Looked After Children* (London: Social Market Foundation, 2006).
16. Jonathan Williams and Ann Rossiter, *Choice: The Evidence* (London: Social Market Foundation, 2004).
17. Simon Burgess, Brendon McConnell, Carol Propper and Deborah Wilson, *Sorting and Choice in English Secondary Schools* (Bristol: Centre for Market and Public Organisation, University of Bristol, 2004).
18. Williams and Rossiter, *Choice*; Tony Hockley and Daniel Nieto, *Hands Up for School Choice!: Lessons from School Voucher Schemes at Home and Abroad* (London: Policy Exchange, 2004).
19. Simon Burgess, Carol Propper and Deborah Wilson, *Will More Choice Improve*

      Outcomes in Education and Health Care?: The Evidence from Economic Research (Bristol: Centre for Market and Public Organisation, University of Bristol, 2005).

20. Claudia Wood, *Making Choice a Reality in Secondary Education* (London: Social Market Foundation, 2005).

21. 'Education and Skills: Find Out More', Department for Education and Skills website, http://findoutmore.dfes.gov.uk.

22. This is one of the conclusions drawn in Burgess et al., *Will More Choice Improve Outcomes in Education and Health Care?*.

23. Commission for Rural Communities, Disadvantage Study, March 2005.

24. Leadbeater, *Learning about Personalisation*.

25. While the police is organised into local forces under police authorities (thirty-nine in England, four in Wales and eight in Scotland), they are essentially part of a national force and a single provider.

26. Adam Lent and Natalie Arend, *Making Choices: How Can Choice Improve Local Public Services?* (London: New Local Government Network, 2004).

27. Paul Corrigan, *Registering Choice: How Primary Care Should Change to Meet Patient Needs* (London: Social Market Foundation, 2006).

28. For example see Chater and Le Grand, *Looked After or Overlooked?*.

Chapter 6

1. A. J. P. Taylor, *Purnell's History of the Twentieth Century* (London: BPC, 1968).

2. C. R. Attlee, *As It Happened* (London: William Heinemann, 1954).

3. *Social Insurance and Allied Services* (1942), often known as the Beveridge plan. The 1948 report which followed was called *Voluntary Action*.

4. Gordon Brown, 'Let the people look after themselves', *Times*, 11 January 2001.

5. Speech at the National Council for Voluntary Organisations (NCVO), December 2006.

6. Speech at NCVO annual conference, February 2006.

7. Ann Blackmore, *How Voluntary and Community Organisations Can Help Transform Public Services* (London: National Council for Voluntary Organisations, 2006).

8. Will Paxton, Nick Pearce, Julia Unwin and Peter Molyneux, *The Voluntary Sector Delivering Public Services: Transfer or Transformation?* (York: Joseph Rowntree Foundation, 2005).

9. Martin Narey, 'Preferential treatment', Society *Guardian*, 10 January 2007.

10. Hilary Cottam, quoted in Jonathan Freedland, 'Reform need not mean privatisation if public services are localised', *Guardian*, 17 May 2006.

11. *Reducing Dependency, Increasing Opportunity: Options for the Future of Welfare to Work* (Department for Work and Pensions, 2007).

12. *It Takes Two to Tango: A Survey of Community Enterprise Involvement in Public Service Delivery* (London: Development Trusts Association, 2002).

13. HM Treasury 2005. Figures given relate to 'voluntary and community organisations', as defined by government.

14. John Williams, 'Transforming Procurement in Light of the Efficiency Review: A

Suppliers' Perspective', speech to the Government Procurement Service conference, 26 January 2005.

15. *Surer Funding: The Acevo Commission of Inquiry Report* (London: Acevo, 2004).

16. *Briefing on Partnership in Public Services: An Action Plan for Third Sector Involvement* (London: National Council for Voluntary Organisations, 2006).

17. Bob Garratt, *Thin on Top: Why Corporate Governance Matters and How to Measure and Improve Board Performance* (London: Nicholas Brealey, 2002).

18. *Looking Forward to Better Governance: Seminar Report* (London: Audit Commission/Charity Commission/Home Office, 2003).

19. Office of the Deputy Prime Minister, *Sustainable Communities: People, Places and Prosperity*, Cm 6425, 2005, p. 43.

20. *Social Return on Investment: Valuing What Matters* (London: New Economics Foundation, 2004).

21. Place shaping is defined by the Lyons Inquiry into Local Government as 'the creative use of powers and influence to promote the general well-being of a community and its citizens'

22. Society *Guardian*, 7 February 2007.

23. *Replacing the State: The Case for Third Sector Public Service Delivery* (London: Acevo, 2003).

24. David Miliband, 'Putting People in Control', speech to National Council for Voluntary Organisations annual conference, 21 February 2006.

Chapter 7

1. Charles Leadbeater and Hilary Cottam are co-founders with Colin Burns of Participle, the public service design agency. This chapter is based on ideas in Charles Leadbeater's forthcoming book *We-Think: The Power of Mass Creativity* (London: Profile), which is available in draft at www.wethinkthebook.net.

2. Ivan Illich, *Deschooling Society* (New York: Harper & Row, 1971).

3. Ivan Illich, *Limits to Medicine: Medical Nemesis: The Expropriation of Health* (London: Marion Boyars, 1977).

Chapter 8

1. Guy Lodge and Ben Rogers, *Whitehall's Black Box: Accountability and Performance in the Senior Civil Service* (London: Institute for Public Policy Research, 2006).

Chapter 10

1. For a progressive private sector view of these developments, see Stelio Stefanou, 'Placing Good Employment at the Heart of Public Sector Tendering: Practice and Policy', in *Private Investment for Public Success* (London: Policy Network, 2006).

2. Similar incongruities in relation to health are discussed in Chapter 16.

3. This explains why, in part, competition based on user choice (e.g. schools) is harder to establish and make work effectively than those where end user choice plays little or no part (e.g. highway maintenance).

4. For the effectiveness of comparative data in driving improvement in healthcare see *Intelligence* (London: Dr Foster Intelligence, 2007).

5. Adjustments made or weightings given to performance information on the basis of the 'mix' of severity/difficulty/riskiness of the illnesses or injuries being treated.

6. Contestability was first introduced to prison services in the early 1990s. There are currently eleven privately managed prisons, catering for around 10 per cent of the prison population.

7. An inappropriate label, as payments are actually made for activity, not outcome (result).

8. For further discussion on this see both Chapter 5 in this book and David Chater and Julian Le Grand, *Looked After or Overlooked?: Good Parenting and School Choice for Looked After Children* (London: Social Market Foundation, 2006).
   Alternatively, conditions in respect of equity and access could be attached to the licence for providers, as they are to a certain extent for utilities.

9. It is critical that it is improvement in performance and not absolute levels that is rewarded, as basing such incentives on the latter would create a cycle of decline for poorly performing organisations. An additional benefit of this proposal would be to obviate the need for targets as, properly designed, this incentive would stimulate continuous improvement.

10. See John Kay, *The Truth about Markets: Their Genius, Their Limits, Their Follies* (London: Allen Lane, 2004) for arguments that competition matters not (just) because it leads to the more efficient allocation of resources but because it supports the trailing of new ideas, therefore increasing innovation.

11. For more on issues of scale and diffusion see Geoff Mulgan and David Albury, *Innovation in the Public Sector* (Prime Minister's Strategy Unit, 2003).

12. There are other significant considerations in approaches to contracting, including ensuring business resilience and service continuity, and balances between spot, block and flexible contracting.

13. For the Europeanisation of healthcare see Scott Greer, *Responding to Europe: Government, NHS and Stakeholder Responses to the EU Health Challenge* (London: Nuffield Trust, 2006).

Chapter 11

1. John Hills, *Income and Wealth: The Latest Evidence* (York: Joseph Rowntree Foundation, 1999).

2. Labour Force Survey, February 2007.

3. HM Treasury, *Pre-Budget Report*, Cm 6984, 2006.

4. Before and after housing costs are taken into account. *Households below Average Income 1994/95–2005/06* (Department for Work and Pensions, 2007).

5. Mike Brewer, Alissa Goodman, Jonathan Shaw and Luke Sibieta, *Poverty and Inequality in Britain 2006* (London: Institute for Fiscal Studies, 2006).

6. Measuring net income but before housing costs have been deducted.

7. Source: OECD.

8. DWP research.

9. Martin Evans, Susan Harkness and Ramon Arigoni Ortiz, *Lone Parents Cycling between Work and Benefits* (Department for Work and Pensions, 2004).

10. See e.g. Lorraine Dearden, Stephen Machin and Howard Reed, 'Intergenerational Mobility in Britain', *Economic Journal* (1997) vol. 107, pp. 47–66; Jo Blanden, Alissa Goodman, Paul Gregg and Stephen Machin, *Changes in Intergenerational Mobility in Britain* (London: Centre for Economic Performance, London School of Economics and Political Science, 2001).

11. Sarah Jarvis and Stephen P. Jenkins, 'How Much Income Mobility Is There in Britain?', *Economic Journal* (1998), vol. 108, pp. 428–43.

12. British Household Panel Survey.

13. Jo Blanden, Paul Gregg and Stephen Machin, *Intergenerational Mobility in Europe and North America* (London: Centre for Economic Performance, London School of Economics and Political Science, 2005).

14. British Household Panel Survey.

15. See Leitch Review of Skills, *Prosperity for All in the Global Economy: Final Report* (HM Treasury, 2006).

16. Youth Cohort Study.

17. HM Revenue & Customs.

18. Communities and Local Government, 2007.

19. Department for Work and Pensions, *Security in Retirement: Towards a New Pensions System* (2006), Cm 6841.

20. Leitch Review of Skills.

21. *Reaching Out: An Action Plan for Social Exclusion* (Cabinet Office, 2006).

22. Leon Feinstein and Ricardo Sabates, *Predicting Adult Life Outcomes from Earlier Signals: Identifying Those at Risk* (London: Centre for Research on the Wider Benefits of Learning, Institute of Education, University of London, 2006).

23. Office for National Statistics longitudinal study.

24. Office for National Statistics.

25. Prabhat Jha, Richard Peto, Witold Zatonski, Jillian Boreham, Martin J. Jarvis and Alan D. Lopez, 'Social Inequalities in Male Mortality, and in Male Mortality from Smoking: Indirect Estimation from National Death Rates in England and Wales, Poland, and North America', *Lancet* (2006), vol. 368, pp. 367–70.

26. 'The Mental Health of Children and Adolescents in Great Britain', in *Social Trends 29* (Office for National Statistics, 1999).

27. *Reaching Out.*

28. OECD Family Database.

29. *Security in Retirement.*

30. Anthony Giddens and Patrick Diamond, *The New Egalitarianism* (Cambridge: Polity Press, 2005).

Chapter 12

1. James Q. Wilson, *Bureaucracy: What Government Agencies Do and Why They Do It* (New York: Basic, 1989).

2. See *Good and Bad Power: The Ideals and Betrayals of Government* (London: Allen Lane, 2006).

3. This was the theme of Shoshanna Zuboff and Jim Maxmin's book *The Support Economy: Why Corporations Are Failing Individuals and the Next Episode of Capitalism* (New York: Viking, 2002), and of a cluster of research institutes in Scandinavia in the 1970s and 1980s whose investigations of the practical meaning of service now look very prescient.

4. I made this argument in 'Democratic Dismissal, Competition, and Contestability among the Quangos', *Oxford Review of Economic Policy* (1994), vol. 10.

5. See Chapter 7 for more on direct payments and In Control.

6. See David Halpern, Clive Bates, Geoff Mulgan, Stephen Aldridge, Greg Beales and Adam Heathfield, *Personal Responsibility and Changing Behaviour: The State of Knowledge and Its Implications for Public Policy* (Prime Minister's Strategy Unit, 2004), which set out many of the theoretical and practical issues that would arise as questions of behaviour change moved to the fore in public policy. David Boyle, Geoff Mulgan and Rushanara Ali, *Life Begins at 60: What Kind of NHS after 2008?* (London: Young Foundation/New Economics Foundation) sets out the implications of these ideas in health policy.

7. Geoff Mulgan and David Albury, *Innovation in the Public Sector* (Prime Minister's Strategy Unit, 2003) provides one of the few overviews of the field.

8. In a recent survey we also looked at other routes for innovation, including business, social enterprise, social movements, academia and philanthropy. *Social Innovation: What It Is, Why It Matters, How It Can Be Accelerated* (London: Young Foundation, 2006) has prompted the creation of a global network on innovation.

9. For more on innovation in the public sector see my pamphlet *Ready or Not?: Taking Innovation in the Public Sector Seriously'* (London: NESTA, 2007).

10. These are provided by the World Bank, and provide useful pointers to the best governments to learn from.

Chapter 13

1. Steven Musson, 'The State of the Union: England', *RSA E-Journal*, February 2007.

2. Communities and Local Government, *Strong and Prosperous Communities*, Cm 6939-I.

3. David Walker, *In Praise of Centralism: A Critique of the New Localism* (London: Catalyst Forum, 2002).

4. Speech by John Healey MP, Financial Secretary to the Treasury, 14 September 2006.

5. Dan Corry and Gerry Stoker, *New Localism: Refashioning the Centre–Local Relationship* (London: New Local Government Network, 2002).

6.   Ibid.
7.   Gerry Stoker, *Transforming Local Governance: From Thatcherism to New Labour* (Basingstoke: Palgrave Macmillan, 2004), p. 216.
8.   Walker, *In Praise of Centralism*.
9.   John Healey, speech at Lyons inquiry conference, 14 September 2006.
10.   'Strong and prosperous communities: Kelly unveils new vision for local government', Communities and Local Government news release, 26 October 2006.
11.   *Newcastle in the North East, United Kingdom* (Paris: Organisation for Economic Co-operation and Development, 2006).
12.   As recommended by Simon Marvin, Alan Harding and Brian Robson, *A Framework for City-Regions* (Office of the Deputy Prime Minister, 2006).
13.   Ed Balls, John Healey and Chris Leslie, *Evolution and Devolution in England: How Regions Strengthen Our Towns and Cities* (London: New Local Government Network, 2006).
14.   Stoker, *Transforming Local Governance*, p. 217.
15.   Adam Marshall and Dermot Finch, *City Leadership: Giving City-Regions the Power to Grow* (London: Centre for Cities, 2006).
16.   Marvin et al., *A Framework for City-Regions*. This quote is taken from a summary of the report on the DCLG website (www.communities.gov.uk), not from the report itself.
17.   *Devolving Decision Making 3: Meeting the Regional Economic Challenge: The Importance of Cities to Regional Growth* (HM Treasury, 2006).
18.   The report is available from the Treasury website, www.hm-treasury.gov.uk.

Chapter 15

1.   I am grateful to the SOLACE Foundation Imprint, who commented on, supported and published an earlier draft of this chapter. The responsibility for the views expressed remains mine alone.
2.   *Closer to People and Places: A New Vision for Local Government* (London: Local Government Association, 2006).
3.   *Delivering Efficiently: Strengthening the Links in Public Service Delivery Chains*, report by the Comptroller and Auditor General, Session 2005/06, HC 940.
4.   Julian Le Grand, *Motivation, Agency, and Public Policy: Of Knights and Knaves, Pawns and Queens* (Oxford: Oxford University Press, 2003).

Chapter 16

1.   Bill Novelli and Boe Workman, *50+: Igniting a Revolution to Reinvent America* (New York: St Martin's Press, 2006).
2.   To underline the volume of consumer spending potentially available for health and well-being services, figures from the Office for National Statistics show that we now spend more on restaurants and takeaways than we do on the NHS.

3. That does not mean, however, that once a country has decided what healthcare its citizens are entitled to, there should not be competitive provider markets or that patients shouldn't be able to choose where to receive care. And this is where the European Court of Justice appears to be taking us.

   Meanwhile, these globalising trends mean we will probably need, for starters: a new legal basis for entitlement to NHS care based on NHS 'membership' and the contributory principle, as against the current common law 'ordinarily resident' test; more systematic cross-European evidence of professional competence; more rigorous management of migration to avoid denuding developing countries of their health professionals; strengthened cross-national communicable disease surveillance and control systems; and a replacement for Britain's long-standing method of controlling drug prices, the Pharmaceutical Price Regulation Scheme, which is no longer fit for purpose in a world where it is almost impossible to track capital deployment decisions within multinational pharmaceutical companies. At the time of writing, none of these is meaningfully being planned for.

4. Recent NHS reforms have explicitly borrowed ideas from other European countries, including foundation trusts (a hybrid of Continental models), cross-charging local authorities for blocked hospital beds (Scandinavia) and patient choice (almost everywhere else). And more generally, it has become recognised that in most of Europe it is possible to combine equitable healthcare funding with more plural provision. So rather than the 'Americanisation' of the NHS (whatever that frequently invoked but vapid slogan actually means), it might be more accurate to talk of its Europeanisation. The more interesting underlying question for the future is whether it will be governments that spread best practice between different European countries' healthcare systems – or whether this will be driven by the European institutions or indeed the individual choices made by citizens.

5. Tony Blair's *Breakfast with Frost* interview on 16 January 2000 (which I have elsewhere described as 'the most expensive breakfast in British history') constituted the key political commitment to raise health spending to the European average, as elaborated by the April 2002 Budget and accompanying Wanless report.

6. Perhaps surprisingly, until the mid-1980s the BMA was campaigning for a reduction in medical school intake – see Clive Smee, *Speaking Truth to Power: Two Decades of Analysis in the Department of Health* (Abingdon: Radcliffe, 2005).

7. Simon Stevens, 'Reform Strategies for the English NHS', *Health Affairs* (2004), vol. 23, no. 3.

8. The government's negotiating position on pay was weakened through clear availability of extra resources to NHS employers; documented recruitment and retention shortfalls, particularly in the south and among nurses; several years preceding of artificially constrained pay settlements; unions with little to lose from not reaching agreement since they could at any time unilaterally revert to the pay review bodies; and sustained media demands that the government end the industrial relations stand-off with health staff.

9. Given these unpropitious circumstances, it is to its credit that the Agenda for Change pay system for most staff – or at least the flexible job grading system at the heart of it – potentially allows innovative local redesign of jobs and patient workflows. It also meets the 'equal pay for work of equal value' tests that were about to bring the old Whitley council system crashing down. But too few of the theoretical local flexibilities on offer have yet been embraced in the average hospital. The same is true of the consultant contract, where hospitals generally failed to take a robust stance on the new consultant job plans, ending up instead with rather expensive 'peace in our time'. By contrast, the type of incentives that GPs are now subject to seem a much more powerful way of driving improvement in clinical performance, although the key test will be whether it is possible in future years to ratchet up the quality standards commensurate with GPs' 30 per cent-plus pay rises in year one.

10. According to Professor Derek Yach, the World Health Organization's former global head of non-communicable disease.

11. John J. Reilly, Louise Kelly, Colette Montgomery, Avril Williamson, Abigail Fisher, John H. McColl, Rossella Lo Conte, James Y. Paton and Stanley Grant, 'Physical Activity to Prevent Obesity in Young Children: Cluster Randomised Controlled Trial', *British Medical Journal* (2006), vol. 333, pp. 1041–3.

12. *Report on NICE Citizens Council Meeting 8–10 June 2006: Inequalities in Health* (London: National Institute for Health and Clinical Excellence, 2006).

13. For example a third of general practices in Knowsley failed to meet national standards for making available convenient surgery appointments compared with less than 10 per cent for the England as a whole.

14. Professor Sir Denis Pereira Gray, *A Dozen Facts about General Practice/Primary Care* (Department of Health, 2006).

15. Mark Hann and Hugh Gravelle, 'The Maldistribution of General Practitioners in England and Wales 1974–2003', *British Journal of General Practice* (2004), vol. 54, pp. 894–8.

16. Joan Higgins, 'A New Look at NHS Commissioning', *British Medical Journal* (2007), vol. 334, pp. 22–4.

17. Some analysts have argued that these adjustments are in fact overly favourable to the NHS in that the underlying driver of much of the productivity gain derives from new medicines which substitute for more costly hospital care, such that the NHS is effectively benefiting from 'imported productivity' that should properly be attributed to the private pharmaceutical sector. Statins for cardiovascular disease are one example of this. This situation is also one reason why the apparent decline in R&D productivity in the pharmaceutical sector is worrying.

18. *Health Strategy Review: Analytical Report* (Cabinet Office Strategy Unit, 2002), p. 78.

19. To make matters worse, despite rapidly rising pay, research shows that as incomes rise, the norm by which they are judged increases too, to the extent that an estimated 40 per cent of an annual pay rise is forgotten a year later. People care more about their relative income judged against a subjective comparator

group, which, as Richard Layard has pointed out, helps explain why East Germans' happiness declined after reunification even though incomes rose, because they started comparing themselves with West Germans rather than their former comrades in the Soviet bloc. Perhaps we now need that effect in reverse, with doctors here being reminded they are now the best paid in Europe – and that it is German doctors who have recently been striking for pay as good as that on offer in the NHS.

20. In time there may also be a case for taking the same approach as other countries in splitting the tariff into one element for paying clinicians and another for paying institutions – see for example the Resource Based Relative Value Scale used for Medicare in the United States.

21. Luigi Siciliani and Jeremy Hurst, *Explaining Waiting Times Variation for Elective Surgery across OECD Countries* (Paris: OECD, 2003).

22. Meg Hillier, Hansard, HC Deb, vol. 450, col. 333, 11 October 2006.

23. *Guardian*/ICM poll, 20–22 October 2006.

24. Other attempts have been less successful. The independent reconfiguration panel, intended to take the heat out of local hospital closures and mergers, has not yet done so. The independent advisory committee on resource allocation has had only an indirect influence on the weighted capitation formula which sets PCT budgets. And there is currently no transparent and predictable method of establishing and enforcing anti-cartel or pro-competitive rules of the road for the health sector as a whole.

25. NHS trusts found their freedoms eroding during the 1990s, partly because they remained directly accountable to the Health Secretary. For that reason a legally independent foundation trust regulator was established in 2004, making it harder for centralisation to reassert itself without explicit legislative change.

26. The BBC example does in fact offer some interesting parallels. If the NHS were to more closely mirror the BBC, it would have to be a lot more radical in its separation of commissioning from providing than is currently the case. By law Parliament requires the BBC to outsource at least 25 per cent of all programme making to independent media companies, and under the terms of its renewed charter it is now required to formally market-test a far larger share of its entire output. It is also subject to competition law to a much greater extent than the NHS.

27. Nevertheless, on grounds of efficiency, hospitals should be prevented from 'vertically integrating' into primary and community health provision. There is now ample evidence from the UK and internationally that hospitals tend to suck in primary and community health resources, impeding the flow of funding the other way. One of the main reasons for putting activities in separate organisations is precisely to dilute this centripetal force and ensure that decisions on community resource allocation are not simply internal and unaccountable budget decisions made within integrated trusts. The alternative strategy of having integrated but competing foundation trusts in every locality across England is simply not practical given our current number and distribution of hospitals.

Where NHS hospitals face little 'horizontal' competition from other hospitals locally, the main challenge to their local monopoly comes from the threat of vertical substitution by primary and community health services. Handing hospitals control of one of their main sources of competition would therefore further weaken commissioners' influence over what acute trusts do.

Chapter 17

1. The description and analysis in this chapter relate to the education system in England. Education is a devolved responsibility in Scotland, Wales and Northern Ireland. They too have seen progress and widespread changes but the nature of the reform has varied.

2. See *Statistics of Education: Trends in Attainment Gaps 2005* (London: National Statistics, 2006).

3. See Kathy Sylva, Edward Melhuish, Pam Sammons, Iram Siraj-Blatchford, Brenda Taggart and Karen Elliot, *The Effective Provision of Pre-school Education (EPPE) Project: Findings from the Pre-school Period* (London: Institute of Education, University of London, 2003).

4. *Education at a Glance 2006: OECD Briefing Note for the United Kingdom* (Paris: OECD, 2006).

5. *ICT in Schools 2004: The Impact of Government Initiatives in Schools Five Years On* (London. Ofsted, 2004).

6. *The Becta Review 2006: Evidence on the Progress of ICT in Education* (Coventry: Becta, 2006).

7. David Jesson and David Crossley, *Educational Outcomes and Value Added by Specialist Schools 2005* (London: Specialist Schools and Academies Trust, 2006).

8. *Ensuring the Attainment of White Working Class Boys in Writing* (Department for Education and Skills, 2005).

9. See *Statistics of Education: Trends in Attainment Gaps 2005*

10. *Making Mathematics Count: The Report of Professor Adrian Smith's Inquiry into Post-14 Mathematics Education* (2004).

11. *Prosperity for All in the Global Economy – World Class Skills: Final Report* (HM Treasury, 2006).

12. *Working on the Three Rs: Employers' Priorities for Functional Skills in Maths and English* (London: Confederation of British Industry, 2006).

13. *14–19 Curriculum and Qualifications Reform: Final Report of the Working Group on 14–19 Reform* (Department for Education and Skills, 2004).

14. The material in this section is based on Jonathan Osborne and Sue Collins, *Pupils' and Parents' Views of the Schools Science Curriculum* (London: King's College London, 2000); Pippa Lord and Annie Johnson, *Pupils' Experiences and Perspective of the National Curriculum and Assessment: Fifth Update of the Research Review* (York: National Foundation for Educational Research, 2005); Robin Millar, 'Science in Education: Implications for Formal Education?', in Jon Turney (ed.), *Engaging Science: Thoughts, Deeds, Analysis and Action* (London: Wellcome Trust, 2006);

Pupils' Views on Language Learning (London: Qualifications and Curriculum Authority, 2006).

15.   Research by the DfES confirms the boredom problem. In *Making Good Progress: How Can We Help Every Pupil to Make Good Progress at School?* (DfES, 2006) the department acknowledges that 'pupils had become disappointed and demoralised. Throughout Key Stage 3, they were never really engaged or motivated by school.'

16.   Survey carried out for the *Times Educational Supplement* in October 2006.

17.   *14–19 Curriculum and Qualifications Reform: Interim Report of the Working Group on 14–19 Reform* (Department for Education and Skills, 2004).

18.   Ibid.

19.   Speech by Ken Boston at the launch of the Institute of Educational Assessors, 9 May 2006.

20.   *Qualifications and Curriculum Authority: Financial Modelling of the English Exams System 2003/04* (London: PricewaterhouseCoopers, 2004).

21.   See David Hopkins, 'Realising the Potential of System Reform', in Harry Daniels, Jill Porter and Hugh Lauder (eds), *The Routledge Companion to Education* (Abingdon: Routledge, forthcoming).

22.   Tony Blair, speech at 10 Downing Street, 24 October 2005.

23.   See Stephen D. Sugarman and Frank R. Kemerer (eds), *School Choice and Social Controversy: Politics, Policy, and Law* (Washington, DC: Brookings Institution Press, 1999) for an excellent discussion of the impact of choice in the US education system.

24.   Professor Charles Desforges and Alberto Abouchaar, *The Impact of Parental Involvement, Parental Support and Family Education on Pupil Achievement and Adjustment: A Literature Review* (Department for Education and Skills, 2003).

25.   David Reynolds, David Hopkins and John Grey, *School Improvement: Lessons from Research* (Department for Education and Skills, 2005).

26.   *Child Poverty: Fair Funding For Schools* (Department for Education and Skills/HM Treasury, 2005).

27.   *2020 Vision: Report of the Teaching and Learning in 2020 Review Group* (Department for Education and Skills, 2006).

28.   Charles Leadbeater, *The Shape of Things to Come: Personalised Learning through Collaboration* (Department of Education and Skills, 2005).

29.   Taken from the KIPP website, www.kipp.org.

30.   See www.horsesmouth.co.uk, for example.

31.   Pippa Lord, Sharon O'Donnell, Ruth Brown and Hilary Grayson, *Learner Motivation 3–19: An International Perspective* (Slough: National Foundation for Educational Research, 2005).

32.   The London Challenge project, begun in 2003, identified seventy schools across London (known as Key to Success schools) that faced the most challenging circumstances. They received intensive support from a team involving the minister for London schools, a government-appointed London Commissioner to lead the change programme, the five local authorities targeted and a group of

expert advisers. The expert advisers helped ensure that schools received and used the right interventions and funding.

33.   *Education at a Glance: OECD Indicators 2006* (Paris: OECD, 2006).

34.   The LSC system has until now been based on actual student numbers. At the time of writing it was considering – mistakenly in my view – of moving to an allocation based on planned numbers.

35.   Sugarman and Kemerer, *School Choice and Social Controversy* illustrates how charter school reforms have necessitated broader funding reforms to create a level playing field and realise the fuller impact of change within neighbouring public schools.

36.   See Sugarman and Kemerer, *School Choice and Social Controversy*.

Chapter 18

1.   See A. Gamble, 'Why Social Democrats Need to Re-think the State', in Matt Browne and Patrick Diamond (eds), *Rethinking Social Democracy* (London: Policy Network, 2003).

2.   See Julian Le Grand, *Motivation, Agency, and Public Policy: Of Knights and Knaves, Pawns and Queens* (Oxford: Oxford University Press, 2003).

3.   See R. H. Tawney, *Equality* (London: George Allen and Unwin, 1931).

4.   Pupils' study at school is divided into four key stages (KS): KS1 runs from ages 5–7; KS2 from 7–11; KS3 from 11–14; and KS4 (GCSE) from 14–16. At the end of each KS, the government assesses and tracks the performance of all pupils in English, maths and science. At KS1, 2 and 3, an expected level of performance is defined for each of the subjects: at KS1 it is Level 2, at KS2 Level 4 and at KS3 Level 5. Study in pre-school settings and in reception classes is covered by the Early Years Foundation Stage (see Chapter 17).

5.   Some of these points are developed in Geoff Mulgan, 'Going with and against the Grain: Social Policy in Practice since 1997', in Nick Pearce and Will Paxton, *Social Justice: Building a Fairer Britain* (London: Politico's, 2005).

6.   The comparison of ethnic minority achievement is complex since, according to the Prime Minister's Strategy Unit, ethnic minority pupils are among the highest and the lowest educational performers in England and Wales.

7.   Gøsta Esping-Andersen, 'A Child Centred Social Investment Strategy', in Gøsta Esping-Andersen, Duncan Gallie, Anton Hemerijck and John Myles, *Why We Need a New Welfare State* (Oxford: Oxford University Press, 2002).

8.   See Michael Rutter, 'Is Sure Start an Effective Preventative Intervention?', *Child and Adolescent Mental Health* (2006), vol. 11, pp. 135–41.

9.   See Norman Glass, 'Surely some mistake', *Guardian*, 5 January 2005.

10.   See *Early Impacts of Sure Start Local Programmes on Children and Families: Report of the Cross-Sectional Study of 9- and 36-Month-Old Children and their Families* (Department for Education and Skills, 2005).

11.   Professor John Hills of the London School of Economics and Political Science uses the term 'selective universalism', indicating that the electorate will tolerate

selective increases in public expenditure for health and education, and benefits for pensioners, low-income families and disabled people.

12. Some critics allege that even the original Sure Start community development model falls far short of real empowerment. Though creating the appearance of community ownership, Sure Start programmes were dominated by professional staff from health, education and social work backgrounds, and large corporate voluntary sector organisations. The structures of power sharing were in reality opaque. For an example of this critique see Margaret Lochrie, 'No Child Left Behind: Making It a Reality', in Margaret Lochrie (ed), *The Learning We Live By: Education Policies for Children, Families and Communities* (Teddington: Capacity, 2006).

13. See David Donnison, *Act Local: Social Justice from the Bottom Up* (London: Institute for Public Policy Research, 1994).

14. See David Marquand, *The Progressive Dilemma: From Lloyd George to Kinnock* (London: Heinemann, 1991).

15. See Peter Clarke, *Liberals and Social Democrats* (Cambridge: Cambridge University Press, 1978).

Chapter 19

1. For example, the 1998 Crime and Disorder Act gave local government a lead role in working with police and other criminal justice agencies to promote community safety. It has encouraged an ethos of engagement throughout the criminal justice system and championed neighbourhood policing in particular – indeed under David Blunkett the Home Office became something of a proselyte of 'civil renewal' and 'active citizenship'. And it has funded and promoted some notable experiments in 'community justice', most notably the North Liverpool Community Justice Centre.

2. D. Prior, K. Farrow, B. Spalek and M. Barnes, 'Anti-Social Behaviour and Civil Renewal' and A. Bottoms and A. Wilson, 'Civil Renewal, Control Signals and Neighbourhood Safety', both in Tessa Brannan, Peter John and Gerry Stoker (eds), *Re-energizing Citizenship: Strategies for Civil Renewal* (Basingstoke: Palgrave Macmillan, 2006).

3. See William Higham, 'Punishment and Social Justice', in Ben Shimshon (ed.), *Social Justice: Criminal Justice* (London: Smith Institute, 2006).

4. Mike Dixon, Howard Reed, Ben Rogers and Lucy Stone, *CrimeShare: The Unequal Impact of Crime* (London: Institute for Public Policy Research, 2006).

5. Ibid.

6. See Tim Newburn, 'Policing since 1945' and Trevor Jones, 'The Governance and Accountability of Policing', both in Tim Newburn (ed.), *A Handbook of Policing* (Cullompton: Willan).

7. Ibid.

8. It also needs to be acknowledged that not all the trends have been in one direction. At the national level, the growth of Home Office powers has been

matched by the development of the Association of Chief Police Officers, HM Inspectorate of Constabulary, the National Audit Office and the Audit Commission, which act to some degree as countervailing forces. Devolution to Scotland (and to a much lesser extent Wales and London) has again somewhat diminished Home Office dominance. Human rights legislation, a more active judiciary and more vigilant and assertive media and civil society ensure that the Home Office and police more generally come under greater scrutiny than was once the case. Finally local government itself has gained some new influence, mainly through new statutory partnership mechanisms, such as crime and disorder reduction partnerships and local strategic partnerships (see Jones, 'Governance and Accountability of Policing').

9.   I have not said anything here about issues of accountability and governance of international policing organisations and partnerships.

10.   Guy Lodge and Ben Rogers, *Whitehall's Black Box: Performance and Accountability in the Senior Civil Service* (London: Institute for Public Policy Research, 2006).

11.   Dixon et al., *CrimeShare*.

12.   Barry Loveday and Anna Reid, *Going Local: Who Should Run Britain's Police* (London: Policy Exchange, 2003).

13.   Mike Hough, 'Policing London, 20 Years On', in Alistair Henry and David J. Smith, *Transformations of Policing* (Aldershot: Ashgate, 2007).

14.   The Home Office public service agreement includes as one of its targets 'Reassure the public, reducing the fear of crime and anti-social behaviour, and building confidence in the criminal justice system without compromising fairness'.

15.   Rachel Briggs, Catherine Fieschi and Hannah Lownsbrough, *Bringing It Home: Community-Based Approaches to Counter-Terrorism* (London: Demos, 2006).

16.   Peter Neyroud, 'Policing and Ethics', in Tim Newburn (ed.), *A Handbook of Policing* (Cullompton: Willan); Barry Loveday, *Police Staff and Service Modernisation: A Reform too Far?* (Birmingham: University of Central England, 2005); Hough, 'Policing London, 20 Years On'.

17.   There are also important problems around the police precept. Though police authorities have the power to set the police precept, they are not effectively held to account for this, or for the way money is spent. It is notable that the precept has in recent years increased faster than other components of council tax, and is often responsible for a sizeable proportion of overall increases in council tax.

18.   Loveday and Reid, *Going Local*.

19.   In particular, it would necessitate a new role for police authorities and regional police leaders, who, no longer responsible for appointing, directing or line-managing local police officers, would become responsible for working with local authority leaders and their police chiefs to develop regional strategies, promoting joined-up working among locally appointed police chiefs, and promoting best practice across the region. Regional-level authorities, however, could remain directly responsible for tackling serious and trans-local crime.

20.   Clearly, moves in this direction – giving local democratic leaders greater authority over local police activity – would have to be accompanied by

safeguards preventing inappropriate political involvement, especially the scapegoating or neglect of vulnerable minorities. There are in fact already many safeguards in place (more effective scrutiny of council decisions, the Equalities Commission, the Human Rights Act, centralised scrutiny and inspection etc.). Nevertheless reform could be matched by (1) clear prohibition of local authority involvement in directing operations, as opposed to setting outputs; (2) a right of appeal to HMIC or another body, if police officers believe that local authority demands are inappropriate.

21. Rachel Tuffin, Julia Morris and Alexis Poole, *An Evaluation of the Impact of the National Reassurance Policing Programme* (Home Office, 2006).

22. Kathryn Farrow and David Prior, 'Togetherness?: Tackling Anti-social Behaviour through Community Engagement', *Criminal Justice Matters* (2006), vol. 64, pp. 4–5.

23. Bottoms and Wilson, 'Civil Renewal, Control Signals and Neighbourhood Safety'.

24. The case for greater accountability at this level becomes all the stronger once it is appreciated that there has been an upward trend across the country in the size of BCUs. In Thames Valley, for instance, there are now just five BCUs, one of which covers the entire administrative county of Oxfordshire (John W. Raine and Eileen Dunstan, 'Enhancing Accountability in Local Policing', *Criminal Justice Matters* (2006), vol. 63). Where London boroughs used to contain two or sometimes three BCUs each, they now contain only one. The sort of reforms I have advocated above, moreover, that would give local authority leaders greater powers could lead to a further increase in the size of areas covered by BCUs.

25. Skogan, *Police and Community in Chicago*.

26. Carol Hedderman, 'Keeping the Lid on the Prison Population: Will It Work?', in Mike Hough, Rob Allen and Una Padel (eds), *Reshaping Probation and Prisons: The New Offender Management Framework* (Bristol: Policy Press, 2006).

27. Patrick Carter, *Managing Offenders, Reducing Crime: A New Approach* (Cabinet Office, 2003).

28. Hedderman, 'Keeping the Lid on the Prison Population'.

29. Carter, *Managing Offenders, Reducing Crime*. None of this is to deny that there are some cases, and types of case, where sentencing is not severe enough – as Carter argued, the system did not and does not always bear down sufficiently on dangerous and highly persistent offenders, nor perhaps on the perpetrators of white-collar crime.

30. David James, Frank Farnham, Helen Moorey, Helen Lloyd, Kate Hill, Robert Blizard and T. R. E. Barnes, *Outcome of Psychiatric Admission through the Courts* (Home Office, 2002); Higham, 'Punishment and Social Justice'.

31. Nick Pearce, 'Crime and Punishment: A New Home Office Agenda', in Nick Pearce and Julia Margo (eds), *Politics for a New Generation: The Progressive Movement* (Basingstoke: Palgrave Macmillan, 2007)

32. Mike Hough, Jessica Jacobson and Andrew Millie, *The Decision to Imprison: Sentencing and the Prison Population* (London: Prison Reform Trust, 2003).

33. Andrew Millie, Jessica Jacobson, Eraina McDonald and Mike Hough, *Anti-Social Behaviour Strategies: Finding a Balance* (Bristol: Policy Press, 2005).

34. See 'Victims say stopping re-offending is more important than prison', SmartJustice press release, 16 January 2006.

35. *Rethinking Crime and Punishment: The Report* (London: Esmée Fairbairn Foundation, 2004); Lawrence W. Sherman and Heather Strang, *Restorative Justice: The Evidence* (London: Smith Institute).

36. *Rethinking Crime and Punishment*; Ben Rogers, *New Directions in Community Justice* (London: Institute for Public Policy Research, 2005).

37. Rogers, *New Directions in Community Justice*; Ben Rogers, 'Courtroom Shake-Up', Open Democracy website, 23 September 2005; see also Peter Neyroud, '21st Century Justice?', 10 Downing Street website, 2006.

38. John W. Raine; 'End-to-End or End in Tears?: Prospects for the Effectiveness of the National Offender Management Model', in Hough et al., *Reshaping Probation and Prisons*.

39. *Reducing Re-Offending by Ex-Prisoners* (Social Exclusion Unit, 2002).

40. Rogers, *New Directions in Community Justice*.

41. *Going Straight: Reducing Re-Offending in Local Communities* (London: Local Government Association, 2005).

42. Rob Allen, 'Communities and the Criminal Justice System', in Shimshon, *Social Justice: Criminal Justice*.

43. Eric Cadora, 'Open Society', *CJM* (2006), no. 64.

Chapter 20

1. This paper represents the Work Foundation's analysis and commentary, as informed by the views of an expert panel. Members of the panel were: David Albury, No. 10 Strategy Unit; Richard Brooks, Institute of Public Policy Research; Stephen Evans, Social Market Foundation; Jane Mansour, Work Directions; Sara Caplan, KPMG; Ben Lucas, FD-LLM; and Andy Westwood, Centre for Economic and Social Inclusion.

2. *Prosperity for All in the Global Economy – World Class Skills: Final Report* (HM Treasury, 2006).

3. See Peter A. Hall and David Soskice, *Varieties of Capitalism: The Institutional Foundations of Comparative Advantage* (Oxford: Oxford University Press, 2001).

4. The five drivers of productivity are competition, innovation, investment, skills and enterprise. See *Productivity in the UK 6: Progress and New Evidence* (HM Treasury, 2006), p. 42.

5. Kathy Armstrong, *Life after MG Rover: The Impact of the Closure on the Workers, Their Families and the Community* (London: The Work Foundation, 2006).

6. *Prosperity for All in the Global Economy – World Class Skills: Final Report*, p. 75.

7. The classic account can be found in George A. Akerlof, 'The Market for "Lemons": Quality Uncertainty and the Market Mechanism', *Quarterly Journal of Economics* (1970), vol. 84, pp. 488–500.

8. See Jeffrey Pfeffer and Robert I. Sutton, *Hard Facts, Dangerous Half-Truths, and Total Nonsense: Profiting from Evidence-Based Management* (Boston: Harvard Business School Press, 2006).

9. Paul Gregg and Jonathan Wadsworth, *More Work in Fewer Households?* (London: National Institute of Economic and Social Research, 1995).

10. Robert Taylor, *Britain's World of Work: Myths and Realities* (Swindon: Economic and Social Research Council, 2002); F. Green, 'The Demands of Work', in Richard Dickens, Paul Gregg and Jonathan Wadsworth (eds), *The Labour Market under New Labour: The State of Working Britain* (Basingstoke: Palgrave Macmillan, 2003).

Index